Jet airline travel today is statistically safer than everyday life. But this standard has been bought at a price: this book is dedicated to the memory of all those – crew and passengers – whose lives were part of that price.

AIR DISASTER

VOLUME 1

by Macarthur Job

ACKNOWLEDGEMENTS

No book encompassing the aviation disciplines and experiences represented in this survey of 18 seminal jet airliner accidents could be prepared without the willing assistance and advice of a number of people.

At the outset, I am indebted to Dr Rob Lee, Director of the Bureau of Air Safety Investigation, for his generosity in allowing me access to the Bureau's library of overseas accident investigation reports, without which the book would have been impossible. I would also express my appreciation to the Bureau's Russell Sibbison, Data Manager of its Safety Analysis Branch, for his unfailing helpfulness; and to Stuart Spinks and Andrew Watson, respectively Manager and Administration Officer of the Bureau's Melbourne Field Office, for placing their facilities at my disposal for necessary research. My thanks too, to the Bureau's Investigator Alan Hobbs for clarifying the source of the comments on aviation psychology quoted in Chapter 17.

Long time aviation colleagues Captain John Laming, Bob Fripp, Norman Clifford, Captain Alan Searle and Drs Paul Matthews and Paddy O'Brien have kindly provided advice spiced with extensive experience whenever asked, as has aviation antiquarian John Hopton out of his extraordinary knowledge of airline history. As with my earlier books, aviation "elder statesmen" Stanley Brogden and John Watkins OBE, have been constantly encouraging and helpful in many ways.

With the author in Melbourne, the illustrator in Sydney, and the publishing office in Canberra, the logistics of collaborating to complete the book on schedule has been a challenge in itself.

Here I would pay tribute to artist Matthew Tesch, commercially qualified pilot in his own right. As creator of the many graphic illustrations which bring the text so much to life, his own aeronautical understanding had ensured technically correct detail. In addition, his encyclopaedic knowledge of the many versions of manufacturer's designs and of world airline fleets, not to mention his enormous enthusiasm for "getting it right", has added much authenticity. In a real sense, it is his book too. On his behalf I would like to thank those in Sydney who assisted his illustration research – Herr Hans Meier and staff at the Swiss Consulate-General, Beth McDougall of KLM's Australian office, Mike Clayton of Aironautica who supplied photographs, Paul Chamney and Mick Hodges.

As before, my thanks go to Jim Thorn and Maria Davey at Aerospace Publications for their trust, their patience, and their enthusiasm for seeing the project through to its worthwhile conclusion.

Finally I would say thank you to my wife, Esma, an editor in her own right, for her patient ongoing efforts to ensure that a technocrat's aviation jargon was not merclessly inflicted upon hapless readers!

Macarthur Job
Lower Templestowe,
Victoria
1994

Published by Aerospace Publications Pty Ltd (ACN: 001 570 458), PO Box 3105, Weston Creek, ACT 2611, publishers of monthly Australian Aviation magazine.
Production Manager: Maria Davey

ISBN 1 875671 11 0

CONTENTS

INTRODUCTION

The advent of the jet airliner in the early post World War 2 era ushered in an age that would change the face of the world, facilitating swift, economic, long distance mass travel on a scale previously undreamed of.

The ultimate development of the propeller driven airliner during these years – the DC-6, DC-7, Lockheed Super Constellation, and the Boeing Stratocruiser, together with their turboprop successors, the Vickers Viscount and Vanguard, the Lockheed Electra, and the Bristol Britannia – popularised air travel in the Western World to the point where it finally overtook the train and the ocean liner as the principal means of long distance public transport. Yet for the most part, intercontinental travel remained the privilege of senior executives and the well-to-do.

It was the jet airliner, and in particular its later giant, widebodied derivations – the Boeing 747, Lockheed Tristar, McDonnell Douglas DC-10 and the Airbus 300 – that at last brought air travel within reach of millions who previously had been unable even to contemplate it. Such aircraft today are arguably the most efficient and economic movers of people over long distances the world has ever seen.

Yet for all the advanced technology that brought the jet airliner into being, for all its vastly improved aerodynamic efficiency and increased reliability, for all its apparent ease of maintenance and economy of operation compared to its piston engined predecessors, its advent was a venture into the unknown – a venture into a realm where the well learned techniques and lore of piston engined airliner operation would not always apply.

Jet aircraft are different and they behave differently. They have higher momentum than piston engined aircraft, much greater thrust, but very low drag, making them highly vulnerable to overspeed situations if not carefully controlled. They fly fast and high, a regime where the previously little known hazards of high Mach number instability, reduced manoeuvrability and restricted speed ranges have to be taken into account. They require variable incidence tailplanes, Mach trimmers and yaw dampers – which can malfunction, adding to a flight crew's problems. And their poor lift at low airspeeds makes their low speed controllability heavily dependent upon complicated high lift devices requiring disciplined speed control and handling.

Because of these totally new characteristics and aerodynamics, because of the jet airliner's vastly increased performance, and the speeds and heights in which this radically new generation of large aeroplanes would operate, new and hitherto unsuspected hazards would be encountered; a host of new and unforeseen operational problems would arise and have to be dealt with.

Many of these would only come to light through harsh practical experience. Stresses imposed by high differential cabin pressurisation, the aerodynamic effect of gusts and turbulence at high altitudes, the stalling characteristics of ultra clean, swept wing designs, more critical fuel management at turbojet consumptions, the changed aerodynamic response with propeller slipstreams no longer blowing over wings, the relatively slow response of jet engines to the application of power and consequent dangers of excessive rates of descent, particularly during visual approaches – these and other traits peculiar to jet operations were but some of the problems encountered on this new aeronautical learning curve.

Air Disaster then is the story of how some of those lessons were learned. The experiences described, for all their individual tragedies, has helped to evolve a global transport system whose reliability is beyond anything the world has ever seen. Considering the frequency and number of jet airliner flights taking place the world over, 24 hours a day every day of the year, in all manner of weather and circumstances, the level of achieved safety is nothing less than astounding.

Even so, it has to be said that the total number of accidents contributing to this learning process far exceeds what could be included within the covers of a single book. Since the inception of jet airliner operations in the late 1950s, several hundred airline jets have been involved in major accidents, including those in the former Soviet Union and China. Those described in this book have been chosen either because they are notable in their own right, or because they are representative of accidents that resulted from similar causal factors.

Their other qualification for inclusion in the book was that comprehensive and reliable reports on the accidents themselves, their circumstances, and their subsequent investigation, were available. It is for these reasons only that the majority of case histories included have come from the United States and from the United Kingdom. It certainly is not meant to suggest that the airline accident record for these leading airline nations is worse than in other countries of the world!

Another point to be made is that all the case histories described are accidents from which significant operational lessons were drawn, and which, by application of what was learnt, led to greater safety. This of course is the evolutionary process by which any technological system develops. Disasters resulting from acts of sabotage or hostile enemy action – such as Korean Airlines' Flight 007 shot down by a Soviet fighter, or the Pan American Boeing 747 which exploded over Lockerbie, Scotland – are not accidents in the true sense of the word. For this reason they have not been included.

The treatment of the fascinating technological and human stories that follow differs from that of other books on airline disasters. Based on official investigation reports, supplemented by research from other available sources, the various chapters not only present and illustrate the technical aspects of the investigations in accurate detail, but try to do so in a way readily understood by readers who are neither pilots nor engineers. They also seek to bring a human face to the dramas. The combination of these different strands probably makes this book unique.

In identifying the pilots and other crew members unfortunate enough to be caught up in the outworking of these unhappy but immensely valuable learning experiences, the book seeks only to be authentic in "telling it as it was". In no sense whatever does it seek to sit in judgement, much less to apportion blame.

Indeed, in preparing the material for publication, the author and the illustrator, both of whom are themselves commercial pilots, were continually reminded that "there but for the grace of God go I".

Macarthur Job
Lower Templestowe, Vic
Oct 1994

ARTIST'S NOTE

Creating the 60 plus illustrations in this book has been both rewarding and draining. Collaborating closely with Mac Job – doyen of Australia's aviation safety writers – my aim has been to add a visual dimension to his already graphic narrative: to interpret technicalities and aerodynamics to enhance readers' appreciation of the *what, how* and *why* of the events described, as much as the *when* and *where* in setting the scene for each chapter.

It is only right to claim a little artistic licence where necessary, but this has been sparingly applied – readers may be assured that any minor omissions or adjustments have been crafted to add to the sketches' clarity. All the words and pictures in this book are in fact founded on the facts and deductions of official investigation reports, reinforced by exhaustive secondary research. Indeed, I am personally indebted to a number of authorities and individuals for their responses to often "curly" queries.

I would draw readers' attention to the two principal styles of illustration. The artist's impressions – the *action shots* – seek to depict the aircraft, livery and environment with as much reality as is possible in black and white rendering. Deliberately more clinical are the clean line drawings of the breakup sequences, "deidentified" for reasons of ethical and moral sensitivity. In permitting a greater focus on graphic reconstruction, this technique also avoids the visual confrontation of "bodies and bits coming away from airline x".

For it is impossible to escape having to face the hurt, the loss of life and the destruction inherent in the subject material, no matter how dispassionate the overview. It is for this reason that I used the word "draining". Despite all my efforts at objectivity, many were the times when emotion involuntarily overtook me at the drawing board – and not always in the reflective stillness of the wee small hours of the morning.

I can but hope that the souls of all those who loved and crewed those magnificent aeroplanes, with those who trusted their lives to comforts of their cabins, are not unhappy with the calibre of my interpretations. For the air transport industry we take so much for granted today is as much a tribute to the price they paid, as it is to the skill and ingenuity of the investigators whose dedication has brought us the benefits of greater safety and understanding.

If Mac's words and my drawings do justice to the lessons of aviation history contained in this volume, the effort will have indeed been worthwhile.

Matthew Tesch
Sydney
October 1994

"The cost of solving the Comet mystery must be reckoned neither in money nor in manpower"

– Sir Winston Churchill

THE COMET
Britain leads
DE HAVILLAND ENTERPRISE

BOAC DH-106 Comet 1 G-ALYP [6003] – January 10,1954;
BOAC DH-106 Comet 1 G-ALYY [6011] – April 8, 1954

In any new field of human endeavour, it is often those who blaze a trail into previously unknown realms who suffer the consequences of their pioneering efforts. Nowhere was this more true than with the development of the world's first jetliner by Britain's de Havilland Company.

In Britain as the end of World War 2 approached, the nation's aircraft industry was facing a dilemma. Throughout the war, the industry had properly concentrated on the development and production of military aircraft, principally fighters to counter the might of Germany's Luftwaffe, and heavy bombers to take the air war into the heartland of Germany itself. As a result there had been virtually no transport aircraft development in its own right for several years. The few transport types being built in Britain were no more than adaptations of existing twin engined and four engined bomber designs.

By contrast, in the United States, the war had provided the stimulus for the development and construction of large transport aeroplanes on a scale never before envisaged. The Douglas C-47 Dakota, the military version of the prewar DC-3, had been turned out in thousands, and its four engined long range successor, the C-54 or DC-4, was proving itself as a superb, highly efficient, intercontinental military aircraft – the world's first true global transport. Meanwhile Lockheed was producing its C-69, an even more advanced high speed, long range four engined

pressurised aircraft, originally designed for TWA as the Constellation. Already Douglas was working on a bigger and faster pressurised version of the DC-4, to be known as the DC-6, while Boeing was developing a two deck transport version of their high altitude B-29 long range bomber.

With the war's end, all these aircraft would of course be instantly adaptable to airline operations. All in all it looked as though, with the coming of peace and the anticipated boom in airline flying the world over, the British industry would be well and truly left at the post.

The Brabazon Committee, a British Government body appointed at the end of 1942 to examine proposals for the development of postwar airline aircraft, decided that, rather than merely design new types of conventional transport aircraft to compete with existing American designs and their derivatives on the world market, the British industry should seek to build civil types that would be technologically well ahead of current design practice. Among the major recommendations of the Brabazon Committee was that a turbojet airliner, capable of operating on the North Atlantic route, should

be developed as soon as possible after the war, a proposal expected to almost halve flying times.

The old established de Havilland Company, because of its experience with the Vampire jet fighter, was keenly interested in the project, and began design work on the world's first jet airliner, to be known as the DH-106 Comet, in 1946.

It would be powered by four Rolls-Royce Ghost engines, carry 36 passengers in a pressurised cabin, and be capable of operating up to 40,000 feet at a cruising speed of almost 500mph (800kph) – nearly twice the performance of the best existing American piston engined airliners. An ambitious plan indeed!

A few months later de Havilland's received official backing for the project when the Ministry of Supply placed a contract for the purchase of several Comet aircraft for the government overseas airline, BOAC.

Some measure of the magnitude of the pioneering design task the de Havilland Company had taken on can be gained from the fact that it was not until mid 1949 that the prototype Comet made its maiden flight – and it was a further two and a half years before the type – now designated the Comet 1 – received a full

Certificate of Airworthiness. After specialised crew training by both BOAC and de Havilland's, BOAC at last began scheduled passenger services with the Comet, initially between London and Johannesburg, on May 2 1952.

The introduction of the world's first jet airliner to everyday operations, offering passengers entirely new standards of comfort and speed, created a furore in the world airline industry. In one masterly stroke, Britain appeared to have regained mastery over the American civil aircraft industry, despite the lead the latter had gained during the long years of war. Orders for the Comet and its proposed faster and higher capacity development, the Comet 2, flowed in from other international airlines – Air France and UAT, Canadian Pacific Airlines, Olympic Airways, Middle Eastern Airlines, United Arab Airlines and Ibn-Saud. The Australian based British Commonwealth Pacific Airlines, though having reservations about the aircraft's long range capability for efficient operations on the trans Pacific service, was keenly interested, while Qantas Empire Airways was under considerable pressure from its Kangaroo Route partner, BOAC, to also place orders for the type.

In September 1952, four months after regular Comet services had begun, de Havilland's announced the development of a longer range variant, the Comet 3, for trans Atlantic services. The jewel in the crown for the British aircraft industry followed shortly afterwards – orders for the Comet 3 from the long established and prestigious Pan American Airways. The US domestic operator,

Capitol Airlines, also placed an order for Comet 2s soon afterwards. A new British era in commercial aviation was dawning!

But now came the first of a series of misfortunes that were ultimately to shatter the fulfilment of the British dream. On October 26 1952, BOAC's Comet G-ALYZ was taking off at night and in rain from Rome's Ciampino Airport with a full load of passengers. On the point of becoming airborne at 112 knots, Captain Foote felt a shudder, followed by a pronounced buffet – the prelude to an aerodynamic stall. Realising the aircraft was no longer accelerating, he eased the control column forward, but the buffet continued and the aircraft bounced on the runway. Foote immediately cut the power and abandoned the takeoff, braking heavily. But too late.

Still travelling at high speed, the Comet plunged off the end of the runway into the dark. The undercarriage was wrenched off as it hit a mound of earth, the port wing and tailplane smashed into two of the airport's post mounted boundary lights, and the aircraft finally slid to a stop on the muddy ground, damaged beyond repair. Mercifully, though kerosine poured from a ruptured fuel tank, no fire broke out and the occupants, though badly shaken, all escaped injury.

An investigation carried out by the Italian authorities found that the tail of the Comet had made contact with the runway several times some distance before its end. The accident was attributed to "pilot error" in raising the nose too high, a finding disputed by the British Airline Pilots' Association. The Italian report was not published and the accident itself

was given little publicity, a situation by no means unwelcome to BOAC and de Havilland's.

Subsequent tests by de Havilland's chief test pilot, Group Captain John Cunningham, established that if the nose of a Comet was raised too far while taking off, the induced drag resulting from the high angle of attack would prevent the aircraft from accelerating to flying speed and would bring on a low frequency buffet – that which Captain Foote had experienced at Rome with such unfortunate results. Comet pilots were accordingly briefed on a revised takeoff technique, requiring the nosewheel to be kept in contact with the runway until the specified takeoff speed was reached, when the aircraft was to be "rotated" into the climb attitude.

Meanwhile the production of Comets continued at de Havilland's Hatfield works and by February, Comet 1 *Empress of Hawaii*, carrying Canadian registration CF-CUN, was ready for delivery to its new owners, Canadian Pacific Airways. A Canadian Pacific delivery crew, led by Captain Charles Pentland, the company's overseas operations manager, arrived at Hatfield to undergo endorsement and engineering training, and the delivery flight to Canada was planned for the end of the month.

De Havilland now saw the delivery flight as the opportunity they had been waiting for. Because of the perceived reluctance on the part of British Commonwealth Pacific Airlines, and particularly Qantas, to actually place orders for the Comet (attitudes, it must be said, that were largely the product of de Havilland's unwillingness to provide either air-

The prototype de Havilland 106 Comet, flown by de Havilland's Chief Test Pilot, Group Captain John Cunningham, becomes airborne at Hatfield for the first time on July 27, 1949. Keen eyed observers will note the single wheel main undercarriage – in contrast to the bogey type undercarriage of the later production Comets. (Temple Press)

The future looked bright for BOAC, de Havilland's and the British aircraft industry when the world's first jet passenger service from London to Johannesburg opened on May 2 1952. Company and national publicity made the most of the historic occasion. (IPC)

line with a detailed analysis of the type's performance), a Comet demonstration to Australia had long been planned "to help the Australians realise that the Comet is in fact an aeroplane and not a pipe dream", as the Chairman of BOAC, Sir Miles Thomas put it.

If the Canadian Pacific Airways Comet could be delivered via Australia and the Pacific instead of across the Atlantic, taking time out while in Australia to be shown to the press and public, it could well swing the balance in favour of Comet orders instead of the Lockheed Super Constellations Qantas were keen to obtain.

A satisfactory arrangement was negotiated with Canadian Pacific and it was agreed that the delivery flight should proceed via Australia, flown by the aircraft's Canadian crew under the command of Captain Pentland. A further incentive to help convince the potential Australian customers was now conceived: if the flight could also smash the elapsed time record for the England/Australia route, public acclaim for the Comet would be all the greater.

The Comet's proposed record breaking flight was widely reported in the press and many excited Australians looked forward to seeing their first jet airliner literally within little more than a day after its departure from England. But now fate struck the whole Comet project a more serious blow.

On March 3 1953, taking off for Rangoon in the early hours of the morning after a quick refuelling stop

at Karachi, Pakistan, CF-CUN was seen to assume an abnormally nose-up attitude early in the takeoff run. After using up the entire length of the runway and its overrun without becoming airborne, the Comet's undercarriage struck the culvert of a perimeter drainage ditch. The aircraft swung, lurched, then plunged into a dry canal bed beyond the airport boundary, exploding violently into flames on impact. The flight crew of five, together with their six passengers — de Havilland technical personnel on their way to Canada to

assist with the Comet's introduction to the airline – all died in the crash and fire. It was an almost exact repetition of the accident at Rome just over four months previously – except for the traumatic and tragic outcome.

The weather at the time was fine and calm, with a visibility of some nine kilometres in haze, but the night was very dark. The Comet was loaded to its maximum permissible takeoff weight of 52,150 kilograms, but the 2288 metres of runway available should have been adequate in the existing conditions. Beyond the end of the paved runway was an overrun of another 180 metres, and the runway was equipped with high intensity lighting and threshold lights at both ends.

In addition to the evidence of eyewitnesses who said the aircraft's nose was abnormally high for almost the whole takeoff run, marks on the runway showed that the Comet's tail bumper had come in contact with the ground a number of times. Unlike the Rome accident, there was nothing to indicate that the crew had made any attempt to abandon the takeoff. But there was evidence that the nose high attitude was corrected towards the end of the runway and the Comet was about to become airborne when the undercarriage hit the culvert.

The Indian investigation concluded that the accident resulted from the excessive nose-up attitude of the aircraft during the takeoff run, producing a partly stalled condition and excessive drag. This prevented

Interior of the comfortable forward passenger cabin of the Comet. Passengers were entranced by the quietness and smoothness of Comet travel – not to mention its slashed timetables! (IPC)

The first production Comet, G-ALYP, which flew the world's inaugural jet passenger service from London to Johannesburg. This aircraft was lost just 20 months later when it exploded over the Mediterranean, killing all on board and casting a heavy shadow over the whole future of Comet operations. (IPC)

normal acceleration to flying speed. Eventually realising the nose was too high, the crew took corrective action, but too late to prevent the undercarriage striking the culvert.

Contributing to the cause of the accident was the captain's very limited experience on Comet aircraft. Though a highly experienced airline pilot, Captain Pentland had little jet experience and had not previously attempted a night takeoff in a Comet. During his conversion training on the Comet, Pentland had been briefed on the Rome accident and its apparent cause. Group Captain Cunningham had also demonstrated the revised takeoff technique to him, stressing the need to keep the nosewheel on the runway until flying speed was reached. Even so, as with the Rome accident, the investigators believed the steep nose-up attitude of the aircraft might not have been apparent to the crew, with no horizon visible in the hazy darkness. (At that stage of their development, Comet aircraft were not fitted with accurate attitude indicators with nose attitude calibrated in degrees, their only attitude instruments being standard Sperry artificial horizons).

It was also thought that the Comet's powered hydraulic flying controls, with no "feel" or "feedback" to the pilot, could easily contribute to over control, especially when no external visual reference was available.

The final contributing factor to the accident was considered to be the pressure on the crew to complete the flight from London to Sydney in the least possible time. Fatigue had undoubtedly played some part.

The Karachi accident was a bitter blow to both Canadian Pacific Airways and the aircraft manufacturer. Apart from the tragic loss of some of its key personnel, de Havilland's much vaunted public relations exercise for the Comet had turned out to be a disaster of nightmare proportions. And its repercussions were by no means limited to the Comet's future in Australia: Canadian Pacific Airways promptly cancelled orders they had placed with de Havilland's for a further two Comets.

Only two months later another Comet, operating BOAC's Singapore/London service, became the victim of an even worse disaster, again on the Indian subcontinent.

On May 2, 1953 – the first anniversary of the aircraft type's inauguration of jet passenger services – Comet 1 G-ALYV, under the command of Captain Maurice Haddon, landed at Calcutta's Dum Dum Airport for refuelling at the conclusion of the leg from Rangoon.

The early summer weather was fine locally, with three eighths of cumulus cloud, but it was the monsoon season and scattered cumulonimbus build ups to 35,000 feet were likely. Following an inflight message from an Indian aircraft operating to the north-west of Calcutta, a special airfield weather report had been issued a few minutes before the Comet landed, warning of a thunderstorm, known locally as the monsoonal "north-wester", approaching Dum

Comet G-ALYZ was written off in a takeoff accident at Rome on October 26 1952 – the victim of industry inexperience with large jet powered aircraft and the techniques required to handle them. (IPC)

Canadian Pacific Airways' CF-CUN, destroyed in a takeoff accident similar to G-ALYZ's. The accident occurred at Karachi during the Comet's delivery flight to Canada via Australia. This time all on board were killed in the crash and fire. (IPC)

Dum, with squalls reaching 50 knots. The thunderstorm was reported to be accompanied by "very strong vertical updraughts".

Soon after arriving at Dum Dum from Rangoon, Captain Haddon went to the meteorological office to discuss the approaching weather and was personally briefed by the duty forecasting officer. The captain evidently did not consider the approaching storm warranted a major diversion from track and elected to continue the flight on to Delhi as planned. The terminal forecast for Delhi's Palam Airport was entirely satisfactory.

At 4.20pm the Comet taxied out for takeoff. On board, in addition to the crew of six, were 37 passengers, most of them Britons resident in the Far East. They included the Leader of the Opposition in the Victorian State Parliament, Mr Trevor Oldham and his wife, on their way to London to attend the Coronation of Queen Elizabeth II. Ten minutes later the aircraft lifted from Dum Dum's Run-

way 19 and set course to the north-west. The surface wind at the time was south westerly at 13 knots.

Contacting Calcutta Area Control at 4.32pm, the Comet reported that its ETA Delhi was 1850 hours and that it was "climbing to 32,000 feet". Three minutes later the Comet was heard calling Delhi, but when Delhi's Communications officer told the Comet to go ahead with its message, there was no response. All subsequent attempts to contact the Comet were unsuccessful.

Around 4.35, workers tilling the soil in paddy fields near the village of Jagalgori, some 40 kilometres west of Calcutta, heard a loud report during the passage of an unusually severe thunderstorm and saw "a blaze of fire" in the sky. Various pieces of aircraft wreckage, some of them burning, then fell to the ground over a wide area.

An investigation team made up of the Indian Department of Civil Aviation's Inspector of Accidents and a Senior Inspector of Accidents from

the Ministry of Civil Aviation in London, found the main wreckage, consisting of the forward fuselage, stub wings and engines, lying inverted in a watercourse 38 kilometres from Dum Dum Airport and right on the aircraft's planned track. The rear fuselage lay in a paddy field 250 metres away, and a wreckage trail of smaller components extended for nearly nine kilometres in a south westerly direction.

It was clear that the Comet had disintegrated in the air, the separated tailplane exhibiting evidence of having failed under excessive downloading. A public inquiry conducted by an Indian High Court judge concluded that the aircraft had encountered severe gusts during flight through the thunderstorm, leading to loss of control and overstressing of the tailplane to the point of failure during an attempt to recover.

Components of the wreckage were afterwards flown to the Royal Aircraft Establishment at Farnbor-

First revenue flight fatality: BOAC Comet G-ALYV broke up in flight during an encounter with a monsoonal thunderstorm, soon after leaving Calcutta en route to Delhi on May 2 1953 – the first anniversary of the commencement of Comet services. (IPC)

"I heard three explosions," a fisherman told investigators. "Then, several kilometres away, I saw something silver flash down out of the clouds. By the time I got to where it hit the water, all was still again."

ough for further investigation. This confirmed the determination of the Indian court – an inflight break up after the aircraft encountered very severe gusts. The crew's reaction to the severe turbulence, resulting in over-control, was probably aggravated by the Comet's non-sensitive power controls and the fact that the captain was a former BOAC flying boat pilot accustomed to applying heavy control forces.

Following the failure of the tailplane under download, the aircraft would have pitched violently nose down, breaking the wings off just outboard of the engines and causing an explosive decompression of the fuselage. The violence of the monsoonal thunderstorm was considered to be of such exceptional severity that it could have produced structural failure in any type of aircraft. There was no reason to suspect the integrity of the Comet design.

But only eight months later, after yet another disaster overtook a BOAC Comet en route from Singapore to London, the picture began to look rather different.

At 10.30am GMT on January 10, 1954, Comet G-ALYP – the same aircraft that had made history nearly two years before by completing the world's first scheduled passenger jet flight – took off from Rome's Ciampino Airport for London on the last leg of its regular service from Singapore. With its normal crew of six – captain and first officer, flight engineer, radio officer and two cabin staff – it was carrying 29 passengers under the command of Captain Alan Gibson, DFC. The passenger list included the distinguished Australian wartime radio journalist, Chester Wilmot.

It was a crisp, calm winter's morning, with only thin and broken layers of middle level cloud which the Comet quickly surmounted as it climbed towards its cruising altitude. Tracking via the Ostia NDB on Italy's west coast, thence north-west up the coast, the Comet reported passing through 26,000 feet over Orbetello, 44 nautical miles south east of the island of Elba, at 0950 hours. A minute later, Captain Gibson called Captain J Johnson, the pilot in command of BOAC Argonaut aircraft, G-ALHJ, which had taken off from Rome 10 minutes ahead of the Comet, apparently to enquire about an inflight weather report he had transmitted a few minutes before. "Did you get my ...," Captain Gibson began. His message was never completed.

At about this time, the crew of a fishing trawler off the coast of Elba, and a farmer out shooting on the island itself, heard a series of loud explosions, followed by a roaring sound, above the clouds. Soon afterwards they saw aircraft wreckage, some of which was on fire and streaming smoke, spiral down into the sea, midway between Elba and the smaller island of Montecristo, 16 nautical miles to the south.

All available vessels from Elba's Porto Ferrario were dispatched to the area as soon as the accident was

Comet G-ALYY, the loss of which off Naples on April 8 1984 while the wreckage of G-ALYP was still being raised from the seabed, finally sealed the fate of the Comet and dashed the high hopes of the British aircraft industry. (IPC)

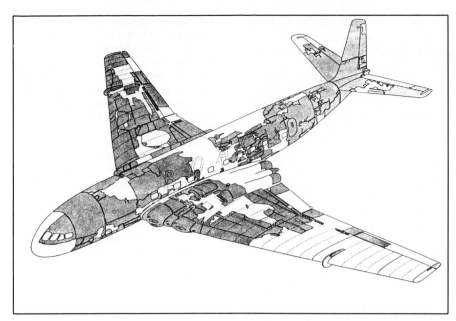

Diagram showing amount of wreckage of G-ALYP eventually recovered from the seabed off the island of Elba.

reported. Assisted by search aircraft, they succeeded five hours later in recovering various small items of floating wreckage – mail bags, cushions, overcoats, a child's teddy bear – and 15 mutilated bodies.

The Italian Government immediately set up a board of inquiry at which the British Ministry of Civil Aviation was represented by the same Senior Inspector of Accidents who had attended the Comet accident near Calcutta. There was much public and press speculation that the inflight break up was the result of sabotage – a possibility that even the British Government would not rule out at this stage. But autopsies conducted on the recovered bodies failed to reveal any telltale signs of metallic fragments that could point to the inflight explosion being caused by a bomb. Rather, all the bodies had sustained violent decompression injuries and the burns inflicted on them had occurred after death from this cause. Clearly, an explosive decompression of the pressurised cabin had occurred,

probably while the Comet was climbing through about 27,000 feet.

But why? The aircraft was exactly three years old the day prior to the accident and it had flown a total of only 3681 hours – about 1200 flights. Fatigue testing by de Havilland's during the development of the Comet up to twice the cabin's designed operating pressure differential of 8¼ pounds per inch had shown the fatigue life of the pressure cabin to be at least of the order of 18,000 flights.

Meanwhile in London, BOAC suspended all its scheduled Comet services for the purpose of completing a detailed examination of its aircraft in collaboration with the Air Registration Board and de Havilland's. Some days later the Italian authorities, in view of the complexity of the case, readily agreed that responsibility for the investigation of the accident should be handed over to the British Ministry of Transport and Civil Aviation.

In view of all that was at stake, it was now essential to recover as much of the aircraft's wreckage as possible, for detailed technical ex-

amination by experts at the Ministry of Supply's Royal Aircraft Establishment at Farnborough, one of the world's most experienced and advanced aviation research organisations.

The Royal Navy's base at Malta was called upon to assist, and three navy salvage vessels, one fitted with underwater television equipment and carrying a deep sea observation chamber, began their search in the 100 fathoms of water into which the wreckage of the Comet had fallen. It was the first time television had been used for an underwater search. The navy ships were assisted by several Italian trawlers, chartered from Porto Azzurio on Elba.

While the search for the wreckage continued, it was decided that pressurisation fatigue tests to destruction would be carried out on one of BOAC's oldest Comets, G-ALYU. Water instead of air pressure, would be used so the fuselage would not fragment when it ultimately failed. To achieve this, a large water tank was constructed around the Comet at the Royal Aircraft Establishment at Farnborough, completely submerging the fuselage while allowing the wings to protrude through the walls of tank. A complex loading cycle to simulate a typical flight, involving transfer of loads from undercarriage to wings, pressurisation, depressurisation, and finally transfer of loads back to undercarriage, was developed to achieve the equivalent of three hours flying time every 10 minutes. The test rig then began operating 24 hours a day.

Meanwhile, a committee comprising technical representatives of BOAC, the Air Registration Board and de Havilland's, had been set up to consider what modifications should be incorporated in the Comet fleet before the resumption of Comet operations could be considered. After examining a number of possible explanations for the accident in detail, a large number of modifications were carried out. The committee still regarded inflight fire

"Reconstruction" of G-ALYP's fuselage and tail assembly at the Royal Aircraft Establishment at Farnborough during the investigation of the G-ALYP and G-ALYY accidents.

as the most likely cause, and all possible sources of fire risk were investigated. To guard against the remote possibility that an engine failure had resulted in the loss of a turbine blade which had punctured the pressure cabin, armour plate was fitted around the engine nacelles in the plane of rotation of the turbines. Because of the extensive testing carried out by de Havilland's during the development of the Comet, it was thought highly unlikely that the accident was caused by a failure of the pressure cabin itself.

Towards the end of March 1954, 11 weeks after the Elba accident, with no real explanation emerging from the investigation and still no sign of structural weakness apparent in the ongoing fatigue testing of the Comet pressure cabin, despite the large number of cycles imposed on the test fuselage, the Air Registration Board could see no reason why BOAC should not resume Comet services. This the company did on March 23. Meanwhile as a precaution, the round-the-clock testing of the pressure cabin at Farnborough would continue.

Unfortunately the decision was to be proven premature. Only a fortnight later on the evening of April 8, in good if overcast weather, BOAC

Comet G-ALYY, on charter to South African Airways, departed Rome for Cairo in the course of a company service from London to Johannesburg. In the hands of an experienced South African Airways crew of seven under Captain Wilhelm Mostert, the Comet was carrying 14 passengers. Lifting off from Ciampino Airport at 7.32pm, the aircraft reported abeam Naples at 7.57pm, climbing to 35,000 feet. At 8.05pm the Comet called Cairo to pass its ETA for that airport. No further transmissions were received from the Comet by any station and all attempts to make radio contact with it were unsuccessful.

At the time of the aircraft's disappearance, the Royal Navy aircraft carrier HMS *Eagle*, accompanied by the destroyer HMS *Daring*, were at sea en route from Malta to Naples. The ships were ordered to join the search for missing Comet and when morning came, *Eagle* flew off her Grumman Avenger aircraft. After sweeping the sea for some time in the vicinity of the area in which the Comet was believed to have gone down, they succeeded in locating floating wreckage close to the volcanic island of Stromboli, some 20 nautical miles to seaward of the Italian west coast and 70nm south east

of Naples. Deformed aircraft seats, personal effects, including a letter being written at the time of the accident by one of the passengers, other floating wreckage and finally five bodies, were later picked up by the warships and taken to Naples. A further body was later washed up on the Italian coast.

The fate that had befallen G-ALYY was clearly a repetition of the Elba accident – the aircraft had disintegrated at approximately the same time after takeoff and at about the same height while climbing to cruising level. BOAC again suspended its Comet operations until more was known of the accident's circumstances. But this time more drastic measures were obviously called for – four fatal Comet disasters had now occurred within the space of 13 months, two of them in highly mysterious circumstances, and public and media confidence in the type had plummeted.

On April 12, 1954, four days after the loss of G-ALYY, the Minister for Transport and Civil Aviation announced to a gloomy House of Commons that the Air Registration Board had withdrawn the Certificates of Airworthiness of all British registered Comet aircraft.

It was a bitter blow to the British

Comet G-ALYU, used as a test fuselage, submerged in the specially built water tank at Farnborough. The fatigue pressure testing went on 24 hours a day until the pressure cabin failed.

aircraft industry and to the nation it-self. No other manufacturer in the world had a jet airliner anywhere near ready for passenger services and until this time a huge potential market had been open to the Comet. In Parliament a few days later the Prime Minister, Sir Winston Churchill, directed that the cost of solving the Comet mystery was not to be reckoned in either money or manpower. As a result, the investigation became the most intense – desperate would hardly be too strong a word – the world had ever witnessed into an aircraft accident.

The question of attempting to salvage the wreckage of G-ALYY for technical examination was considered, but quickly rejected as totally impractical. The sea where the flotsam and bodies were found was more than 2000 feet deep, precluding any possibility of recovery with existing deep sea salvage technology. With no hope of being able to examine the remains G-ALYY, it thus became all the more vital to recover as much of the airframe of G-ALYP as humanly possible. The two accidents would become the subject of a joint public inquiry, the Government decided. "Exhaustive tests will be carried out as a major national research policy'" it announced.

The Navy search off Elba for the remains of G-ALYP, painstakingly continuing in the meantime, had proved an extraordinarily difficult task. There was first of all the enormous problem of locating the relatively small pieces of wreckage in a wide area of sea. Descriptions of position by the few witnesses who had seen the Comet falling into the sea varied by up to 10 nautical miles each way, making it akin to looking for the proverbial needle in a haystack. Fortunately, circumstances now intervened to the Navy's advantage. It was learned that a survey aircraft of Skyways Ltd had flown over the disaster area shortly after the inflight catastrophe, and had photographed vessels picking up wreckage and some of the bodies. In one of the photographs, a corner of the island of Elba was visible, so providing a more accurate guide. Even so, more than a month passed before the first piece of Comet wreckage was located with the aid of the underwater television camera. Then there was the task of actually raising the numerous wreckage pieces from the sea bed, 500 to 600 feet below the surface – 300 feet or more deeper than the maximum at which Navy divers could work.

The chartered trawlers systematically swept the sea bed in the hope

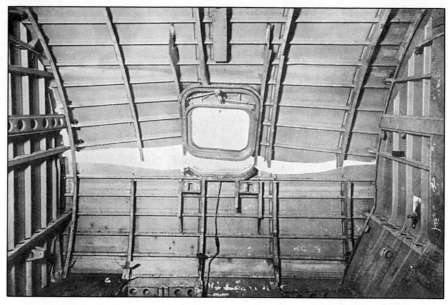

Where the pressure cabin ultimately failed in the test tank – at the forward escape hatch and window on the port side.

of scooping up small items of wreckage in their nets, the Navy ships used their Asdic, dropping maker buoys whenever a significant "ping" was registered, and the salvage vessels followed up with the television camera and the deep sea observation chamber, its crew peering out through port holes as the sea bottom was scoured a few metres at a time. As pieces of wreckage were progressively recovered, they were brought into Porto Azzurio, washed down with fresh water, then examined and identified. After being photographed, they were air freighted to Farnborough for detailed examination and inclusion in the Comet "reconstruction" which Royal Aircraft Establishment investigators were piecing together on a wooden "skeleton" mock-up of the aircraft. The tedious process dragged on until the end of August, nearly eight months after the loss of G-ALYP.

As more and more salvaged pieces of wreckage were placed in their relative positions on the fuselage skeleton, the sequence of break up became increasing clear, though its origin still remained a mystery. The middle section of the fuselage had failed first, after which the rear fuselage, then the nose section, had separated as complete entities. Shortly afterwards the outer sections of both wings had broken off. All four pieces of airframe had detached in a downward direction, leaving the centre section, including the four engines and the remains of the centre fuselage, by this time on fire, to plummet into the sea on its own.

At Farnborough too, the time con-

suming testing of the Comet pressure cabin in the water tank went on day and night, surpassing in simulated hours, the maximum time so far flown by any Comet. Meanwhile the seabed search continued off Elba, week after week, without any significant progress.

But by late May, when G-ALYP's broken off tail assembly was recovered from the seabed, the investigation began to take a more dramatic turn. When the tail unit was eventually assembled on the fuselage mock up at Farnborough, it was seen to have been heavily scored by a metal object which had left traces of blue paint. The score marks matched similar ones further forward on the port side of the aft fuselage, indicating that the object had slid along the fuselage before striking the tail and possibly knocking it off. Chemical analysis of the paint showed that the object responsible for the scoring was a cabin chair – it had somehow been catapulted from the cabin before the tail failed. Embedded in the tail structure itself was further proof that the cabin had been violently disrupted – a piece of carpet from the cabin floor. The only way this could have happened was if the carpet had been hurled against the tail before the tail assembly broke off.

Now other recovered pieces of wreckage pointed to an explosive failure of the fuselage. Score marks and paint were found running across the upper surface of the port wing – and the paint was that used for the heavy blue "cheat line" running the length of the fuselage! In other words the port side of the fuselage had been violently blown out on to the upper surface of the port wing while the wing was still attached. On June 16 a piece of the port side of the fuselage was recovered from the seabed and sent to Farnborough. Its scratched blue cheat line paint and jagged edges exactly matched those on the portion of port wing!

Even more was to come. At the end of June, as the test fuselage was being pressurised to simulate yet another climb to cruising altitude, there was a further dramatic development – the gauges registering the pressure difference between that of the cabin and that in the surrounding tank suddenly dropped to zero. The fuselage had failed after the equivalent of 9000 hours flying!

Draining the tank revealed a massive split in the fuselage skin eight feet (2.4m) long and three feet (30cm) high, located above the port wing and just below the forward cabin window and escape hatch. The failure had originated from a fatigue crack at a rivet hole at the lower rear corner of the escape hatch cut out. Further examination of the fuselage then revealed similar hairline fatigue cracks emanating from rivet holes around the cut out for the ADF antenna in the top of the cabin.

Yet there was not a sign of a similar fatigue failure in the wreckage of G-ALYP's fuselage – unless it still lay on the bottom of the sea. Certainly a good deal of the fuselage was still missing, especially in the vicinity of the centre section. The trouble was that the Navy search seemed to have scraped the seabed clean.

In desperation, the investigators now turned their attention to the likely trajectories of G-ALYP's wreckage after the inflight explosion, in the hope that this might help locate the vital still missing sections of the fuselage. If there had been a violent structural failure of the pressure cabin, the effect, it was calculated, would be similar to a 500 pound bomb exploding inside the aircraft. To simulate what this might have done to the various sections of the airframe, a large number of wooden scale flying models of the Comet were constructed with their major components detachable, but held in place by sliding pins, to which lines of varying length were attached. When the models were launched from a tethered balloon, the lines pulled out the pins in a predetermined sequence to simulate the inflight breakup of G-ALYP. As the components fluttered down, their trajectories were recorded by movie cameras. From these experiments, a pattern of the way in which the components scattered was established. This information, scaled-up, was then applied to the areas of sea off Elba to estimate where the missing sections of fuselage were most likely to be found.

On July 6 the systematic sea search off Elba was modified accordingly. The problem now was deeper water, confining the work to the trawlers. Nothing of significance

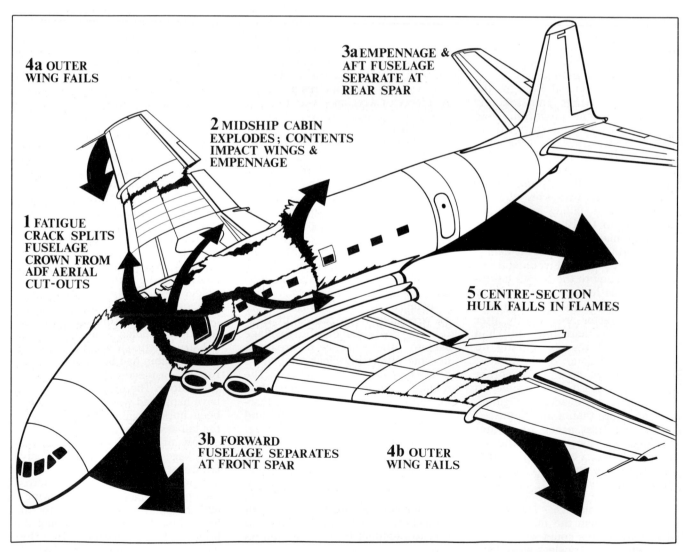

Main structural failures of G-ALYP airframe following inflight fracture of pressure cabin. (Matthew Tesch)

was found for a month, but on August 12 the trawl net of one of the Italian fishing vessels at last snagged a substantial piece of wreckage. When hauled to the surface it proved to be a large piece of the top of the cabin, including the roof "window" for the ADF antenna where the hairline fatigue crack had been found on the test fuselage. At a rivet hole in the corner of the window cut out, not far from the section of fuselage that had scored the port wing, there was an unmistakable fatigue crack – marking the origin of the fuselage structural failure that had destroyed the aircraft!

The mystery was at last solved. As G-ALYP climbed to cruising altitude over the Mediterranean on the morning of January 10, 1954, its pressure cabin had burst like an over inflated balloon with the force of a bomb, flinging the centre fuselage structure and its contents into space. Some had hit the wings, others the tail. Immediately afterwards, with the integrity of the fuselage thus destroyed, the nose and rear sections had separated, falling relatively intact until they hit the water. Aerodynamic forces acting on the tumbling centre section, still with the four engines attached, had then torn off the outer wings, leaving it to fall, now burning from disruption of the fuel lines, into the sea on its own. For all on board, death would have been instantaneous as the aircraft exploded.

Had exactly the same thing happened to G-ALYY only three months later? All the circumstances certainly pointed to it. But with no examination of the wreckage of G-ALYY possible to confirm the origin of failure or pattern of break up, how could it be known for certain?

The evidence was provided by the Italian and British pathologists who examined the bodies recovered from the sea after both disasters. The pattern of injuries sustained in the accidents was identical in both cases, pointing to a common cause of trauma. It was the first instance of aviation pathological evidence confirming the circumstances of a major air accident.

So ended what was undoubtedly the most intense and costly accident investigation in the history of aviation. The formal Court of Inquiry into the two accidents began in London under a judge of High Court in October 1954. The transcript of its proceedings ran to 800,000 words and a document 10 inches (25cms) thick. Its report, published in February 1955, found no just cause to criticise de Havilland's: they had proceeded at all times in accordance with good engineering practice. But they were working at the very frontier of technology and had paid a high price for their pioneering work.

Did the inquiry's findings cast any further light on the earlier structural failure of Comet G-ALYV after take-off from Calcutta on May 2 1953? The official inquiry report did not refer to it, but in retrospect, Senior Inspector of Accidents T R Nelson who participated in the Indian investigation privately believed that its basic cause was probably similar to the Elba and Naples accidents.

On the other hand, a distinguished Australian aeronautical engineer who was seconded to the Indian investigation as an observer had an entirely different theory which never came out in the official report. John Watkins, Director of Engineering for TAA and a man with a keen professional interest in the future of the Comet at the time, believed the precipitating factor in the Calcutta accident was a lightning strike in the cumulonimbus cloud of the monsoonal squall line.

At Calcutta when G-ALYV was refuelled, the wing tanks were filled to capacity, but at Captain Haddon's request only a small amount of fuel was pumped into the Comet's empty belly tank. As it happened, the tanker vehicle which refuelled the Comet had been standing in the hot Calcutta sun for two and a half hours before the aircraft arrived. After refuelling, the Comet's belly tank thus contained a relatively small quantity of hot kerosine – and by the time of takeoff, a large quantity of highly explosive vapour. In these circumstances, John Watkins believed, a lightning strike could have touched off the vapour, initiating the structural failure. Watkins examined the wreckage himself and was convinced the remains of the belly tank exhibited evidence of such an explosion.

Be that as it may, the findings of the massive and definitive British investigation made aviation history. Its effects were far reaching, other aircraft manufacturers with jet airliners on the drawing board, particularly the Boeing and Douglas corporations in the United States, benefiting enormously from the British industry's costly lessons.

Throughout the world, new design standards for the structural safety of jet powered airframes and pressure cabins were adopted, and the spectre of metal fatigue became an ever present consideration in the minds of designers. Manufacturers were alerted to the fact that even the smallest fatigue crack resulting from repeated pressurisation of a fuselage had the potential to lead to a disastrous structural failure.

The Comet investigation also pointed out the problems inherent in designing cutouts in pressure cabins. The result is that today's pressurised jet airline aircraft fuselages have heavier skinning and smaller windows. Their design also incorporates a cross-webbing type of fuselage wall structure intended to stop any crack extending unimpeded along the cabin skin. The resulting gain in design knowledge and safety is plain to see – since the Comet disasters, no other airline jet has exploded in flight as a result of a pressure cabin fatigue failure.

But none of this could compensate the aircraft manufacturer and the airline that had blazed the trail into the unknown realm of high speed jet airliner operations at 40,000 feet – Britain's de Havilland Company and BOAC. The fleet of five surviving Comet 1s remained permanently grounded. The RAF's Transport Command took delivery of a few Comet 2s with modified fuselages. Only one Comet 3 was completed to flying status and became an airborne test bed for Rolls-Royce's new and more powerful Avon engines.

The general public was not to have the opportunity to fly again in a Comet until BOAC introduced the redesigned and longer fuselage Comet 4s to the North Atlantic service in October 1958. But only three weeks later Boeing's new, much bigger and longer range 707 jetliner, an aircraft developed from the KC-135 flying tankers Boeing had developed for the USAF's Strategic Air Command, entered the same market – a market which the Seattle manufacturer, by the overall excellence of its product, would take by storm.

Britain's de Havilland Company, the pioneer, has missed the bus.

CHAPTER 2

"We can see it out ahead ... it looks pretty bad"

– F/O to Miami Departures

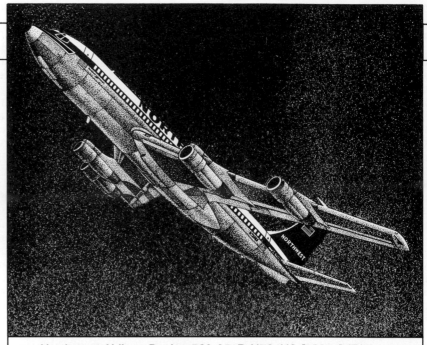

Northwest Airlines Boeing 720-051B N724US [18354] (F/n N724) – February 12, 1963

Nothing less than a major disaster could fully reveal the hazards that await large jets in turbulent air.

In the pre-jet, pre-turbine era, aircraft designers dreamed of the day when technology would allow airliners to "cruise in the stratosphere", flying serenely between ports of call high "above the weather", a realm thought to be free of the discomfort generated by convective cloud and the more pernicious turbulence of frontal storms.

The advent of Boeing's piston engined 307 Stratocruiser in 1940, the world's first pressurised airliner, seemed to bring that dream a little closer, its fulfilment apparently frustrated only by the intervention of World War 2, resulting in the decision to cease production after only 10 Stratocruisers had been built. It was not until jet airliners began to invade regions of the atmosphere above 30,000 feet in the late 1950s and early 1960s that the long sought ideal of "above the weather" flight was finally seen for the myth it was – that turbulence could be encountered at these levels in every way as severe as that afflicting flight at less ambitious altitudes.

But as has been the pattern so often in the march of aviation technology over the years since man's first faltering successes with heavier than air flight in 1903, it took a major disaster to fully reveal the hazards that can await large jet aircraft plying their high corridors in angry air.

Northwest Airlines Inc, based at Minneapolis, Minnesota, USA, had taken delivery of Boeing 720B, N724US, late in 1961. Fitted with the latest Pratt & Whitney JT3 turbofan engines, it had flown more than 4500 hours on the company's domestic route network in the 18 months it had been in service. A lighter version of the better known Boeing 707, it was America's first short to medium range passenger jet and had been ordered by a number of US domestic airlines.

On February 12 1963, N724US was scheduled to operate Flight 705, the company's transcontinental service from Miami, Florida, to Portland, Oregon, with intermediate landings at Chicago, Spokane and Seattle, departing Miami at 1.30pm local time. The aircraft had arrived from Chicago at 12.40pm after an uneventful trip, the crew reporting only a slight problem with the pressurisation controls, which was quickly rectified at Miami.

A change of crew for the return flight took place at Miami. Captain Roy Almquist, a veteran airline pilot with nearly 18,000 hours experience, was in command. His first officer, Robert Feller, was also highly experienced, with a total of nearly 12,000 hours. But because Boeing 720 aircraft were still relatively new to the airline, neither pilot had a great deal of experience on the type, most of their flying having been logged on the company's DC-4s, DC-6s, DC-7s and, in the case of the captain, Lockheed 188 Electra turboprops. First Officer Feller had gained just over 1000 hours on the Boeing 720, but the captain, who had completed his type rating only three months before, had only 150 hours. As usual in American airline operations, the flight engineer, officially designated the second officer, was also pilot rated with 5000 hours experience. His flight engineer experience on Boeing 720 aircraft amounted to 523 hours. Five stewardesses, all in their twenties, made up the rest of the crew.

The weather at Miami was threatening as the 35 passengers boarded the aircraft for the first leg to Chicago, just after 1.15pm. A prefrontal squall line lay to the north west of the city, moving south east at eight knots. Associated with this squall line was a broken area of thunderstorms with cells up to 20 miles in diameter and cloud tops reaching to

30,000 or even 40,000 feet in some cases. Freezing level was between 11,000 and 12,000 feet. The Miami weather bureau had issued a Sigmet forecasting moderate to severe turbulence in the thunderstorms, with a chance of extreme turbulence in the heavier storms, and the crew were well aware they could be in for a rough ride on their initial departure route.

At 1.25 the Boeing taxied out for takeoff, the crew asking the Miami ground controller what routes other aircraft were using to avoid the approaching weather. He told them that most flights were departing either on "a south west climb or a south east climb, then back over the top of it". The crew asked for a "south east vector" and at 1.35 the Boeing was cleared for takeoff from Runway 27 Left.

Turning left after takeoff, and radar vectored by Miami Departure Control, the aircraft then followed a circuitous routing to avoid the expected worst areas of turbulence. Eight minutes later, while maintaining 5000 feet on a heading of 300 degrees, the crew asked for a clearance to a higher altitude. "We're in the clear now," the first officer told the controller. "We can see it out ahead ... looks pretty bad."

At 1.43, after co-ordination with Miami Air Route Traffic Control, Departure Control cleared the Boeing 720B to climb to flight level 250 (25,000 feet). Acknowledging the clearance, the first officer said they would turn left "about 30 degrees and climb". Seeking to clarify the crew's intentions, the controller then asked if 270 degrees was their selected climbout heading. The first officer replied that this would take them "out into the open again," and after reporting the turbulence as "moderate to heavy", he advised the controller: "OK, you better run the rest of them off the other way."

Two minutes later Departure Control terminated the radar service and transferred the Boeing to the Miami Air Route Control frequency. When Air Route Control asked for the aircraft's position and altitude, First Officer Feller reported they were climbing through 17,500 feet and told the controller to "standby for our DME position". His transmission, at 1.48pm, was the last received from the Boeing.

Soon after this time, a number of people on the ground in different areas of the Everglades National Park, some 60 kilometres south west of Miami, where it was raining heavily, heard a loud explosion in the air and a short time later felt a ground tremor. One woman who heard the explosion immediately looked up in the direction from which it came and in a moment saw what seemed to be "a ball of flame in the edge of a cloud." As she frantically pointed it out to her companions, it "dropped straight down, became a streak, and disappeared behind trees." This group heard a second explosion shortly afterwards. Their position was some 11 kilometres south of where the disintegrated main wreckage of the Boeing was later found.

Search helicopters dispatched by the Civil Aeronautics Board later established that the wreckage was scattered widely over an inaccessible area of the Everglades National Park in flat open country interspersed with clumps of trees, rocky outcrops, and marshland. The distribution of the wreckage, extending over an area 25 kilometres long and two kilometres wide and aligned on a heading of about 260 degrees, left no doubt that the Boeing had broken up in flight. Ground access to the wreckage was extremely difficult, four wheel drive vehicles taking three hours to cover the 25 kilometres from the nearest road.

Some 90% of the aircraft's structure, including all the major sections, was concentrated in the westernmost three kilometres of the wreckage trail. The main section of

A Boeing 720B similar to the one that broke up in flight over the Everglades National Park, Florida. In appearance closely resembling its stretched fuselage, longer range, Boeing 707 stablemate, the type was used extensively by US domestic airlines in the 1960s. (Boeing)

(left) Weather warned of in the crew's Sigmet was all too evident as passengers boarded the fight at Miami. (right) Artist's impression of accident as described by witnesses in the Everglades National Park. (Matthew Tesch)

the fuselage had been gutted by fire, the wings and tail surfaces had separated in flight, and there was clear evidence also of a severe break up of the forward fuselage in flight. The Boeing was equipped with a Fairchild four trace flight recorder and this was recovered in readable condition. The smaller sections of wreckage, scattered to the east of the main concentration, consisted mainly of lighter material which had drifted with the wind as it fell.

To the Civil Aeronautics Board investigators, the extensive disintegration at once suggested a single catastrophic inflight event. But what could possibly have caused it? An explosion resulting from an act of sabotage? A fatigue or control system failure? More likely, was it something induced by the intense thunderstorm activity and its associated turbulence? An excessive gust loading, or even control system flutter? Or, as the aircraft had been involved in a landing accident some months before, was it the result of failure of a previously damaged component?

In a preliminary attempt to narrow these possibilities, the investigators attempted to "reconstruct" the wreckage at the accident site, confident this would soon reveal evidence pointing unmistakably to the origin of the structural failure. But as this work progressed without the slightest indication of any clear pattern emerging, the mystery deepened and it soon became obvious that a far more detailed study of the wreckage would be required.

So began what was to prove one of the most intense aircraft accident investigations in United States aviation history – one that would result in a wide reaching airline industry review of the recommended techniques for flying high speed swept wing jetliners in heavy turbulence.

★　　★　　★

Arrangements were first of all made to transfer the entire wreckage recovered from the Everglades National Park piece by piece to a US Coast Guard hangar at Opa Locka Airport at Miami. This was accomplished using a US Army H-37 helicopter, which airlifted the components to waiting trucks, or directly to the hangar itself in Miami.

Six weeks after the accident, a "reconstructed" mock-up of the Boeing 720, similar to that of the de Havilland Comet G-ALYP put together at Farnborough nine years previously, had been completed in the Opa Locka hangar, utilising all the recovered wreckage components. The detailed study was then resumed and it progressively became possible to eliminate inflight explosion, fatigue failure, control system failure and previous damage as possible causes. Yet it seemed to bring the investigators no nearer to determining what had caused a perfectly sound aeroplane to break up in flight.

The investigators found that the Boeing's wings and tailplane had failed symmetrically in downward bending, the forward fuselage had broken off upwards, and the fin had failed to the left. All four engines had separated upwards and outwards. The tailplane trim jackscrew was found to be in the full nose down position, and examination of the cockpit instruments showed that the nose down pitch stops of both vertical gyros had been severely damaged as a result of the aircraft rotating rapidly about its pitch axis.

There was no indication of arcing or burning in the electrical system, and the fuel tank vents showed no sign of fire damage. Similarly, there was no evidence of internal wing tank fires having occurred before the inflight break up, and nothing to suggest the aircraft had been damaged by lightning or hail.

Meanwhile, a readout of the recovered Flight Data Recorder's traces of altitude, airspeed, heading, and vertical acceleration showed that after takeoff at 1335.22 (1.35pm and 22 seconds), the Boeing made a series of turns while climbing in light turbulence. At 1342.36 it encountered heavier turbulence which lasted until it turned left on to a heading of 200 degrees three minutes later. During this time, the aircraft continued climbing to 15,000 feet, its airspeed fluctuating between 210 and 320 knots. It then turned on to a heading of 320 degrees as it climbed to 17,250 feet. At this point the climb ceased and the altitude remained constant for 12 seconds.

At 1347.25 the Boeing began to climb again at a rapidly increasing rate, reaching an extraordinary 9000 feet per minute 13 seconds later at 1347.38. The rate of climb then fell off quickly, dropping to zero within nine seconds as the altitude momentarily peaked at 19,285 feet. In the course of this brief but steep and abrupt climb, the airspeed fell from 270 to 215 knots and, as the altitude peaked, the vertical acceleration suddenly reversed from a normal plus 1g to minus 2g.

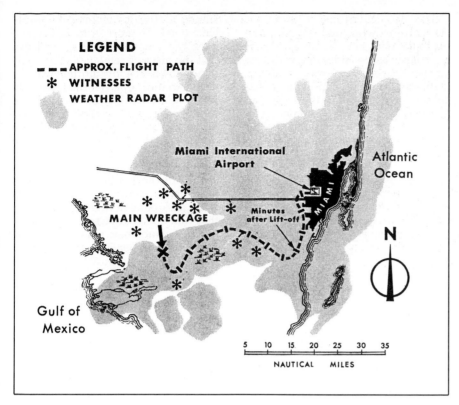

LEGEND
‑ ‑ ‑ APPROX. FLIGHT PATH
* WITNESSES
▓ WEATHER RADAR PLOT

Miami International Airport

Atlantic Ocean

MAIN WRECKAGE

Minutes after Lift-off

Gulf of Mexico

N

5 10 15 20 25 30 35
NAUTICAL   MILES

Diagram showing track flown by the Boeing 720B after takeoff from Miami, location of thunderstorm areas, crash site, and positions of witnesses on ground. (Aviation Safety Digest)

During the ensuing eight or nine seconds, the negative g increased even more, with rapid fluctuations, to minus 2.8g, while the aircraft began losing height at an increasing rate. This continued with the airspeed rapidly building up, while the vertical acceleration trace changed from the high negative peak to plus 1.5g (apparently as the crew attempted to regain control), when it again reversed. During the last nine seconds of flight the altitude continued to plummet, the airspeed rose until the stylus in the flight recorder hit its mechanical stop, the negative g increased again, and the heading remained fairly constant at 330 degrees. From the beginning of the final climb from 17,250 feet at 1347.25, all these manoeuvres occupied only 45 seconds.

Data provided by the Boeing Company, derived from aerodynamic studies of the Boeing 720's control response, graphically illustrated N724US's final moments. They showed that no less than full nose down deflection of both the elevators and the adjustable tailplane would have been required to achieve the unusually high negative load factors recorded. Moreover, the elevators would have had to be intact to achieve the partial recovery that followed the nose over and build up of speed. The studies also showed that N724US's pitch attitude had ranged

from 22 degrees nose up during the sudden climb, when it reached a rate three times greater than normal, to beyond the vertical after it pitched nose down and dived towards the ground at dramatically increasing speed.

Because of the massive control inputs revealed, the Boeing Company sought to determine to what extent the aircraft could have been affected

by vertical air currents – updraughts and downdraughts in the heavy turbulence of the thunderstorm. This was achieved by comparing the airspeed and altitude traces obtained from the flight recorder with the aircraft's known climb performance. The comparison showed that although vertical currents of high intensity were acting on the aircraft at the time of the steep climb and subsequent dive, these were not in themselves sufficient to cause structural failure.

Nevertheless, it was obvious that the aircraft's response to such high intensity draughts could have been extremely misleading to a pilot flying in instrument conditions. Although the overall effect of an updraught is to produce an increase in altitude and a nose up attitude, an aircraft flying into an updraught initially tends to "weathercock" nose down. A pilot trying to counteract this initial bunt with nose up elevator could thus amplify the overall effect of the updraught. The converse would happen in a sudden encounter with a downdraught. Further studies by the Boeing Company, conducted by simulating flights in a variety of gust conditions, showed vertical air currents alone could not have been responsible for the vertical acceleration forces shown on the flight recorder. Rather, it seemed highly probable that the effect of the gusts was magnified by the crew's attempts to counter them.

A US Weather Bureau analysis of the gust intensities recorded at the time in the area of the accident dem-

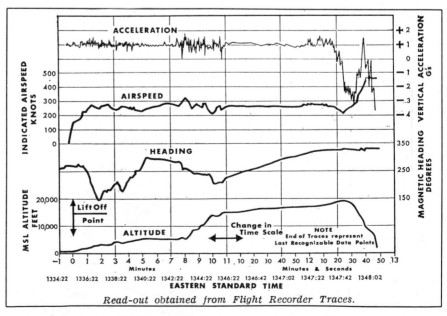

Read-out obtained from Flight Recorder Traces.

Readout of the Boeing 720B's flight recorder, showing traces for vertical acceleration, airspeed, magnetic heading, and altitude. Note the high negative accelerations coinciding with the abrupt decrease in altitude and rapid gain in airspeed. (Aviation Safety Digest)

onstrated that while the frontal weather was severe, it was not unusual and that, apart from the statistically remote chance of an extreme gust encounter, the maximum gusts the Boeing would have encountered were within the design limits of the aircraft type.

It was now apparent that, contrary to what the investigators had first suspected, no single catastrophic event had been responsible for the accident after all. A study of the trajectories followed by the various components of the aircraft after the inflight break up, in conjunction with the data derived from the flight recorder, confirmed this belief.

A detailed analysis of the various wreckage trajectories established that the Boeing remained intact throughout most of its final dramatic manoeuvres, and that components did not begin to separate until it had dived to below 10,000 feet and substantially exceeded its design limit speed.

Design regulations required the structure to withstand only a minus 1g limit load, but the actual design strength was considerably in excess of this. The tailplane was capable of withstanding the high minus 3.2g load imposed on it in the early part of the nose over and should not have failed at this load factor unless the elevators were suddenly pulled nose up at a rate considerably greater than that revealed by the flight recorder. The way in which the elevators and tailplane did finally fail suggested that a loading of this sort was imposed on them later in the high speed dive – presumably during the crew's attempts to recover level flight.

The forward section of the fuselage was also capable of withstanding the initial high negative loading and would not have failed until after the tailplane did so. The design strength of the wings would have been exceeded at each of the high negative loadings, but the second in-

stance at the lower altitude would have been the more critical. But perhaps the most convincing evidence that the aircraft remained essentially intact down to a low altitude was the determination that the final manoeuvres required full nose down elevator trim, together with full nose down elevator, both held for about eight seconds, followed by a return to full up elevator as the crew attempted to recover from the dive.

Two further factors which could have had a bearing on the accident were also considered. The first was that rain could have frozen in the elevator balance bay, resulting in icing of the balance panel seals and restriction of elevator movement. There had been numerous instances of longitudinal control difficulties arising from this problem, usually characterised by stiffness in the control column with a corresponding lack of response by the aircraft, or by a cycling force in the column with a consequent porpoising aircraft motion.

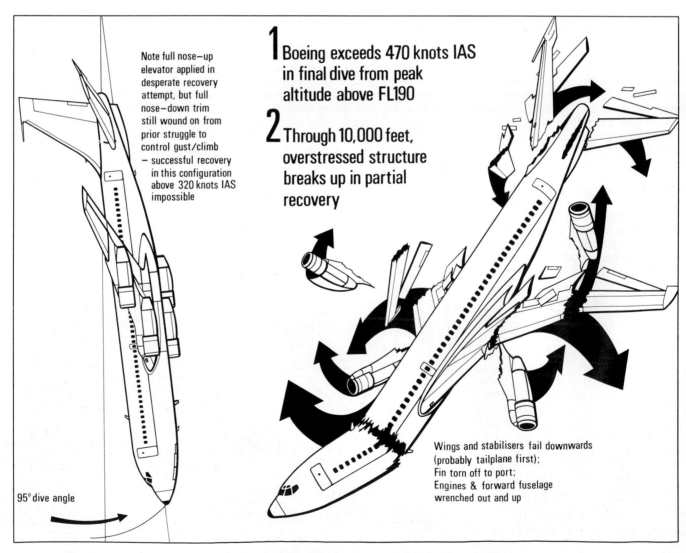

Note full nose–up elevator applied in desperate recovery attempt, but full nose–down trim still wound on from prior struggle to control gust/climb – successful recovery in this configuration above 320 knots IAS impossible

1 Boeing exceeds 470 knots IAS in final dive from peak altitude above FL190

2 Through 10,000 feet, overstressed structure breaks up in partial recovery

95° dive angle

Wings and stabilisers fail downwards (probably tailplane first); Fin torn off to port; Engines & forward fuselage wrenched out and up

Probable breakup sequence of Boeing 720B, N724US. (Matthew Tesch)

In some cases additional force on the control column overcame the difficulty, but in a few instances the controls were so stiff that elevator trim had to be used to control the aircraft. Some crews had overcome the problem by descending to a lower altitude, allowing the ice to melt. In no case however had the ice caused a loss of control.

The other factor to be considered emerged from the results of calculations made by aerodynamicists. Mathematical analysis of the Boeing's longitudinal control system indicated that at full down elevator deflection, control forces could lighten or even reverse. A full scale wind tunnel test was required to resolve the question and this was carried out using a Boeing 720 half tailplane and elevator.

It was found that from level flight, control forces varied normally with increases in elevator angles, but that during pitching manoeuvres with constant tailplane angle settings, the push force required for down elevator reached a maximum at 10 degrees down, then decreased as the angle was increased. The aero elastic properties of the aircraft structure also tended to decrease the amount of control column force required to perform nose down pitching manoeuvres.

The picture of the Boeing's final manoeuvres that initially emerged from the investigation was that of an intact aircraft following a grossly abnormal flight path resulting from highly unusual longitudinal control displacements.

It was inconceivable that a pilot of Captain Almquist's experience would have imposed such displacements unless prompted by the most exceptional circumstances. It was equally difficult to imagine a control difficulty that could account for the tailplane and elevator movements the manoeuvres required. No possible control malfunction, such as a runaway tailplane trim drive or a hard over autopilot, could produce such drastic results.

One likely explanation appeared at first to be the control restriction caused by icing in the elevator balance bay theory. But after further consideration of the facts as demonstrated by actual flight testing, this explanation could not be substantiated.

The other possible explanation was the misleading effect of the aircraft's response to severe gusts while the crew were flying in instrument conditions, precipitating an upset and a steep high speed dive from which the crew were unable to recover.

The performance analysis by the Boeing Company to support the belief that the manoeuvres leading to the accident had developed from an "out of phase" relationship between the aircraft's response to severe turbulence and the crew's control inputs, was critically examined in conjunction with the wind tunnel test results.

The wind tunnel tests proved extremely useful in confirming many of the results obtained by calculation. Although elevator control forces did not actually reverse in the tests, they showed that considerable lightening of control forces occurred at large down elevator angles. Small variations in tailplane rigging such as might be found on aircraft in service, were found to be capable of a further lightening effect, or even a mild control force reversal.

A further Boeing Company study to assess the possibility of recovering from a high speed dive showed that a Boeing 720 in a 95 degree dive at 320 knots with full nose down trim was recoverable provided that full up elevator was used. Beyond this speed however, it was no longer possible to achieve a return to level flight while the elevator trim remained fully nose down.

At the start of the recovery, full up elevator required a pull force of 84 kilograms on the control column and imposed a load factor of 4g on the aircraft. This load factor decreased throughout the recovery, but at the same time the control force needed to hold full up elevator increased, reaching a maximum of 145kg shortly before the aircraft levelled out. While demonstrating the theoretical ability of the Boeing 720 to recover in such a situation, the study emphasised the enormous difficulty facing a crew confronted with the task, particularly in severe turbulence and in instrument conditions with no outside reference.

Some of the findings of the rough air penetration studies being conducted independently at the time by the National Aeronautics and Space Administration (NASA), were also of assistance. They showed that in certain circumstances, the unfavourable coupling of a pilot's control inputs and aircraft motion induced by heavy turbulence, could create a hazardous situation. Pilot workload and technique, acceleration forces, cockpit instrumentation and aircraft characteristics could all become factors in precipitating an upset.

In a Boeing 720 simulator, it was shown that an aircraft, properly trimmed for straight and level flight, could be flown "hands off" through the most severe gusts without inducing excessive g loadings or large air-

The recovered wreckage of the Boeing 720B being "reconstructed" in the Coast Guard hangar at Opa Locka Airport, Miami. An Army helicopter was used to lift the wreckage piece by piece from the inaccessible crash site in the Everglades National Park. (Aviation Safety Digest)

Boeing 707/720 cockpit: The cockpit layout of the Boeing 720 is virtually identical to that of the better known 707. (Boeing)

speed and altitude variations. The gusts produced large changes in pitch attitude, but in each instance the aircraft's inherent stability restored the trim condition. By contrast, with a pilot "flying" the simulator, the variations in load factor depended on how closely the pilot tried to maintain a constant pitch attitude. Some of the attempts resulted in large oscillations in pitch, indicating the pilot's control inputs were out of phase with the effects of the gusts. In a few cases, the oscillations increased to the point where an upset occurred. Large pitch oscillations also occurred when pilots were instructed to ignore the pitch attitude indicator and concentrate on maintaining a constant airspeed during a simulated turbulence penetration.

Other studies made after the accident on the human factors, aircraft design, and operational aspects of rough air penetration were also examined. Notable among these were

papers by Captain Paul Soderlind, manager of Northwest Airlines' Operations Research and Development Division, which discussed potential "miscues" that could be obtained from primary flight instruments, and sensory cues that could be misleading in particular flight conditions. The importance of using the attitude indicator as the primary instrument reference in turbulence, together with the need for improvement in the design of attitude instruments were other important conclusions reached by Captain Soderlind.

Although the Civil Aeronautics Board and its investigators were unable to agree with all the findings presented by various parties during the investigation, they believed the accumulated evidence was sufficient to draw a broad picture of the events that befell N724US and its crew in the final 45 seconds of their lives.

It was evident that shortly after 1.47pm, only 12 minutes after takeoff, the Boeing 720 entered an area

of heavy turbulence at 17,250 feet. The climb that began at this point could have been the result of vertical air currents or initiated by the captain, but probably resulted from a combination of both. The dramatic way in which the rate of climb then increased, the alarming nose up aircraft attitude, and the rapidly falling airspeed would have led the captain to believe a stall was imminent.

Reacting accordingly, probably while being severely buffeted by the turbulence, the captain apparently applied full-down elevator and tailplane trim. These large control inputs would certainly have checked the high rate of climb and decrease in airspeed and returned the aircraft to a near level attitude, but would also have produced high and extremely disorientating negative g forces.

The actual negative g forces revealed by the flight recorder would have caused chaos in the cockpit. As well as the distraction of warning bells and lights triggered by the negative g conditions, the crew would have to contend with brief cases, charts, manuals, pencils and any other loose articles violently thrashing around the cockpit as they were hurled towards the ceiling. The crew members themselves would be forced upwards, hard against their seat belts, finding it almost impossible to keep their hands on the control column and feet on the rudder pedals. The instrument indications would become a blur and the crew would probably lose all track of time.

In the passenger cabin, even greater bedlam would have reigned. Any passenger or flight attendant not restrained by a seat belt would have been flung hard against the ceiling, together with hand luggage, books, newspapers, personal items, and any catering equipment not securely locked down. All this would have been accompanied by severe buffeting from the turbulence, and the noise of ripping, tearing and smashing, not to mention the terrified screaming and shouting of the passengers. The contents of the toilets would also have been forcibly ejected on to their compartment walls and floor and probably into adjoining sections of the cabin.

But why had this appalling situation been allowed to continue for eight or more seconds, a condition that could be maintained only by full down elevator, with the control column hard against its forward stop? It is inconceivable that it could have been the action of the crew. The far more likely explanation is that the elevator control forces lightened nearly to zero, and both untended control columns simply remained in the fully forward position.

It seems that one or other of the pilots were finally able to take hold of the control column again, but by this time the aircraft was diving vertically through 16,000 feet with the

airspeed building up frighteningly. The flight recorder indicated that one of the pilots initially pulled the control column back to the neutral position where it remained for a few seconds before being drawn right back, probably by both pilots acting together, into the full up elevator position as they desperately attempted to regain control.

But by this time the aircraft had dived to 10,000 feet, the airspeed had exceeded 470 knots, and the excessive airloads on the elevators prevented a successful recovery. The crew's attempt to retrim the tailplane nose up would also have been foiled by the trim drive motor stalling under the high elevator loads.

Although a recovery might have been theoretically possible from this appalling situation a little earlier if the pilots had acted more promptly, their failure to do so was hardly surprising in view of the extremely high control forces required and the conditions in the cockpit. It is even possible the rapid upward elevator movement needed for the theoretical recovery at this stage might only have resulted in the elevator and tailplane failing structurally earlier than they did.

Some characteristics of the aircraft undoubtedly played a part in the events leading to the accident. The acceleration forces in the cockpit induced by flexing of the fuselage in heavy turbulence and amplified by the combined effect of the pilots' seat cushions and their tightly fastened seat belts, undoubtedly blurred the crews' view of the instruments. This unpleasant characteristic, common to all large swept wing aircraft, would certainly be detrimental to the pilots' ability to act, and with the aircraft out of control and in a grossly abnormal attitude, would have been frightening.

The lightening of the elevator control forces at large down elevator angles also made matters worse for the

crew, as did the powerful effect of the moveable tailplane. Though of course essential to the design of the aircraft, the Civil Aeronautics Board believed that a moveable tailplane's operation should be such as to preclude serious out-of-trim situations developing.

Finally there was the calibration of the attitude indicators with which the Boeing was equipped. These were among the newer types of attitude indicators available at the time and provided adequate attitude reference for all normal pitch attitudes. At large pitch angles however, the horizon line disappeared from the face of the instrument, making interpretation of attitude extremely difficult. During the pitch down manoeuvre and the crew's efforts to regain control, this could have added to their disorientation and indeed become the "last straw" in the inevitability of the accident.

Altogether it was obvious to the Civil Aeronautics Board that many factors, which in isolation would not have presented a great hazard, had combined in a particularly unfortunate way to cause the accident. Perhaps above all, the investigation clearly demonstrated that instrument flight in severe turbulence could become dangerous if pilots did not follow the practice of using the attitude indicator as their main reference. Undue emphasis on any other instrument during a pilot's normal instrument scan could lead to serious misinterpretations with extremely drastic results.

Similarly, attempts to maintain a "perfect" flight attitude could be equally hazardous because of the high loadings involved, the danger of overcontrolling, and the possibility of inducing an oscillatory motion in the aircraft. A "loose" attitude control, using moderate counteracting control inputs, appeared to be by far the safest pilot technique when penetrating heavy turbulence.

CHAPTER 3

" ... Taxi onto the runway ... to have a look around ...?"

– Caravelle crew to Zurich Ground Control

Swissair SE-210 Caravelle III [147] HB-ICV {147} *Schaffhausen –* September 4, 1963

Jet blast seemed one way to clear fog from the runway for takeoff. But the consequences would exact a terrible price the crew could not foresee.

Wednesday, September 4, 1963, was to be a big day for the tiny Swiss village of Humlikon, to the north of Zurich. Forty three of its leading citizens – a quarter of its population, including its mayor and town councillors – were leaving early in the morning for Geneva where they would attend an agricultural show of interest and importance to their close knit rural community.

It was an occasion to which the farmers and their wives had been looking forward for months. Moreover, instead of the tortuous train journey of more than 300km through the mountains, they were going to fly there, a rare experience for many of them and one that should be highly exciting – they were booked to Geneva on one of Swissair's new Caravelle twin jets. In the village the early autumn day promised to be fine and clear, and the whole party of men and women was in high spirits as they set off together by coach for Zurich's Kloten Airport.

Swissair Flight SR306, Zurich to Rome via Geneva, departing Zurich at 7am, was to be operated that morning by Caravelle III, HB-ICV. It was an aircraft the company regarded as "almost new", having being delivered by the manufacturer at Toulouse less than a year before. Indeed, in Europe the whole concept

of jet travel was still relatively new, Air France's Sud Aviation SE-210 Caravelle Is, delivered only four years previously, being the first European jet to enter service after the ill starred de Havilland Comets. It was also the first airline jet design to have its twin engines mounted on either side of the rear fuselage, and was proving an excellent aircraft.

In command of Flight SR306 that morning was Captain Eugen Hohli, a pilot with Swissair for the past 10 years. His first officer was Rudolph Widmel, while one steward and two stewardesses were rostered to look after the Caravelle's capacity load of 74 passengers. In addition to the lively party from Humlikon, the passenger list included Swissair's personnel manager and six other staff. Except for six foreign businessmen, including a London banker and an American sales executive, the remainder were all Swiss citizens, most of them bound for Rome.

Though the day was fine and cloudless on the mountains, shallow morning fog lay in the valleys, and Kloten Airport was still closed to operations as the flight's departure time approached. Captain Hohli nevertheless decided to have a look at conditions on the runway and the passengers were ushered aboard at the normal time.

After the engines had been started, the aircraft called the tower to ask for the surface visibility on the airport's 16-34 runway. The controller told the crew the visibility from the Runway 16 threshold was only 60 metres, but from the 34 threshold in the reciprocal direction it was 210 metres. The crew then asked the tower for a guide vehicle to lead them to the threshold of Runway, 34 as well as for approval to "taxi on the runway – on 34 – and back again to have a look around."

The tower approved the request, a guide vehicle was despatched to the tarmac where the Caravelle was waiting, and it began leading the slowly taxiing aircraft out towards the threshold for Runway 34. The fog on this part of the airport was particularly dense, and the guide vehicle driver soon lost his way, mistakenly leading the Caravelle into Taxiway 4 instead of Taxiway 5. The result was that the aircraft joined Runway 34 about 400 metres from the threshold instead of at the threshold itself. However, it turned on to the runway, and with the engines roaring loudly, began taxiing slowly in the direction of takeoff.

After covering about 1400 metres, the Caravelle slowed, turned 180 degrees, and taxied slowly back, this time continuing right to the thresh-

A Sud Aviation Caravelle III of the type which caught fire after takeoff from Zurich, Switzerland. All eighty occupants were killed instantly when the aircraft dived steeply into the ground. (Michael Maton)

old, still with engines set to high power. Workmen on the airport in the vicinity of the runway particularly noticed the engine noise was a good deal louder than normal for a taxiing Caravelle.

At 7.09am the aircraft called the tower again, reporting that the fog appeared to be lying in banks, with varying visibility, and that the jet blast from the engines had some effect in clearing the fog from the runway itself. The crew indicated they were preparing for takeoff, and three minutes later requested approval to do so. The tower promptly passed the aircraft its clearance, and the Caravelle apparently took off normally. Shortly afterwards the crew reported they were now in clear conditions on top of the fog bank at 1700 feet and climbing to cruising level, and communications were transferred to the Zurich departure frequency in the normal way.

But only eight minutes later, one of the crew transmitted a Mayday call in a highly agitated voice. His words then became almost incoherent, and when Air Traffic Control

The picturesque Kloten Airport at Zurich, Switzerland, as it looked in the mid 1960s. The aircraft taxiing past in the foreground is an Austrian Airlines Caravelle of the same type as the Swissair aircraft involved in the accident. Also visible in the picture are (left to right), another Caravelle, this time belonging to the Spanish airline Iberia, a British European Airways Comet 4, a Swissair Convair 440, a KLM Boeing 707, and a Swissair Convair 880.

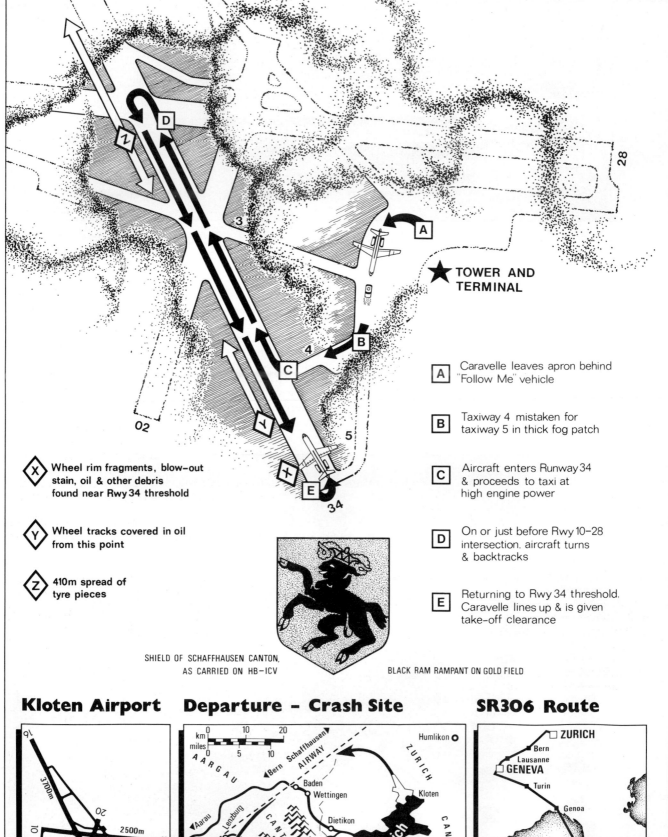

TOWER AND
TERMINAL

3

4

5

02

34

A Caravelle leaves apron behind "Follow Me" vehicle

B Taxiway 4 mistaken for taxiway 5 in thick fog patch

C Aircraft enters Runway 34 & proceeds to taxi at high engine power

D On or just before Rwy 10–28 intersection, aircraft turns & backtracks

E Returning to Rwy 34 threshold. Caravelle lines up & is given take-off clearance

X Wheel rim fragments, blow-out stain, oil & other debris found near Rwy 34 threshold

Y Wheel tracks covered in oil from this point

Z 410m spread of tyre pieces

SHIELD OF SCHAFFHAUSEN CANTON,
AS CARRIED ON HB-ICV

BLACK RAM RAMPANT ON GOLD FIELD

Kloten Airport

19

3700m

20

2500m

1535m

10

02

34

28

Departure – Crash Site

km
miles

0   10   20

0   5   10

AARGAU

Bern Schaffhausen AIRWAY

Humlikon

ZURICH

Lenzburg

CANTON

Baden

Wettingen

Dietikon

Kloten

Zurich

CANTON

Aarau

DÜRRENÄSCH

BETTWIL

Zurichsee

SR3O6 Route

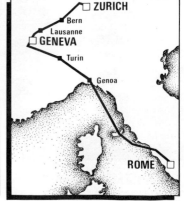

ZURICH

Bern

Lausanne

GENEVA

Turin

Genoa

ROME

Diagram showing pretakeoff movements of Caravelle HB-ICV at Zurich's Kloten Airport, and location of undercarriage debris found later. Insets show layout of airport and Caravelle's departure route. (Matthew Tesch)

A Sud Aviation twin jet Caravelle 225 operated by the Scandinavian Airlines System in the early 1960s. The Caravelle was the first jet airliner design to have its engines mounted on either side of the rear fuselage. The Swissair Caravelle which caught fire after takeoff from Zurich was substantially similar in appearance.

asked for details of the emergency, he gasped with obvious desperation: "No more ..." Silence followed, and all further attempts to communicate with the Caravelle went unanswered.

About this time, a farmer working high on a valley side not far from the village of Dürrenäsch in the Canton (State) of Aargau, 19 nautical miles south west of Zurich, sighted the Caravelle in flight. Flying in a clear sky well above the blanket of fog that still covered the lower areas of the country, it appeared at first to be climbing normally at a moderate altitude from the direction of Zurich. But as it neared his position, the farmer noticed whitish smoke streaming from its port side. As he continued to watch, he was horrified to see flames burst out along the port side of the fuselage. The aircraft flew on for a time, seemingly unaffected. But then it entered a gradual turn to the left and began to lose height. Finally it nosed over into a dive and, steeply nose down, plunged from sight into the bank of fog.

Meanwhile, on the outskirts of fog enshrouded Dürrenäsch, retired farmer and local businessman Heinrich Lienhard was breakfasting in the kitchen of his two storey house. Gradually he became aware of the sound of an approaching jet aircraft. But instead of receding as the aircraft passed over, the noise increased, rising in note until it became an ear shattering, spine chilling scream.

Seconds later there was a tremendous explosion that rocked the house like an earthquake, its flash of fire lighting up the whole room, despite the heavy fog. A moment afterwards, there was a second, much closer impact as debris sliced into the roof on the far side of the house,

carrying away the tiles and roof beams. Lienhard was unhurt, but the side of the house that had been struck was left burning. A short distance away from Lienhard's house, tavern proprietor Kurt Walti had rushed outside when he heard the screaming of the descending jet and actually saw it emerge from the fog an instant before it dived into a potato field on the edge of the village with "a great burst of fire". Flames were "shooting from its left side" before the crash.

The force of impact in the soft agricultural ground gouged a crater 20 metres long and 10 metres deep, with debris from the crash scattering over half a square kilometre.

Some of the burning wreckage flung from the impact point set a barn on fire in an adjoining field.

The sound of the impact explosion was heard for kilometres around, and ambulances and fire engines from Dürrenäsch and nearby Aarau rushed to the scene. The two building fires were promptly extinguished, but it was all too evident there could be no possible hope of survivors. Not a single body could be found in the impact crater or the wreckage trail extending beyond it. Of the Caravelle's 80 occupants, the only sign was fragmented human remains.

It was the worst air disaster in Swiss aviation history. It also marred

View looking inboard and aft of the port main undercarriage bogie of a Caravelle III. The No 3 tyre (on the right of the photo) exhibited evidence of both brake rim overheating and fire; the No 4 wheel assembly – the source of the fire – is obscured.

A house on the outskirts of the Swiss village of Dürrenäsch, badly damaged by wreckage from the stricken Caravelle.

vestigation laboratory, gave few clues to the nature of the catastrophe. Apart from showing that the Caravelle had climbed to 8780 feet before it began to lose height, the FDR revealed little that the investigators did not already know from eyewitness evidence.

This witness evidence now confirmed that the aircraft had been on fire in the air well before it crashed. Eyewitness reports from other villages in fact indicated the aircraft was on fire several minutes before. Farmers working on the land near the village of Bettwil, 14 kilometres south east of Dürrenäsch where some fog still lay, could not see the Caravelle itself, but they saw a "glowing fire" moving at great speed through morning mist, accompanied by loud roaring. Parts of the aircraft, from the port undercarriage area, the port wing and rear fuselage, were later found on the ground under the last six nautical miles of the Caravelle's flightpath.

Fragments of the outer rim of the aircraft's No 4 landing wheel (the inner rear wheel of the port undercarriage bogie) were also found near to the threshold of Zurich's Runway 34. Close to it on the runway was a blowout stain, an earthing cable and its attachments, and traces of burnt hydraulic oil. The blowout stain lay between the tracks of the two pairs of wheels of the port main undercarriage, and beyond this point the wheel tracks were covered in hydraulic oil. Pieces of the tyre from No 4 wheel were found further still

the excellent safety record of Swissair which had previously lost only seven passengers since being founded 32 years before – four in a Junkers accident at Constanz, Germany in 1939, and three when a Convair ditched in the English Channel in 1954.

The villagers of Dürrenäsch had themselves had an extremely narrow escape from disaster. Still trembling from shock, Heinrich Lienhard told newspaper reporters: "I was tremendously lucky – my room was at the far end of the house from the crash. I missed death by a hairsbreadth." Local textile factory owner, Oskar Sager said: "It was a stroke of fate the aircraft did not come down 50 metres further to the left. Had it done so, all 70 workers in the factory would have been killed. We were extremely lucky."

The cause of the accident initially defied explanation. It was clear that the aircraft had been on fire in the air shortly before the crash, but what could have led to it so quickly after an apparently perfectly normal takeoff and climb?

The Swiss Federal Air Accidents Investigation Office quickly convened a Commission of Inquiry under Colonel Karl Höenegger, and its investigators set about the daunting task of piecing together the available evidence.

The exact time of the crash needed little enquiry – it was evident to the whole district. In the instant before it hit the ground in its near vertical dive, the Caravelle had sliced through power and telephone lines and all electric clocks had stopped at the moment of the accident. But a preliminary examination of the crash site yielded little information of any use: the wreckage in the impact crater was so fragmented that only an almost impossibly thorough excavation and detailed examination of each piece of wreckage could point to any pattern of fire damage and structural failure.

Nevertheless the investigation team did succeed in recovering the aircraft's Flight Data Recorder. But even this, when read out in the in-

Aerial view of the Swissair Caravelle crash site. The 10 metre deep crater made by the aircraft's near vertical dive into the ground can be seen in the lower centre of the picture.

along the runway, between 1230 and 1640 metres from the threshold.

After a long and detailed investigation and analysis of all the circumstances that could have contributed to the accident, the investigators found that three interrelated factors could be used as a starting point from which to reconstruct the likely sequence of events. These were the fracture of the No 4 wheel before or at the beginning of takeoff, the outbreak of fire in the aircraft while climbing, and the final dive to destruction.

It was evident to the investigators that the rim of the No 4 landing wheel broke away and its tyre burst while the Caravelle was turning to line up on the takeoff heading at the threshold of the runway. The condition of the wheel's brake mechanism, recovered with much effort from the crash site, led to the conclusion that the mechanism had been grossly overheated by the prolonged manoeuvres on the runway before takeoff, with the crew using high engine power settings to disperse the fog while deliberately holding the aircraft to a slow taxiing speed with the brakes. Tests showed that such overheating could lead to a wheel fracture similar to that which occurred in the Caravelle's No 4 wheel.

The external picture of the events leading to the crash, as obtained from eye witnesses, was one of rapid change, only a few minutes after takeoff, from a trail of white smoke issuing from the aircraft, to a sudden

Artist's impression of the horrifying sight that confronted a farmer working on a valley side high above the fog enshrouded village of Dürrenäsch. (Matthew Tesch)

major fire in the vicinity of the retracted port undercarriage while the Caravelle was still climbing. In reviewing the circumstances that could have led to this sudden outbreak of fire, the investigators were faced with two alternative possibilities.

Firstly, it was known that hydraulic oil escaped from the braking system immediately after the blowout of No 4 tyre, and that this oil was

burning as the takeoff began. If the fire started when the No 4 tyre blew out and was still burning when the crew retracted the undercarriage, it could be expected to spread to the other wheels of the port main undercarriage bogie and eventually burst out of the undercarriage housing.

Alternatively, there was evidence to show that there had also been a primary fire in the No 3 wheel (the rear outer wheel on the port bogie,

(left) Wheel brake disk recovered from the Caravelle's No 4 wheel assembly. The deep grooves made by heavy braking while taxying at high engine power are clearly visible. (right) A typical blowout stain similar to that found by investigators near the threshold of Zurich's Runway 34.

adjacent to No 4), and its brake disks too showed unmistakable signs of overheating. Tests and calculations established that wheel rims of the type fitted to the Caravelle do not reach their maximum temperature until a few minutes *after* the braking effort that produced the overheating. For this reason, it was quite possible that No 3 wheel rim had also burst after takeoff, causing damage to fuel lines and ignition of a separate fire which eventually ate its way out of the undercarriage housing.

In either event, there could be no doubt that the fire which eventually destroyed the aircraft and all its human cargo of 80 souls – a tragedy that orphaned no less than 43 children in the little village of Humlikon

– was brought about simply by the overheating of the brakes before takeoff.

In their final reconstruction of the various phases in the accident process, the investigators concluded that the flight was normal for the first five minutes, with the crew and passengers blissfully unaware of the potentially disastrous situation that was developing in the port undercarriage bay. Data derived from the FDR showed that the first obvious effects of the problem were a falling off in aircraft performance. This was followed soon afterwards by a deviation to the left as the fire took hold, and a loss of height. The final phase, in which the Caravelle entered its fatal steep dive, was probably induced by a loss of rigidity in the port wing

structure as a result of the intense fire, loss of hydraulic power for the control system, and structural damage to the port tailplane.

Apart from the obvious dangers inherent in the technique used by the crew to achieve a takeoff in the fog prevailing at Zurich at the time of their flight's scheduled departure, the most significant safety lesson to emerge from the disaster was the fact that the temperature of wheel rims continues to rise *after* heavy braking has ceased. It is vitally important therefore, for pilots to keep this fact in mind when assessing the time they should allow between abandoning a takeoff for any reason (nearly always with heavy braking), and beginning another takeoff run.

The principle of using jet blast to clear fog from a runway – attempted with such disastrous results by the Swissair Caravelle crew – is sound in itself, provided the jet engines are not on an aircraft! At Orly Airport, Paris, the experimental "Turboclair" system was used successfully for this purpose. Comprising a row of eight turbojet engines mounted on the ground beside the runway, the Turboclair system could clear a path for a takeoff or a touchdown in only a minute. This aerial photograph, taken on infrared film from directly above the runway, shows the obliquely angled jet effluxes dispelling fog from the landing area. (National Geographic)

CHAPTER 4

"Have you still got the runway OK?"

– Cincinnati Tower to Boeing 727

American Airlines Boeing 727-123 N1996 [18901] (F/n 996)
– November 8, 1965

Haste, high rate of descent, poor visibility, lack of crew co-ordination and visual illusions – all combined to forge a chain to disaster.

For 39 year old Captain Bill O'Neil, Flight 383 from New York to Cincinnati on the evening of November 8 1965, was to be another of the final steps to his long sought upgrading to jet airliner command.

Not that he was any newcomer to airline flying. But American Airlines, as befitted its status and reputation, did not promote lightly or unadvisedly. O'Neil had been a pilot with the company for 14 years and a captain on its piston engined DC-6s, DC-7s and Convair 240s for eight of those years. Three weeks before, with an enviable total of 14,000 hours in his log book, he had completed three months intensive training on the company's new Boeing 727 trijets. Now he was well into the final stage of his transition to captaincy on the type – the 25 hours of line flying "in command under supervision" required by Federal Aviation Agency (FAA) regulations.

The probation period was no great hardship. David Teelin, 46, the check captain assigned to supervise his 25 hours, was well known to him. Though a veteran American Airlines pilot with considerably more experience than his own in terms of both flying hours and years of service, they got on well and their respect for each other's abilities was not in question.

★   ★   ★

The forecast for the hour and a half flight to Cincinnati, scheduled to depart New York's LaGuardia Airport at 5pm, though by no means perfect, held no terrors for the experienced crew. At their planned cruising level of 35,000 feet, they expected to be on top of the weather until descending into Cincinnati. Though some thunderstorms were forecast, their briefing indicated that a route via Charleston, Virginia, involving a 90 nautical mile diversion to the south, should position them well clear of this weather. The terminal forecast for Cincinnati read: "Ceiling 1200 feet broken, 3500 feet overcast, visibility four miles, light rain, fog. Variable to 1000 feet overcast, visibility two miles, thunderstorms, moderate rain."

After a 20 minute delay, occasioned by the aircraft's late arrival at New York from an earlier flight, Boeing 727-123, Registration N1996, taxied out. With Captain O'Neil in nominal command in the left hand seat, Captain Teelin was carrying out the duties of First Officer in the right hand seat. Their Flight Engineer was 33 year old John Lavoie, also highly experienced, with more than 6000 hours as a crew member. Three young stewardesses, all in their

early twenties, looked after the aircraft's 56 passengers.

After takeoff from LaGuardia Airport, the flight made a standard instrument departure, then requested a clearance to Charleston at 35,000 feet, thence direct to Cincinnati at the same flight level. Some 40 minutes later however, when about 90nm from Charleston (apparently because the expected thunderstorms were not materialising), the crew requested a clearance to the York VOR, some 55nm northwest of Charleston's radio beacon, thence direct to Cincinnati. Air Traffic Control cleared the Boeing 727 accordingly.

At 6.45pm, the crew called Cincinnati to report their ETA was now 1905 hours (7.05pm). They were told that the QNH was 30.01 inches, with the airport barometric setting (QFE) 815 feet "above". (For approaches to land, it was American Airlines' practice to set both pilots' altimeters to the airport QFE, while leaving the centre altimeter set to the QNH). Ten minutes later, when the Boeing was 24nm from the airport, communication was transferred to Cincinnati Approach Control. The weather was clear to the east and northeast of the airport, but there was cloud, with some lightning, to the northwest.

A Boeing 727-100 similar to the type involved in the Cincinnati accident.

Descent clearances were issued to the aircraft and two minutes later the crew reported: "Out of 5000 for 4000 (feet) – how about a control VFR? We have the airport in sight."

The Approach Controller replied: "Continue to the airport – cleared for a visual approach to Runway 18, precip lying just to the west boundary of the airport and its ... southbound." The crew acknowledged the clearance and the controller cleared them to descend to 2000 feet at their discretion.

Three minutes afterwards, the Approach Controller told the Boeing its radar position was now six nm southeast, and instructed the crew to change frequency and call Cincinnati Tower. Their exchanges with the tower controller then went as follows:

Aircraft: "Cincinnati Tower ... we're six miles southeast and ... control VFR."

Tower: "Runway 18, wind 230 degrees, five knots, altimeter 30."

Aircraft: "Roger, Runway 18."

Tower: "Have you in sight – cleared to land."

Aircraft: "We're cleared to land, roger. How far west is that precip line now?"

Tower: "Looks like it's just about over field at this time, sir. We're not getting anything on the field however ... if we have a windshift, I'll keep you advised as you turn on to final."

Aircraft: "Thank you – we'd appreciate it."

Tower: (10 seconds later – just after 7.00pm) "We're beginning to pick up a little rain right now."

Aircraft: "OK".

Tower: (A minute later) "Have you still got the runway OK?"

Aircraft: "Ah ... just barely ... we'll pick up the ILS here."

Tower: "Approach lights, flashers and runway lights are all on high intensity."

Aircraft: "OK."

This transmission, 22 seconds af-ter 7.01pm, was the last to come from the crew. Five seconds later, apparently under full control, the Boeing flew into the wooded slopes of the west bank of the Ohio River valley, three kilometres north of the approach end of the runway. Cutting a swathe through foliage and scrub for 300 metres, it collided violently with a stand of trees, exploded into flame and burnt to destruction. One stewardess and three passengers were the only survivors.

Greater Cincinnati Airport, three kilometres south of the two kilometre wide Ohio River valley, has an elevation of 890 feet. At the time of the accident, Runway 18, its main instrument runway, was 2623 metres long and equipped with high intensity runway lights and a standard "A" approach lighting system with sequenced flashing. All lights were at their highest intensity during the Boeing's approach, and the Instrument Landing System (ILS) was fully serviceable.

Examination of the wreckage by investigators of the Civil Aeronautics Board (today the National Transportation Safety Board), established that the Boeing's starboard wing had first struck a tree while the aircraft was on a heading of 235 degrees in a level attitude, but 225 feet *below* the level of the airport. The side of the river valley into which it had descended has an upward slope of about 10 degrees, rising to the approximate elevation of the airport.

There was no evidence of any aircraft malfunction prior to impact. The tailplane trim setting was within the normal range, the undercarriage was still locked in the retracted position, the trailing edge flaps were extended 25 degrees and all leading edge devices fully extended. All spoilers were retracted.

All three engines had ingested tree branches, mud and twigs, the debris being distributed from the air inlets through to the turbine sections of each engine. A thorough examination of the engines, together with the aircraft's hydraulic and electrical systems, revealed no evidence of any failure.

The remains of the aircraft's three Kollsman drum pointer type altimeters were examined by the manufacturers. The subscale of the captain's altimeter was set at a barometric indication of 29.06 inches of mercury, with the index marker set on 800 feet. The "thousands of feet" drum position could not be determined because of damage. The copilot's altimeter subscale was set to 29.03 inches, with the index marker positioned at 815 feet. Both these settings closely approximated the airport QFE setting passed to the crew by Air Traffic Control. No information could be obtained from the remains of the centre panel altimeter.

Of the four survivors of the crash, only one, a company pilot travelling in the first class passenger cabin, could recall any details of the accident. Seated at the front window on the starboard side, he believed the flight from LaGuardia was normal in every way. But the descent into Cincinnati seemed fast, with the lights of the city visible to the north after the aircraft levelled out. He could also see reflections from the airport's approach lighting on scud clouds below the aircraft. The next time he looked out the window, "It seemed like we were very low ... I sat there unconcerned, and it seemed we had started another left turn and we were in a 10 to 15 degree bank." The next thing he recalled was hearing the flap motors being actuated again, and immediately afterwards they crashed.

The violent impact threw him out of his seat on to the floor. Though momentarily stunned, he saw flames coming from the rear of the cabin. He succeeded in extricating himself from the cabin debris piled on top of him, found his way forward and stepped out the front of the aircraft, the nose of which had been demolished. A few moments later the Boeing exploded and burnt fiercely. It was not raining when he clambered out of the wreckage, but a heavy downpour began about half a minute later.

The Cincinnati arrivals radar controller gave evidence that, as the Boeing was approaching the airport, areas of rain were visible on his radar screen. The heaviest was to the west of the airport, moving southwards, with lighter areas to the north and north west. When he last observed the Boeing on radar it was two miles to the north east, and appeared to be at the leading edge of the lighter area of rain.

A number of witnesses on the ground watched the Boeing during its approach. They saw it flying downwind about four miles to the east of the airport, then crossing the Ohio River valley at low altitude before turning left on to base leg, parallel to and immediately to the north of the Ohio River. Its landing lights were on and it appeared to be flying level or making a gradual descent. It then turned in towards Runway 18 as it crossed the wide river valley for the second time. Light rain was falling as it did so, and heavy rain began shortly afterwards.

One witness in the river valley watched the Boeing's last 10 seconds of flight. He first saw its four landing lights coming towards his position from the east, then saw it bank rapidly to the left and crash violently into the valley's southern slopes. There was nothing unusual about the aircraft except that it was flying too low in the valley to clear its sides.

The pilot of a Cessna 310, inbound to Cincinnati from the northeast at the time of the accident, said he saw "a streak of light" (which he later took to be the Boeing's landing lights), progressing from left to right across his field of vision. The lights appeared to diminish in length over a period of between five and 10 seconds, then abruptly went out. Seconds later flames erupted from the ground. Conditions were generally visual to the north, but there were thunderstorms to the west and northwest. There was a line of rain over the Ohio River to the north of the airport, with patches of low scud in the area. Heavy rain was begin-

ning to fall in the immediate vicinity of the accident.

Boeing 727-123, N1966, had been delivered new to American Airlines only four months before the accident and had flown a total of only 938 hours. At the time of the accident, both its gross weight and centre of gravity were well within prescribed limits.

The Boeing was not equipped with a cockpit voice recorder, but its four trace Flight Data Recorder was recovered from the wreckage and a detailed readout of the recorder traces covering the final six minutes of the flight produced a ground track and rapid descent profile corresponding with the evidence of air traffic controllers and other witnesses. There was no significant turbulence throughout this whole

descent except during the last 50 seconds when some light turbulence was recorded.

The FDR showed a continuous descent from 7000 to 2000 feet on a northwesterly heading of 305 degrees, during which the airspeed was progressively reduced from 350 to 250 knots with a descent rate of around 3000 feet per minute. At 2000 feet (1100 feet above airport elevation), the Boeing levelled off, turned north on to a downwind leg, and remained at this approximate altitude while the airspeed bled off to 190 knots. It then entered a gentle left turn on to base leg. At this point it began descending again at a steady rate of about 800fpm for just over one minute, with the airspeed gradually decreasing to 160 knots.

Half a minute before impact, the

Plan of the Boeing 727's night approach to Greater Cincinnati Airport as reconstructed from witness evidence. When about to turn final for Runway 18, the aircraft descended into the wide Ohio River valley and impacted against the valley side. (Aviation Safety Digest)

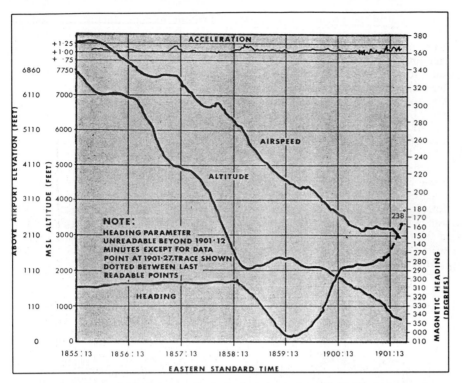

Readout of the Boeing 727's flight recorder for its final six minutes of flight. The times are shown in US Eastern Standard Time. (Aviation Safety Digest)

Boeing began another left turn, this time on to final approach. Ten seconds afterwards the descent rate increased again to just over 2000fpm and the aircraft descended below the level of the airport into the Ohio River valley. During the final 10 seconds the descent rate decreased again to 625fpm and the airspeed to 147 knots.

★　　★　　★

Study of all the evidence indicated that the cause of the accident was directly related to the way the crew conducted the approach to land. There were also a number of specific factors which could have influenced the crew's judgement.

Analysis of the FDR recordings, together with a study of American Airlines' approach procedures, showed that the Boeing entered the airport traffic pattern at 210 knots with the spoilers retracted and two degrees of flap extended. The airspeed decreased as it began its turn on to base leg, and the flaps were extended to five degrees at 170 knots. Midway along base leg, the crew selected 15 degrees of flap, and as they turned on to final, increased this to 25 degrees.

These flap extensions, though conforming to the company's stipulated speeds, were "bunched up" on base leg because of the excessive airspeed at which the approach was flown. Indeed, except for a brief period at the beginning of the base leg,

the crew succeeded in reducing the airspeed to the successive flap extension figures only by conducting the entire descent at or near idle engine thrust. It was evident that if they had extended the downwind leg, or used a substantially lower rate of descent while the flaps were being lowered, the airspeed would have reduced more easily and the flap extensions could have been accomplished more progressively.

Thus, with the aircraft slowed and

the proper degree of flap extended, it would have been possible for the crew to use higher, more desirable thrust settings, allowing them to control the approach with greater precision, and to complete the landing checklist in an unhurried manner. As it was, a number of configuration changes, including lowering the undercarriage, still remained when the aircraft was turning on to final.

The investigators had difficulty in understanding how two highly experienced captains could spend almost two minutes descending from only 1200 feet above the airport at night in adverse weather, without adequately monitoring their altitude. It could only be assumed that, preoccupied with expediting the approach in the face of deteriorating visibility, neither pilot gave due attention to the altimeter readings.

Yet, given the experience of both pilots, this explanation seemed over simplistic and inadequate. Rather, it seemed that the real solution to the cause of the accident lay with several complex, closely related factors that evidently developed during the approach.

Weather

Before the Boeing turned on to base leg, better than VFR conditions existed along the flightpath. But after making this left turn, the crew would have encountered light rain and low scud, rapidly reducing visibility. At this point, to maintain visual conditions, they might have had to descend from the altitude at which they intended flying the leg.

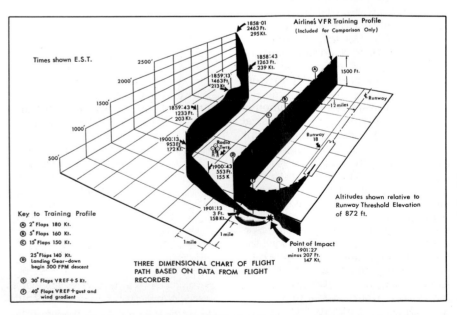

Three dimensional diagram of the Boeing 727's final flight path, reconstructed from data read out from the aircraft's flight recorder. American Airlines' VFR circuit training profile for Boeing 727 aircraft is included for comparison. (Aviation Safety Digest)

Further along base leg, the rain became heavier and visibility dropped to two miles or less. At this stage the sequenced "flashers" of the airport's approach lighting system would probably have been the only airport lights still visible, and the pilots would have been preoccupied in trying to keep them in sight.

Terrain

At this stage of the approach too, the Ohio River valley lay just to the left of the flightpath. The river itself is 400 feet lower than the airport, with its unlit, wooded valley sides rising steeply to the elevation of the airport. In their efforts to keep the airport approach lights in sight, the crew would of course have been looking out to the left of the aircraft. But as the only other lights in this direction would have been those of houses on the river bank, in the poor visibility these could easily have given the pilots an illusion of adequate altitude above the airport.

Altimeter Presentation

Another factor was the possibility that the crew could have misinterpreted the altimeter readings. The Kollsman drum pointer type of altimeter installed in the Boeing 727 has a range from minus 1500 feet to plus 50,000 feet. Hundreds of feet are indicated by a single radial pointer: thousands of feet are shown on a rotating drum, the relevant portion of which is viewed, like the barometric subscale, through a "window" in the face of the dial. To increase the significance of the indication at readings of less than 1000 feet, there is a crosshatched marking on the drum adjacent to the figures. The barometric subscale, (calibrated in inches of mercury in the USA at the time of the accident), is conventional, its adjusting knob also positioning the index on the periphery of the dial to indicate airport pressure altitude.

In reading this type of altimeter, the pilot first looks at the number below the index on the drum for the thousand foot level, and then at the radial pointer for the hundreds of feet indication. At constant altitudes or low rates of climb or descent where the drum is almost stationary, the pilot has to be careful to associate the correct thousands of feet reading with the hundreds of feet reading. For example, a reading of 900 feet would show "1" slightly above the drum index with the "0" below the index, while the radial pointer would indicate "9" on the dial. A misinterpretation could occur if the pilot mistakenly associated the

Kollman single pointer altimeter as fitted to Boeing 727 aircraft at the time of the Cincinnati accident.

pointer indication with the "1" slightly above the drum index, rather than the "0" below it. The result would be a reading of 1900 feet rather than the 900 feet actually indicated.

In descending to a "below zero" elevation, as occurred in this case, the radial pointer, rotating anticlockwise, does not point to the actual number of feet below zero. For instance, a reading of 100 feet below zero elevation would be portrayed with the radial pointer indicating "9" on the dial, and the zero on the drum slightly above the index, requiring the pilot to interpret the 900 feet indication as actually meaning 100 feet below zero. Thus with negative values, the number above the drum index rather than the number below the index provides the correct thousands of feet reading. In other words, the drum presentation reverses at below zero readings.

Experienced pilots should have no difficulty interpreting the correct reading, but the investigators considered that, under conditions of infrequent or distracted altitude monitoring, a misinterpretation could occur.

Crew Workload and Co-ordination

According to American Airlines' procedures, the Boeing when it turned on to final approach should have been in the full landing configuration with the undercarriage lowered, 40 degrees of flap extended, and the airspeed and rate of descent stabilised so that only small adjustments to the glidepath, approach speed and trim would be necessary from that point on. But because higher than normal airspeeds had been maintained throughout most of the approach, only 25 degrees of flap had actually been extended at this stage, the undercarriage had still not been lowered, and a number of other items on the landing checklist remained to be completed. Less than two nm from the runway threshold by this time, the crew would have been extremely busy.

A further consideration was the fact that the two experienced captains had flown together on seven previous flights, knew each other well, and had no doubt established a high degree of reliance on one another. It was possible that Captain Teelin, fully confident of his 'pupil's'

Viewed from the Flight Engineer's position, this artists's impression captures the scene on N1996's flight deck during the Boeing 727s turn on to what was truly 'final approach'. (Matthew Tesch)

capability, could have assumed that Captain O'Neill was monitoring the instruments, and that he could safely concentrate on keeping the airport approach lights in sight in the deteriorating weather. Similarly, O'Neill, secure in the knowledge he had a highly experienced check captain in the copilot's seat and assured in his mind that Teelin would be monitoring the instruments, could also have believed he could concentrate on the approach lights.

American Airlines' procedures require the pilot not making the landing to call airspeed, altitude, and rate of descent when the aircraft descends to 500 feet above airport elevation. The rate of descent is to be called again if at any time it exceeds 700fpm after this.

The FDR showed that the Boeing descended through 500 feet on base leg 42 seconds before impact, but that the rate of descent remained in excess of 700fpm throughout the remainder of the approach. It follows that either the altimeter monitoring procedures were not being followed, or the crew misread the altimeters.

If the pilot not making the landing, in this case Captain Teelin in the copilot's seat, was concentrating on

the airport approach lights out to the left of the aircraft, the limits of his line of vision would have been between 45 and 80 degrees of straight ahead. With his high workload of extending the flaps, performing the landing checklist in co-operation with the flight engineer, and making the radio transmissions, all the while trying to keep the airport approach lights in sight, he would have little opportunity to swing his gaze back to his own instrument panel on the right hand side of the cockpit. Rather, with O'Neill's altimeter on the left hand side of the cockpit almost in his line of vision and set to the same QFE as his own, it seems likely he would have used this instrument for reference. However, it is well known that the probability of error is increased when an instrument is read from a side angle, which in this case would have been about 55 degrees. The flight engineer, occupied with the landing checklist, was unlikely to have been monitoring the flight instruments at this stage of the flight.

★   ★   ★

Overall, the investigators gained the impression that the entire flight

to Cincinnati was conducted so as to expedite the Boeing's arrival in the shortest possible time, prompted no doubt initially by the 20 minute delay in departing New York, but latterly by the crew's anxiety to beat the deteriorating weather into Cincinnati. The crew obtained clearances en route which provided a shorter, more direct route, and the aircraft's average ground speed within the Cincinnati terminal area (a radius of 30nm from the airport) was in excess of 325 knots, in contravention of FAA regulations which limit terminal area airspeeds to 250 knots below 10,000 feet. In addition, despite the obviously deteriorating weather, the crew elected to make a visual rather than an instrument approach.

This situation alone of course, should not have precluded proper monitoring of the aircraft's altitude, but the evident haste to complete the flight could only be regarded as another factor contributing to the pilots' inattention to the flight instruments.

The last point at which the accident could have been averted was some 13 seconds before impact when the Boeing was descending below the level of the airport. At that point, when any remaining visual contact with the approach lights would have been finally lost, a missed approach could have been accomplished within the performance capability of the aircraft.

In concluding its report, the Civil Aeronautics Board re-emphasised that the responsibility and authority committed to airline captains requires the continual exercise of sound judgement and strict adherence to prescribed operational procedures. Any deviation from such standards can only compromise aviation safety. Airline management too, has a heavy responsibility for implementing practices that ensure crews constantly exercise a conservative and prudent approach to their daily work.

The pertinence of the Board's statement was tragically borne out almost exactly two years later, when a four engined Convair 880, making a night approach to land on Cincinnati's Runway 18 in reduced visibility, also struck trees and crashed three kilometres short of the runway threshold in circum-

stances remarkably similar to that of the Boeing 727. In this case all but 12 of the Convair's 82 occupants were killed.

Subsequent studies of the likely illusory effects produced the lights on the river bank, viewed in conjunction with the more distant but 400 foot higher runway lights, demonstrated that pilots making approaches to land on this runway in limited visibility could receive visual cues that produced powerful sensations of being much higher than their aircraft's actual altitude.

As a result of these and similar accidents elsewhere, dangerously misleading illusions of this type were publicised for the world airline industry in a paper produced by the Boeing Company, entitled *Night Visual Approaches to Lighted Sloping Terrain*.

The Cincinnati accident also drew attention to the general danger of allowing high descent rates to develop at low altitudes in the newer short haul domestic jet transports such as the Boeing 727 which, because of their need to make frequent landings, have more versatile flight char-

acteristics than earlier, longer range jet types.

Nevertheless, these favourable aspects could give pilots the impression that greater liberties may be taken with the aircraft, especially during approach and landing. Because of the large amount of flap available, high descent rates could develop more easily than in previous jet designs, and should be avoided close to the ground. For example, with full flap, the Boeing 727 requires 47 per cent power simply to maintain a normal three degree approach glidepath. With engine power reduced to idle, it descends at 2,060 feet per minute, a rate impossible to arrest quickly, requiring substantial application of power, time for the engine in spool up, as well as a rotation of the aircraft itself.

All these findings, together with the newly developed visual Approach Slope Indicator Systems (VASIS) being installed at major airports throughout the world, would do much to overcome the problem of undershoot accidents.

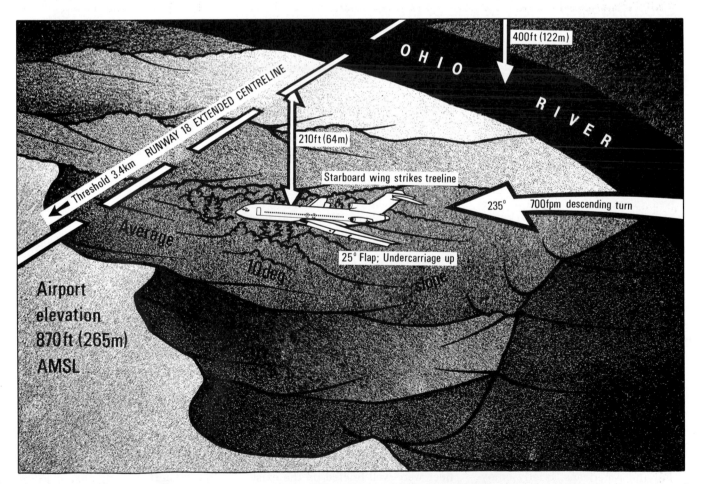

Schematic drawing of the accident site, with impact imminent. The accident resulted from a combination of factors, not least the juxtaposition of the airport and the terrain below the approach path, in combination with poor visability. (Matthew Tesch)

CHAPTER 5

"When the sky is blue, Fuji is angry"

– Traditional Japanese proberb

BOAC Boeing 707-436 G-APFE [17706] – March 5, 1966

That mountains create turbulence in their lee in strong winds was well known – but no-one could have suspected the invisible fury that lay in wait for 124 people savouring a rare view of one of the world's most spectacular volcanic cones.

Unlike conditions on the previous day, the weather over central Japan on March 5 1966 was unusually clear and cloudless. Conditions were so clear in fact, that the spectacular 12,400 foot cone of Mt Fuji could be seen from Tokyo, a distance of more than 110km.

For a party of 75 American tourists, all dealers or executives of a Minnesota based company and their wives, taking a trip to Asia as a reward for a successful marketing campaign, the clear weather in Tokyo that morning was something of a welcome relief. Only the previous evening, during the party's overnight stay in the Japanese capital, a Canadian Pacific Douglas DC-8 en route to Vancouver had crashed during its attempt to land at Tokyo's Haneda International Airport at the conclusion of a flight from Hong Kong. Approaching in poor visibility, darkness and fog, the DC-8 had touched down prematurely, striking the high intensity approach lighting structure and a sea wall short of the runway threshold. Sixty four of its 72 occupants lost their lives in the fierce fire that followed.

For the Americans, briefly enjoying the night life of Tokyo, the devastating news of the accident was a chilling reminder of their vulnerability: they were booked to fly to Hong Kong the following day with British Overseas Airways – the same route, though in the opposite direction. But with the dawning of a bright, cloudless day and its promise of excellent visibility for the scenic, three and a half hour flight to Hong Kong, their fears of the night before suddenly seemed groundless.

BOAC Flight 911, scheduled to depart from Tokyo's Haneda Airport for Hong Kong's Kai Tek at 1.30pm, was to be operated that day by Boeing 707, G-APFE, under the command of Captain Bernard Dobson. The flight was but one segment of a BOAC round the world service, originating and concluding at London Heathrow Airport. For the Tokyo-Hong Kong service, the aircraft was almost fully booked. In addition to the American tourists, there were 38 other passengers, and the flight and cabin crew numbered 11 for a total of 124 occupants in all.

The Boeing 707 landed at Tokyo at the conclusion of its previous leg at 12.40pm, and while on the ground both Captain Dobson and his first officer were well briefed on the existing weather situation by BOAC's Tokyo based duty operations officer.

The flightplan the crew prepared provided for an Instrument Flight Rules departure via the island of Oshima, 50 nautical miles due south of Tokyo, climbing to flight level 310 (31,000 feet) to join the designated airway direct to Hong Kong.

The passengers boarded the aircraft and at 1.42pm the crew were cleared to start the engines. But while taxiing for takeoff from Runway 33L, Captain Dobson requested an amendment to their planned departure route, asking instead to be cleared to climb initially in Visual Meteorological Conditions via Mt Fuji, presumably to allow his passengers a rare view of the majestic volcanic cone in the exceptionally clear conditions.

This was approved by Air Traffic Control, and after taxying past the still smouldering wreckage of the Canadian Pacific DC-8 near the threshold of Runway 33R – a grisly and daunting sight to passengers seated close to the Boeing's right hand cabin windows – G-APFE was cleared for takeoff at 1.58pm.

Making a wide, continuous right hand climbing turn over Tokyo Bay after takeoff, the Boeing overflew Yokohama, some nine nautical miles south of the airport, straightening up

Fateful departure: In bright sunshine at Tokyo International Airport early in the afternoon of March 5 1966, BOAC's Boeing 707 G-APFE is loaded and prepared for its flight to Hong Kong – the next leg of its westerly round the world trip from London.[1]

on a south westerly heading to pass to the north of Odawara City, still climbing. Nearing Gotemba City, seven nm to the east of Mt Fuji, now at a height of nearly 17,000 feet, the aircraft turned right on to a north westerly heading directly towards the mountain and soon afterwards began a gradual descent.

No indication of any emergency came from the Boeing, but soon after passing over Gotemba City, witnesses on the ground who happened to see it passing overhead in the crystal clear sky noticed it was trailing white vapour. Ten seconds later

and still in a shallow descent, its wing tips appeared to be trailing vapour also. Shortly afterwards, pieces were seen falling from the aircraft.

This was quickly followed by a sudden large puff of white vapour from the Boeing's tail – described by some witnesses as "like a firework" – which turned black very soon afterwards. After a few more seconds of flight in its shallow nose down attitude, the Boeing pitched sharply nose up and lost forward speed, puffed out more vapour, then entered a descending flat spin. By this stage the tail assembly and engine

pods were seen to be missing from the aircraft and, as it spiralled down, the outer section of the starboard wing broke away.

When the stricken aircraft had fallen to about 6500 feet, the forward section of the fuselage also broke away, plunged to the ground, and burnt fiercely. The remains of the fuselage, still with most of the wing attached, continued to descend more slowly in a flat spin, finally hitting the ground in a level attitude in a forest at the foot of Mt Fuji. Although this section of the wreckage did not explode, all on board were killed instantly.

★   ★   ★

The wreckage of the Boeing 707 was later found to be scattered over an area 16 kilometres long and nearly two kilometres wide. Clearly, it was a case of another structural failure in the air. But what had caused it this time?

The structural integrity of the Boeing 707 design was not in question, and the aircraft, unlike the Boeing 720B in Florida three years before, could certainly not have encountered any thunderstorm activity on such a clear day. Nor had ground witnesses seen it perform any violent manoeuvres that could have precipitated an inflight break-up.

The mystery only deepened when investigators found that the Boeing's Flight Data Recorder, probably the best potential source of information for answers to the enigma, had been destroyed by fire with the nose section of the fuselage, and that no readout would be possible. The Boeing was not fitted with a Cockpit Voice Recorder.

BOAC's Boeing 707 G-APFE taxis for takeoff from Tokyo International Airport's Runway 33L shortly before 2pm on the afternoon of March 5 1966. In the foreground is the burnt out wreckage of the Canadian Pacific DC-8, CF-CPK, which crashed during an approach to land the previous evening, killing 64 of its 72 occupants. Little did the crew and passengers of G-APFE realise that a similar fate awaited them in less than half an hour.

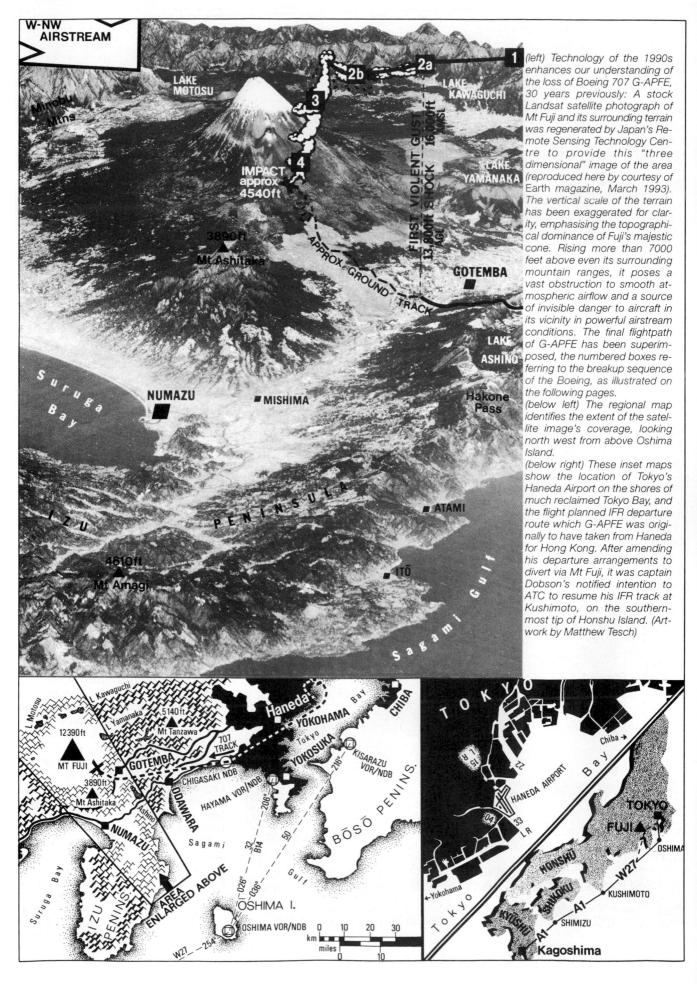

(left) Technology of the 1990s enhances our understanding of the loss of Boeing 707 G-APFE, 30 years previously: A stock Landsat satellite photograph of Mt Fuji and its surrounding terrain was regenerated by Japan's Remote Sensing Technology Centre to provide this "three dimensional" image of the area (reproduced here by courtesy of Earth magazine, March 1993). The vertical scale of the terrain has been exaggerated for clarity, emphasising the topographical dominance of Fuji's majestic cone. Rising more than 7000 feet above even its surrounding mountain ranges, it poses a vast obstruction to smooth atmospheric airflow and a source of invisible danger to aircraft in its vicinity in powerful airstream conditions. The final flightpath of G-APFE has been superimposed, the numbered boxes referring to the breakup sequence of the Boeing, as illustrated on the following pages.

(below left) The regional map identifies the extent of the satellite image's coverage, looking north west from above Oshima Island.

(below right) These inset maps show the location of Tokyo's Haneda Airport on the shores of much reclaimed Tokyo Bay, and the flight planned IFR departure route which G-APFE was originally to have taken from Haneda for Hong Kong. After amending his departure arrangements to divert via Mt Fuji, it was captain Dobson's notified intention to ATC to resume his IFR track at Kushimoto, on the southern-most tip of Honshu Island. (Artwork by Matthew Tesch)

A reconstruction of the trajectories of the various pieces of wreckage, based on their distribution over the ground and the wind velocities at various altitudes at the time of the accident, established that the Boeing's fin and port tailplane had broken away first – before the failure of the starboard outer wing, and the nose section of the fuselage. But beyond this, investigators were not able to determine the exact sequence of inflight break-up.

Detailed examination of the wreckage itself showed that the fractures in the starboard wing had occurred in upward bending. All engine mounting pylons were fractured at their wing mounting points as a result of a predominantly leftward load, and the failures of the ventral fin, the tail fin and the forward section of the fuselage were also to the left.

The tail fin had fractured at its attachments to the fuselage, the starboard rear attachment fitting having failed at its upper bolt holes in tension. Fatigue cracks were found on the fracture face of one of these bolt holes. Damage to the port side tailplane was extensive, scratches and paint markings matching the colour scheme of the fin, showing that the tailplane had been struck forcibly by the fin as it collapsed. The blow had snapped the port side tailplane off at its root fittings. Damage to the starboard side tailplane was minimal, it having broken away from the fuselage later, together with the centre section of the tail structure.

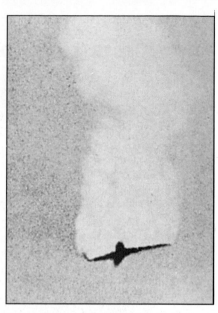

The Boeing 707, trailing vaporising fuel from its disrupted tanks, begins its downward plunge in the lee of Mt Fuji.

The aircraft, minus its tail assembly and engine pods, but still disgorging tons of fuel, descends in a flat spin only two nautical miles from the slopes of Mt Fuji.

Apart from the fatigue cracks in the tail fin attachment fittings, no structural defects could be detected in the Boeing's airframe. There was no evidence of any flying control or system malfunction, or of any precrash defects. Nearly all the aircraft's instruments were destroyed in the fire which devoured the nose section of the fuselage, and no useful information could be derived from them. The jack screw of the tailplane trim mechanism corresponded with a cockpit pitch trim setting of 1.4 units nose down – a perfectly normal setting for a fully loaded Boeing 707 in a gentle descent from level flight at around 335 knots.

So what could possibly have gone so suddenly and catastrophically wrong so soon after takeoff on such an apparently perfect day?

Was it the previously undetected fatigue cracks in the fin attachment fitting? Were these tiny cracks, as in the case of the de Havilland Comet over the Mediterranean, responsible for initiating the process that broke up the entire aircraft? It hardly seemed likely in view of the service history of the Boeing 707 as a type, but what other explanation could there be?

Metallurgical tests carried out by the Boeing Company on the failed attachment fitting recovered from the wreckage showed that the fracture started from the upper outboard attachment hole. Two fatigue cracks in the bolt hole were 1.9 and 1.4 millimetres deep. But the final

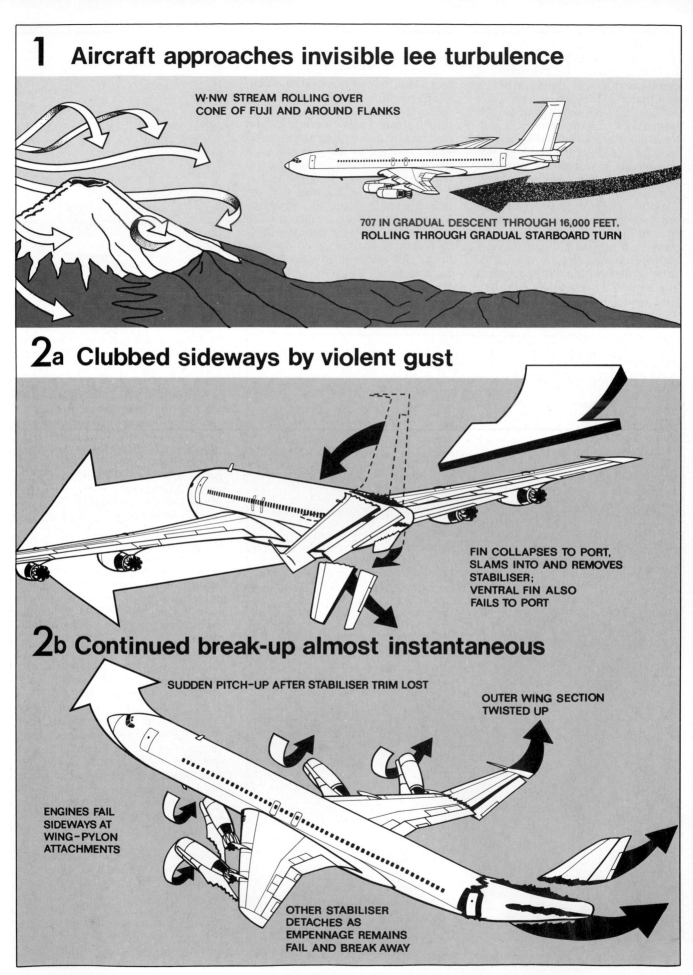

1 Aircraft approaches invisible lee turbulence

W·NW STREAM ROLLING OVER
CONE OF FUJI AND AROUND FLANKS

707 IN GRADUAL DESCENT THROUGH 16,000 FEET,
ROLLING THROUGH GRADUAL STARBOARD TURN

2a Clubbed sideways by violent gust

FIN COLLAPSES TO PORT,
SLAMS INTO AND REMOVES
STABILISER;
VENTRAL FIN ALSO
FAILS TO PORT

2b Continued break-up almost instantaneous

SUDDEN PITCH-UP AFTER STABILISER TRIM LOST

OUTER WING SECTION
TWISTED UP

ENGINES FAIL
SIDEWAYS AT
WING-PYLON
ATTACHMENTS

OTHER STABILISER
DETACHES AS
EMPENNAGE REMAINS
FAIL AND BREAK AWAY

(above and opposite) Sequence showing inflight breakup of Boeing 707 G-APFE, following its encounter with extreme rotor turbulence in the lee of Mt Fuji. (Matthew Tesch)

3 Hulk drops in near-vertical flat spin

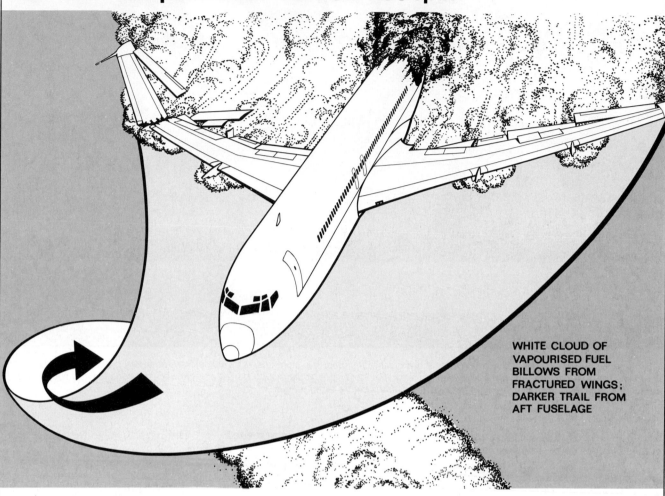

WHITE CLOUD OF
VAPOURISED FUEL
BILLOWS FROM
FRACTURED WINGS;
DARKER TRAIL FROM
AFT FUSELAGE

4 Forward fuselage fails before impact

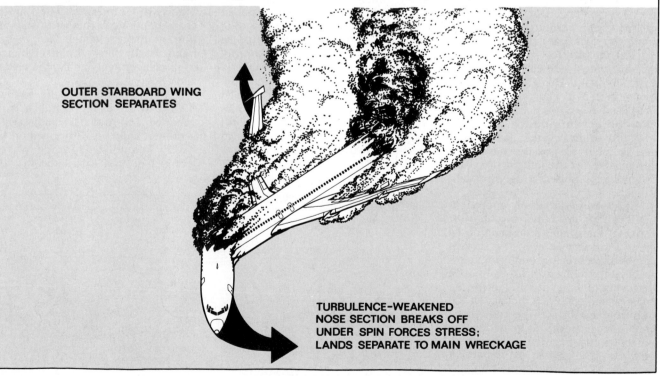

OUTER STARBOARD WING
SECTION SEPARATES

TURBULENCE-WEAKENED
NOSE SECTION BREAKS OFF
UNDER SPIN FORCES STRESS;
LANDS SEPARATE TO MAIN WRECKAGE

Taken from a low flying helicopter not long after the accident, this graphic picture shows investigators (upper left) probing the remains of the Boeing 707. The disposition of the wreckage shows clearly that the aircraft hit the ground in a flat attitude with little or no forward speed. Note the main undercarriage bogies, still in their retracted position, in the centre of the picture.

fracture of the fitting which resulted in the failure of the fin was caused by a sudden load substantially greater than the load which had produced the fatigue cracks in the first place.

The mechanical qualities of the material used in the manufacture of the attachment fitting were to the correct specification. The Boeing Company then conducted a further test on an identical attachment fitting in which fatigue cracks were first simulated. This showed the fitting only failed when the load was increased to a figure 110% greater than the tail fin's design limit gust load. In other words, the fatigue cracks could not possibly have been responsible for the inflight break up in anything like normal flying conditions.

With the investigation approaching a baffling dead end, and the root cause of the Boeing's destruction as great a mystery as ever, the investigators had a breakthrough from a totally unexpected source – the discovery of an eight millimetre cine camera amongst the wreckage of the unburnt section of the passenger cabin. The camera was loaded with a partly exposed colour film spool, and though damaged by impact, it was possible to process the film.

The processed film was screened and found to have been taken by a passenger, possibly one of the party of American tourists. The first of the footage was shot on the ground before the passengers boarded the flight and showed scenes of Tokyo International Airport. The next section of the film had been taken in flight through the starboard side windows of the passenger cabin as the Boeing was approaching Gotemba City on a south westerly heading, only about two minutes before the aircraft broke up. It showed normal views of the Tanzawa Mountains, 10 nautical miles to the north of the aircraft's flightpath, and had been taken from an altitude of just under 17,000 feet.

The next footage began some five nautical miles further south west after the aircraft had turned towards Mt Fuji on a north westerly heading and descended to 16,000 feet, and showed a view towards Lake Yamanaka, about the same distance north of the flightpath as the Tanzawa Mountains. The camera was still taking in this view when the film suddenly skipped two frames, momentarily showed blurred images of passenger seats and cabin carpet, and ended abruptly.

It was obvious that the camera, filming while being handheld to a cabin window, had been subjected to a sudden shock and dropped on the floor. From the footage photographed, it was calculated that the

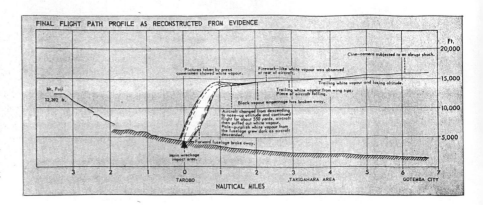

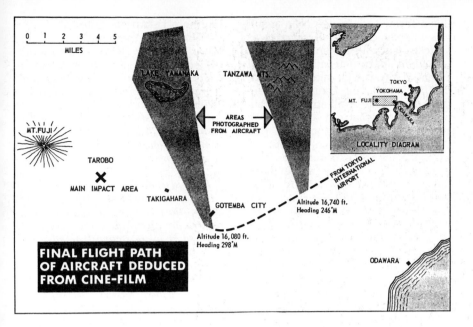

MILES 0 1 2 3 4 5

LAKE YAMANAKA

TANZAWA MTS.

AREAS
PHOTOGRAPHED
FROM AIRCRAFT

MT. FUJI

TAROBO

X
MAIN IMPACT AREA

TAKIGAHARA

GOTEMBA CITY

Altitude 16,080 ft.
Heading 298° M

Altitude 16,740 ft.
Heading 246° M

FROM TOKYO
INTERNATIONAL
AIRPORT

ODAWARA

**FINAL FLIGHT PATH
OF AIRCRAFT DEDUCED
FROM CINE-FILM**

Locality Diagram: TOKYO, YOKOHAMA, MT. FUJI, ODAWARA, LOCALITY DIAGRAM

aircraft's speed when this occurred was between 320 and 370 knots, figures consistent with that estimated from the setting of the tailplane trim screw jack at the time of the inflight break up.

But what had caused a shock sufficient to cause the compact and sturdy camera to skip two frames before it was dropped – an occurrence probably simultaneous with the sudden and extremely severe aerodynamic side loading on the aircraft that had caused the fin attachment fittings and the engine pylons to fracture?

The investigators next turned their attention to the meteorological conditions prevailing on the day of the accident. A depression centred over the South China Sea had intensified during the previous night and moved quickly northeast across Japan into the northern Pacific Ocean. With an anti-cyclone over continental east Asia, a steep meteorological pressure gradient from west to east lay over Japan, producing strong, west to north west winds blowing from the Asian inland. It was this clear, dry airstream that was responsible for the unusually good visibility.

At the time of the Boeing's departure from Tokyo International Airport, these west to north west winds were still blowing strongly, with wind velocities increasing with height. At the weather station at the summit of Mt Fuji at the time, the wind was from the north west at between 60 and 70 knots.

These conditions, in addition to producing the excellent visibility, were highly conducive to the formation of atmospheric "mountain wave" systems, a disturbance of the

airstream broadly analogous to that of a river flowing over a rocky bed, the ripples and "breakers" on the surface of the water corresponding to the standing waves and turbulence found in the airstream above mountainous terrain. The higher the mountains and the faster the airflow over them, the greater the resulting air disturbance. The worst turbulence in such conditions is found in a "standing rotor", a highly agitated body of air rotating about a horizontal axis downwind from and parallel to the mountain ridge producing the air disturbance. If the airstream is sufficiently moist, the rotor will become visible as a characteristic roll cloud, similar to but more defined and intense than that often seen at the leading edge of a line of thunderstorms marking a cold front. Appearing at first glance to be a harmless band of ragged cumulus downwind of the mountain ridge, it is seen on closer inspection to be rotating quite fiercely.

The strongest rotors usually form in the first mountain wave downwind from the ridge and are therefore close to and somewhat above the level of the ridge crest. Within such rotors, vertical gust velocities up to 100 feet per second or more could be encountered – enough to cause structural damage to any aircraft.

Weather satellite photographs that happened to be taken only half an hour before the accident showed lenticular (lens shaped) and rotor clouds characteristic of mountain waves in the lee of the Suzuka Mountains, 240 kilometres to the south west of Mt Fuji. Characteristic mountain wave clouds did not form

in the lee of Mt Fuji or other mountains further to windward, but probably only for the reason that the airflow was too dry.

Reports from 100 other aircraft that flew within 80nm of Mt Fuji on the day of the accident showed that the majority of them had encountered moderate to severe turbulence. Four had experienced severe turbulence within a 27nm radius of Mt Fuji on its eastern side. And the pilot of a US Navy Douglas Skyhawk jet fighter based at Atsugi, who had been asked to look for the scattered wreckage of the Boeing shortly after the accident, encountered turbulence in the lee of the mountain so extreme that he thought his own aircraft was going to break up:

"I flew into the same turbulence and truly thought the airplane was going to come unglued," the pilot said after he landed. "My oxygen mask was pulled loose, my head was banging on both sides of the cockpit canopy, the instruments were unreadable, and the controls just about useless. Somehow I managed to get the nose pointed up more times than down and eventually climbed out of the turbulence. When I got back to Atsugi, the A-4's g meter had registered plus 9 and minus 4g, and the fighter was grounded for inspection."

The fate that so unexpectedly overtook the BOAC Boeing 707 now became clear. Some 10nm south east of Mt Fuji, just after the unsuspecting Captain Dobson swung his aircraft on to a heading directly towards the mountain, descending slowly to give his passengers one of the most spectacular views of their lives, they suddenly flew into an unseen cauldron of fiercely boiling air – the vicious rotor zone of the severe atmospheric turbulence the 70 knot wind was creating in the lee of the 12,000 foot mountain, the summit of which was now only 4000 feet below them.

The shock would have felt something like colliding with an invisible wall – violent and injurious to the aircraft and all its occupants, and in this case sufficient to immediately snap off the tail fin, together with all four engines in their mountings beneath the wing. The fin, slamming down hard against the port tailplane, broke this off also, instantly destroying the aircraft's longitudinal trim and causing it to suddenly pitch nose up. The violence of this manoeuvre, together with tremendous buffeting of the rotor turbulence, not only tore off what remained of the tail assembly, but disrupted the structural integrity of the wings and forward fuselage, allowing them to break off as the aircraft fell into a spin towards the ground. The copious quantities of vapour seen streaming from the Boeing as it fell like a wounded bird, were its many tons of turbine kerosene pouring out into the airstream from the ruptured fuel tanks.

The formal conclusion of the investigation was that the Boeing 707 broke up very quickly after encountering an abnormally severe gust which induced a sudden leftward load on the entire aircraft in excess of its structural design limit.

Severe to extreme turbulence would certainly have existed in any mountain wave rotor system downwind from Mt Fuji on the day of the accident. But in the case of this high, isolated and symmetrical volcanic cone, it was likely that the turbulence was even further intensified by the rapid mixing of the air currents swirling around the mountain with those formed in its lee. The result was turbulence of such severity as to destroy any jet transport aircraft.

It could not be determined to what extent, if any, the fatigue cracking in the fin attachment fitting had contributed to the overall structural failure, but it was not considered significant to the outcome of this tragic and unforeseen encounter with extreme rotor turbulence. Nevertheless, inspections were instituted on the tail assemblies of all Boeing 707 and 720 aircraft which had flown more than 1200 hours, with more stringent inspections being required on aircraft with flight times in excess of 1800 hours. Twenty-two instances of cracks were found in 63 aircraft, as a result of which the Boeing company introduced tail modifications, together with a further schedule of inspections, to eliminate the fatigue cracking problem.

Footnote 1 – Artists Note:

Sharp eyed readers may notice the unfamiliar BOAC cheatline depicted in this chapter's illustrations. Called the 'Golden Speedbird' livery, this short lived paint scheme was used between that of the early postwar era (see the DH Comets in Chapter 1), and the more familiar scheme of the later 1960s (shown on the Boeing 707 in Chapter 7).

Introduced with the first of BOAC's standard VC-10s in April 1964, the 'Golden Speedbird' had the fin design of the later livery, but teamed it with a cheatline edged in gold and blue, with a broad stepped section on the forward fuselage.

Barely 11 months later, BOAC's first Super VC-10 brought a smooth, cleaned up blue cheatline, and the handful of Boeing 707s and standard VC-10s wearing the 'Golden Speedbird' look were repainted.

CHAPTER 6

"Are you painting the weather on your radar now?"

– Chicago Centre Controller to BAC-111

Braniff International Airways BAC-111-203AE N1553 [70] – August 6, 1966

Violent turbulence at the leading edge of thunderstorms was well attested. But in clear air too?

The old established Braniff Airways, operating in the midwest of the USA since 1930, and one of the few American airlines to operate British manufactured aircraft, was proud of its fleet of new BAC-111s. The first of the new generation of medium sized, T-tailed twinjets, the 89 passenger type had entered service with Braniff in April 1966, eight months ahead of the similar looking DC-9, which first began flying with Delta Airlines in December.

Designed for short haul, medium density routes, the BAC-111, powered by two Rolls-Royce Spey turbojet engines, was proving highly satisfactory for the domestic services Braniff Airways operated throughout the midwest.

Braniff's Flight 250, a regular nightly south-north "milk run" from New Orleans, Louisiana, to Minneapolis, Minnesota, via Shreveport, Fort Smith, Tulsa, Kansas City and Omaha, was being flown on the evening of August 6, 1966 by BAC-111, N1553. The night flight was under the command of Captain D G Pauly, a pilot with more than 20 years experience with the company and nearly 21,000 hours total flying time. Captain Pauly had been flying the BAC-111 for more than a year and had logged nearly 600 hours on the type. His first officer, J A

Hilliker, had a total of nearly 10,000 hours experience with some 680 hours on the BAC-111.

Departing New Orleans at 6.35pm, Flight 250 continued in bright moonlight without incident as far as Kansas City. But after landing at Kansas City, Captain Pauly became concerned about the weather ahead. An extensive cold front lay between south western Kansas and north eastern Nebraska (ie nearly astride Flight 250's proposed route), moving south east. With the passage of the front, the weather bureau predicted isolated severe thunderstorms, with hail and wind gusts to 70 knots. Moderate turbulence was expected in showers, increasing to severe near thunderstorms.

Before returning to his aircraft to join his first officer, two stewardesses, and the 38 passengers booked on the next leg of the flight to Omaha, Captain Pauly discussed the weather with another Braniff crew who had just landed from Chicago. They told him there was "a solid line of very intense thunderstorms with continuous lightning and no apparent breaks." The captain of the Chicago flight said the front was "as long and mean" as he'd seen in a long time, and that he "didn't feel the radar reports gave a true picture of its intensity." Captain Pauly com-

mented that he hoped he'd be to the west of the frontal line.

The planned cruising height for the flight to Omaha was flight level 200 (20,000 feet), but while the crew were taxiing for takeoff at 10.55pm, Kansas City Air Traffic Control instructed the BAC-111 to maintain 5,000 feet "until advised" because of conflicting inbound traffic.

The aircraft departed normally and when 12 nautical miles north on track for Omaha, its communications were transferred from the control tower frequency to Kansas City Air Route Traffic Control. After being identified on radar, it was finally cleared to climb to flight level 200. However, after some discussion on the radio about the weather ahead, the crew told the controller they would prefer to remain at 5,000 feet.

Shortly afterwards, the BAC-111 also sought permission to deviate to the left of track. This was approved, and a few minutes later at 11.06pm, Kansas City Air Route Traffic Control cleared the aircraft to maintain 5,000 feet and instructed the crew to contact Chicago Air Route Traffic Control. On doing so they had a further radio discussion on the weather as it was displayed on the Chicago controller's radar. The controller then mentioned that another Braniff BAC-111, operating Flight 255 from

An early model BAC-111 of the type operated by Braniff Airways in the late 1960s. N1553, which broke up in severe turbulence near Falls City on August 6, 1966 was identical to this aircraft. (Michael Maton)

Omaha to Kansas City, was at that moment climbing through 10,000 feet after departing Omaha.

The captains of the two Braniff BAC-111s spoke with each other by radio, the Kansas City bound crew telling Captain Pauly that they were encountering "light to moderate chop" which had begun about 15nm south east of Omaha. From condition displayed on their radar, they expected to be out of it in another 10nm. Captain Pauly's acknowledgement of this information at 11.08pm proved to be the final transmission from N1553.

A few minutes later at about 11.12pm, a number of people living on farms some 10 kilometres north east of Falls City, Nebraska, sighted the BAC-111 by moonlight as it came into view in clear conditions from the south east at a height of only about 4000 feet. At the time the moon was nearly full and stars were visible, but there was an unbroken line of angry looking thunderstorms approaching from the northwest. It was because the storm front looked so threatening that people were outside watching the weather.

Ahead of the storm front itself was a shallow shelf of overcast cloud, the leading edge of which was "boiling" and "rolling forward". The base of this cloud appeared to be between 1000 and 2000 feet above the ground. The front that lay beyond the shelf appeared to be U-shaped in plan, and the BAC-111 appeared to be heading towards "a light spot in the cloud wall'. The BAC-111 was lost to

view as it passed over the cloud shelf, but very soon afterwards those watching from the ground saw a sudden "brilliant flash in the sky", after which "a ball of fire" fell through the cloud shelf. Those who were closer were aghast to see it was the BAC-111 on fire. Fascinated, they watched it spiral down and explode as it struck the ground. Two large pieces of the aircraft fell separately and more slowly.

Shortly afterwards the light wind from the south swung violently to the north, simultaneously increasing in strength to about 50 knots, and it began to rain. Several minutes later two funnel clouds had formed within half a mile of the crash site.

★　　★　　★

Sistership of N1553, BAC-111 N1542 displays Braniff's livery of the day: black "forehead" over the cockpit windows, white fin and engine nacelles, white upper and lower surfaces of wings and tailplanes and overall "jelly bean" fuselage colouring with black titles and logo.

The BAC-111, less the outer section of its starboard wing and its T-tail, had crashed in a flat attitude in rolling farm country 12 kilometres north northeast of Falls City. Except for the flightdeck area, the fuselage, from nose wheel well back to the rear pressure bulkhead, was gutted by fire, as was the still attached port wing. National Transportation Safety Board investigators found portions of the starboard wing and the T-tail assembly that had separated in flight spread over 2.6 square kilometres (one square mile) to the south east of the main wreckage. All these components were untouched by fire.

A detailed examination of the wreckage showed that the starboard wing had broken away in downward bending, while the T-tail had failed in bending to the left. The upper part of the fin was still intact, with the port tailplane and portion of the starboard tailplane still attached. The starboard tailplane itself had failed in upward bending. The rudder and elevators had separated from their attachments, both elevators having overtravelled upwards. The rudder had overtravelled in both directions, while the flying control cables had all failed in tension.

The tailplane trim actuator was at a setting consistent with an airspeed of about 270 knots at 5000 feet, while the flaps and undercarriage were in the retracted position. There was neither evidence of flutter on any of the control surfaces, nor of any pre-impact malfunction of the engines or aircraft systems. Similarly, there was no evidence of airframe damage resulting from hail, lightning strikes, or a static discharge. Metallurgical examination of the fracture faces of the failed airframe components showed no evidence of fatigue, corrosion or previous damage. Altogether the wreckage examination established that the BAC-111 was fully airworthy, intact and operating normally until the moment of structural failure.

The BAC-111 was equipped with a Flight Data Recorder, but it was badly damaged and no useful data could be recovered from it. But the Cockpit Voice Recorder yielded a recording of the pilots' voices and their radio communications. This showed that after the crew's request to maintain 5000 feet to Omaha, there was a brief conversation between the pilots about a "hole" in the line of frontal cloud and, at 2304 hours (11.04pm), they requested permission to deviate to the left of track. Two minutes later, in response to their query, the Chicago controller told them the line of thunderstorms was "pretty solid all the way from west of Pawnee to Des Moines". Intermittent cockpit discussion concerning a diversion via Pawnee City followed for several minutes, ending with First Officer Hilliker saying: "We're not that far away from it – Pawnee is 112.4 [the frequency of the Pawnee VOR] if you want it."

Thirty seconds later at 2311.23 (11.11pm and 23 seconds) the tape recorded the words "Ease power back," and at 2311.42 a "rushing air" noise began which continued until the end of the recording 25.8 seconds later. Towards the end of the tape, the sound of the stall warning horn was superimposed on the "rushing air" noise four times in succession, the last being terminated by impact with the ground.

To try and determine the sequence of the inflight break up, the National Aeronautics and Space Administration conducted an analysis of the likely trajectories of the various pieces of wreckage from the position and height of the aircraft at the moment of structural failure. This showed the breakup was rapid, probably within only about two seconds, and that the T-tail separated first, followed by the starboard wing. The analysis also indicated that the time interval from the initial failure of the tail to impact with the ground was between 25 and 28 seconds.

In the absence of any information from the FDR, the investigators turned again to the Cockpit Voice Recorder as a possible source of further information on the sequence of the structural failure. A test flight in another BAC-111 showed the ambient noise level recorded by the cockpit microphone varied with airspeed, and that the level recorded aboard N1553 shortly before the time of break up could be reproduced at about 270 knots. It was also found that the "rushing air" noise that was continuous over the last 28.5 seconds of N1553's tape could be reproduced by increasing the airspeed by about 50 knots and introducing a large angle of sideslip. Overall, the CVR showed that the BAC-111 was flying normally at or near its recommended turbulence penetration speed of 270 knots until some 29 seconds before impact with the ground, when it was suddenly subjected to an extremely violent manoeuvre.

No less than 300 people living in the area provided eyewitness evidence of the BAC-111's approach from the south towards the severe frontal weather. All were adamant that though it appeared to be heading towards a "light spot" in the wall of cloud, it never reached the main line of thunderstorms which still lay further to the north when the aircraft broke up. Those nearer the accident site believed the aircraft entered cloud before they saw the

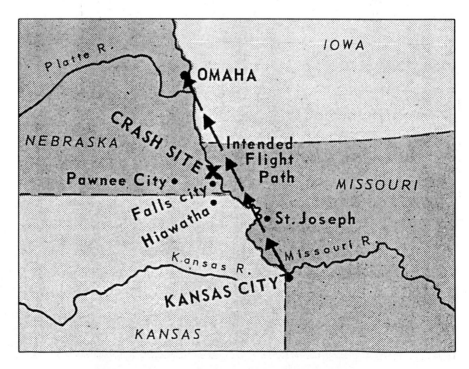

The route being flown by BAC-111 N1553 at the time of the accident. The site of the accident near Falls City, Nebraska, is indicated. (Aviation Safety Digest)

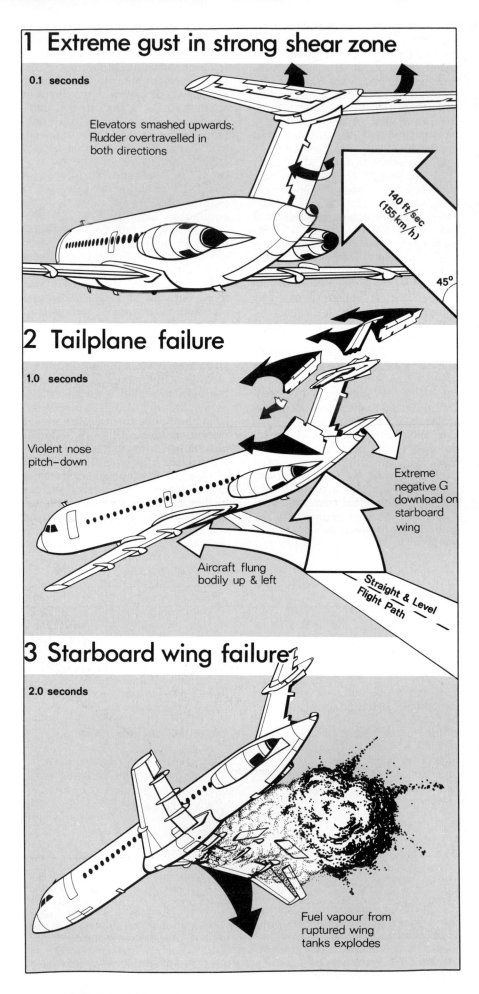

1 Extreme gust in strong shear zone

0.1 seconds

Elevators smashed upwards;
Rudder overtravelled in
both directions

140 ft/sec
(155 km/h)

45°

2 Tailplane failure

1.0 seconds

Violent nose
pitch–down

Extreme
negative G
download on
starboard
wing

Aircraft flung
bodily up & left

Straight & Level
Flight Path

3 Starboard wing failure

2.0 seconds

Fuel vapour from
ruptured wing
tanks explodes

inflight fire, but witnesses further away said it was *above* the shelf of cloud preceding the squall line and still in clear air when the fire broke out.

In view of the proximity of the severe weather at the time of the accident, together with evidence of a "boiling roll cloud" in its immediate vicinity, the investigators conducted studies to determine the nature and magnitude of the aerodynamic forces required to cause the structural failures evident in the wreckage.

The results indicated that the primary failures could only have been produced by a sudden encounter with an exceptionally powerful gust. Causing both the fin and tailplane to fail in the way they did would require a gust of at least 140 feet per second, applied at a 45 degree angle upwards to the left and at right angles to the aircraft's fore and aft axis. Moreover, the gust would have to reach its maximum strength in only 0.125 seconds.

The results of this study supported the findings of the trajectory analysis, and it was concluded that the BAC-111, while flying straight and level, encountered a gust of extreme magnitude which forced it violently upwards and to the left. As the starboard tailplane and fin failed under this assault, the aircraft pitched nose down with a violence that exceeded the starboard wing's negative ultimate design load. As the wing failed, rupturing its integral fuel tank, it released its fuel into the atmosphere. This immediately ignited, creating the "ball of fire" described by eyewitnesses. The aircraft then began tumbling, a motion that finally stabilised into a flat spin.

Because the BAC-111 was more than five nm south of the nearest rain area when it disappeared from the Chicago controller's radar screen, it was evident that a cold outflow of turbulent air from the advancing storm front had reached out as far as the accident site. A US Weather Bureau analysis of conditions existing at the time of the accident confirmed they were likely to produce severe low level turbulence.

Sequence showing inflight structural failure of BAC-111, N1553, in clear air ahead of an approaching line of thunderstorms. The extreme gust which resulted in the failure of the tailplane was probably generated by a combination of roll circulation and horizontal eddies inside a zone of powerful shear, produced by the windshift line the aircraft had just crossed. (Matthew Tesch)

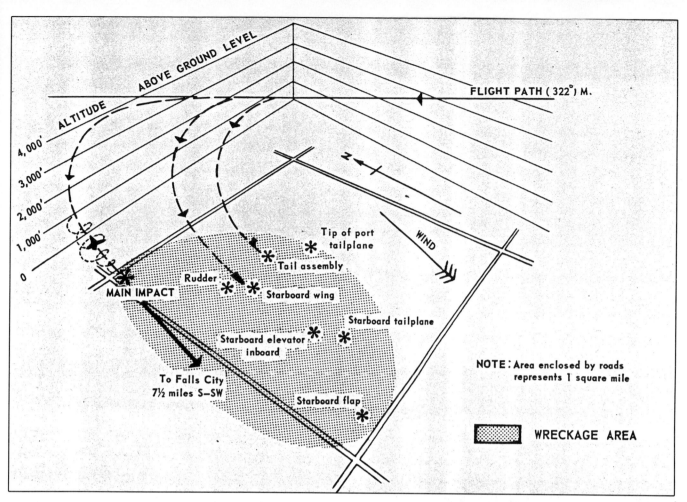

Three dimensional drawing showing trajectories of major components of the BAC-111 after its inflight break up, and distribution of wreckage on the ground. (Aviation Safety Digest)

At the request of the British Aircraft Corporation, manufacturers of the BAC-111, an independent study of these conditions was also undertaken by Dr T Fujita, Professor of Meteorology at the University of Chicago. Dr Fujita had been studying the characteristics of squall lines in the midwest of the USA – the so-called "tornado alley" – since 1953, and was commissioned to make the study because of his experience in thunderstorm research.

After checking all the weather data available for the night of the accident, Dr Fujita plotted the position of the storm front and determined what he believed to be the areas of most severe windshear. To demonstrate the validity of his theories, he did this without any detailed knowledge of the BAC-111's flight path. But when the flight path was added to Dr Fujita's weather plot, it was found that the aircraft had just passed through this wind shear zone when it broke up.

In a prelude to his report, Dr Fujita pointed out that a well devel-

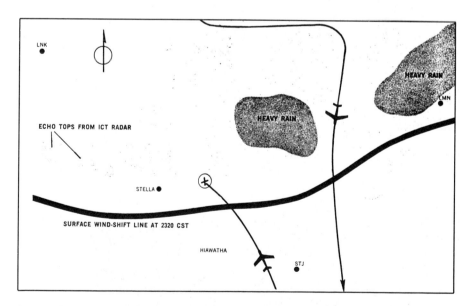

Layout of the weather system that faced the crews of two Braniff BAC-111s flying between Kansas City and Omaha on the night of August 6, 1966 in south east Nebraska. The line of intense thunderstorms that spread across their planned north and south bound tracks was moving south east. Using their airborne weather radar for guidance, both aircraft altered heading to fly through "holes" in the storm front. N1553, the north bound BAC-111, attempted to do so at 5000 feet and broke up in extreme turbulence before reaching the storm front. The south bound aircraft penetrated the line of storms at higher altitude and came through unscathed. (Aviation Safety Digest)

oped line of thunderstorms
pushes ahead of it a mass of cold
air. Storm cells force down the
cold air from high altitudes to
balance powerful updraughts of
warm air within the cells. On
reaching the ground, this cold
air spreads out to form a cushion
or "cold dome". As the line of
thunderstorms moves forward,
pushing the cold dome ahead of
it, warm air at ground level is
forced up, forming more thunderstorm cells. The leading edge
of cold air becomes the wind
shift line and may be invisible,
though sometimes its presence
can be detected by dust raised
on the ground. Sometimes too,
the line is marked by a roll
cloud, but windshear at the line
can be vicious even if there is no
cloud.

The advancing cold dome can
also develop an overhang when
stronger winds at higher altitudes push the leading edge of
cold air ahead of its ground level
position. Warm air trapped in
this overhang produces even
greater wind shear as it strug-
gles to rise through the overhanging cold air mass. An air
circulation system associated
with a well developed squall line
can thus contain several roll
zones which harbour the worst
turbulence of the whole squall
line.

The BAC-111 crossed the wind
shift line ahead of the advancing
storm front at 11.10pm, doing so
at an altitude of 5000 feet – a little over 4000 feet above the
ground. Captain Pauly no doubt
flew into this area because his
weather radar showed it was a
weak spot in the squall line. The
point where the aircraft penetrated the wind shift line was
between two thunderstorm cells
and would certainly have shown
up on the aircraft's radar as a
weak area. Indeed, at 11.12pm,
within only a few seconds of the
inflight break up, the Chicago
controller advised the BAC-111:
"Your present heading appears to be
taking you through the lightest area
to the south west of Omaha. Are you
painting the weather on your radar
now?" There was no reply.

According to Dr Fujita's analysis,
the BAC-111 crossed the wind shift
line at the point where conditions
were most favourable for the formation of roll circulations – just where
horizontal windshear was greatest –
and at an altitude which would have
placed it right in the roll zone. The

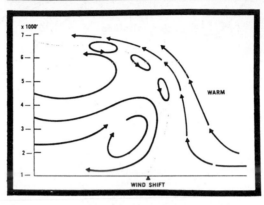

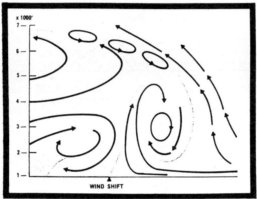

*Development of a highly turbulent roll zone begins with
a cushion of cold air or "cold dome" being pushed
ahead of an advancing line of thunderstorms, forcing
warm air upwards and creating an area of pronounced
wind shear. As stronger winds at higher altitudes push
the leading edge of cold air ahead of its ground level
position, an "overhang" develops. Struggling to rise
through this overhanging cold air mass, the trapped
warm air produces progressively greater shear with a
powerful rolling motion. A well developed roll zone can
contain the worst turbulence of a squall line.*

convective overturning in this air
circulation would have been violent,
with large and sudden directional
changes occurring in very short distances.

But in addition to turbulence in
thunderstorms created by powerful
vertical currents, and the dangerous
roll cloud resulting from their forward movement, Dr Fujita believed
some storms have zones of horizontal circular movement within them.
He had photographs of storm clouds

clearly showing such movement, and believed that torna-
dos may be spawned by this
column-like circulation.

In the case of the BAC-111
therefore, as well as encountering the shear resulting from roll
circulation, the aircraft was
probably subjected to powerful
horizontal eddies formed inside
the zone of strong shear produced by the wind shift line.

Reviewing the findings of the
overall investigation, the National Transportation Safety
Board concluded that, although
the gust velocities present in the
weather system into which the
BAC-111 flew could not be computed, extreme turbulence was
undoubtedly present.

There was no reason to believe that the initial part of the
BAC-111's flight from Kansas
City was conducted any differently from other regular flights
in similar conditions. But it was
evident that the intensity of the
weather system lying across the
BAC-111's intended flight path
was seriously underrated by airline staff responsible for forecasting the weather and dis-
patching the aircraft.

The National Transportation
Safety Board believed that if lessons were to be learned from
the BAC-111 accident, they must
take the form of increased
knowledge of operations in turbulent conditions; of the nature
of expected turbulence, especially at lower levels; of operational procedures to be followed
if turbulence is to be penetrated
safely; and of the forces that
may be produced on an aircraft
by such turbulence. Although
the emphasis on low level weather phenomenon "might seem
incongruous" because most experience in pre-jet airline operations had been gained at lower
altitudes, the Board believed
that jet operations in such conditions could be more critical than
ever. Obvious operational differences now were increased speeds,
and increased reliance on radar to
enable crews to avoid turbulent areas.

Indeed, since the advent of airborne weather radar, more and more
aircraft were being dispatched in
marginal weather, with the captain
having the primary responsibility for
avoiding severe conditions. Yet with
the existing limited knowledge of
turbulence characteristics, too much

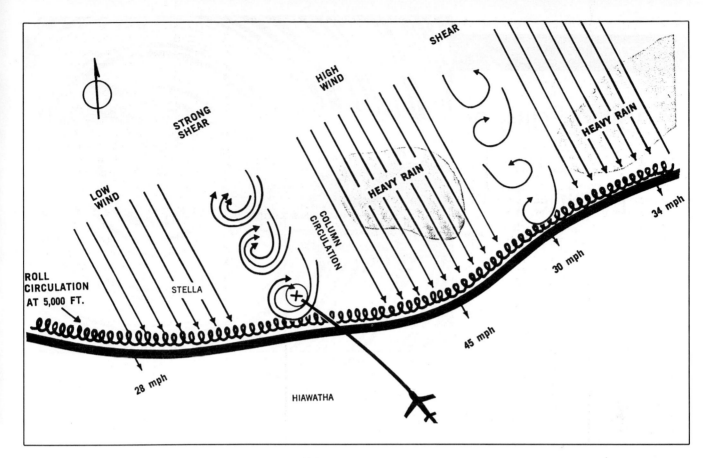

BAC-111 N1553 crossed the wind shift line at an altitude which placed it right in the roll zone. But in addition to vicious vertical shear resulting from the roll circulation, the aircraft probably encountered powerful eddies formed by strong horizontal shear behind the wind shift line. The resulting extreme turbulence subjected the aircraft to forces in excess of its ultimate design strength. (Aviation Safety Digest)

reliance was probably being placed on an instrument which could not "see" the turbulence itself.

The Board believed that the turbulence which destroyed BAC 111 N1553 would have caused the structural failure of any modern civil transport aircraft. Available data on measured gust velocities showed that the extreme 140 feet per second gust necessary to fail the BAC-111's tail assembly was beyond the limits of measured experience, but not excessively so. While weather conditions as extreme as this appeared to be very rare, they were probably more prevalent than statistics indicated. This was because the statistics reflected turbulence avoidance procedures employed in the past.

The probability of encountering a gust of large magnitude increased many times when aircraft were regularly flown in areas where turbulence could be expected. Also, because of the tremendous increase in hours now flown by jet airliners, the vast gap that once existed between the statistical distance an aircraft must fly before encountering an ultimate gust, and the distance actually being flown, had considerably reduced. At the same time the passenger capacity of the average jet transport was continuing to rise, with the result that far more passengers were at risk. Seen in this light, the National Transportation Safety Board believed turbulence avoidance procedures should assume greater importance than ever.

In summing up his own study of the weather system that broke up the BAC-111, Dr Fujita recommen-ded that if an aircraft *has* to fly through a line squall, it should remain *above* the wind shift line until it has passed the roll zone where shear turbulence can be greatest. The cushion of cold air being pushed ahead of a storm front does not extend above the base of a thunderstorm.

For this reason, Dr Fujita advised pilots by all means to seek a "soft spot" in the squall line, but to fly through it *above* the base of the cloud to avoid possible roll turbulence. The old practice of going *beneath* a thunderstorm halfway between the base of the cloud and the ground, he considered dangerous. He also advised against flying through thunderstorms in areas of heavy precipitation where vertical draughts were bound to be greatest.

CHAPTER 7

"Engine Failure Drill ... Engine Fire Drill ..."

– Captain to crew of Boeing 707

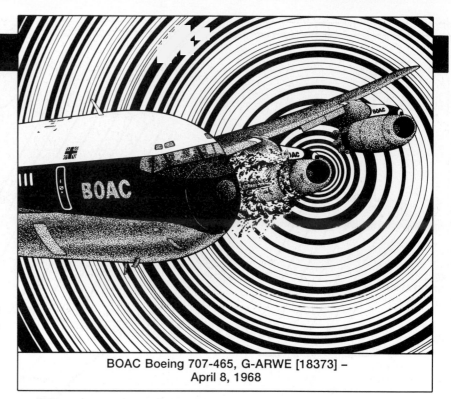

BOAC Boeing 707-465, G-ARWE [18373] –
April 8, 1968

Every pilot's nightmare, a serious engine fire just after takeoff – the most critical time for any emergency – and its tragic consequences showed that even well rehearsed drills and a highly experienced crew could not prevent confusion on the flightdeck when overtaken by a particular combination of circumstances.

British Airways Flight BA 712, London to Sydney, to be operated on April 8, 1968 by Boeing 707 G-ARWE, was scheduled to depart Heathrow Airport at 3.15pm.

The crew for the first leg of the flight to Zurich, Switzerland – Captain C W R Taylor, First Officer F B Kirkland, Second Officer J C Hutchinson, and Engineer Officer T C Hicks – were all well experienced on the company's Boeing 707 aircraft. In addition to the normal flight crew, Check Captain G C Moss was also aboard G-ARWE. His function was to conduct a routine check of Taylor's operational standards, and for this purpose he occupied the jump seat immediately behind the captain. The second officer, who normally monitored operations from this seat during takeoff and landing, was relegated to the navigator's position. The aircraft's cabin crew numbered six – three stewards and three stewardesses.

With 116 passengers aboard, most of them bound for Australia, G-ARWE taxied out from Terminal 3 shortly after 3.15pm in fine and sunny conditions with almost no wind. The heavily laden Boeing was cleared to the holding point for Runway 27 Left, and after pretakeoff

checks that were normal in every way, took off at 3.27pm.

But just after the undercarriage retracted, when the captain was about to call for the power reduction stipulated for noise abatement at Heathrow, there was a jolt throughout the airframe, accompanied by a distinct bang from the port side. Simultaneously, the power lever for the No 2 engine kicked towards the closed position, and instrument indications showed the engine to be running down. Captain Taylor called: "Engine failure drill," and Engineer Officer Hicks immediately began the required emergency action.

As he fully retarded the No 2 throttle lever, the undercarriage warning horn sounded loudly in the cockpit, prompting both him and the check captain to reach quickly for the horn cancel switch on the pedestal. As Captain Moss operated the switch, Hicks also instinctively but erroneously pressed the fire bell cancel button. He then reached for the engine fire shutoff handle on the glare shield above the pilots' instrument panel but, apparently realising this emergency was not a fire drill, did not pull it.

Seconds later, Captain Moss, look-

ing out the port side cockpit window, saw the No 2 engine was in fact on fire – and the fire was a major one. Urgently pointing it out to the crew, he told Captain Taylor: "You'd better turn back and land as quickly as you can." The fire warning light in the No 2 fire shutoff handle was now seen to be illuminated and Taylor called: "Fire drill!".

"What about a Mayday call?" Moss added. With Taylor's consent, First Officer Kirkland responded, telling the Heathrow Tower controller they were returning for an emergency landing.

Alerting the airport fire service and initially offering the aircraft a clearance to complete a circuit and land back on Runway 27 Left, the controller then offered Runway 05 Right, as this would result in a shorter flight path. Captain Taylor accepted the clearance and the tower instructed other aircraft approaching to land to overshoot to ensure a clear path for G-ARWE and to keep the airport movement areas open for firefighting vehicles.

Meanwhile Hicks, having began the prescribed engine failure drill, changed to fire drill and completed its Phase 1 from memory as re-

A BOAC Boeing 707 similar to the one lost at Heathrow.

quired. Opening his own copy of the aircraft check list, he then went through Phase 2 of the drill. At this stage Kirkland, having completed his radio transmissions, began reading the fire drill check list aloud to assist Hicks, but Hicks told him it had already been done.

While this was going on, Moss was watching the engine fire through the cockpit side window and offering advice to Taylor to assist him in positioning the aircraft for a landing. It was a far from easy approach, the Boeing having already reached a height of 3000 feet and a speed of 225 knots when the fire broke out, and the turn back onto a final approach to Runway 05 Left had to be made abnormally close in to the threshold. Furthermore, there was no approach slope guidance to this relatively short 2360 metre runway.

A minute and a half after the start of the fire, just as Taylor called for the undercarriage and full flap to be lowered, the flames weakened the structure of the No 2 engine pylon to the point of failure, and the engine fell away as it was designed to do. Although the wheels locked down normally, the hydraulic contents and pressure gauges were then seen to be falling and the flaps stopped extending at 47 degrees, three degrees short of the full flap position.

Despite the loss of the engine, the fire continued to burn fiercely. Even so, Taylor judged the approach well, the Boeing touching down smoothly less than 400 metres in from the run-

way threshold. To help bring the aircraft to a standstill in the shortest possible distance, he then used reverse thrust on Nos 1 and 4 engines down to a very low speed, succeeding in stopping in only 1250 metres. Unfortunately it also deflected the flames in towards the fuselage.

As soon as the Boeing came to rest, Hicks began the engine shutdown drill, but almost straight away Taylor ordered fire drill on all three remaining engines. Before Hicks and Kirkland could act however, there was a massive explosion in the port wing, intensifying the fire and flinging burning debris over the top of the fuselage to the starboard side of the aircraft. Immediately Taylor ordered his crew to abandon the flightdeck.

Meanwhile, in the passenger cabin, the cabin crew and some of the passengers had felt the aircraft shudder just after takeoff. Looking out through the port side windows as the aircraft climbed, they saw the No 2 engine on fire. Senior Steward Davis Gordon went briefly to the flightdeck to confirm they were returning to land then, in the short time available, directed the cabin crew in preparing for an emergency evacuation. Even before the aircraft had come to a stop, they had both starboard overwing escape hatches open. Immediately it stopped they unlatched the starboard front and rear galley doors and the port forward main door, and began rigging the inflatable escape chutes.

Urged on by the cabin crew, the passengers began leaving through the overwing hatches and, as soon as the escape chutes inflated, from the rear galley door and then the front galley door on the starboard side. The explosion in the port wing and the burning debris it scattered, then prevented further escapes through the overwing hatches.

Captain Taylor, after assisting one of the stewardesses to inflate the chute for the port forward main door, and satisfying himself the evacuation was going satisfactorily, left the aircraft through the starboard flightdeck window, using the crew's escape rope to lower himself to the ground. Hicks, helping cabin staff in the forward section, then saw that the bottom of the chute for the port forward main door had "kinked". He climbed down and straightened it, but immediately it inflated fully, burning fuel spreading out over the concrete runway set the chute on fire and it burst.

More explosions in the port wing followed, releasing more fuel from the breached tanks. This quickly spread, greatly enlarging the area of fire. Because of the spread of burning fuel under the rear fuselage, the rear chute also caught fire and burst after only five passengers had escaped down it. As a result, most passengers had to wait their turn to leave through the forward galley door on the starboard side, using its escape chute.

Kirkland, who could not get into

the forward galley to help with the evacuation, followed Captain Taylor through the flight-deck starboard window and down the crew escape rope. Second Officer Hutchinson, after initially helping direct the passengers, came after him. Check Captain Moss left the aircraft via the forward galley door chute during a brief gap in the stream of passengers evacuating the cabin.

Inside the cabin the exit of passengers was at first orderly, except for some confusion when the rear door and over-wing exits became unusable. Conditions in the cabin remained satisfactory in the early stages of the fire, but quickly deteriorated when the rear section of the fuselage was breached by an explosion. Four passengers in this part of the cabin, including an elderly woman normally confined to a wheelchair, together with Stewardess B Harrison who had been marshalling them to the rear galley door chute before it burst, were overcome by heat and smoke before they could escape and died in the fire that consumed the rear fuselage.

With the exception of these five, the cabin evacuation was almost complete by the time the fire services arrived. The remaining cabin crew, apart from a steward who had climbed down from the rear door while rigging the escape chute for Stewardess Harrison, were the last to leave, following the passengers out via the forward galley door chute. Although the fire services saved the Boeing's starboard wing fuel tanks from catching fire, they were unable to prevent fire destroying the port wing and the rear fuselage.

Thirty eight of the 112 passengers who escaped from the burning aircraft sustained injuries of varying degrees, the more serious from jumping down to the concrete runway from the starboard wing, or in a few cases, from the cabin doors after the escape chutes had succumbed to heat.

★   ★   ★

Examination of the aircraft after the fire was extinguished, showed that none of the four fire shutoff handles (one for each engine) on the flightdeck had been pulled, and that neither the fuel booster pump

Taken by an amateur photographer near London Heathrow Airport, this graphic picture shows the Boeing 707's No 2 engine falling from the still burning port wing as the aircraft was returning to land. The aircraft's magnesium alloy engine pylons are designed to burn through in the event of an uncontrollable engine fire, allowing the complete engine pod to drop off before damage is done to primary wing structure. (Aviation Safety Digest)

switches for the main wing tanks, nor the switches on the engineer's panel for the fuel shutoff valves, had been turned off.

The No 2 engine was recovered from a water-filled gravel pit near Egham, about eight kilometres from the threshold of Runway 05 Right. Despite having fallen some 2000 feet, it was substantially complete and only slightly damaged by fire. A section of the rim of its No 5 stage low pressure compressor wheel was found nearby.

An intensive search of the area beneath the flight path yielded other fragments of the No 2 engine. Some severely damaged stator and rotor blades from the low pressure compressor were found close to the upwind end of Runway 27 Left, to-

gether with fragments of the compressor casing. Not far away lay the starboard section of the engine cowling which had been pierced by engine debris and torn from its mountings.

Further along the flight path, portions of the No 5 compressor wheel rim were found, and finally the main fuel feed pipe for the engine. Normally routed around the starboard side of the engine, the pipe had been torn away by the bursting of the compressor wheel rim and engine casing.

A strip examination of the recovered engine showed the No 5 low pressure compressor wheel had disintegrated as a result of metal fatigue, hurling several pieces of its rim through the engine casing. The fire broke out when fragments severed the main fuel feed pipe, allowing fuel to gush onto the hot engine under pressure from the booster pumps at the rate of about 225 litres a minute. Because the fuel shutoff valves remained open, the fire continued to burn fiercely, quickly eating through the alloy structure of the engine pylon and allowing the engine to fall from the wing. Even after the aircraft came to a stop on the runway, the fuel pumps continued to run, feeding the fire for another 20 seconds or so until it disrupted their electrical wiring. But soon after this the explosion in the port wing released much more fuel, greatly intensifying and spreading the fire.

Boeing 707 aircraft are equipped with a fire extinguisher system that uses bottles of inert gas to smother a fire within an engine cowling. The system is controlled through the fire shutoff handle for each engine, located on the pilots' glareshield. In the event of an engine fire, a red warning lamp illuminates in the appropriate fire shutoff handle and the flightdeck fire warning bell rings.

Pulling out the fire shutoff handle, among other actions, closes the fuel shutoff valve for that engine, shuts off the supply of hydraulic oil to its engine driven hydraulic pumps, and electrically arms the fire extinguisher discharge switch. Only after the fire shutoff handle has been pulled can the fire extinguisher bottles be discharged.

If the engine fire continues to burn despite these discharges, the fire ex-

Firemen tackling the blazing Boeing 707. Fuel pouring from the breached port wing tanks rapidly spread the fire, consuming the port wing and the rear fuselage, before it could be brought under control. Four passengers and one stewardess trapped in the rear fuselage were overcome before they could escape. But for the professionalism of the cabin crew, the loss of life might have been even greater. (Aviation Safety Digest)

tinguisher transfer switch is selected to "transfer" and by pressing the same fire extinguisher button again, the contents of the bottles in the adjacent engine can be used.

Examination of the failed engine's two fire extinguisher bottles showed that both were discharged but this was as a result of overheating, rather than being fired electrically from the flightdeck. On the flightdeck itself, the port side fire extinguisher switch on the engineer's panel was found in the "transfer" position. There was no evidence of any defect in the fire extinguisher system other than that sustained in the ground fire.

It was clear that after the No 2 engine fell from the aircraft, the wing fire continued to burn fiercely because it was being fed from fuel gushing from the stub of the severed fuel pipe ahead of the leading edge of the wing. This in turn was the result of the crew's failure to pull the No 2 engine fire shutoff handle on the flightdeck, as required in the aircraft's emergency check list for fire in flight.

This omission was further substantiated by the rapid loss of hydraulic fluid after the engine fell away. As the fire shutoff handle also operates the hydraulic shutoff valve for that engine, pulling it would have prevented this loss of hydraulic fluid.

The disastrous result of this omission, aided and abetted by the crew's further failure to switch off the fuel booster pumps before abandoning the flightdeck, became far more evident after the Boeing was back on the ground. Despite an excellent landing in the circumstances by Captain Taylor, with the aircraft being brought to a stop on the runway intact in a relatively short distance, the growing ferocity of the fire countered much of the advantage gained by handling skill in the air. The end result was the needless loss of five lives and the destruction of the aircraft.

The focus of the investigation was therefore directed towards the reasons for the crew's failure to properly complete the fire drill actions prescribed in the aircraft's emergency check list.

★   ★   ★

BOAC's emergency drills for the Boeing 707 in force at the time had been regularly practised by the crew and there was no doubt they could be successfully accomplished. But as the accident so unfortunately demonstrated, with a sudden engine fire of this intensity, with Fire Drill quickly supplanting Engine Failure Drill in an atmosphere of genuine urgency, confusion could occur over what vital actions had been completed and what remained to be

done. Apart from the action to silence the fire warning bell, the two drills differed in only one critical action – the pulling of the fire shutoff handle.

In this instance, the difference between the two drills was inadvertently obscured by Hicks when he initially reached for, but did not actually pull, the fire shutoff handle while carrying out the Engine Failure Drill. This evidently gave both him and Kirkland the impression the fire shutoff handle had already been pulled when Captain Taylor called for Fire Drill only a short time later.

From the flight engineer's seat position during takeoff, it is difficult to see at a glance whether or not a fire shutoff handle has been pulled, because its movement is directly towards him. Viewed from either pilot seat its position is more easily recognisable. Even so, because its movement is only about 25mm, it is questionable whether its position would be readily apparent to pilots concentrating on an emergency approach of the sort required in this instance.

BOAC in fact believed that Captain Taylor was so preoccupied with physically handling the aircraft that he was unable to monitor his crew's performance. He therefore had to rely on the crew members' report that the fire drill had been completed.

Check Captain Moss, in the jump seat behind Taylor, could not monitor the fire drill either, because he was watching the progress of the engine fire, keeping Taylor informed, and verbally helping him position the aircraft for landing. For these reasons he did not notice the fire shutoff handle had not been pulled. Furthermore, with the physical loss of the engine from the aircraft, the red warning lamp in the fire shutoff handle would have gone out, and from that point on the crew's attention would not have been drawn to it.

A serious weakness in the prescribed fire drill was the fact that the vital action of pulling the fire shutoff handle relied solely on memory and called for no further check that it had been accomplished. Another factor leading to the breakdown of the drill was Kirkland's workload. In the short time available, in the midst

of his other tasks as first officer in preparing for the landing, he was instructed to transmit a Mayday call. Also, when he began to read the emergency checklist aloud to Hicks as required by BOAC's operations manual, Hicks told him the check had already been completed. But even if he *had* read back all the listed fire drill actions, they would not have included a check of the fire shutoff handle.

It was evident to the investigators that the fire warning bell on the flightdeck did not ring when the engine fire broke out because Hicks, hearing the undercarriage warning horn a moment before, misidentified the action to be taken and pressed the fire bell cancel button at the instant the bell would have begun to ring. Had it actually rung however, and his first fire drill action had been an *intentional* cancellation of the warning bell, it is highly likely that

there would have been no confusion over completing the other memory items of the fire drill check list.

In the passenger cabin, there was little time to prepare the passengers for the landing and emergency evacuation. Even so, from the mass of favourable comment from the surviving passengers and other available evidence, it was clear that everything possible was done and that the cabin staff, under the leadership of Senior Steward Gordon, acted with a dedication, coolness and efficiency that enabled the evacuation to progress in an orderly manner and without panic. Indeed, Stewardess B Harrison, the only member of the aircraft crew to lose her life, did so as a result of her concern to help passengers trapped in the rear of the cabin in rapidly deteriorating conditions. There could be no doubt it was the cabin crew's extremely professional conduct that

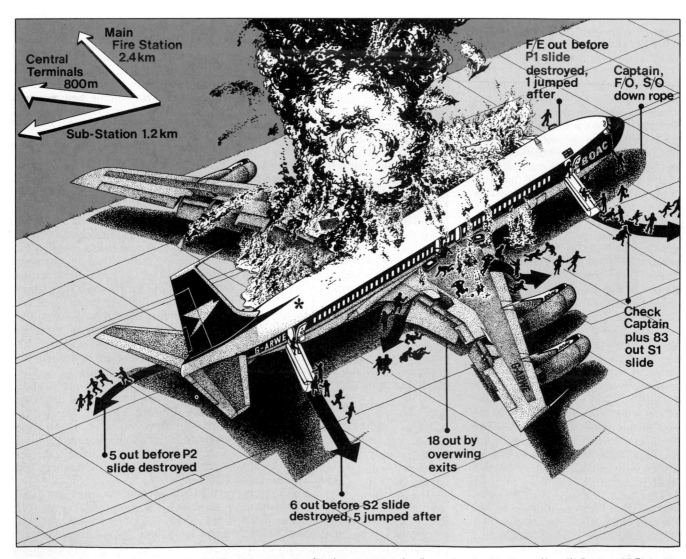

Evacuation paths followed by 122 of G-ARWE's 127 occupants after the emergency landing on London Heathrow Airport's Runway 05 Right. The airport's fire and rescue services were still on their way when a port wing fuel tank exploded as shown. Burning debris then caused three of the four inflatable escape slides to burst while the evacuation was in progress. The asterisk indicates where a stewardess and four passengers died after fire breached the rear fuselage. (Matthew Tesch)

A sad end to G-ARWE as it burns at Heathrow Airport April 8, 1968.

prevented greater loss of life after the aircraft came to rest on the runway.

This evacuation under real life emergency conditions showed that great concern of many passengers to take small belongings with them tended to block the cabin aisle and seriously delay the general movement of passengers towards the available exits.

It was clear from the accident also, that the inflatable escape chutes in use were far too vulnerable to heat and flame. Because a large number of passengers can escape down even one chute in a short space of time, further research was needed in the design of inflatable chutes in general and in the development of fire resistant materials for use in their manufacture. Even a half minute's additional use of a chute in deteriorating conditions could save many lives.

As a result of the investigation of this unfortunate accident, BOAC modified its emergency check lists for the Boeing 707 in several respects. The two engine emergency drills were combined into one – "Engine Fire or Severe Failure Drill" – unconditionally requiring the fire shutoff handle to be physically pulled, whether or not a fire warning had occurred. In addition, the first item of Phase 2 of the drill now required the pilot in command to confirm that the fire shutoff had been pulled. The company's operations manual for the Boeing 707 was also revised to more specifically define

The pilot's instrument panel in a Boeing 707, showing position of fire shutoff handles. (Aviation Safety Digest)

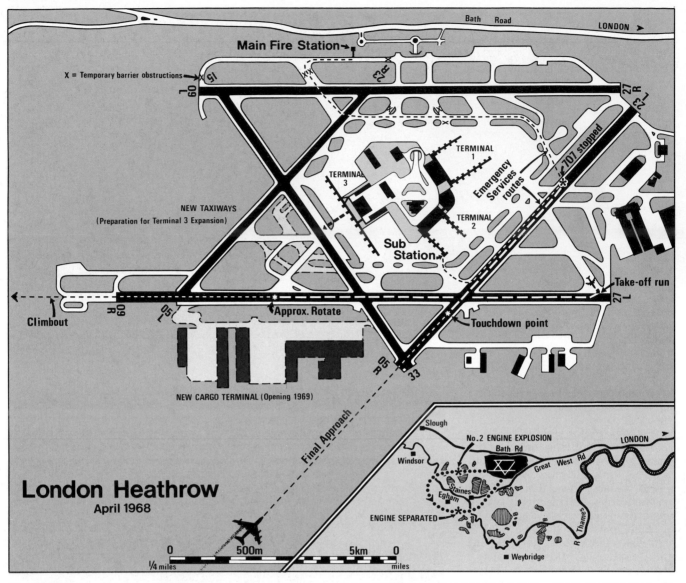

London Heathrow
April 1968

X = Temporary barrier obstructions

Main Fire Station→

Bath Road

LONDON →

TERMINAL 1

TERMINAL 3

TERMINAL 2

Emergency Services routes

707 stopped

NEW TAXIWAYS
(Preparation for Terminal 3 Expansion)

Sub Station

Take-off run

Climbout

Approx. Rotate

Touchdown point

NEW CARGO TERMINAL (Opening 1969)

Final Approach

Slough

No.2 ENGINE EXPLOSION
Bath Rd

Windsor

LONDON →

Great West Rd

Staines
Egham

R Thames

ENGINE SEPARATED

Weybridge

0   500m   5km   0
¼ miles   miles

Diagram of London Heathrow Airport at the time of the accident, showing G-ARWE's takeoff and approach paths, and routes followed by fire service vehicles to where the aircraft was burning on Runway 05 Right. (inset) Approximate circuit flown by G-ARWE during its scant minutes of flight.

the emergency check list procedure to be followed by crew members.

Overall, the accident was undoubtedly the result of an untimely combination of circumstances. Prominent among these, in addition to the actual emergency, was the additional crew member on the flightdeck in the person of Check Captain Moss. His official function was that of observer "to ensure that agreed standards of operation were maintained". BOAC's brief for such routine checking was that the "check captain ... in general is expected to be as unobtrusive as possible".

In the undoubted fear and tension that an emergency of this sort generates, it is probably unrealistic to expect any senior airline captain to remain "as unobtrusive as possible".

Even so, it has to be said that it was probably the check captain's action in silencing the undercarriage

warning horn when the flight engineer began the engine failure drill that produced the initial confusion in the latter's mind, leading him to inadvertently silence the fire warning bell.

This in turn led to the omission that had such drastic and tragic consequences – the failure to pull the No 2 fire shutoff handle. Furthermore, the check captain's verbal warning to the crew in general that the No 2 engine was on fire just when the warning lamp on the fire shutoff handle would have illuminated, might have diverted the flight engineer's attention to the extent that the warning light failed to prompt him to pull the handle. Again, at the very time when the first officer might have "picked up" the fact that the fire shutoff handle was displaying a red warning light and had not been pulled, the check captain's suggestion of a Mayday call

effectively diverted his attention also.

All these promptings by the check captain were perfectly normal reactions and entirely understandable in the circumstances. But they nevertheless point to a "too many cooks" situation which could have detracted from the crew's concentration on the emergency drills they were trained to carry out, thereby contributing to the confusion that developed on the flightdeck.

Had the fire drill been properly accomplished when Captain Taylor called for it, there can be little doubt that the engine fire could have been promptly extinguished in flight. What turned out to be a tragedy, involving the loss of five lives and a valuable Boeing 707, would have been no more than an uncomfortable incident, resulting in the aircraft having to return for an inspection and a subsequent engine change.

CHAPTER 8

"I may have to ditch this aircraft"

– Captain to San Juan Control

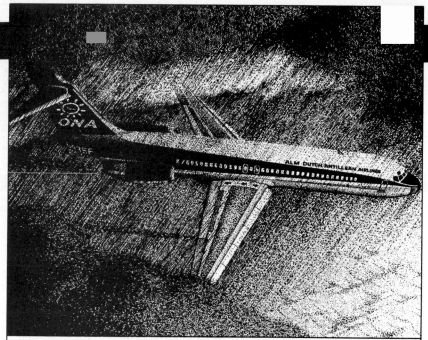

Overseas National Airways McDonnell Douglas DC-9-33F, N935F [47407] *Carib Queen*, operating on behalf of ALM Dutch Antillean Airlines – May 2, 1970

With the advent of the jetliner, the ocean ditchings that too often befell the slower, less reliable piston engined airliners, were throught to be a thing of the past. But the industry had yet to learn that the fortunes of a long range jet flight could change with dramatic suddenness if liberties were taken with fuel reserves.

Flight 980, departing Kennedy International Airport, New York, at 11am on May 2, 1970, was not the type of service usually operated by domestic airliners.

Though flown by the near new DC-9-33F, N935F, it was in fact an international flight by the US carrier, Overseas National Airways Inc, operated under a lease agreement on behalf of the Dutch colonial airline, Antilliaanse Luchtvaart Maatschappij, a subsidiary of KLM. Its destination was Juliana Airport, serving the tiny Dutch settlement on St Maarten, Netherlands Antilles, two groups of small islands forming part of the West Indies.

The flight crew, Captain Balsey DeWitt, First Officer Harry Evans and Navigator Hugh Hart, were American citizens and members of ONA's staff, but the cabin crew – Purser Wilford Spencer, Steward Tobias Cordeiro and Stewardess Margaret Abraham – were employees of the Dutch airline. All were well experienced and four months previously the cabin crew had undergone a course emphasising the differences in the equipment used by the two airlines. ALM operated three DC-9s of its own, but these were all short fuselage Series 15 aircraft.

The en route weather for the 1400 nautical mile trip was expected to be overcast and showery, with south easterly winds off the Atlantic and scattered thunderstorms. The terminal forecast for St Maarten predicted a wind from the southeast at 10 knots, two octas of cumulous cloud at 2500 feet, and possible showers and thunderstorms with a base of 500 feet. Visibility was expected to be 10km, reduced to 2.5km in showers.

Selecting St Thomas Airport in the US Virgin Islands, 110nm west of St Maarten, as their alternate, the crew filed an IFR plan direct to St Maarten at Flight Level 290 (29,000 feet), with a time interval of 206 minutes. The DC-9 carried 28,900 pounds (13,120kg) of fuel, giving it a calculated endurance of 274 minutes. The required reserve fuel for the flight, including fuel to the alternate and 30 minutes holding, was calculated as 6400 pounds (2905kg). The fuel actually on board exceeded the planned requirement by 900 pounds (409kg).

When the 57 passengers had boarded and the DC-9 was ready to taxi, the flight crew discovered their public address system was not working. Although this would be a nuisance during the three and a half

hour flight, the PA system within the passenger cabin itself was functioning, and the fault, apparently in the flightdeck microphone, was considered insufficient to delay the aircraft's departure.

Taxiing from the International terminal at 11.02am, the DC-9 was cleared for takeoff 12 minutes later. The climb was normal, and on levelling off at FL 290, cruising flight was established. Some 750nm southeast of New York, the aircraft encountered thunderstorm conditions, necessitating minor diversions from track and a reduction in airspeed to turbulence penetration speed. At 1.36pm, the aircraft descended to FL 270, where it resumed cruising flight.

But the thunderstorm encounters continued, and with 400nm still to run to St Maarten, the crew requested a further descent to FL 250. Passing an en route position report to the San Juan Air Route Traffic Control Centre on the US island of Puerto Rico at 2.24pm, when the DC-9 was 180nm northwest of St Maarten, the crew noted they had 8600 pounds (3900kg) of fuel remaining and estimated they would arrive at St Maarten at 3pm with 6000 pounds (2725kg) on board.

N935F, a McDonnell Douglas DC-9-33F powered by Pratt & Whitney JT8D-9 engines, as delivered new to Overseas National Airways Inc on March 7, 1969, only 14 months before it was lost (see footnote below).

Some 15 minutes later, San Juan Control advised the DC-9 the weather at St Maarten's Juliana Airport had deteriorated and was now below the landing minima of 600 feet cloudbase and three km visibility. Captain DeWitt's response was to ask for a clearance to San Juan at FL 210, and at 2.46pm, less than 15 minutes from Juliana, the DC-9 diverted for San Juan.

Five minutes later however, Juliana Airport's tower controller reported the weather had improved again. Below the general overcast at 5000 feet there was now only broken cloud at 1000 feet, with six to eight kilometres of visibility in rain. The captain decided to attempt a landing at Juliana after all, and at 2.51pm, San Juan Control passed the DC-9 a new clearance to St Maarten.

At this point Captain DeWitt saw that 5800 pounds (2635kg) of fuel remained and estimated they would arrive at the Juliana terminal with 4400 pounds (2000kg) still in the tanks. At 3.08pm the crew reported over the Juliana NDB at 2500 feet and the controller advised there was now scattered cloud at 800 feet and broken cloud at 1000 feet, with visibility fluctuating between three and five kilometres.

The airport, on a narrow neck of land on the southwest coast of the island, has an elevation of only 13 feet. Its single east west runway is 1600 metres long, with little land extending beyond either end. Hills on the main body of the island, rising to more than 1000 feet, lie three km across a bay immediately to the east of the runway.

Carrying out an NDB approach with the undercarriage lowered, 25 degrees of flap extended, and Captain DeWitt handling the aircraft, the crew finally became visual at 3.15pm. Immediately ahead of them was the airfield, but it was too late to properly align the aircraft with the runway. Still flying visually, the captain immediately applied power and began a low level left hand circuit for another attempt.

The second approach four minutes later again had to be abandoned because of difficulty in lining up with the runway in the poor visibility. A heavy shower on base leg was making a visual approach particularly hard to judge. After adding power to go around for the second time, the captain called for full flap and brought the airspeed back to 130 knots for a third attempt to land.

This time he succeeded in getting the alignment right on final approach, but when the runway became fully visible through the rain, he realised they were too high and too close in for a landing without reducing engine power below acceptable limits. Forced to go around yet again, the captain this time carried out the instrument procedure for a missed approach, and after briefly discussing the fuel situation with Navigator Hart, called the Tower to report they would have to divert to St Thomas after all. The controller cleared the DC-9 direct to St Thomas at 4000 feet, and the crew set course for the Virgin Islands airport, 110nm distant, at 3.31pm.

Re-establishing contact with San Juan Control, they were informed they would be assigned a higher altitude shortly, the controller alerting them to the presence of a slower aircraft only 10nm ahead. During the brief climb to 4000 feet, all three members of the flight crew were suddenly alarmed to see the fuel gauges and the fuel totaliser giving erratic readings, and as they levelled off at 4000 feet, the totaliser stabilised momentarily at only 850 pounds (396kg).

"It can't be right," DeWitt blurted, his face ashen. "None of the cross checks we made en route showed any discrepancies.

"It only showed 850 the once when we levelled off," Navigator Hart reassured him. "Look, it's bobbing around now between 1350 and 1400 pounds, and fluctuating higher into the 2000 range."

DeWitt shook his head in disbelief. "There's just no way we could possibly be as low as 850." As if to convince himself, he added: "In my judgement there's no way could have less than 2000."

Shortly after 3.33pm, San Juan Control called the DC-9: "What altitude are you requesting to St Thomas?" Deeply worried, the captain responded: "Anything you've got that's higher – I'm a little short on fuel and I've got to get up."

"Roger, you're cleared to Flight Level 120," (12,000 feet).

(right) The DC-9's great circle route from New York south east to St Maarten. The track flown after the initial diversion towards San Juan leads into the enlargement depicting the final 45 minutes of flight, terminating in the ditching less than five minutes flying time from St Croix. St Maarten is one of the small north eastern trio of the six scattered Caribbean islands that comprise the Netherlands Antilles. The three bigger islands lie some 560 nautical miles south west, just off the Venezuelan coast. (Matthew Tesch)

Artist's note: Research has failed to confirm details of ALM's lease of the ONA DC-9 'Carib Queen'. Even so, the former company's name may well have been carried on the aircraft as shown in the artist's impression. ONA appears to have had a substantial leasing presence in the region, evidenced by its other DC-9s bearing similar names such as 'Island Queen' and 'Calypso Queen'. ALM's own trio of short bodied DC-9-15s were replaced by DC-9-32s in 1975.

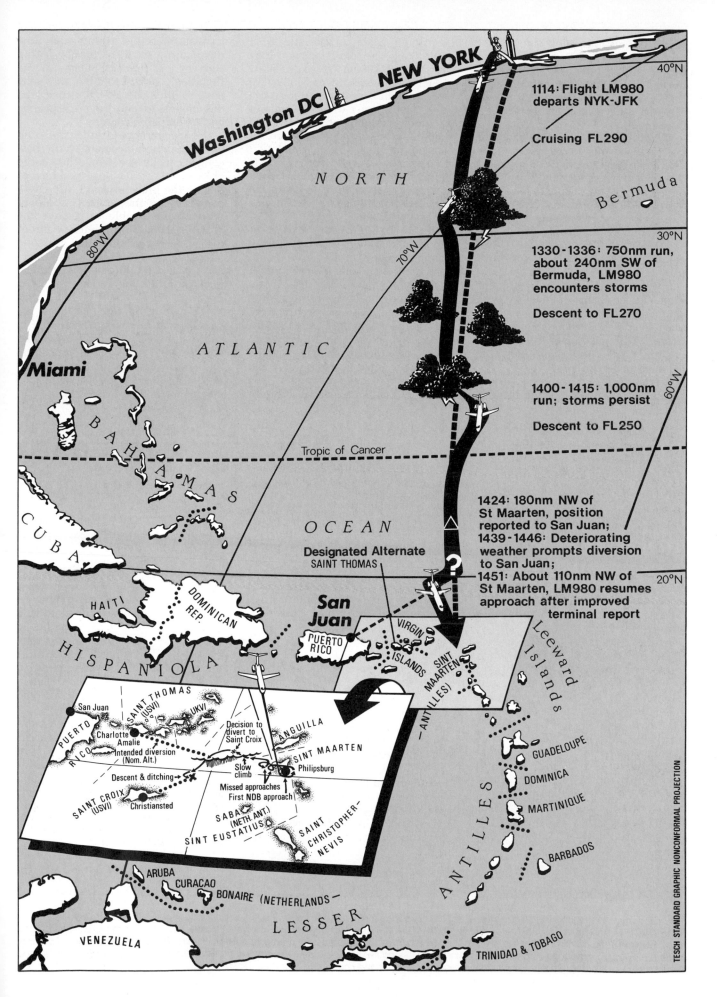

NEW YORK

Washington DC

1114: Flight LM980 departs NYK-JFK

Cruising FL290

N O R T H

Bermuda

40°N

30°N

70°W

1330-1336: 750nm run, about 240nm SW of Bermuda, LM980 encounters storms

Descent to FL270

A T L A N T I C

Miami

60°W

1400-1415: 1,000nm run; storms persist

Descent to FL250

Tropic of Cancer

B A H A M A S

O C E A N

Designated Alternate
SAINT THOMAS

1424: 180nm NW of St Maarten, position reported to San Juan;
1439-1446: Deteriorating weather prompts diversion to San Juan;
1451: About 110nm NW of St Maarten, LM980 resumes approach after improved terminal report

C U B A

HAITI

DOMINICAN REP.

San Juan

PUERTO RICO

VIRGIN ISLANDS

20°N

H I S P A N I O L A

L e e w a r d I s l a n d s

SINT MAARTEN
(ANTILLES)

San Juan

SAINT THOMAS (USVI)

UKVI

PUERTO RICO

Charlotte Amalie

ANGUILLA

Decision to divert to Saint Croix

Intended diversion (Nom. Alt.)

SINT MAARTEN

Philipsburg

GUADELOUPE

Slow climb

Descent & ditching

Missed approaches
First NDB approach

SAINT CROIX (USVI)

Christiansted

SABA (NETH. ANT.)

SINT EUSTATIUS

SAINT CHRISTOPHER-NEVIS

DOMINICA

MARTINIQUE

A N T I L L E S

BARBADOS

ARUBA
CURACAO
BONAIRE (NETHERLANDS-

VENEZUELA

L E S S E R

TRINIDAD & TOBAGO

TESCH STANDARD GRAPHIC NONCONFORMAL PROJECTION

Still shaken by the fuel indications, the captain gingerly coaxed the DC-9 into a climb, using less power and a lower airspeed than normal in an attempt to conserve their now precious remaining fuel. The fuel gauges continued to give erratic readings.

"What do you think?" he asked Hart, still seriously concerned.

"It's hard to know from the gauges," the navigator answered. "But just to be sure, why not head for St Croix instead of St Thomas? It's a bit closer from where we are now." The US island of St Croix, 44nm due south of St Thomas, was 10nm closer to their position en route from St Maarten.

DeWitt agreed and in a moment First Officer Evans called San Juan again: "Could we have that clearance to St Thomas amended to St Croix?" This was approved, and the captain turned left on to the new heading for St Croix.

Continuing the reduced power climb, the DC-9 entered the base of the overcast and at about 7000 feet, the captain again became uneasy. "I don't like it," he told Evans and Hart shortly after 3.35pm. "If we *are* short of fuel, and there's any possibility we have to ditch – we ought to keep the sea in sight. Don't want to flameout in cloud – and have to make a dead stick approach through the overcast with no time to set up a ditching."

The crew agreed and DeWitt added, "I think we'd better get back down below the cloud." To Evans, he said: "Ask San Juan for a clearance to descend again."

San Juan approved the request and about a minute, later as the DC-9 was descending through 5000 feet in zero visibility, the captain again spoke what was on his mind. "You know, there's no way for me to decide whether those gauges are accurate or inaccurate," he said to Hart. "I have to believe them. And if we do in fact have this low fuel, it would be best to get down near the water and try to find a place to ditch now."

Calling San Juan Control himself, he told the controller: "OK, I may have to ditch this aircraft – I'm now descending to the water." Asking Hart to call Purser Spencer to the flightdeck, DeWitt told him they may have to ditch. He was to instruct the passengers to don their lifejackets, and to prepare generally.

Spencer returned to the cabin and made the announcement to the passengers while the two other cabin crew members demonstrated how to put on the lifejackets. All three then assisted the passengers, some of whom were unable to remove the jackets from their pouches under the seats, while others had difficulty adjusting the fit of the jackets themselves. In a few minutes Hart came back into the cabin to help the cabin crew.

Meanwhile on the flightdeck the captain and the first officer were in radio contact with San Juan concerning their likely ditching position and the availability of rescue facilities. They were assured that rescue efforts were already in hand.

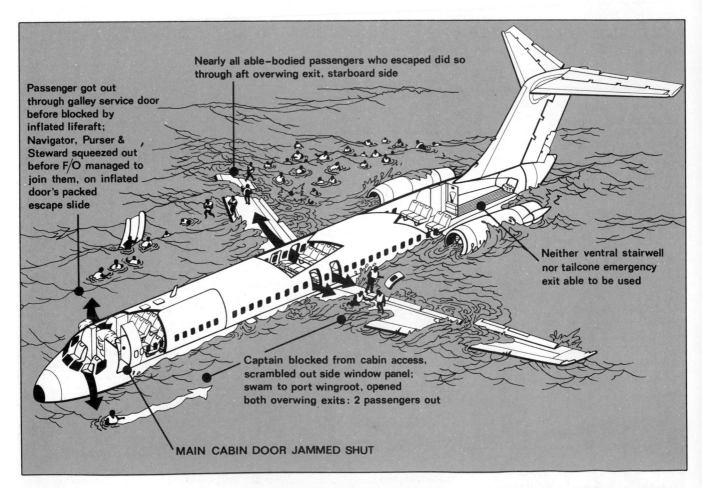

Nearly all able-bodied passengers who escaped did so through aft overwing exit, starboard side

Passenger got out through galley service door before blocked by inflated liferaft; Navigator, Purser & Steward squeezed out before F/O managed to join them, on inflated door's packed escape slide

Neither ventral stairwell nor tailcone emergency exit able to be used

Captain blocked from cabin access, scrambled out side window panel; swam to port wingroot, opened both overwing exits: 2 passengers out

MAIN CABIN DOOR JAMMED SHUT

Key aspects of the world's first (and to date only) successful ditching of a civil jet transport are portrayed in this schematic view of survivor evacuation. As one British commentator has put it, "hitting water at speed is like hitting concrete". Some occupants who were standing in the DC-9's aisle at the moment of impact were either killed or incapacitated and did not escape from the aircraft. Others whose seatbelts failed suffered a similar fate. Of the 63 occupants, 35 passengers and five of the six crew members were winched from the sea by helicopter. It is not known how many others left the aircraft but were lost at sea while awaiting rescue. (Matthew Tesch)

Just before 3.48pm, the DC-9 was down to 500 feet, just below the base of the overcast. The sea and its grey swell, rolling in from the southeast, was now plainly visible beneath the aircraft, but it was raining heavily and horizontal visibility was limited to about 600 metres. The fuel gauges now indicated the engines would fail very shortly and, at the captain's instruction, Evans called San Juan Control again. "We're ditching," he radioed.

Levelling off, DeWitt positioned the aircraft directly over the crest of a swell, laying off a small amount of crosswind drift to fly along the crest as he progressively reduced speed and height, pausing briefly in 100 foot increments to improve his depth perception. Down to 20 feet above the water at an airspeed of 145 knots, he lowered 15 degrees of flap and allowed the airspeed to decrease further. As soon as the low fuel pressure warning lights began to flicker, he lowered full flap. Soon afterwards both engines flamed out. Flashing the Fasten Seat Belt and No Smoking signs on and off several times to warn those in the cabin the ditching was imminent, he raised the nose about six degrees and flew the DC-9 onto the swell at about 90 knots.

In the cabin, Hart was helping Purser Spencer remove one of the aircraft's five 25 man inflatable liferafts from its storage in the forward coat cupboard on the port side of the cabin. Carrying it across the aisle into the galley directly opposite on the starboard side, they placed the liferaft beside the galley loading door, ready for deployment in the water as soon as the aircraft came to a stop.

Steward Cordeiro was also in the galley securing equipment when Hart, hearing the engines spooling down and seeing the seat belt lights flashing, suddenly realised they were about to ditch. In the cabin, several passengers were still standing in the aisle, putting on their life jackets, together with Stewardess Abraham, who was helping them. At least five others did not have their seat belts fastened.

Desperately shouting for everyone to sit down, Hart and Spencer quickly seated themselves on the aft facing jumpseat on the forward cabin bulkhead, while Cordeiro sat down on the life raft with his back against the bulkhead. Neither Hart nor Spencer had time to fasten their seat belts.

Passenger reaction to Hart's warning varied. Some, seemingly oblivi-ous to what was happening, simply relaxed in their seats, looking out the window, assuming the DC-9 was completing its overwater approach to the runway at St Croix. A few, including Stewardess Abraham, not appreciating the urgency of the situation, were still on their feet when the aircraft hit the water. Others acted immediately on the navigator's command and used pillows and the 'crash position' to brace themselves, bending forward with their arms over their heads in accordance with the safety instructions on the cards in each of the cabin seat pockets.

Even so, most were unprepared for the severity of the impact. Passengers who still did not have their seat belts fastened, and those still standing, were flung violently forward through the cabin, sustaining incapacitating injuries. At least six more were injured when their seat belt fastenings failed.

Yet the aircraft itself remained essentially intact and none of the other crew members was injured. Immediately the aircraft lurched to a stop in the sea swell, Spencer and Hart attempted to open the port side forward main door. It was jammed and would not budge. Cordeiro meanwhile had opened the galley loading door on the starboard side, and a young woman passenger had already scrambled through it into the water.

The navigator and the purser then went to help Cordeiro retrieve the liferaft from beneath galley debris – ovens, bins and drawers – that had tumbled on top of it in the impact. They had just been joined by Evans from the flightdeck when the liferaft inadvertently inflated, pinning Evans against the cabin bulkhead and blocking the others' way back into the main cabin. They did the only thing possible and jumped into the sea via the galley door, as did Evans as soon as he was able to extricate himself.

In the meantime, with the DC-9 rapidly taking water and part of the cabin floor already awash, the passenger sitting next to the aft overwing exit on the starboard side had opened it. A seasoned air traveller, it was his habit to sit next to an emergency exit whenever possible, and to make a mental note of its operation. He and most of the able bodied passengers, all wearing lifejackets, quickly left the aircraft through this exit.

Alone on the flightdeck, Captain DeWitt saw that the inflated liferaft in the galley blocked his way to the cabin too. Scrambling out through his windscreen hatch and entering the water, he immediately swam back to the port side overwing exits and opened them from the outside. After assisting two passengers out, he looked inside for more, but could

Survivor's view of N935F shortly before it slipped beneath the waves of the Caribbean. Despite empty fuel tanks, the DC-9 sank in less than 10 minutes, suggesting that the underside of the fuselage was breached in the impact with the sea. At the time of the ditching the cloudbase was low, it was raining heavily, and visibility was only a little over half a kilometre. (M Tesch)

see none. By this time the DC-9 was close to sinking and it was vital for those in the water to swim well clear. The aircraft finally disappeared beneath the waves less than 10 minutes after the ditching.

Fortunately for the survivors, though all five liferafts carried on the DC-9 went down with the aircraft, the inflatable escape slide for the galley door had dropped into the water when the crew were escaping. Navigator Hart, swimming about in his lifejacket, came upon it, still packaged and barely floating. With the help of a swimming woman passenger, he inflated it. First Officer Evans, who had been forced to leave the aircraft without a lifejacket, then climbed onto the slide and took command of the survivors bobbing about in the waves, enjoining them all to swim towards him, gather round the slide, and find a handhold. Survivors' belts and neckties were used to provide additional handholds.

Meanwhile, a Pan American World Airways flight which diverted to the area to provide what assistance it could, confirmed the position of the ditching on radar, passing the coordinates to San Juan Control.

Before long, a US Coast Guard HU-16 Albatross amphibian from Puerto Rico arrived overhead and dropped two liferafts but, in the extremely poor visual flying conditions, both fell too far away to be recovered. Next came a Shorts Skyvan, which dropped another two liferafts, this time closer to the survivors. Dewitt swam to one and Hart to the other, but neither were able to manoeuvre the rafts back to the main group.

An hour and a half after the ditching' two HH-52 Coast Guard helicopters arrived over the scene and their crews began winching the survivors aboard one by one, taking 11 in all. Then came a massive US Navy SH-3A Sea King which uplifted 26. Finally, an hour later, with only three remaining survivors to be rescued, a US Marine Corps CH-46 Sea Knight arrived. The last survivor to be winched up was First Officer Evans.

When a tally was finally made of those rescued, it was found that 22 passengers, including two children, together with Stewardess Margaret Abraham, were missing – either lost with the aircraft, or drowned while awaiting rescue in the water.

★　　★　　★

The DC-9 had sunk in 5000 feet of water and its salvage could not be contemplated. But as there had been

no malfunctions of its engines or systems, it was obvious to National Transportation Safety Board investigators that the accident had resulted from inadequate fuel management.

There was no question of optimism on the part of the captain in not allowing adequate fuel for the flight at the planning stage. In addition to fuel to be used en route, the flight plan provided, in accordance with Federal Aviation Regulations, for a 10% reserve, fuel to the St Thomas alternate, and 30 minutes holding fuel. These reserve requirements totalled 28,000 pounds, but over and above this figure, the aircraft carried an additional 900 pounds of fuel, giving a total endurance of 274 minutes, 68 minutes more than the planned flight time of 206 minutes.

Furthermore, the captain's original calculation of the aircraft's endurance when preparing the flight plan proved to be remarkably accurate. Although the en route flight procedures differed from those indicated in the flight plan because of thunderstorm avoidance, the actual time of fuel exhaustion was within only a minute of the estimated endurance.

Of particular concern to the investigators therefore, were the events that followed the captain's decision to divert to San Juan after being told that weather conditions at St Maarten had deteriorated. Clearly, if the DC-9 had continued to San Juan at this time, the accident would not have happened. The factors influencing the captain to alter this decision, together with what followed as a result, were thus vital links in the chain of circumstances that led to the accident.

Given that there is an obligation upon an airliner captain to deliver passengers to their planned destination whenever it can be accomplished safely, it is understandable that Captain DeWitt was influenced by Juliana Tower's advice that conditions at the airfield had now lifted well above minima and showed an improving trend. But the governing factor in making this judgement should have been the amount of fuel needed to continue to St Maarten, carry out an NDB approach and then, if still necessary, divert to the planned alternate.

Because of weather conditions en route, the trip up to this point had taken longer than provided for in the flight plan. At 2.51pm, when the captain reversed his decision to divert to San Juan and elected to continue to St Maarten instead, the DC-9 had

already been in the air for 217 minutes – 11 minutes longer than the total flight planned time of 206 minutes.

At this stage, according to the captain, 5800 pounds (2635kg) of fuel remained in the tanks. As his revised ETA for St Maarten was 3.05pm, he expected to arrive at Juliana Airport with 4400 pounds (2000kg) of fuel remaining. His calculations were based on an 800 pound (365kg) burnoff in the descent from 21,000 feet, with a further 600 pounds (270kg) for the ADF approach and landing. If a straight in visual approach proved possible, he expected to be on the ground with only a little less than 5000 pounds (2270kg) still in the tanks. On this basis, the DC-9 was expected to arrive at St Maarten with prescribed fuel reserves intact, its remaining endurance being 57 minutes.

However, the DC-9 did not reach the St Maarten NDB until 3.15pm, 10 minutes later than the captain's revised estimate. Most of these extra minutes were flown at only 2500 feet at an airspeed of 210 knots and would have consumed around an additional 800 pounds (365kg) of fuel. The aircraft thus reached the St Maartin NDB with only about 4200 pounds (1910kg) of fuel remaining, some 100 pounds (450kg) less than the prescribed alternate fuel requirement.

The remaining endurance was now only a critical 33 minutes, necessitating an immediate diversion to the alternate if an approach and landing could not be completed promptly. After the first approach was abandoned because of poor visibility, only 29 minutes remained to fuel exhaustion. But instead of diverting at once, the captain began tight, low altitude circuits to make two more attempts to land. This took 11 more minutes, the DC-9 all the while in the landing configuration at power settings demanding high fuel consumption.

The investigators calculated that some 1400 pounds (635kg) were consumed during this time, leaving only about 2200 pounds (1000kg) in the tanks when the aircraft finally began its diversion to St Thomas. Though slightly more than the fuel allowed for the diversion in the flight plan, which in theory should have enabled the DC-9 to reach St Thomas or St Croix, this figure was based on zero wind conditions, not taking into account variables that could affect the precise track and flight profile required to obtain the optimum performance from the aircraft. Moreover, there was no way at this late stage that the flight crew could be certain of the precise amount of fuel remaining in the tanks.

But even given the aircraft's critical fuel state when the captain informed Juliana Tower they were diverting to St Thomas, he did not immediately request an economical altitude. Nor did he make any mention of the low fuel state when he called San Juan Control shortly afterwards. As a result, the San Juan controller waited until another aircraft was out of the way before clearing the DC-9 to climb to FL 120. And even after beginning this delayed climb, the captain did not use full power, choosing instead a low power, low airspeed climb in the belief that it would conserve fuel. This was in fact much less efficient in terms of distance covered than would have been a full power climb. Any remaining opportunity the aircraft still had to reach St Thomas or St Croix was thus diminished even further.

For all practical purposes the aircraft was by this time committed to a ditching somewhere to the west of St Maarten. But it was not until six minutes later, when the DC-9 was descending again from 7000 feet, that the captain made his first reference to the possibility of ditching. And it was only at this stage that he called the purser to the flightdeck to tell him they might have to ditch. Even then, the purser gained no impression of the true gravity of the situation, understanding the captain's warning to be no more than a precautionary measure. Indeed,

from the captain's tone, he assumed that, with the flightdeck public address system inoperative, further instructions would be forthcoming if a ditching did become necessary.

The result, only 10 minutes later, was that the cabin crew had no idea the ditching was actually about to take place, and had no time to adequately warn the passengers. Although the captain flashed the No Smoking and Fasten Seat Belts signs several times just before the aircraft hit the water, this meant little to the cabin crew or the passengers, because they had neither been briefed to expect such a signal, nor were they watching for it. Had it not been for Navigator Hart's shouted instruction at the last moment, those in the cabin would have had no warning whatever that impact with the water was imminent.

This lack of communication between the flightdeck and the passenger cabin seriously undermined the effectiveness of the cabin crew's preparations for ditching, and undoubtedly affected the survival prospects of the passengers during and after the ditching.

Nevertheless, the ditching itself was well planned and most successfully accomplished under adverse conditions, the captain demonstrating exceptional skill in handling the aircraft. And certainly the leadership shown by all three flight crew members after the ditching did much to minimise the loss of life while awaiting rescue in the water.

It seems that the captain, after being told of the improving conditions at Juliana Airport and deciding it should be possible to land there

after all, became so preoccupied with his efforts to do so that he "lost the plot" concerning the aircraft's remaining endurance.

Finally forced to give up on Juliana Airport, he was then shaken to the core by the fuel gauge indications, even though both he and the navigator should have known the aircraft's fuel state had by that time become highly critical for their intended diversion.

Devastated by the sudden and appalling prospect of needlessly losing his fully serviceable, near new DC-9, he seemingly again became so preoccupied, this time with planning the ditching itself, that he gave scant thought to adequately warning his cabin crew and the passengers themselves.

As a result of the accident, the US National Transportation Safety Board made several recommendations to the Federal Aviation Administration:

• That the item "warn passengers" be included as one of the last items on all airlines' emergency landing or ditching checklists to ensure that passengers have time to brace for impact.

• That no flight be dispatched without an operable public address system from both flightdeck and cabin crew station.

• That all fabric to metal seat belts fastenings be replaced with metal to metal types with a standardised release.

• That methods for storing lifejackets be re-examined to eliminate obstructions to their easy release in the event of an overwater emergency.

CHAPTER 9

"Let's go!"

– Captain handing over the takeoff to First Officer

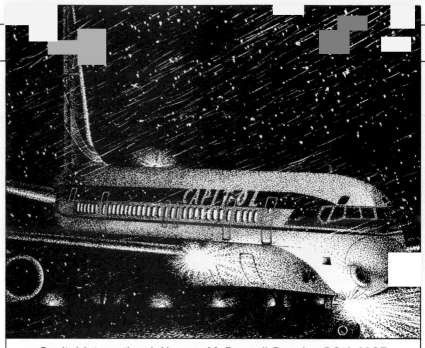

Capitol International Airways McDonnell Douglas DC-8-63CF,
N4909C [46060] – November 27, 1970

With full power applied and all engine gauges indicating normal, it was reasonable to assume acceleration and liftoff would be normal too. But there was no way this unfortunate crew could know an insidious malfunction was progressively frustrating the takeoff – until it was too late.

Capitol International Airways' DC-8-63CF, N4909C – a long range "stretched" version of the well known McDonnell Douglas four engined jet – had been chartered by the United States Military Airlift Command to fly a party of 219 service personnel from Tacoma, in Washington State, to Vietnam.

Departing McChord Air Force Base at midday on November 27 1970, the flight would make only two en route refuelling stops – at Anchorage, Alaska, and Yokota Air Force Base, Japan. The crew – Captain William Reid, First Officer James Downs, Flight Engineer Edward Fink, and Flight Navigator Robert Leonard – were all veterans of the airline, each with around 14,000 hours total experience and more than 2000 hours in DC-8 aircraft. Six young stewardesses comprised the cabin staff, four of whom had been with Capitol International Airways for more than a year.

Taking off on schedule from Tacoma, the DC-8's three and a half hour flight to Anchorage was uneventful. Night falls early in that latitude (less than 350 nautical miles south of the Arctic Circle) at this time of the year and it was dark and overcast with light sleet falling when

N4909C touched down on the international airport's icy runway 06 Left just after 3.30pm.

While the passengers waited in the warmth of the terminal building, the DC-8 was refuelled and inspected, and a minor fault in an engine instrument was checked. When all was ready for departure again, the tarmac crew sprayed the wings, tailplane, and all control surfaces with a heated ethylene glycol solution to remove any ice that had accumulated while the aircraft was standing in the freezing drizzle.

The engines were started at 4.50pm and the aircraft taxied out, cleared this time to the 3325 metre runway 06 Right. The night sky was overcast by a layer of cloud at 1600 feet, with visibility reduced to eight kilometres in light sleet. The wind was from the northeast at six knots, and the temperature was minus four degrees Celsius.

With Captain Reid handling the controls from the left hand seat, the crew completed their takeoff checks while the aircraft was rolling, and as they approached the holding point, landing lights now ablaze, the tower controller cleared them to taxi into position on the runway.

Using the brakes carefully be-

cause of the icy surface, the captain taxied slowly on to the runway, lined the aircraft up, and held it in position with the brake pedals rather than setting the parking brake.

First Officer Downs was to make the takeoff, but before handing the aircraft over to him, the captain briefed the crew that he would handle the brakes, set the engine power, and make the required airspeed calls during the takeoff run. With the aircraft loaded to just below its maximum allowable gross weight of 159,000 kilograms, the calculated reference speeds for this takeoff were V_1 (decision speed) 138 knots, V_R (rotation speed) 153 knots, and V_2 (takeoff safety speed) 163 knots.

As soon as the takeoff clearance came from the tower, Captain Reid, still holding the aircraft on the brakes, advanced the power levers to 80%, then took his feet off the pedals. "Let's go," he said, nodding to First Officer Downs.

As the aircraft began to move, Downs made a slight directional correction to properly align the aircraft with the runway centreline, while Reid quickly increased the throttle settings to takeoff power.

Accelerating normally at first, all appeared well with the DC-8, and at

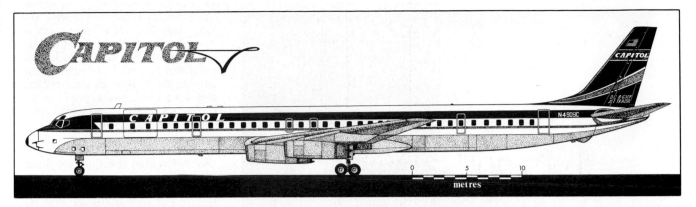

McDonnell Douglas DC-8-63CF, N4909 white and red livery used by Capitol International Airways at the time of the Anchorage accident. (M Tesch)

80 knots Downs checked the engine instrument indications to his satisfaction. Even so, it seemed to take "a few moments longer" than usual before Reid called "V₁". But then the acceleration definitely fell off a little, though the speed was still increasing. Around 145 knots there was an even more pronounced lag in acceleration. Yet plenty of runway still remained to complete the takeoff.

At 153 knots Reid called "Rotate!", and Downs raised the nose about nine degrees into the liftoff attitude, Reid meanwhile "following through" on his controls. Some 500 metres of runway now remained – less than expected, but still sufficient, in the view of the experienced crew, to become airborne and climb away.

To their alarm, the DC-8 failed to lift off. Six seconds later, still in the liftoff attitude, it overran the end of the runway on to ploughed ground. Finally accepting the appalling fact they were not going to fly, Reid snapped all four power levers shut in a desperate attempt to save the aircraft.

It was too late; the DC-8 tore its way through a substantial wooden barricade, demolished the ILS localiser support structure, and bounced across a four metre deep drainage ditch. The impact with the ditch fractured the rear fuselage and tore open the starboard wing, allowing its capacity load of fuel to pour out. The aircraft, its undercarriage torn off, both wings burning fiercely, and its back broken, finally shuddered to a stop more than 1000 metres beyond the end of the runway.

Captain Reid, who was not injured, immediately opened his side window and yelled to passengers already scrambling out through the forward main door to move quickly away from the burning aircraft. Trying to go back into the passenger cabin, he found the flight deck door blocked by galley equipment. Scrambling out quickly through the port side cockpit window, he ran back to the main entry door to help passengers out. When no more passengers appeared at the door, he ran round to the starboard cockpit window to assist First Officer Downs get the flight engineer and navigator out, both of whom had been injured.

Despite the efforts of the airport fire service, whose vehicles began reaching the scene within three minutes, the DC-8 burnt to destruction, several successive explosions in the wreckage hampering their attempts. Forty six of the 219 passengers, together with one of the cabin crew, died in the blaze before they could escape.

★　★　★

Surviving passengers said that soon after the nose was raised into the liftoff attitude, the aircraft ran beyond the end of the runway and the ride became "extremely bumpy". Three distinct impacts followed.

Still firmly on the ground in its nose high liftoff attitude DC-8 demolishes the ILS Localiser support structure 300 metres beyond the end of the runway. The impact tore off the No 2 engine and started a fire in the port wing. (Matthew Tesch)

Completely burnt out except for the nose and tail assembly, the remains of the Capitol International Airways DC-8-63F smoulder after the main fire has been extinguished. The aircraft overran the runway by more than 1000 metres. (Aviation Safety Digest)

break in the fuselage itself. Some said that fuel from the starboard wing tanks formed a pool some 18cm deep around the aircraft. Large quantities of fuel also accumulated in the bottom of the fuselage, a factor that no doubt prevented the escape of many passengers when it caught fire shortly afterwards.

★　　★　　★

But why had the fully serviceable DC-8 failed to become airborne from a runway of more than adequate length and in conditions that theoretically should have been ideal for a maximum performance takeoff?

Two of the surviving passengers, both US Air Force pilots, said that when the takeoff began, the aircraft's initial acceleration seemed slow, and after they had run about

The first was when the DC-8 hit the ILS structure, wrenching off the No 2 engine, badly damaging the inboard section of the port wing, and setting it on fire. The second impact, as the aircraft crossed the drainage ditch, was the most severe, demolishing most of the starboard wing, breaking open the rear fuselage, and tearing loose cabin fittings – galley equipment, overhead racks, ceiling panels, and life raft storages. All the cabin lights went out at the same time. Fuel pouring from the ruptured starboard wing tanks erupted into an intense fire on this side of the aircraft as it continued to slide over the ground.

Passengers close to this fire released their seat belts to move quickly down the aisle away from it. The third and final jolt, as the DC-8 came to a sudden stop, threw them to the floor, injuring some. One of the stewardesses who had loosened her seat belt to try to restrain loose equipment, was thrown from her seat and knocked unconscious. A passenger carried her from the aircraft.

Other survivors said the fire that broke out in the port wing after the first impact also continued to burn throughout the aircraft's ground slide. One passenger opened a port side overwing exit during this time, and a tongue of flame momentarily licked into the cabin.

The majority of those who lost their lives in the fire after the aircraft jolted to a stop, including the stewardess who died, were occupying the section of the cabin behind the wing but ahead of the fracture in the rear fuselage. Most of the survivors seated behind this position quickly left the aircraft through the

Aerial view of Anchorage's runway 06 Right, looking in opposite direction to that of the takeoff. The photograph was taken the morning after the accident. The burnt out wreckage is visible in the foreground. Note the blackened areas left by the fire, even before the DC-8 slid to a stop. (Aviation Safety Digest)

1000 metres there was a series of loud reports which they thought were the main wheel tyres blowing out. Most of the other surviving passengers also heard these reports.

Though none of the flight crew heard these noises, nor felt any unusual vibration they would have associated with blown tyres, evidence found on the runway confirmed the passengers' statements, showing clearly that there had been a progressive deterioration and destruction of the DC-8's main wheel tyres throughout the attempted takeoff run.

Normal wheel tracks left by the port undercarriage bogie progressed from the taxiway on to the runway, where a well defined static "footprint", melted by the warmth of the tyres though the thin layer of ice on the runway, showed where the DC-8 had awaited its takeoff clearance.

There was no evidence of skidding in the wheel tracks leading to this footprint, but from it, skid marks extended along the runway in the direction of takeoff. Skid marks made by the starboard undercarriage bogie tyres also led from the point at which the takeoff commenced. Evidence of deterioration of all the main undercarriage tyres, beginning from this point, continued for the entire length of the runway. The first scrap of reverted rubber was found only 170 metres from the start of takeoff, and by 820 metres the amount of fibre remaining in the rubber scraps showed that at least some of the tyres had been scrubbed down to their reinforcing cords. By 1300 metres from the beginning of takeoff, all the port tyres were blown out, and all starboard tyres by 2650 metres. Inspection of all tyres and wheels not extensively damaged by fire showed that all had been ground down in one place only on their circumferences – in other words none of them had been rotating during the takeoff run. The tyre damage and blowout patterns were typical of that caused by skidding with the wheels locked. X-ray examination of the tyres established that none of them had rolled after they had blown out.

Detailed examination of the brake assemblies of the crashed aircraft indicated that they should have been capable of normal operation and that all the damage they sustained had been caused by impact forces and the fire that followed. The cockpit parking brake handle was in the off position and there was no evidence of any malfunction in the parking brake mechanism.

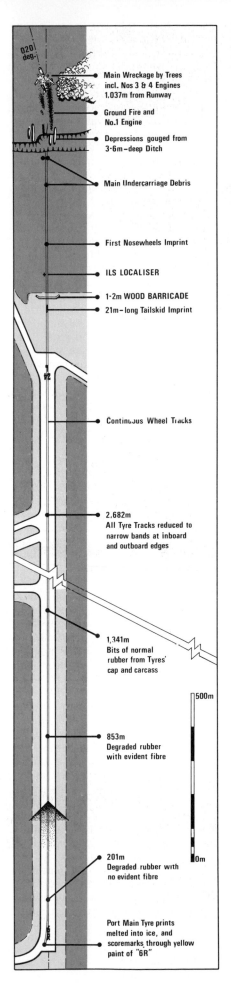

020 deg.

Main Wreckage by Trees incl. Nos 3 & 4 Engines 1,037m from Runway

Ground Fire and No.1 Engine

Depressions gouged from 3-6m-deep Ditch

Main Undercarriage Debris

First Nosewheels Imprint

ILS LOCALISER

1-2m WOOD BARRICADE

21m-long Tailskid Imprint

Continuous Wheel Tracks

2,682m All Tyre Tracks reduced to narrow bands at inboard and outboard edges

1,341m Bits of normal rubber from Tyres' cap and carcass

500m

853m Degraded rubber with evident fibre

201m Degraded rubber with no evident fibre

0m

Port Main Tyre prints melted into ice, and scoremarks through yellow paint of "6R"

At the request of the National Transportation Safety Board, the National Aeronautics and Space Administration (NASA) conducted tests on rolling and sliding friction forces generated by aircraft tyres at low ground speeds. In view of the fact that skid marks were left in the parking footprints when the aircraft started to move, consideration was given to whether a tyre that had skidded momentarily on ice could then develop skidding friction coefficients so low that it would not begin to roll when the brakes were released. In all cases, it was found that a tyre would rotate normally and spin up following brake release.

The breakaway starting friction coefficients on frosted ice and glazed ice were measured at 0.16 and 0.14 respectively. Thus, as long as the initial aircraft thrust-to-weight ratio exceeded these values, the aircraft would move forward with the brakes on and the wheels locked. It was also found that, immediately the wheels began to slide on the ice, water melting in the tyre footprints from friction heating dropped the average sliding friction coefficient to only 0.025, a value of the same order as the normal wheels-rolling friction coefficient of 0.019. A takeoff could thus be continued under these conditions with little initial effect on the aircraft's acceleration – but with a progressively catastrophic effect on its tyres.

The reason why the crew of N4909C did not detect the wheels were skidding initially becomes easier to understand when the runway frictional data is examined. With a total weight of just over 158,000 kilograms on the DC-8's undercarriage, and a breakaway coefficient of 0.14, only 22,200 kilograms of frictional drag would have existed. With the aircraft's total engine thrust of 74,600 pounds (33,868 kilograms of thrust) only 65% power would have been required to begin moving the aircraft forward with the brakes hard on and the wheels locked. And since the sliding coefficient of friction (0.025) is almost a full order of magnitude less than the breakaway coefficient (0.14), the crew would have felt a minor surge of acceleration similar to a normal brake release as the DC-8 began to move. Furthermore, as the sliding coefficient is only slightly higher

Plan of Anchorage's Runway 06 Right, showing positions of tyre and wheel marks, together with distribution of wreckage beyond the end of the runway. (Matthew Tesch)

than the undercarriage's normal rolling coefficient of friction, the aircraft's initial acceleration would have seemed little different from that of a normal takeoff.

As the speed increased however, the rapidly deteriorating condition of the tyres would have nearly doubled their sliding coefficients of friction. When they blew out further down the runway, their coefficients would have increased significantly, probably to about 0.2 or 0.3. As the takeoff progressed therefore, the DC-8's acceleration would have deteriorated at an increasing rate, particularly in the latter stages.

The aircraft's Flight Data Recorder, recovered from the wreckage relatively free of damage, in fact established that the maximum speed attained during the attempted takeoff was only 152 knots, slightly less than the computed rotation speed and 11 knots less than the takeoff safety speed. Yet comparison of the aircraft's actual initial acceleration (using figures derived from the FDR) with that of a DC-8 taking off normally under the conditions existing at the time showed that, up to a speed of about 100 knots, the performance would have been little different. For this reason it would have been difficult, if not impossible, for the crew to have sensed that all was not well until the aircraft had run well over a third of its normal takeoff distance. Even then, there was no definite symptom evident on the flight deck to alert them to the fact that the wheels were not rotating.

The investigation showed beyond doubt that the accident resulted from the main wheels remaining locked after power was applied for takeoff. There was nothing to suggest any phenomenon such as aquaplaning could have inhibited their rotation; rather it was clear that a sustained braking torque remained applied to the wheels throughout the takeoff. The possibility of some malfunction within the aircraft's hydraulic system resulting in this condition was considered, but fire damage to the system's components precluded any definite conclusions. All main wheel bearings were examined for evidence of high friction, but none was found.

Consideration was also given to the possibility that either the captain or the first officer inadvertently maintained some foot pressure on the brake pedals during the takeoff.

Captain Reid told the investigators he held the brakes on with his feet while he initially set the power, but that he released the brakes and transferred his feet to the rudder pedals as he opened the throttles wider to full takeoff power. First Officer Downs was equally certain his feet were on the rudder pedals, with his heels on the floor, throughout the takeoff, and that he maintained directional control with rudder alone. He did not feel the captain depressing the brake pedals at any time during the takeoff.

On the slippery, icy runway, only slight brake pressure would have been sufficient to skid the wheels when the aircraft began to move. But as it began to slide faster, the rise in coefficient of friction would have soon overcome any inadvertent braking by one or other of the pilots. In this case, there would have been some evidence of tyre rotation, either on the runway or the tyres themselves. None was found and it is impossible to imagine braking being applied and maintained equally on all mainwheels throughout the attempted takeoff without the pilots being conscious of it.

Although both pilots were adamant they had not applied the parking brakes at any time after taxiing from the terminal, the investigators had to consider the possibility that the pilots set the parking brakes on the runway while awaiting their takeoff clearance, and subsequently overlooked releasing them. For such a possibility to occur however, the flight crew would also have had to overlook the antiskid "not armed" warning light. This light is on whenever the antiskid system is not armed, or at any time the antiskid switch is in the armed position with the parking brake engaged. The crew said the light was on while they were taxiing to the runway, but that when the system was armed in accordance with the checklist just before entering the runway, the light went out. It did not come on again at any time after this. Again, it is impossible to imagine this warning light being overlooked by all crew members, particularly as the takeoff was being made at night, making the bright amber light highly conspicuous in the darkened cockpit.

While the unusual combination of circumstances which kept the wheels locked, yet still permitting the crew to unknowingly go ahead

with the takeoff, was certainly the main factor in the accident sequence, the investigators had also to examine the crew's response.

Though the initial part of the takeoff no doubt seemed quite normal, there can be little doubt that the lack of acceleration was noticeable by the time the DC-8 reached 100 knots. And by the time it reached V_1 (Decision Speed), nearly half a minute later, the takeoff run had occupied a whole minute instead of 39 seconds. As well, the aircraft had travelled more than 70% further down the runway than in normal circumstances. Put another way, after 39 seconds (the normal time to V_1), the aircraft had accelerated to a speed of only 110 knots instead of the expected 139 knots. At this point, having used up some 1130 metres of runway to attain a speed that was still 29 knots below V_1, the takeoff could have been abandoned and the aircraft brought to a stop with runway to spare.

It is obvious however, that the insidious nature of the aircraft's decreasing performance made recognition and assessment of the problem extremely difficult. Though the crew finally realised that the acceleration was deteriorating, their only reasonable option, once the aircraft had attained V_1, was to continue with the takeoff.

Only by recognising the lack of acceleration at an earlier stage, and immediately abandoning the takeoff at that point, could the crew have avoided the accident. Yet this could have been achieved only if there had been some means of determining that the required acceleration over a given time or distance was being achieved.

As a result of the accident to N4909C, the National Transportation Safety Board recommended that the Federal Aviation Administration should "determine and implement" takeoff procedures to provide crews with a time and distance reference by which they can appraise their aircrafts' acceleration to V_1.

Although the investigation established beyond doubt that brake pressure, sufficient to lock all the aircraft's main wheels, was somehow imparted to the brake system before the fatal takeoff began, investigators were finally unable to determine the nature of the malfunction that produced this condition.

CHAPTER 10

"... Caution - Wake Turbulence!"

– Tower Controller to DC-9

Delta Air Lines McDonnell Douglas DC-9-14, N3305L [45700]
(F/n 205) – May 30 1972

The advent of the first of the 'widebodies', the Boeing 747, the McDonnell Douglas DC-10 and the Lockheed Tristar – introduced an unforseen hazard to major airports. Though wake turbulence was recognised in earlier years, it was considered a risk only to light aeroplanes. It took a spectacular DC-9 disaster to show than an encounter with the wake of a heavy jet could be as dangerous as any extreme turbulence.

Set in flat country midway between Fort Worth and Dallas, Texas, USA, Greater Southwest International Airport was the venue selected by two major airlines for crew training early on the morning of May 30, 1972. The crews and the aircraft they would be flying were all based at Love Field, Dallas, some 20 nautical miles to the east.

Shortly after 5.15am, an American Airlines DC-10 departed Love Field and, on arrival in the Greater Southwest circuit a few minutes later, began an extended period of circuits and landings, using Runway 13. The airport has two runways, 13/31 of 2575 metres, and 17/35 of 2745 metres, intersecting 800 metres southeast of the threshold of Runway 13. The weather was fine, clear and almost calm, with only a five knot wind from the northwest – ideal for type rating training on the DC-10 for two of the company's first officers.

An hour and a half later, Delta Air Lines' DC-9-14, N3305L, also took off from Love Field for Greater Southwest International Airport for crew training. On board the DC-9 were company check captain G G Grey, two line pilots, F M Cook and J M Martin, both undergoing command training, and FAA operations inspector L R Hull who was conducting a proficiency check on Captain Grey. One trainee was flying the aircraft from the left hand seat, Captain Grey was in the right hand seat, Hull occupied the jump seat, while the other trainee sat in the passenger cabin awaiting his turn to fly. The DC-9 carried no cabin crew or other passengers.

The DC-10s circuits were still continuing when the Delta DC-9 arrived over Greater Southwest Airport and requested a practice ILS approach to Runway 13. In clearing the DC-9 accordingly, the tower controller informed its crew that the DC-10 was conducting "touch and go" landings on the same runway, with both aircraft operating on the same tower frequency.

The separation between the two aircraft in the circuit pattern was more than six nautical miles, and after carrying out their approach and landing to a full stop, the DC-9 crew taxied to the threshold of Runway 13 and asked to be cleared for a second ILS approach. This also was approved and the Tower passed the DC-9 appropriate climbout instructions and cleared it for takeoff. "Maintain VFR," the controller told the aircraft.

Instead of landing off the second ILS approach which was again flown about six nm behind the DC-10, the DC-9 put on power and executed a deliberate go round. The crew then sought a clearance for a VOR approach to Runway 35, also to be terminated by a "go-round". This too was approved by the tower controller.

On final for Runway 35 after completing the VOR procedure, the DC-9 crew next asked for and received a clearance to circle to the left to rejoin the circuit for a simulated low visibility approach and full stop landing on Runway 17. But after the DC-9 had climbed out and turned onto a low level downwind leg for Runway 17, the DC-9 crew amended this request, asking instead to be cleared to land on Runway 13 behind the DC-10, now inbound on the

N3305L shortly before its loss, wearing the revised Delta Air Lines livery. Note the minor widget variation between the engine nacelle and forward fuselage positions – the latter has disproportionate "Delta" titles to ensure they can be seen when the forward door is open.

ILS for Runway 13. The requested amendment was to avoid the possibility of the two approach paths conflicting.

The tower controller responded, "OK. That'll be fine – use 13 for full stop." He then added the advisory, "Caution – wake turbulence", in accordance with air traffic control procedures for non-radar VFR approaches behind an arriving heavy jet with less than 2500 feet (760 metres) separating the two aircraft.

However, the separation between the two was still well in excess of this. After turning on to its new heading of 310 degrees magnetic to fly a downwind leg for Runway 13 at the "low visibility" circuit height of 500 feet, the DC-9 reported passing abeam the runway threshold. The DC-10 at this stage was on final approach, some 2.5 nautical miles from touchdown. Almost half a minute later, when the DC-9 reported "Turning base – full stop," the DC-10 was a little over one nm from touchdown. By the time the DC-10 actually touched down, the DC-9 was just beginning its turn on to final, with the distance separating the two aircraft still a little over two nm.

Watched by the tower controller, the smaller jet continued its final approach to Runway 13 as the DC-10 applied power and lifted off for yet another circuit. With its undercarriage lowered and flaps extended, the DC-9's flight appeared perfectly normal in the calm conditions until, only about 10 seconds from touchdown, the port wing dropped as the aircraft suddenly rolled to the left. This appeared to be over corrected by the crew, resulting in a roll to the right, followed by a second, more moderate wing drop to the left as it continued its approach and crossed the threshold. Then, without warning, and with the DC-9 only 50 feet above the runway, the lateral move-

ment abruptly reversed, the aircraft rolling violently to the right, bringing its starboard wingtip into contact with the runway as the angle of bank passed through the vertical.

By now some 380 metres beyond the threshold, the DC-9 fell heavily on to the runway on its back, the impact snapping off the tail assembly as the aircraft exploded into flames and slid upside down. The burning wreckage finally came to rest more than 720 metres further on, 50 metres to the right of the runway centreline. Although the airport crash crew were on the scene in the shortest possible time, they could do nothing to save the DC-9s four occupants, all of whom died in the impact or the fire.

The entire circumstances of this totally unexpected tragedy suggested to National Transportation Safety Bureau investigators that it

could have only one explanation, however unlikely it might seem for an aircraft the size of a DC-9: the loss of control was the result of flying into an extremely powerful but totally invisible vortex generated by the DC-10 during its approach about a minute earlier.

An accurate time-related comparison of the tracks flown by the two aircraft showed that both had traversed the same path during the final part of their approaches, the actual time separation between them being 53-54 seconds. Further detailed computer studies established that the DC-9 descended into the influence of the vortex generated by the DC-10's port wing, approaching it at a height of about 60 feet above the ground. The studies also showed that, in the atmospheric conditions existing at the time, this vortex would have remained in the

The ill-fated aircraft as delivered to Delta Air Lines in November 1965. The 'Wiget' insignia was aligned off the vertical in this new, cleaned up livery, introduced with the company's Series 14 and Series 32 DC-9s. (Matthew Tesch)

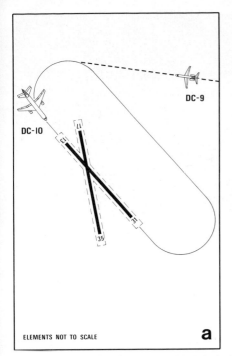

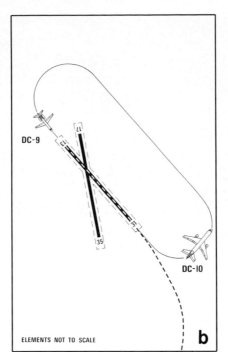

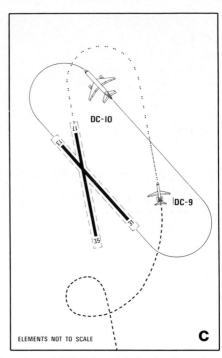

(a) DC-9 joins Greater Southwest circuit for its ILS to Runway 13 behind DC-10 carrying out 'touch and goes'; DC-9 does full stop landing, takes off again and makes second circuit again 6nm behind DC-10. (b) Cleared for deliberate missed approach, DC-9 overflies Runway 13 to make VOR approach to Runway 35. (c) VOR approach to Runway 35 terminated by clearance to Runway circle left and join low level 'bad weather' circuit at 500 feet AGL for landing on Runway 17. (Matthew Tesch)

runway threshold zone for more than two minutes.

The turbulent wake left by any aircraft in flight has been well known for many years. Back in the era of biplane flying training, it was regarded as a measure of a student pilot's skill if he could "hit his own slipstream" on completing a well executed 360 degree steep turn. The effect in light training aeroplanes was little more than a sudden jolt which, though throwing the machine about momentarily, was easily corrected. Yet the sharpness of this "slipstream" encounter – the suddenness with which it was met and passed – left no doubt of its identity. It was unlike any other form of inflight turbulence the student had encountered. These so-called "slipstream" effects were originally attributed to "propeller wash", but as aircraft became bigger and heavier with higher wing loadings, it was found that by far the greater portion of an aircraft's turbulent wake is vortex turbulence, generated at each wingtip as a side effect to the lift being produced by the wing.

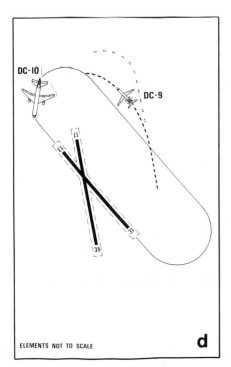

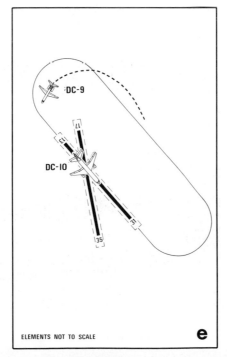

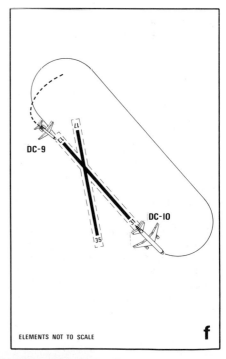

(d) On low level downwind leg for Runway 17, DC-9 crew reassess position of DC-10 in circuit and request landing on Runway 13 instead, to avoid possible confliction with DC-10's approach. (e) DC-10 touches down on Runway 13; its crew immediately apply power to lift aircraft off again for another circuit. Meanwhile DC-9, 2.25nm behind DC-10, begins shallow turn on to final at 500 feet AGL. (f) DC-10 is climbing out when DC-9, now 400 metres from runway threshold at 200 feet AGL, encounters outer influence of DC-10s port wingtip vortex and initially rolls to left.

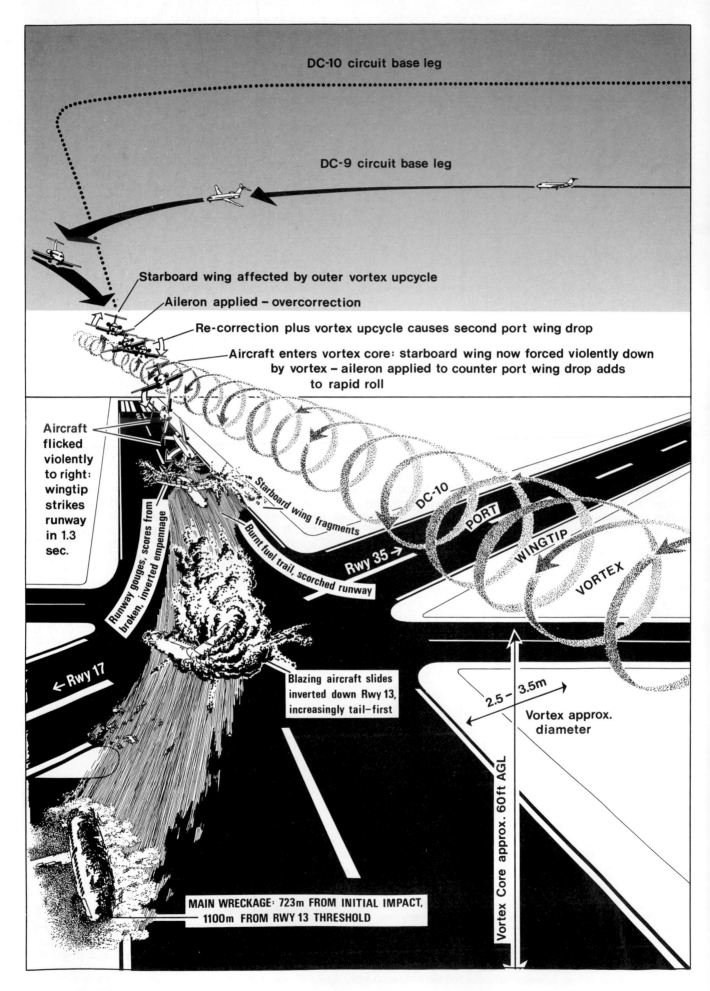

DC-10 circuit base leg

DC-9 circuit base leg

Starboard wing affected by outer vortex upcycle

Aileron applied – overcorrection

Re-correction plus vortex upcycle causes second port wing drop

Aircraft enters vortex core: starboard wing now forced violently down by vortex – aileron applied to counter port wing drop adds to rapid roll

Aircraft flicked violently to right: wingtip strikes runway in 1.3 sec.

Runway gouges, scores from broken, inverted empennage

Starboard wing fragments

Burnt fuel trail, scorched runway

Rwy 35 →

DC-10

PORT

WINGTIP

VORTEX

← Rwy 17

Blazing aircraft slides inverted down Rwy 13, increasingly tail–first

2.5 – 3.5m

Vortex approx. diameter

Vortex Core approx. 60ft AGL

MAIN WRECKAGE: 723m FROM INITIAL IMPACT, 1100m FROM RWY 13 THRESHOLD

The vortices are formed by air from the region of high pressure beneath the wing spilling around the wingtip into the region of low pressure which the aerofoil shape is producing above the surface of the wing. Coupled with the forward motion of the aircraft, this airflow results in a horizontal whirlwind-like movement of air funnelling back from each wingtip. The twin vortices, induced in this way behind all aircraft in flight, spin in opposite directions, are narrow in diameter, and when generated by heavy aircraft can be very powerful, their magnitude being inversely proportional to the aircraft's speed and directly proportional to its wingspan loading.

The most powerful vortices are in fact generated by large, heavily laden aircraft flying at low speed with all high lift devices extended, such as during an approach to land. In calm conditions, such vortices can persist for several minutes. As a

(opposite page) This diagram, following on from the sequence on the previous page, illustrates the dramatic final seconds of the DC-9s last approach behind the DC-10. As the DC-9 converged on the powerful but invisible horizontal vortex from the DC-10s port wingtip, held almost stationary over the runway by the light crosswind, the loss of control became progressively irretrievable. (Matthew Tesch)

result of their own motion, the vortices tend to settle below the height of the generating aircraft and, if it is flying low (such as during an approach to land), the vortices will sink to the ground and fan out laterally while still retaining their momentum. A critical combination of this lateral movement and a light crosswind can result in a vortex lingering directly over a runway on which a heavy aircraft has landed.

Because the vortices rotate at about 80 degrees a second – double the rate of roll of many aircraft, even with full aileron deflection – the hazard they can pose to light aeroplanes was well known. During the 1960s, there were a number of accidents of varying severity in the United States and Canada in which light aircraft approaching to land flew into the unseen wake turbulence of large four engined propeller driven aircraft that had touched down ahead of them – and in some cases when they took off behind a heavy aircraft using the same runway. These prompted further studies of the phenomenon by the US Federal Aviation Agency (FAA) and the National Aeronautics and Space Administration (NASA), resulting in air traffic control procedures providing stipulated separations for aircraft operating behind "heavy jets" in airport circuit patterns. A heavy jet was defined as one having a takeoff weight of 300,000 pounds (136,200kg) or more (eg a Boeing 707-320 or bigger).

Even so, it was widely believed in the industry that the vortices were a hazard only for light aircraft, and though possibly uncomfortable for moderately large transports, were not dangerous to this class of aircraft.

But the Flight Data and Cockpit Voice Recorders recovered from the burnt out wreckage at Greater Southwest International Airport now left no doubt that this horrifyingly spectacular accident to the DC-9 was entirely the result of its encounter with the wake turbulence generated by the DC-10 that had landed ahead of it.

The recorders confirmed that the DC-9's approach was perfectly normal until it was on short final when, only 400 metres short of the threshold at a height of slightly less than 100 feet, the DC-9 encountered a 1.7g gust, prompting Captain Gray to exclaim, "A little turbulence here!" This was at the point when the aircraft was seen to make its initial roll to the left.

The Flight Data Recorder's vertical acceleration trace continued to show turbulence of the same order for about five seconds, prompting Captain Grey to tell his trainee: "Let's go round." But almost at once, as the trace recorded a small negative g excursion, his tone changed to one of urgency and he commanded: "Takeoff power,"

Before there was any response from the engines, the stick shaker

The FAA, NASA and Continental Airlines flight tested this winglet configuration on one of the carrier's DC-10-30s for a period during the 1980s. The object of the exercise was to see if there was any appreciable reduction in wingtip vortice drag and hence a reduction in drag and fuel burn. The experiment was reasonably successful but did not warrant a fleet wide conversion programme for existing airliners. The knowledge gained was used to good effect in ultimately fitting winglets to the DC-10's successor, the MD-11. (MDC)

stall warning activated and the check captain, evidently attempting to take over control, called: "I've got it". Immediately the stall warning sounded again. A second later the recorder trace leapt to minus one g as the aircraft's roll suddenly reversed, and one of the pilots involuntarily called out, "God ... !" Less than a second later there was the noise of initial impact.

In the course of the investigation, evidence was taken from three captains who had had inflight encounters with wake turbulence while flying DC-9 aircraft. One, a training captain, experienced a violent roll while making a practice approach three nm behind a landing L-1011 Tristar. He responded by applying power and going round. The second instance involved a DC-9 taking off on a scheduled airline flight behind a preceding Boeing 727. While climbing out normally, the DC-9 suddenly rolled 30 degrees to the right, the nose dropped a similar amount, then the roll violently reversed 30 degrees to the left. The captain recovered control and the climb then

continued normally. He estimated the Boeing 727 to be three to four nm ahead at the time of the encounter.

The third case involved a military version of the DC-9 on a medical evacuation operation. Approaching to land in instrument conditions on a coupled ILS approach, the aircraft suddenly rolled 45 degrees and the nose dropped 20 degrees. It lost 200 feet in altitude before the captain could override the autopilot. Disengaging the autopilot and applying power, he called the Tower to report they were making a missed approach and was told they were following a heavy jet.

To assist in the investigation of the DC-9 accident, as well as to help devise more realistic wake turbulence avoidance procedures, the FAA conducted a field study of the intensity of wingtip vortices generated by the DC-10 and another widebody jet of similar size, weight and configuration, the L-1011 Tristar. The tests were made by flying a series of low level passes upwind of a steel tower on which velocity sensors and smoke generators were mounted. As the

vortices generated by the aircraft drifted past the tower, the sensors recorded the vortex flow velocity gradient, while the smoke, drawn swiftly into the vortices, rendered them clearly visible.

Some 20 passes, flown by each aircraft type in various configurations – takeoff, cruise, approach and landing – showed that the vortices generated by the DC-10 and the L-1011 were of similar intensity. Their tubular core "structure" had a diameter of eight to 10 feet (about three metres) with peak tangential velocities of the order of 150 feet (approx 50 metres) per second, well above the design limit gust loads for transport category aircraft. The maximum peak tangential velocity measured during the tests exceeded a frightening 220 feet (67 metres) per second. The persistence of such vortices in calm air was also demonstrated during the tests, in one case the upwind vortex reaching the tower as much as two minutes and 20 seconds after the DC-10 had flown past.

The results of these tests were computer analysed to determine the

A wingtip vortex made visible: In the mid 1970s, wake turbulence experiments similar to those conducted by the FAA in the USA (see text) were carried out in light wind conditions by the Aeronautics Department of the University of Sydney at RAAF Base Richmond NSW, for the Australian Department of Transport. To begin the experiment, a Lockheed Hercules was flown just upwind of a mast on which a smoke generator was mounted (a). A few seconds later, the smoke generator was ignited (b). As the vortex generated by the Hercules' port wing drifted over the mast, the rising smoke was suddenly whipped into the rapidly rotating horizontal column of air (c). The smoke, captured first by the more open, induced spiral airflow surrounding the vortex, was quickly drawn into the core of the vortex itself (d). In the final stage of smoke development, the compact spiral character of the vortex core becomes plainly visible (e). (Aviation Safety Digest)

During 1994 the FAA introduced a mandatory four nautical mile separation between the Boeing 757 narrow bodied twinjet and following aircraft after the loss of a corporate jet at San Diego caused by wake turbulence from a 757. Even fighter aircraft have been destroyed while landing astern of larger types. (Boeing)

effect of a vortex flow, generated by the DC-10's port wingtip with the aircraft in the landing configuration, on the DC-9. The computer simulation showed that initially, the outer influence of the clockwise circulation of the vortex core, acting *upwards* on the underside of the DC-9s starboard wing as it descended, caused the DC-9 to enter a moderate left roll. Application of counteracting right aileron produced an over correction, causing the DC-9 to overshoot the wings-level attitude and roll to the right. The subsequent re-correction resulted in the aircraft rolling again to the left, but at a lower rate. But by this time the DC-9 was entering the vortex core itself and its starboard wing now came under the influence of the *downward* loads produced by the clockwise vortex flow. This, combined with the right aileron being applied to correct the second roll to the left, now produced a rapid roll to the right. Even with the immediate application of full left aileron, the lag in the control system was such that it was impossible to prevent the roll rate reaching 57 degrees per second, allowing the starboard wingtip to strike the ground in only 1.3 seconds. The simulation also showed that any action with the flight controls to counter the initial vortex-induced left roll, invariably carried the DC-9 further into the vortex core, causing a violent right roll.

While this computer simulation was being carried out, McDonnell Douglas conducted an independent study to assess the rolling moment induced on a DC-9 placed *directly* in the core of a DC-10 wingtip vortex. This established that the rate of roll induced by the vortex was actually 12% greater than the maximum roll control capability of the DC-9.

The investigation thus showed beyond all doubt that, far from not posing a hazard to moderately large aircraft, the turbulent wake of a widebodied heavy jet could be every bit as dangerous to medium sized transport aircraft such as the Boeing 727 and the DC-9, as the wake of those aircraft was to light aeroplanes.

In this instance, tragic as it was for the aircrew involved, only four fatalities resulted, because the flight during which the accident occurred was a training exercise. But such an accident could just as easily have overtaken a DC-9 operating an airline flight with a full load of passengers, and it was obvious there was continuing potential for far greater disasters. So the nub of the problem was this: What could be done to avoid future encounters with wake turbulence, with all their likely consequences?

The knowledge gained from the study of vortex turbulence following the spate of light aircraft accidents resulting from this phenomenon during the 1960s had been widely disseminated and used as the basis for air traffic control procedures designed to prevent accidents from this cause. Basically, air traffic controllers were required to provide five nm or two minutes' separation behind a heavy jet for all IFR aircraft, and VFR aircraft being radar vectored. In the case of VFR aircraft not under radar control, pilots were expected to maintain their own separation, the phrase "caution – wake turbulence" being used by controllers as a warning to such pilots if their separation behind a heavy jet was less than 2500 feet (760 metres).

But one of the problems with this cautionary system was that actual encounters with wake turbulence were rare compared to the number of warnings issued by Air Traffic Control. As a result, pilots tended to become the victims of the "cry wolf" syndrome – experience conditioned them to believe they would not actually encounter wake turbulence, despite an ATC caution. The result was that such warnings were rarely taken seriously.

In this case, although the crew of the DC-9 were cautioned on the possibility of wake turbulence in the early stages of their ill-fated approach and, in acknowledging the tower's transmission, they accepted the responsibility for avoiding it, it was evident from their conversation (as transcribed from the Cockpit Voice Recorder) that it gave them no concern. Rather, their chief preoccupation seemed to be with flying the "low visibility" circuit in accordance with the procedures specified in their company's DC-9 operations manual and in maintaining inflight separation from the other aircraft in the circuit.

Certainly the precise combination of meteorological circumstances required for a powerful wingtip vortex to linger over the threshold of a runway for long enough to become a hazard to a following aircraft are extremely rare. In this instance, the calm and stable atmospheric conditions, together with the relatively flat terrain in which Greater Southwest Airport is located, produced no disturbing influences to break up the vortex flows left by the DC-10, allowing them to persist for some time. And the very light wind from the northwest not only counteracted the natural lateral motion of the vortices in ground effect, allowing the DC-10s port wing vortex to remain stationary over Runway 13 – the slight tailwind component on the runway further aggravated the situation by moving the turbulent air mass bodily from the final approach path to over the runway threshold.

Such a situation raised the other difficulty in wake turbulence avoidance: even if the crew of an aircraft *do* heed a prescribed warning from ATC, how can they effectively exercise caution to ensure their aircraft avoids the invisible hazard? Again in the case of this DC-9 accident, although the crew were warned to expect wake turbulence, they had no information to assist them in accurately evaluating the hazard or estimating the location of the vortices.

Obviously therefore, FAA directives placing responsibility for avoiding wake turbulence solely on the crews of aircraft operating visually without the benefit of radar guidance, were unrealistic. No data whatsoever was available to pilots to indicate what distance from a preceding aircraft constituted safe separation. And even if this criteria were established, the estimation of separation distance in flight is extremely difficult. Tests showed that even an experienced pilot's ability to estimate an actual aircraft separation of three nm could be in error by as much as 2.5nm. Furthermore, recommended wake turbulence avoidance procedures involved maintaining an approach path above that of the preceding aircraft to effect a touchdown further down the runway. Yet again, a pilot's ability to judge the vertical dimension of an aircraft's descent path, from perhaps two nm distant, was highly questionable.

In addition, data available on vortex measurements at the time of the accident were insufficient to assume that a two minute or five nm separation between aircraft was adequate to ensure avoidance of the hazard under *all* conditions. Much more needed to be known about the persistence of vortices after the passage of a generating aircraft. Indeed, inflight tests conducted by NASA to examine safe separation distances showed that a corporate jet could be uncontrollably upset by the wake turbulence of a Boeing 747 no less than *eight* nm behind it. Other ground based tests showed that, in calm conditions, vortices under the influence of ground effect could consistently be tracked for well over two minutes.

Altogether it was evident that far more research was needed on the whole problem of wake turbulence avoidance. As a direct result of the DC-9 investigation, the National Transportation Safety Board made a number of recommendations to the Federal Aviation Agency:

• That wake turbulence separation criteria for aircraft operating behind heavy jets be re-evaluated.
• That alert notices be issued to all pilots and aircraft operators stressing the urgent need to maintain an adequate separation from heavy jets.
• That, pending the results of further extensive research into the problem of wake turbulence avoidance, the FAA implement the following measures:

1. Revise pilot publications to more specifically describe avoidance techniques.
2. Publish the meteorological parameters that allow vortices to persist in the vicinity of a runway.
3. Include wake turbulence warnings on ATIS broadcasts whenever those conditions allow vortices to pose a significant hazard.
4. Develop new ATC separation standards, taking into account the relative wingspan loadings of the vortex generating aircraft and the aircraft following it.
5. Pending the development of these standards, instruct air traffic controllers to increase separation times to at least three minutes whenever conditions are conducive to the persistence of vortices.
6. Develop methods by which tower controllers can assist pilots in maintaining adequate separation to avoid wake turbulence.

CHAPTER 11

"Bealine 548 is climbing as cleared, passing 1500"

– Trident Captain to London Departures

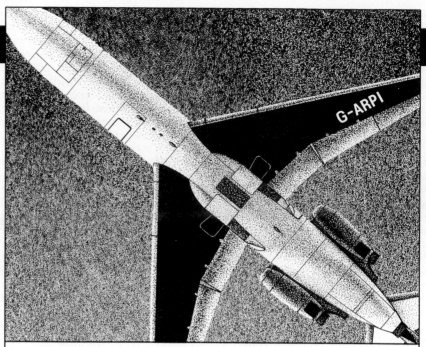

British European Airways Hawker Siddeley (DH-121) Trident 1C
G-ARPI [2109] – June 18, 1972

Who could have thought that a violent verbal clash and a loss of temper in an airline crew room could be the prelude to a major airline disaster?

The London base of British European Airways was a far from happy workplace in June 1972.

A long-standing industrial dispute between the airline and the British Airline Pilots' Association over working conditions and rates of pay was straining relationships, not only between management and flight crew, but between individual pilots themselves.

A general meeting of BEA pilots on June 13 indicated that a majority were in favour of strike action, but there were a number, in particular senior pilots of "the old school", who considered such conduct unbefitting and unprofessional. A further meeting to resolve the issue was scheduled for Monday, June 19.

In the crowded BEA crew room at London Heathrow Airport early in the summer afternoon of Sunday, June 18, 1972 – the day before the second pilots' meeting – the ill-feeling manifested by the dispute boiled over into an angry verbal altercation between 51 year old Captain Stanley Key, preparing for a flight to Brussels, and a senior first officer who was not a member of his crew.

Key, a highly experienced captain, was vehemently opposed to the strike action mooted by the more militant BEA pilots, and had been enlisting the backing of other senior

captains for this position. His stand on the issue had earnt him considerable criticism, if not vilification, among more junior flight crew members of the airline.

Questioned about his campaign while in the crew room, Captain Key exploded, his outburst being described by some present as "the most violent" they had ever heard. Although the argument subsided almost as quickly as it flared and Captain Key afterwards apologised for his outburst, it was plain to all who heard him that the proposed strike was a source of great tension for him, and that his fury with the first officer concerned was extreme.

Among the numerous other pilots who witnessed the exchange was Second Officer Keighley, one of two copilots rostered for the flight to Brussels with Captain Key.

In accordance with the "monitoring system" BEA had developed as an integral part of its flight procedures, it was the airline's practice to crew its Hawker Siddeley Trident aircraft with three pilots, normally a captain and two copilots. Most of BEA's European services were being operated by the Rolls-Royce Spey-engined Tridents, a type which had entered service with the airline in March 1964.

With the captain and one copilot

occupying the control seats, the airline's monitoring system provided for all critical stages of flight to be monitored by the third pilot, seated in a position similar to that of the flight engineer in other jet airliners.

According to BEA's operations manual, the monitoring pilot's function was to "continue to monitor the flight instruments, select frequency changes as requested by ATC, and advise the captain." This latter instruction meant that the monitoring pilot was to bring any variation from normal procedures to the captain's immediate attention. The flightdecks of BEA's Tridents were laid out to enable the third pilot to carry out most of his duties in the forward facing position.

The two copilots in the crew normally alternated in their duties on successive legs of a trip, taking turns in the right hand control seat while the other took the monitoring pilot's position. To ensure a balanced level of flightdeck experience was maintained under the three pilot system, BEA crew rosters paired copilots with less than 12 months on the Trident with ones with greater experience on the type. Training for the monitoring function was additional to that for normal copilot responsibilities in the right hand seat, and was carried out during line flying under the command of a Training Captain. On such flights, the trainee would act in the monitoring position under the direction of a fourth pilot on the flightdeck, a Supervisory First Officer, occupying the jump seat behind the captain's position.

In the course of the industrial dispute, BEA's monitoring system had become the source of further discontent among crews. Because the airline's Supervisory First Officers had withdrawn their services for the training of monitoring pilots, there were now a number of junior pilots in the airline who, though fully trained and qualified for right hand seat flying, had not yet been able to qualify for the monitoring pilot function.

BEA had dealt with the problem by rostering such pilots for right hand seat duties only. But this action not only excluded more senior copilots from their turn in the right hand seat; it also inhibited the authority of captains, requiring them to have their less experienced copilot in the right hand seat at all times, regardless of conditions on a particular flight.

It was against this unsettling background that BEA's Trident 1C, G-ARPI, operating Flight BE 548 to Brussels, Belgium, with a full complement of 112 passengers, taxied out from Lon-don Heathrow Airport's Terminal 2 at 4.03pm on June 18, 1972.

Captain Stanley Key was in the left hand seat, with Second Officer J W Keighley, a 22 year old pilot who had been line flying with BEA only a short time, in the right hand seat. The more experienced copilot, Second Officer S Ticehurst, 24, was in the monitoring pilot's position. Keighley was one of the company's junior flightcrew who had not had the opportunity to qualify as a monitoring pilot because of the industrial dispute, and so was limited to right hand seat duties.

The Trident's passenger list included a BEA Vickers Vanguard freighter crew of three travelling to Belgium who had boarded Flight BE 548 at the last minute. Vanguard First Officers C K Ware and R E Wilde were accommodated in the passenger cabin, while Captain J Collins, himself a qualified Trident captain, took the jumpseat on the flightdeck behind Captain Key. The passenger cabin was under the supervision of Senior Steward F Farey, assisted by Stewardesses A Lamb and J Mowat.

The weather at Heathrow as the Trident was cleared to taxi for Runway 27 Right was mild but overcast, with some drizzle from the 1000 foot cloudbase, and a moderate wind from the southwest.

Reaching the runway holding point at 4.06pm, the Trident was given a Standard Departure Clearance via Dover and instructed to select its transponder to *Standby*. A few seconds later the crew reported "Ready", and Heathrow Tower cleared the aircraft for takeoff. At this point however, the crew told the tower controller a "slight problem" had developed, and the aircraft remained at the holding point for an additional 42 seconds before being recleared for takeoff. What the problem was the crew did not disclose, but shortly after 4.08pm they released the Trident's brakes and applied power.

The takeoff run appeared perfectly normal, the Trident rotating after 42 seconds and leaving the runway two seconds later. Half a minute afterwards, still on a westerly heading but now at a height of a little over 700 feet, it banked into a 20 degree turn to the left towards the Epsom NDB and some 10 seconds later again was lost to the tower controller's view as it entered the overcast cloud.

At about this time the crew reported, "climbing as cleared" and were instructed to call London Air Traffic Control Centre on 128.4 MHz. Their next call 17 seconds later was on this frequency, the aircraft reporting: "Passing 1500 feet". London Control then cleared the Trident to continue climbing to Flight Level 60

The second aircraft of BEA's initial order for 24 Trident 1s, G-ARPB, is seen here in the airline's earlier "red square" livery. The leading edge droop can be seen in the extended position (plainly visible on the starboard wing). Taken during certification test flying, this photograph shows the original wing fences inboard of the landing lights. These were later deleted and an additional droop segment fitted in their place. With additional fuel tankage as well, the modified Trident 1s were redesignated Trident 1Cs.

Three more views of BEA's second Trident 1, G-ARPB, taken for publicity purposes early in the aircraft's life. The old established de Havilland Aircraft company at Hatfield, which originally designed the Trident as the DH-121 before being absorbed into the Hawker Siddeley Group, pioneered the concept of the centre engine mounted in the tail cone of the fuselage, with the air intake incorporated into the design of the fin. The layout was later adopted by Boeing for the 727, by Lockheed for its widebodied L-1011 Tristar, and by the Soviet Union for both its Tupolev Tu-154 and its Yak-40, while McDonnell Douglas produced its own variation for the DC-10 and MD-11.

BEA's "High Speed Jack" livery which replaced its "red squares" from the end of 1968, seen here on Trident 2, G-AVFI. Trident 1C G-ARPI was painted in this scheme at the time of its final flight.

and instructed it to "squawk" 6615 on its transponder. This message was tersely acknowledged by the voice of Captain Key with the brief transmission: "Up to six zero". There were no further radio messages from the Trident and it subsequently failed to respond to calls from London Control.

Less than a minute later, Trevor Burke, a 13 year old schoolboy, walking along the footpath by the sparsely settled A30 Staines bypass road near the King George VI reservoir, some five km southwest of the airport, heard a roaring above him that was rapidly increasing in volume. Looking up, he saw a big rear-engined jet emerge from the base of the overcast cloud. To his utter bewilderment, though its engines were obviously under power, it seemed to have little forward speed and was falling almost vertically in a flat, nose up attitude.

Trevor Burke watched transfixed as the unbelievable unfolded before his very eyes – the sickening near-vertical fall continuing until the huge aeroplane, narrowly missing a major powerline pylon, finally smashed down into a field on the outskirts of Staines. There was an enormous metallic sound of impact as the Trident, still in its flat attitude, hit the ground with great force, bounced, and broke apart, the tail snapping off bodily with the three rear-mounted engines. Despite the spillage of fuel from ruptured wing tanks, no fire broke out.

Immediately Trevor Burke began running to the nearest house (some 400 metres away) to raise the alarm. Its occupant, a Mrs Castledine, had been a nursing sister at nearby Ashford Hospital with experience in casualty, and as soon the boy blurted

out his story, she ran with him to the scene to render what assistance she could. Moving quickly amongst the wrecked sections of the cabin, she did her utmost to seek out passengers who were still breathing, but found only one, deeply unconscious. The high vertical decelerative forces had killed all the others outright.

Firefighting vehicles and ambulances were on the scene within a few minutes and the surviving passenger was rushed to Ashford Hospital, but died soon afterwards.

The worst disaster in the history of aviation in the British Isles, and the first fatal accident involving a Trident in normal airline operations, the unusual and extremely puzzling crash made headline news around the world.

★ ★ ★

The fact that there was no post-crash fire greatly assisted both the detailed inspection of the wreckage by personnel from the Accidents Investigation Branch of the UK Department of Trade and Industry, and the postmortem examination of the flight crew by aviation pathologists.

Despite a most searching examination, no defect or evidence of malfunction was found in the aircraft or its various systems and it was clear that the Trident was fully serviceable in every way up to the moment of its impact with the ground. Indeed, the only factor apparently preventing it from flying normally was its almost complete lack of airspeed.

Regrettably, the Trident was not equipped with a Cockpit Voice Recorder, but readouts of the two Flight Data Recorders fitted to the aircraft, one of which was a newly developed 64 channel unit, utterly removed any lingering doubts as to

the aerodynamics of the accident: the Trident's wing leading edge droops had been retracted prematurely at too low an airspeed and the aircraft had stalled. Following the crew's failure to recover, for reasons unknown, from this aerodynamic condition, the nose had pitched up steeply and the aircraft had finally entered a "deep stall" (a phenomenon peculiar to T-tailed aircraft), from which recovery was not possible.

The Trident was the first British civil aircraft to be equipped with retractable leading edge high-lift devices, then known as "droops". Hinged at the bottom of the leading edge of the wing, they move outwards from the top when extended. Extension of the droops markedly decreases the speed at which the wing stalls – in the case of a Trident at a weight of 50,000 kilograms, the stalling speed is decreased by about 30 knots. Conversely, when the droops are retracted, the stalling speed is increased by the same figure.

Trident aircraft are also equipped with both a stall warning system in the form of a "stick-shaker", and a pneumatically powered "stick-pusher" stall recovery system which operates automatically to lower the nose at a wing incidence approaching that of a true aerodynamic stall. The stick pusher can be inhibited by moving a lever on the left side of the central control pedestal on the flightdeck.

The FDR readout revealed that, some six seconds after the last radio transmission from the Trident – Captain Key's terse acknowledgement of London Control's clearance to climb to FL 60 – as the aircraft was climbing through 1770 feet in cloud at an airspeed of only 162 knots, a crew member unaccountably retracted the wing leading edge droop, putting the Trident into an incipient aerodynamic stall, and triggering both the stick shaker stall warning and the stick pusher stall recovery system. This automatically disengaged the autopilot and pitched the aircraft's nose down, causing the stick push to cease as the wing incidence decreased and the wing became unstalled again.

But with the autopilot now inoperative, the wing leading edge droop retracted, and the elevator trim unaltered, the aircraft had become tail heavy. As a result, the nose pitched up again and, eight seconds after the first stick push, the stall recovery system operated a second time. Three seconds afterwards, as this pattern repeated itself, the stick-pusher forced the nose down yet again. But this time its operation was inhibited – at this highly critical point, some member of the crew selected the system off.

It was a fatal mistake. Deprived of the counteracting effect of the stick pusher, the Trident then pitched rapidly and steeply noseup in excess of 30 degrees. Losing speed and height,

the aircraft quickly entered a true aerodynamic stall, then a deep stall from which recovery was impossible. The Trident struck the ground in this condition 22 seconds later.

The FDR readout showed also that, even up to the time the leading edge droop was retracted, the manner in which the Trident was flown differed disturbingly from standard BEA practice – it had consistently

failed to achieve the appropriate airspeeds for the various phases of flight. Indeed, had the Trident's speed been only 10-15 knots higher when the droops were retracted, recovery would have been comparatively simple.

The airline's standard operational procedure for London Heathrow departures involved commencing the takeoff with 20 degrees of flap and

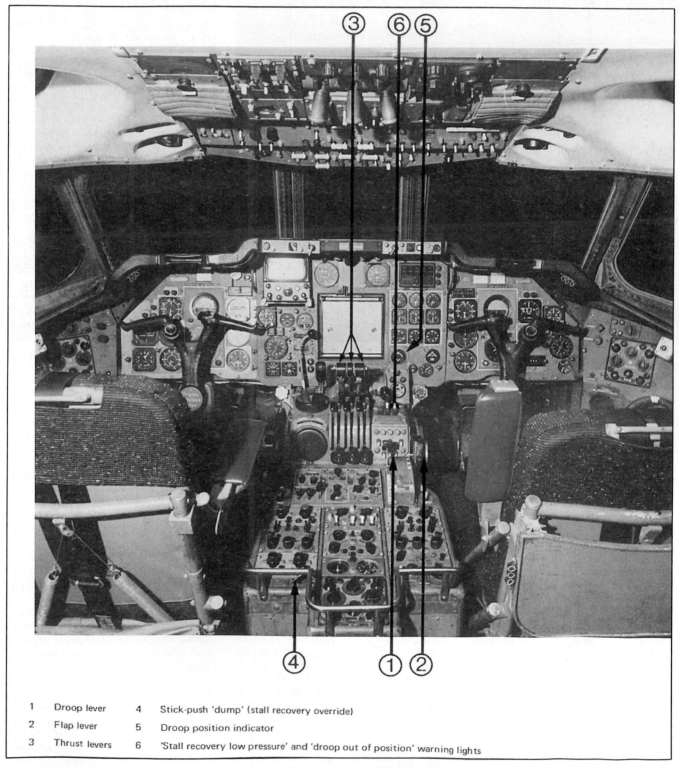

1	Droop lever	4	Stick-push 'dump' (stall recovery override)
2	Flap lever	5	Droop position indicator
3	Thrust levers	6	'Stall recovery low pressure' and 'droop out of position' warning lights

BEA Trident 1C flightdeck, showing position of controls and indicators pertinent to the Staines accident. The accompanying diagram (opposite) shows the seat positions of each of the four pilots on the flightdeck.

A wider angle view of the later Trident 2's flightdeck, substantially similar to that of the Trident 1C. On Trident 2 and Trident 3 aircraft the original wing leading edge droops were replaced by leading edge slats, but these were actuated by a similar lever in the same position as the Trident 1C's droop control on the right hand side of the pedestal. In this picture, both the slat lever and the adjacent flap lever immediately to its right, are in the fully extended positions. This particular aircraft, photographed new at the manufacturer's facility at Hatfield, UK in July 1974, is G-BABP, one of several Trident 2Es destined for China, where its registration became B-252.

the leading edge droop extended, and after takeoff, increasing speed to the predetermined noise abatement safety speed (in this case 177 knots). At 90 seconds from brake release, the flaps were to be selected up, and engine power reduced to noise abatement settings. On reaching 3000 feet, the power levers were to be advanced again to normal climb power settings and, as the aircraft accelerated through 225 knots, the leading edge droop was to be retracted and en route climb established.

In the takeoff that led to the accident, after lifting off at 145 knots, the speed was increased over the next 19 seconds to 170 knots. At this point the autopilot was engaged some seven knots below the noise abatement climb speed. By the time the flaps were raised 94 seconds from brake release and 50 seconds from liftoff, the speed had decayed to 168 knots. After engine thrust was reduced in accordance with noise

abatement procedures, it fell further over the following 15 seconds to 157 knots, 20 knots below noise-abatement climb speed. The wing leading

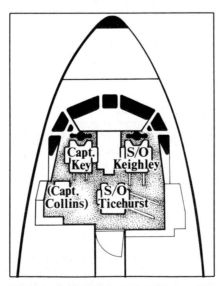

Diagram showing crew seat positions on the flightdeck of G-ARPI.

edge droop was retracted another six seconds later while the aircraft was in a banked turn.

This untimely and inexplicable action immediately placed the aircraft in an aerodynamically stalled condition. The minimum droop retraction speed of 225 knots is placarded by the droop lever on the flightdeck, and is well known to all Trident pilots, as is the airline's injunction against retracting the droop during a turn.

But grave though this action was at such a low airspeed, all was not yet lost. Even at this stage, though the engine thrust still remained at the reduced power noise abatement setting, the Trident could have been quickly recovered from the stall to resume normal flight if any one of the following actions had been taken:
• Increasing speed at least 10 knots by reapplying climb power.
• Immediately extending the leading edge droop again.

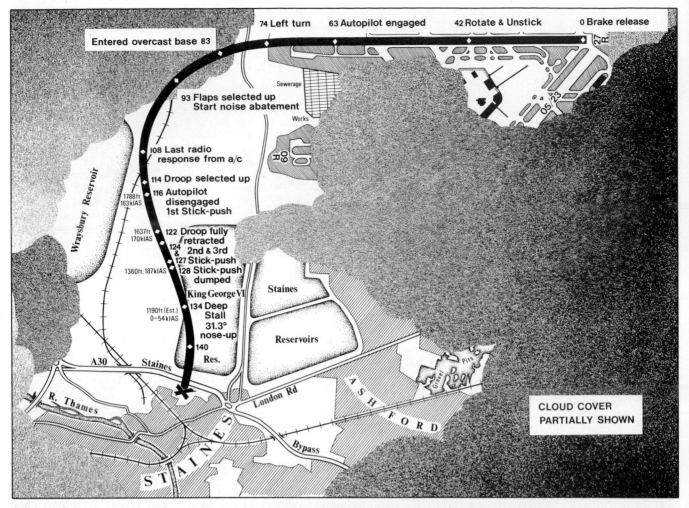

74 Left turn   63 Autopilot engaged   42 Rotate & Unstick   0 Brake release

Entered overcast base 83

Sewerage

Works

93 Flaps selected up
Start noise abatement

108 Last radio
response from a/c

114 Droop selected up

116 Autopilot
disengaged
1st Stick-push

1788ft
163kIAS

1637ft
170kIAS

122 Droop fully
retracted
124 & 2nd & 3rd
127 Stick-push
1360ft; 187kIAS   128 Stick-push
dumped

King George VI

Staines

1190ft (Est.)
0–54kIAS

134 Deep
Stall
31.3°
nose-up

Reservoirs

140
Res.

A30   Staines

R. Thames   London Rd   A S H F O R D

Gravel
Pits

CLOUD COVER
PARTIALLY SHOWN

S T A I N E S

Bypass

Map showing G-ARPI's all too brief flightpath. Just how brief this was is evident from the numbers denoting seconds from the beginning of takeoff.

• Holding the control column forward after the stick-pusher operated to maintain the attitude regained by the stall recovery system.

Yet none of these actions were even attempted, despite the repeated stall warnings and automatic stall recovery operation. To the investigators therefore, it seemed the underlying cause of the tragedy lay in answers to several highly significant unknowns:

• Why was there such a serious and persistent speed error in the flying of the aircraft up to the point at which it stalled?

• Who was responsible for retracting the leading edge droop and why was it retracted so prematurely?

• Why did BEA's much vaunted inflight monitoring system fail to avert the stall – and why did the crew not fly a recovery after the stall warnings?

• Why did the crew fail to diagnose the reason for the stall recovery system operating repeatedly, and why was the system turned off at such a critical point?

A pointer to where the solution to these enigmas might lie came dra-

matically to light when pathologists examined the bodies of the four pilots occupying the flightdeck.

The autopsies revealed nothing abnormal in the cases of Second Officers Keighley and Ticehurst, or the supernumerary pilot, Captain Collins. But it was a very different matter with the autopsy performed on the body of 51 year old Captain Key.

The pathological examination revealed a severe case of atherosclerosis – a narrowing of the arteries resulting from a buildup of fatty deposits in the heart – and there was a tear in the lining of the wall of one artery. This tear was likely to have been the end result of an initial rupture of small blood vessels in the thickened artery wall, caused by a sharp rise in blood pressure, not more than two hours before the accident. The resulting haemorrhage, creating its own buildup of pressure, then progressively forced the artery lining to separate.

The several eminent cardiologists participating in the investigation agreed that, under physical or emotional stress, weak blood vessels in

Captain Key's thickened arteries had ruptured. The symptoms of the internal haemorrhage that resulted could range from a slight indigestion-like pain in the chest to collapse and unconsciousness. At the very least, it was considered they would have caused some "disturbance of thought processes".

There can be little doubt that tension on the flightdeck of the Trident, as it taxied out from the terminal at Heathrow that afternoon, would have been high. Key, struggling with what he probably thought was an attack of indigestion after his altercation in the crew room, would probably have been responding tersely under the effect of his pain as he went through the pre-takeoff checks with his crew.

But his two young and relatively inexperienced copilots, Keighley and Ticehurst, could well have been mistaken their captain's demeanour for short temper and intolerance. Keighley had been a witness to the captain's vitriolic outburst in the crew room, and both he and Ticehurst were probably very much on edge – fearful of saying or doing the slightest thing that might upset this senior captain with the obviously violent temper.

In this emotionally charged flight-deck atmosphere, the copilots would have been extremely reluctant, regardless of their official BEA brief, to point out any operational oversight or shortcoming on the part of the captain. And the presence of another senior captain on the flight-deck in the person of Captain Collins would have done nothing to assuage this reluctance.

In this situation, the most reasonable explanation for the Trident's steady deterioration in airspeed between the time the crew reported "Climbing as cleared" and Captain Key's final "Up to Six Zero" transmission, was simply that Key was trying to cope with increasing pain, and his concentration and judgement were affected. In normal circumstances, Captain Key, being the sort of pilot he was, would have corrected any discrepancy in airspeed immediately. As it was, neither copilot was apparently sufficiently con-cerned with the discrepancy in airspeed to risk upsetting the captain further by pointing it out. In such circumstances, their natural inclination would be to accept that their highly experienced captain "knew what he was doing."

The events that led to the premature retraction of the leading edge droop were more difficult to account for. The droop mechanism is controlled by a lever on the centre pedestal to the right of the power controls quadrant, close to, but distinct from the flap lever. For this reason apart from any other, it was thought highly unlikely that Second Officer Ticehurst, seated in the monitoring pilot's position, would have been responsible for moving it.

While it was physically possible that Keighley, in the right hand control seat, could have retracted the droop a this point, this also was considered highly unlikely. Though not a very experienced line pilot at this stage, Keighley was nevertheless competent and fully trained for his duties, training which included considerable instruction in handling stalling in the Trident simulator. Keighley would thus have been well aware that speed, height, timing and aircraft bank angle were all wrong for droop retraction at that point.

Overall, it seemed far more likely that the movement of the droop lever at such a grossly inadequate airspeed and Captain Key's physical condition were somehow linked. At this stage of the flight, though no doubt feeling extremely uncomfortable because of the increasing pain in his chest, Key was probably aware that the aircraft's speed was too low. In his existing state of mind it seems possible that he might have associated this low airspeed with a need to raise the flaps, not appreciating the fact that the flaps were already fully up. With his reasoning thus impaired, he might have moved the droop lever, believing he was retracting the flaps.

Even so, the "how and why" of moving the droop lever was only part of the answer. Still to be explained was the reason for the failure of the airline's monitoring system to detect and correct the error. It was precisely this sort of error that the monitoring system was

The severed tail assembly of the Trident, with portion of the fuselage in the background. The fully stalled aircraft struck the ground in a near vertical descent but in a flat attitude, breaking apart on impact.

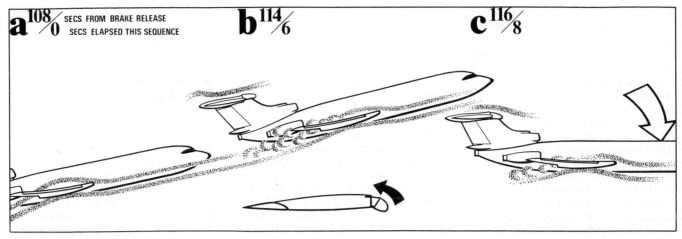

(a) Trident climbing normally with leading edge droop extended. (b) Leading edge droop lever inadvertently moved to retracted position – aircraft enters incipient aerodynamic stall as droop progressively retracts over period of six seconds. (c) "Stick pusher" stall recovery system operates, automatically lowering nose. Wing becomes unstalled as incidence decreases. (Matthew Tesch)

designed to overcome. Indeed, had it done so on this occasion, there would have been no accident. So why was the movement of the droop lever not picked up and immediately reversed by Ticehurst in the monitoring pilot's position? Or even by Keighley in the right hand seat?

On the assumption that Captain Key was responsible for moving the droop lever, there were two possible reasons for Keighley not noticing the movement. Firstly, if he had had his left armrest in the horizontal position, it could have obscured his view of the droop lever. Secondly, if he had still been adjusting engine power to the correct noise-abatement level, his attention would have been on the engine instruments as he moved the power levers, and his extended left arm could have hidden what Captain Key was doing.

Ticehurst's failure to notice the error is perhaps harder to understand

at first sight. But at this critical moment it is likely he was logging the Flight Level to which they had just been cleared. The Flight Level 60 entry in Ticehurst's log, found in the wreckage after the accident, could only have been made in the few seconds prior to the movement of the droop lever and the first stick push.

If Captain Key was exhibiting signs of imminent collapse about this time, this could also have distracted Ticehurst's attention from the control console, particularly if there had been some comment or reaction from Captain Collins, sitting immediately behind Captain Key. Furthermore, if Captain Key's final collapse had coincided with the operation of the stall warning and stick pusher operation, that in itself could explain the crew's failure to correctly diagnose the reason. At the time of course, the aircraft was flying in cloud with no visual reference.

If, on top of the copilots' failure to notice that the leading edge droop had been retracted, both copilots and Captain Collins were suddenly confronted with a collapsed and possibly dying Captain Key, it is understandable that he would have been their preoccupation for the moment. As the aircraft had been flying and climbing normally in cloud at a safe speed up to that time, the sudden and unexpected onset of stick shaker and stick pusher operation at no change in airspeed or aircraft attitude may well have been regarded as a false alarm, perhaps somehow associated with something the captain had inadvertently done in his last moments of consciousness.

There was a belief among BEA pilots (originating in several false alarms in the development stages of the stall recovery system some years before), that the system could be unreliable at times. It is also significant

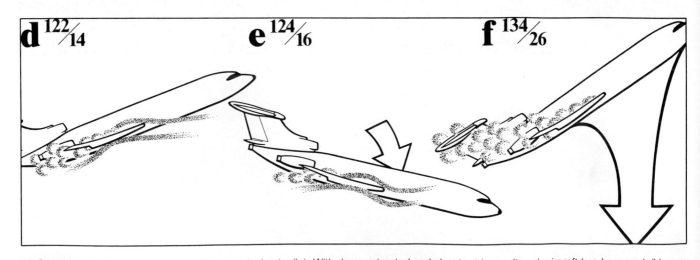

(d) Operation of stick pusher has also disconnected autopilot. With droop retracted and elevator trim unaltered, aircraft has become tail heavy. Nose pitches up again and Trident again enters stalled condition. (e) Eight seconds after first stick push, stall recovery system operates again, once more forcing aircraft's nose down and unstalling wing. (f) For reasons unknown, crew select automatic stall recovery system off. Deprived of counteracting effect of stick pusher, Trident's nose pitches up rapidly in excess of 30 degrees. Losing speed and height, aircraft quickly becomes fully stalled, then enters deep stall. High set T-tail loses all control effectiveness over the aircraft's pitch attitude, rendering recovery impossible.

that neither of the copilots had been warned during their airline training of the possibility of a change-in-configuration stall as occurred in this instance, or of what a sudden and completely unexpected stick push might indicate.

So when the stick shaker operated, apparently without valid reason, for the third time, quite probably interrupting whatever assistance the pilots were trying to give the collapsed Captain Key, the immediate and understandable response was to inhibit the system to enable them to get on with dealing with the medical emergency on the flightdeck.

Had they realised that the only reason that could account for what they were experiencing was an untimely retraction of the leading edge droop, or had they appreciated that retracting the droop at the speed and attitude of the aircraft at the time, would immediately place it in an incipient stall, they might well have taken the action required to recover from the stall before the situation worsened into one that was irretrievable.

Like so many major airline accidents, the loss of BEA Trident G-ARPI resulted from an untimely combination of a number of unfavourable but relatively minor factors, any one of which, had it been recognised and appropriately allowed for, could have averted the accident. The Public Inquiry into the accident to G-ARPI concluded with 10 recommendations to BEA and the airline industry generally. Chief among these were:
• The incorporation of speed operated baulks into the design of aircraft fitted with leading edge droops or slats to prevent their inadvertent retraction at low speed.
• That specific training be in future given to pilots on stalls resulting from "change in configuration".
• That Cockpit Voice Recorders be fitted to all British civil passenger aircraft with an all up weight of 27,000kg or more.
• That the attention of pilots be drawn to the dangers of subtle as well as obvious crew incapacitation.
• That the question of subjecting aircrew to "stress test" electrocardiograms rather than "resting" ECGs during medical examinations be kept under review as the reliability of such testing improved.

Another view of the wreckage. The disruption of the fuselage structure, resulting from the high vertical forces at impact is clearly evident.

CHAPTER 12

"Hey – What's happening here?"

*– Tristar captain to crew
a moment before impact*

Eastern Air Lines Lockheed L-1011 Tristar 1 N310EA [193A-1011] –
December 29, 1972

*"Because of the nail, the shoe was lost; because of the shoe the horse was lost.
Because of the horse, the battle was lost. Because of the battle – the war was lost."*

Long established Eastern Air Lines, a major US company with a history dating from the pioneer years of commercial aviation, was justifiably proud of its new 254 passenger, Rolls-Royce engined Lockheed L-1011 Tristars.

The launch customer for the widebodied design that had flown for the first time in November 1970, Eastern Air Lines had ordered no less than 50, to serve as flagships of Eastern's huge fleet.

"The quietest, cleanest plane in the skies," an Eastern executive had enthused, extolling the name *Whisperliner* which each of the company's white and blue Tristars bore on the massive air intake for the tail mounted centre engine. Not only did the giant trijet offer domestic passengers a superior standard of comfort, spaciousness and quietness in flight: its highly sophisticated Lockheed Avionic Flight Control System (AFCS) provided its crews with the latest in autopilot technology, permitting the aircraft to be flown in different "modes" or degrees of automatic flight.

N310EA, one of the 12 Tristars so far delivered to Eastern, is the aircraft scheduled to operate Flight 401 from New York to Miami on Friday night, December 29, 1972. Only four months old, it has not yet logged

1000 hours in the air and is in superb condition.

The three flight crew members rostered to take Flight 401 to Miami are as competent as their age, background and experience would suggest. Veteran Captain Robert Loft, in his middle 50s and one of Eastern's senior captains, has been an airline pilot all his adult life and has accumulated the astonishing total of almost 30,000 hours. First Officer Albert Stockstill, 39, also highly experienced and a light aircraft enthusiast as well, has more than 300 hours on the new Tristars. Flight Engineer Don Repo, 50, a former airline ground engineer who himself holds a commercial pilot licence, is a perfectionist with a great admiration for the Tristar and its advanced systems.

With New York in the grip of midwinter cold, the Christmas holiday season has ensured the Miami-bound flight is fully booked – so much so that company technical officer Angelo Donadeo, returning to Miami from an assignment in New York, has to settle for the jump seat on the flightdeck if he is to travel on the flight at all.

In the event, not all those booked have arrived by Flight 401's departure time of 9pm, and by the time the cabin crew of 10 flight attendants

are securing the doors, only 162 of the Tristar's 254 passenger seats are filled. Even so, Donadeo decides to remain on the flightdeck. He is an expert in the Tristar's systems, and the jump seat is a far more interesting place to travel than the passenger cabin.

A few minutes after 9pm, N310EA taxies from the terminal at New York's John F Kennedy International Airport to join the queue of passenger jets lined up at the runway holding point awaiting their takeoff clearances. But the tower controllers are handling the heavy holiday traffic expeditiously and by 9.20 the Tristar is lifting off, its huge Roll-Royce RB211 engines humming reassuringly as it climbs and turns over a sparkling carpet of ground lights to set course for Miami. On board, the passengers are in high spirits as they look forward to the balmy night air of southern Florida in place of New York's frigid cold.

For air travellers inclined to be nervous, flight aboard one of the huge new widebodied airliners seems especially comforting. Since the Boeing 747 was introduced to service three years earlier, followed by the slightly smaller McDonnell Douglas DC-10 and Lockheed L-1011 Tristar two years later, not one of the giant new generation aircraft has

The magnificent Tristar: A L-1011 Tristar in Lockheed livery cruises serenely above the snow capped Rockies during certification flying from the manufacturer's facility at Palmdale, California in 1971. The first production Tristar was delivered to Eastern Air Lines, the launch customer for the type, in April 1972. The Tristar involved in the accident was the 10th produced for Eastern and was only four months old.

been involved in a fatal accident. Tonight's flight, as it progresses, does nothing but reinforce this happy impression. At cruising altitude, it is uneventful, smooth and pleasant, with the cabin service excellent.

Less than two and a half hours later, as the Tristar, now in radio contact with Miami Approach Control, descends from cruising level with the lights of the city visible in the far distance beyond the unbroken blackness of the Everglades National Park, Captain Loft speaks to the passengers over the cabin PA system: "Welcome to Miami," he declares enthusiastically. "The tem-

perature is in the low seventies, and it's a beautiful night out there tonight."

Though the night is dark with no moon, the weather is indeed fine, with almost no wind, only scattered cloud at 2500 feet, and more than 10 nautical miles' visibility.

At 11.32pm, Miami Approach Control clears the Tristar, now only a little more than five nm to the northwest, to join the ILS for Miami International Airport's Runway 09 Left, and instructs the crew to call the control tower on its frequency of 118.3 Mhz:

Captain Loft acknowledges:

"Cleared to ILS 09 left, call Miami Tower on 118.3." He concludes informally: "Eastern 401, so long."

While Loft quickly changes frequency as instructed, First Officer Stockstill eases the huge aircraft into a gentle turn to the left to line up with the twin row of lights marking Runway 09L that are gleaming in the distance. Then Loft calls the tower: "Miami Tower, Eastern 401 – just turned on to final."

There is no immediate response, the Tristar's transmission apparently having been blocked by a call from another aircraft on the tower frequency. As the crew wait, Loft turns

All three Rolls-Royce RB211 engines at full takeoff thrust, another Tristar in Lockheed livery lifts effortlessly into its natural environment. The L-1011 was the first aircraft type to use the newly developed, fuel efficient Rolls-Royce RB211 engine and represented a major marketing breakthrough for the renowned British manufacturer. The Tristar itself was a major corporate gamble by Lockheed to regain its airliner reputation after the turboprop Electra debacle of the 1950s. Though it was to prove something of a commercial disaster, principally because the widebody market at the time was not big enough to sustain three competing manufacturers, the aircraft itself was a superb technical achievement and the type is still in wide use today. (Lockheed)

This Lockheed mockup of the Tristar's spacious two aisle passenger cabin provides an idea of the interior layout of the Eastern Air Lines Tristar involved in the accident – a standard of comfort and a feeling of security that probably helped to sooth the nerves of nervous flyers who boarded Flight 401 at New York that fateful night of December 29, 1972. Air safety authorities in fact believed that, because of the scale of their structures, the new generation widebodied jets might well be safer for their occupants in a "survivable" crash than their narrow body forbears such as the 707 and the DC-8. The Everglades experience showed this to be so – though sadly it required an accident to prove it. (Lockheed)

again to Stockstill: "Go ahead and throw them out," he tells him. Stockstill moves the undercarriage lever to its down position and there are the usual series of grinds and thumps below the floor as the three undercarriage legs extend and lock down.

Captain Loft calls the tower again: "Miami Tower – do you read Eastern 401? Just turned on to final."

This time the tower controller answers at once: "Eastern 401, heavy – continue approach to 09 Left." (The "heavy" denotes for other aircraft that Eastern 401 is a widebodied jet and there may be wake turbulence considerations for smaller aircraft).

"Continue approach – roger," Loft acknowledges.

Flight Engineer Repo begins calling the prelanding checklist, to which Captain Loft responds, item by item, while First Officer Stockstill flies the aircraft. As Loft scans the instrument panel, his gaze rests on the undercarriage position indicator lights. Only two of the three greens are showing!

"Bert," he asks, addressing Stockstill in the right hand control seat, "Is that [undercarriage] handle in?"

Repo, at his engineer's console behind the two pilots, is unaware of the interruption and continues for the moment with his checklist calls. Stockstill meanwhile scans the instrument panel himself, assessing the implications of the captain's question. After a pause, he replies: "No nose gear!"

The pilots recycle the undercar-

riage retraction mechanism, first raising then lowering the wheels again. But still the green "down" indicator lamp for the nose leg fails to illuminate. Either the nose leg has not locked down safely or, far more likely, to judge from the sound of the

mechanism when the undercarriage lever was moved to the "down" position, the indicator system itself is at fault.

It is a problem that occurs occasionally on all retractable undercarriage aeroplanes, regardless of size.

An interesting feature of the Lockheed Tristar was its optional underfloor galley which allowed more passenger seating in the main cabin. Serving trolleys were carried to and from the main deck via two small lifts. Two cabin crew were on duty in the galley aboard Flight 401, but both had returned to the passenger cabin in preparation for landing before the aircraft flew into the ground. Both of them survived the accident. (Lockheed)

The cockpit of the Lockheed L-1011 Tristar. The autopilot controls can be seen on the glareshield.

However, the doubt will have to be resolved one way or another before they attempt to land. But there is no cause for alarm. As a last resort, the undercarriage can be cranked down manually.

Laconically, the veteran airline captain calls Miami Tower again: "Well. Tower, this is Eastern 401. It looks like we're going to have to circle – we don't have a light on our nose gear.

"Eastern 401 heavy, roger," the controller replies at once, also taking the minor emergency in his stride, "Climb straight ahead to 2000 – go back to Approach Control on 128.6."

"OK", Loft acknowledges, "going up to 2000 – 128.6."

Stockstill's hand moves to the undercarriage selector lever to raise the wheels again, but the captain checks him. "Put power on first, Bert – leave that damn gear down until we've found out what we've got."

As Stockstill advances all three power levers to the climb power setting, Repo asks Loft: "Do you want to test the lights?" He means the electrical circuit for the undercarriage position indicators.

"Yeah – check it," Loft answers.

Stockstill, continuing to fly the aircraft, interposes to the captain: "Bob, it might just be the light [itself]. Could you jiggle it?"

The undercarriage position indicator lamps are mounted on the instrument panel on the first officer's side of the flightdeck, just below the undercarriage selector lever. Repo moves forward from his engineer's seat to see what he can do to help. At that moment the aircraft reaches 2000 feet and Stockstill levels it out in accordance with Miami Approach Control's instruction. He speaks again to the captain: "We're up to 2000 – you want me to fly it, Bob?"

Loft doesn't answer directly. Rather, he is thinking about what he should tell Approach Control. He checks with Stockstill: "What frequency did they want us on, Bert?"

"128.6," Stockstill confirms.

Loft changes to the required frequency on the VHF selector panel. "I'll talk to them," he says.

Repo, still trying to help with the faulty indicator light, asks the pilots: "It's right above ... that red one, isn't it?

Loft responds, "Yeah – I can't get at it from here."

Leaning over Stockstill's shoulder,

Repo pulls unsuccessfully at the indicator lamp assembly: "I can't make it pull out either," he declares.

Loft presses the microphone button on his control wheel again: "Approach Control – Eastern 401," he transmits. "We're right over the airport now, climbing to 2000 feet – in fact we've reached 2000 – and we've got to get a green light on our nosegear."

"Eastern 401, roger," the controller replies, "Turn left, heading 360, maintain 2000 [feet] – vectors to 09 Left on final.

"Left – 360," Loft acknowledges, and Stockstill swings the Tristar through 90 degrees on to a northerly heading – one that will take the huge aircraft out over the vast pitch black expanse of the Everglades again. It is 11.35pm – just after the time the Tristar crew had expected to touch down at Miami.

With the undercarriage indicator lamp assembly on the first officer's side of the instrument panel, neither Loft nor Repo can get at it properly. Loft is becoming exasperated. "Put the damn thing on autopilot," he tells Stockstill, who is still flying the aircraft manually. "See if *you* can get it out."

When Stockstill has engaged the autopilot, Loft instructs: "Now push the switches just a little bit forward – you've got to turn it sideways." Then: "No, I don't think it'll fit." When this advice doesn't succeed, he adds: "You've got to turn it a quarter turn to the left"

At 11.36pm, Miami Approach Control, monitoring the Tristar's position on radar to keep it well separated from other traffic in the busy airport control area, calls the aircraft again: "Eastern 401, turn left – heading 300."

Loft acknowledges the instruction and Stockstill complies, then both pilots turn their attention to the troublesome lamp assembly again. While Stockstill works away at it, Loft's patience is running out. A minute later he turns around to Repo: "Hey – get down there and see if that damn nosewheel is down – you better do that."

The captain means the spacious electronics bay below the flightdeck and just forward of the nosewheel well. The bay is accessible via a manhole in the flightdeck floor and, from the rear of the bay, it is possible to view the position of the nose leg mechanism through an optical sight. If the two rods that are visible through the sight are aligned with a red line in the sight, the noseleg is down and locked.

Stockstill meanwhile, has managed to remove the lamp lens assembly from the instrument panel but is now having difficulty unscrewing the offending peanut sized light bulb. "Got a handkerchief or something so I can get a better grip?" he asks. "Anything I can do it with?"

The captain hands him a tissue, then technical officer Donadeo, sitting in the jump seat and unable to contain himself any longer, finally offers some advice on how to do it: "... pull down and turn to your right," he tells Stockstill. "Now turn it to your left one time ..."

"It hangs out and sticks," Stockstill complains.

"Try it my way," Donadeo insists.

Stockstill's efforts are still unsuccessful. He looks across at the captain: "It won't come out, Bob – if I had a pair of pliers, I could cushion it with that Kleenex."

Repo, who has opened the manhole and is about to climb down the ladder into the electronics bay, interjects: "I can give you a pair of pliers. But if you force it, you'll break it – believe me."

Miami Approach calls again: "Eastern 401, turn left – heading 270."

Loft acknowledges the call while Stockstill swings the Tristar on to the new heading. It is still flying on autopilot in the "altitude hold" mode at 2000 feet.

Loft gives up on the lamp assembly. "To hell with it!" he declares emphatically. He turns around to Repo again. "To hell with this – go down and see if it's lined up on that red line – that's all we care!" He laughs at himself. "Screwing around with a 20 cent piece of light equipment – on this plane!" The other crew members laugh too.

Loft presses his microphone button to speak to Miami Approach Control again: "Eastern 401 will go out west a little further if we can ...

see if we can't get this light to come on."

"All right," the controller replies. "We've got you headed westbound now, Eastern 401."

With Repo now below in the electronics bay, Loft and Stockstill continue over the next two minutes or more to manipulate the lamp assembly. "Always something," Stockstill grumbles. "We could have made it on schedule."

They discuss the situation and conclude that the noseleg *has* to be down – the problem is no more than a faulty lamp. "Leave it there," Loft tells Stockstill with an air of finality, referring to his further efforts to remove it.

At this point Repo climbs the ladder and raises his head through the manhole in the floor of the flightdeck. "I can't see it down there," he tells the pilots.

"For the nosewheel there's a place in there where you can look and see if it's lined up," Loft reminds him.

"I know – a little like a telescope."

"It's not lined up?"

"I can't see it," Repo replies. "It's pitch dark."

Still anxious to help, Donadeo undoes his jumpseat harness and stands up to join Repo in the electronics bay. "Wheel well lights on?" he asks.

"Yeah," Repo answers. "Wheel well lights are always on if the gear's down."

As Donadeo crosses to the manhole, Repo disappears down the ladder. Donadeo follows him down, walking aft to the nosewheel well bulkhead where he should be able to

Photo taken from a low flying helicopter the morning after the accident, looking back along the wreckage trail towards get initial impact area. The tail section – the biggest single piece of wreckage – is in the foreground. An idea of scale can be gained from the man standing on the wreckage at right. The remains of the fuselage centre section and starboard wing can be seen in the upper right background.

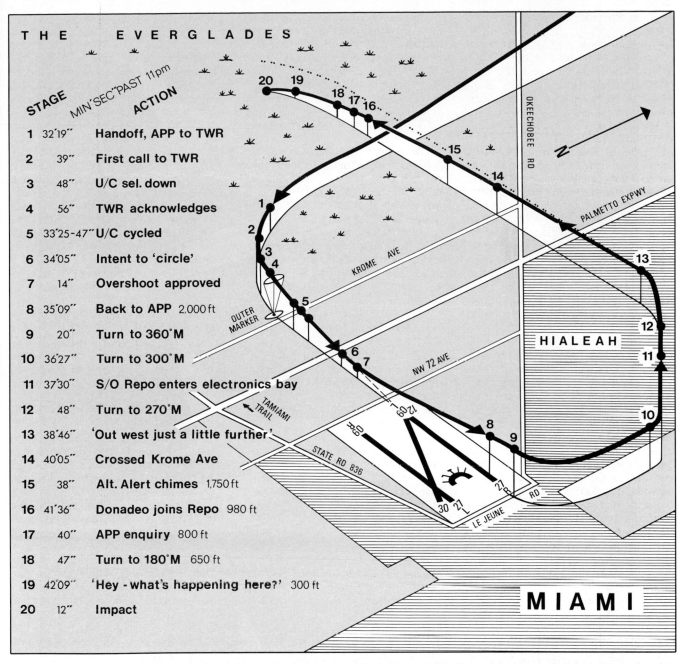

STAGE	MIN'SEC"PAST 11pm	ACTION	
1	32'19"	Handoff, APP to TWR	
2	39"	First call to TWR	
3	48"	U/C sel. down	
4	56"	TWR acknowledges	
5	33'25-47"	U/C cycled	
6	34'05"	Intent to 'circle'	
7	14"	Overshoot approved	
8	35'09"	Back to APP	2,000 ft
9	20"	Turn to 360°M	
10	36'27"	Turn to 300°M	
11	37'30"	S/O Repo enters electronics bay	
12	48"	Turn to 270°M	
13	38'46"	'Out west just a little further'	
14	40'05"	Crossed Krome Ave	
15	38"	Alt. Alert chimes	1,750 ft
16	41'36"	Donadeo joins Repo	980 ft
17	40"	APP enquiry	800 ft
18	47"	Turn to 180°M	650 ft
19	42'09"	'Hey - what's happening here?'	300 ft
20	12"	Impact	

Aerial perspective depicting the Tristar's final flight path to accident site – initial approach to Miami International Airport Runway's 09L, subsequent go around, and gradual unintentional descent to point of impact. (Matthew Tesch)

view the undercarriage leg mechanism through the optical sight.

Miami Approach Control calls the Tristar again: "Eastern 401 - how are things coming along out there?"

Six and a half minutes have elapsed since the Tristar overflew the runway as it carried out its missed approach – it is now well out over the totally dark and uninhabited Everglades to the west of the airport.

Loft replies at once: "OK – we'd like to turn round now and come back in."

The airspeed over the past few seconds had increased from 174 knots to 188, which Stockstill compensates for by retarding the power levers slightly.

"Eastern 401 – turn left, heading 180," the Miami controller instructs.

As Stockstill swings the Tristar into another gentle turn, he senses something isn't right. Yet the "ALT" annunciator light on the glareshield in front of him is illuminated as it should be, indicating that the autopilot is still engaged in the "Altitude Hold" mode – the setting he selected after they had climbed back to 2000 feet. His gaze falls on the altimeter on the panel in front of him below the glareshield. Momentarily confused by the contradictory instrument indications he has just seen, he blurts: "We did something to the altitude!"

"What?" Loft asks.

"We're still at 2000 – right?" Stockstill demands, unable to accept the evidence of his own eyes.

There is a moment's silence as Loft scans his own instrument panel. Then he yells: "Hey – what's happening here!"

At the same time the radio altimeter warning begins beeping at an increasing rate, indicating proximity with the ground. In a moment there is metallic impact out on the port wing and the aircraft lurches alarmingly. In another instant there is a totally disorienting nightmare of extreme violence and noise that seems to go on and on ... but finally there is silence ... and blackness.

★   ★   ★

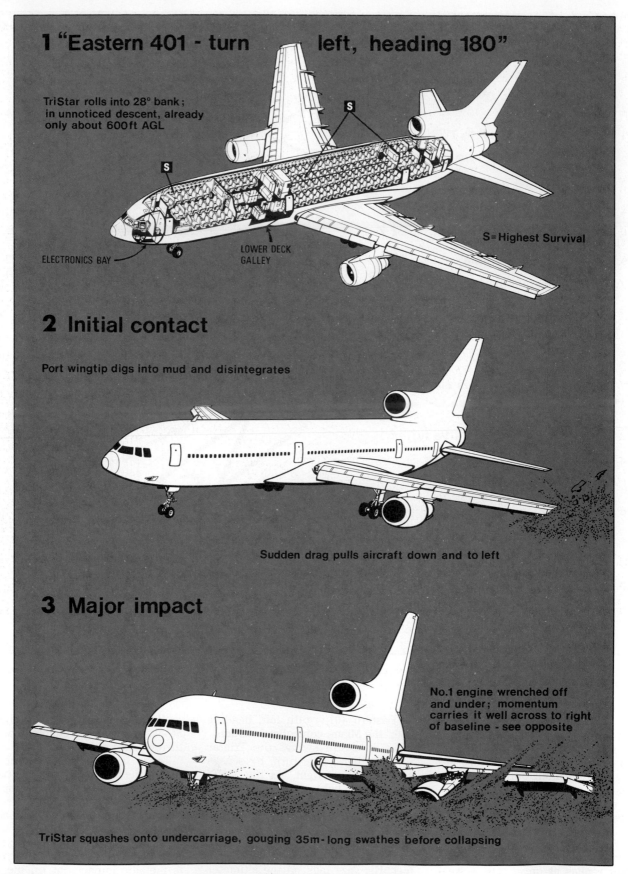

1 "Eastern 401 - turn   left, heading 180"

TriStar rolls into 28° bank;
in unnoticed descent, already
only about 600ft AGL

S

S

ELECTRONICS BAY

LOWER DECK
GALLEY

S=Highest Survival

2 Initial contact

Port wingtip digs into mud and disintegrates

Sudden drag pulls aircraft down and to left

3 Major impact

No.1 engine wrenched off
and under; momentum
carries it well across to right
of baseline - see opposite

TriStar squashes onto undercarriage, gouging 35m-long swathes before collapsing

These six diagrams graphically portray the way in which the Tristar broke up after its port wing first made contact with the mud of the Everglades swampland. The initial cutaway view of the aircraft, depicting its approximate turning attitude just before impact, shows the layout of the cabin in Eastern's 40 first class, 214 economy, configuration. The shaded seat blocks represent the main cabin areas in which passengers and crew survived the impact and breakup forces. Also shown is the avionics bay beneath the flightdeck. The distribution of the wreckage as found by investigators concludes the sequence of drawings. It is interesting to compare this with the aerial photographs taken the following morning (see preceding and following pages). That so little wreckage remained visible can be attributed to inertia forces driving debris into the quicksand like mud of the swamp, with its covering of shallow water and sawgrass up to two metres high. This was borne out by evidence from survivors and rescuers of widespread, jagged, subsurface wreckage. Note also that the tail assembly – rear fuselage, No 2 engine, and remains of the empennage – finally came to rest almost at the end of the wreckage trail, substantially further forward than other major sections. This was probably the result of the No 2 engine continuing to deliver thrust – even if only for seconds – during the actual breakup of the aircraft. (M Tesch)

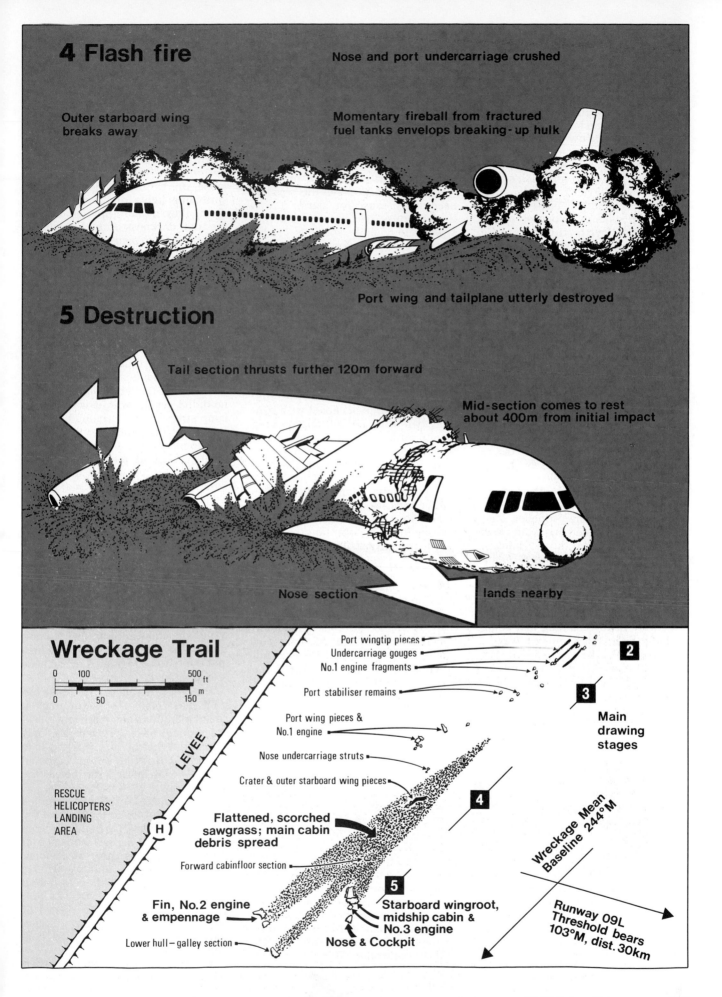

4 Flash fire

Nose and port undercarriage crushed

Outer starboard wing breaks away

Momentary fireball from fractured fuel tanks envelops breaking-up hulk

Port wing and tailplane utterly destroyed

5 Destruction

Tail section thrusts further 120m forward

Mid-section comes to rest about 400m from initial impact

Nose section **lands nearby**

Wreckage Trail

0 100 500 ft
0 50 150 m

LEVEE

RESCUE HELICOPTERS' LANDING AREA

(H)

Port wingtip pieces •
Undercarriage gouges •
No.1 engine fragments •

2

Port stabiliser remains •

3

Main drawing stages

Port wing pieces & No.1 engine •

Nose undercarriage struts •

Crater & outer starboard wing pieces •

4

Flattened, scorched sawgrass; main cabin debris spread

Forward cabinfloor section •

5

Fin, No.2 engine & empennage →

Starboard wingroot, midship cabin & No.3 engine

Lower hull—galley section •

Nose & Cockpit

Wreckage Mean Baseline 244°M

Runway 09L Threshold bears 103°M, dist. 30km

In the pitch dark marshland wilderness of the Everglades, many miles from any habitation, there was only one ground witness to the horrific accident.

Bob Marquis, a former Florida fisheries and wildlife officer, was prowling the marshes in his airboat, a flat bottomed scow powered by an engine driving an air propeller high in its stern. Steered by twin air rudders mounted in the propeller's slipstream, the awkward craft was the only type of vehicle capable of negotiating the swampy expanses of the Everglades, with their prolific growth of sawgrass in water ranging from a few inches to many feet deep. In favourable conditions, airboats like his could skim the marshes at more than 60km an hour.

Marquis was hunting for sulphur-belly frogs, a local delicacy and wore a battery powered lamp on his head to pick his way through the "trails" in the swampland. Tonight he had ventured a long way from the access track where he had left his car and airboat trailer, and was some 20 miles northwest of Miami. But it was getting on for midnight and, with a good quantity of frogs in the flat bottom of his boat, it was almost time to head back.

Sitting up high, just in front of the steel wire cage that provided protection from the flailing propeller, Marquis expertly guided his craft with the lever that moved the air rudders, his foot on the accelerator pedal controlling the engine. Close to the horizon to the north, he could see the lights of a big airliner. There was nothing unusual about that – big aircraft were always coming and going over the Everglades on their way to and from Miami International Airport. But this one did seem low – though it was hard to tell in the dark. It was perhaps five miles away, heading southwest.

Steering the airboat demanded his full attention for a short time and when he looked to the north again the lights of the airliner were nowhere to be seen. Instead, in a moment, there was a brilliant orange flash on the horizon, glowing for about five seconds. Then all went black again.

Unbelievable though it might seem, he realised instantly what it was – the airliner had gone down! Despite his shock, he swung his airboat in that direction and gave the engine its head, pushing the little vessel as hard as he dared through the marshes, the lamp strapped to his head his only illumination.

★   ★   ★

Back at Miami Airport, in the radar control centre below the tower, approach controller Charles Johnson was mystified to see that Flight 401 had disappeared from his radar screen.

A minute before, when he had instructed the Tristar to turn on to a heading of 180 degrees prior to vectoring it back to Miami Airport, his radar screen display had shown the aircraft at a height of only 900 feet instead of 2000. But this was not necessarily cause for alarm: it was the response to only one antenna sweep and could be spurious – radar altitude readout errors were not uncommon. More antenna sweeps were needed to indicate whether the altitude readout was reliable. In any case, the Tristar crew's response on the radio was relaxed and detached. Apparently their undercarriage problem had been solved, for it was hardly a tone of voice to indicate anything wrong. But before he could check the Tristar's altitude readout against more antenna sweeps, Johnson became occupied with handling two other aircraft approaching Miami. And now, 40 seconds later, when he looked at the screen to confirm Flight 401's height, there was no sign of it!

Uncertainly, Johnson keyed his microphone and spoke: "Eastern 401 – are you requesting emergency equipment for your landing?" He meant the airport fire service – did the captain want them to standby the runway while the Tristar landed in case there was any further problem with the noseleg?

There was no immediate reply, but then a Chilean aircraft inbound to Miami called, its transmissions and requirements occupying the next full minute. Finally Johnson called the Tristar again. "Eastern 401, I've lost you on radar – and your transponder. What is your altitude?"

Twelve seconds of silence followed and he was about to try to contact the Tristar again, when another inbound aircraft called: "Miami Approach, this is National 611. We just saw a big flash – looked like it was out west. Don't know what it means, but we wanted to let you know."

The Chilean flight called again immediately afterwards: "Lan Chile 451 – we saw a big flash – a general flash, like some kind of explosion."

At almost the same moment, a private aircraft which had just taken off was calling Miami Tower to report seeing a "tremendous flash". Its pilot told the controller: "It looked like an airplane dived right into the ground."

★   ★   ★

The Coast Guard Air Station at Miami's Opa-Locka Airport received word of the appalling accident by telephone at 11.45pm. The position of the Tristar when it disappeared from the radar screen was given as 18 miles west northwest of Miami International Airport.

Within minutes, two Coast Guard helicopters based at Opa-Locka were on their way. Leaving the sprawling lights of the city behind them, they quickly pressed on into the total darkness of the Everglades, a featureless expanse on such a dark night that stretched to the barely discernable horizon.

By 12.10am the first helicopter, flown by Lieutenant M McCormack, was in the area of the crash, sweeping the swamp with his aircraft's powerful "Nightsun" floodlamp from a height of 500 feet. He could sight nothing for a time, but then, some distance away, he was able to make out a faint, flickering light. Though he didn't yet know it, it was the tiny lamp strapped to Marquis's head.

Turning his helicopter towards it, his floodlight soon began to reveal small pieces of aircraft wreckage, widely scattered across the marshland, then finally three major sections, the biggest of them obviously the tail assembly of the Tristar. It was lying on its port side, still with the No 2 engine in position. The other two major pieces of wreckage were harder to recognise, such was the extent of the damage they had sustained. A further look as the helicopter hovered showed them to be the centre section of the fuselage, minus the cabin roof, but with a portion of the starboard wing attached, and the battered remains of the nose and flightdeck.

The destruction of the huge aircraft was total – to McCormack it seemed impossible than any occupants could have survived. The only sign of life below him was the man with the little light, whom he could now see was in an airboat near the wreckage.

Then, as McCormack descended for a closer look and the glare of the helicopter's powerful floodlight continued to move across the scene of desolation, to his utter amazement he saw people – small pathetic groups of them, dishevelled and mud-covered, some near-naked, clustered near the main pieces of wreckage. Some of them were painfully waving their arms at the helicopter.

McCormack descended further, seeking amongst the flooded swampland ground solid enough to set the helicopter down near the wreckage. But the rotor wash began picking up small fragments of wreckage, flinging them about dangerously. The man in the boat desperately waved him off, and after several more thwarted attempts, McCormack had to settle for landing on a flood control levee bank, nearly 200 metres away.

The airboat skimmed across the swamp to meet him and its driver introduced himself as Marquis. Breathlessly he told McCormack there were many injured survivors lying amongst the sawgrass in the shallow water, some still strapped to their seats. All it seemed were soaked in kerosene from the Tristar's ruptured fuel tanks, and there was the risk of fire. Some survivors, in danger of drowning because they were face down and unable to move, he had freed and moved on to sections of wreckage out of the water. But there were many others still call-

ing out for help in the darkness whom he had not yet been able to reach. The task of finding and rescuing them in time seemed overwhelming. There were many dead too, some of whom had drowned after the crash because they could not keep their heads above water.

Quickly McCormack and Marquis devised a temporary plan. Using his airboat, Marquis would continue to help as many survivors as he could, moving them to flat sections of wreckage where they could lie in relative safety until rescued. McCormack, after radioing for ambulances and rescue vehicles to drive out to the crash site along the rutted, single lane dirt track that ran for some 13km along the top of the levee bank, would seek to make a landing on firm ground as close as possible to the wreckage and ferry out as many casualties as the helicopter could carry.

Soon another Coast Guard helicopter, carrying a crew of three

joined them in the rescue operation. After helping other victims, they found the flightcrew still in the broken off nose section. First Officer Stockstill had been killed in the impact, and Captain Loft and Flight Engineer Repo badly injured. Donadeo, the L-1011 technical officer, was less seriously injured.

As the rescue work continued throughout the early hours of the morning, difficult, dangerous and agonisingly slow in the darkness and treacherous mud, other helicopters and their crews arrived, swelling the team effort and operating shuttle services to Miami with loads of survivors for admission to the city's hospitals.

More airboats soon arrived to assist, and so did the emergency road vehicles, having finally succeeded in making their way slowly and precariously out along the 13km levee bank. Under an unspoken arrangement, the dead were left for the time being, so as to give priority to find-

Another view of the wreckage, taken from a helicopter on the morning after the accident. The initial impact point is out of the picture, some 400 metres to the right. The tail section, together with the tail-mounted No 2 engine, lies at the extreme left. The battered, broken off nose and flightdeck can be seen at the bottom right, with the remains of the fuselage centre section and starboard wing directly above it. The round object nearby is an undamaged, fully inflated rubber dinghy, one of a number carried on the Tristar. The breakup of the fuselage freed it from its stowage and triggered its inflation.

ing and rescuing survivors. By the time first light was brightening the eastern horizon, all the living, mud encrusted, bloody, many of them crying out in pain, had been located and flown to hospital, and it remained only to account for the silent dead.

The coming of daylight that Saturday morning revealed the extent of the desolation. From where the Tristar's port wingtip had first gouged into the swamp, a trail of fragmented wreckage extended for almost 500 metres in a southwesterly direction. Only small fragments of metal marked the wingtip's first contact, followed 15 metres further on by three massive 35 metre swaths cut through the mud and sawgrass by the aircraft's extended undercarriage before two of the legs were sheared off. Then came scattered parts from the No 1 (port) engine, and fragments from the port wing itself and the port tailplane. One hundred and fifty metres from the wingtip mark, the massive fuselage had begun to break up, scattering components from the underfloor galley, the cargo compartments, and the cabin interior. At 250 metres along the wreckage trail, the outer section of the starboard wing tore off, gouging an 18 metre long crater in the soft ground as it did so.

From this point on, the breakup of the fuselage became more extensive, scattering metal fragments, cabin fittings, and passenger seats widely. The three major sections of the fuselage, the most intact of which was the tail assembly, lay in the mud towards the end of the wreckage trail.

Incongruously, not far from the roofless fuselage centre section with the inner portion of the starboard wing still attached, lay a large, undamaged and fully inflated rubber dinghy, one of a number carried on the Tristar. The breakup of the fuselage had obviously freed it from its stowage and activated its inflation mechanism.

Viewing the full extent of the Tristar's destruction, it seemed no less than miraculous that *any* of the 176 occupants could have survived. In fact, when a tally of survivors was finally completed, a task not made easier by the fact that they had been admitted to a number of major hospitals, it was found that 77 had lived through the ordeal, though 60 of them had serious injuries. Incredibly, 17 suffered only minor injuries.

The survivors included eight of the Tristar's 10 flight attendants, and technical officer Donadeo who was down in the nose electronics bay with Flight Engineer Repo at the moment of impact. Repo was also evacuated to hospital, but later succumbed to his injuries. Captain Loft had died in the wreckage of the flightdeck before he could be moved to hospital.

★   ★   ★

News of the accident, the first in the world involving a so-called "jumbo" jet, was flashed around the globe, raising contradictory questions about the much vaunted safety of the new generation of widebody commercial airliners.

Crews of helicopters reported that the aircraft's three undercarriage legs had left deep tracks through the soft mud of the swamp. Other reports that the Tristar was in a normal flying attitude at the time of impact were reinforced by the condition of the aircraft's nose radar dome, which did not appear to have suffered major damage.

Prior to the crash there had been no radio communication from the crew indicating that any serious problem was developing. Indeed, the tone of the captain's final transmission suggested the situation on the flightdeck was entirely under control. It was completely mystifying that the veteran crew had no warning of the disaster that obviously overtook their highly sophisticated aircraft in a moment of time.

On the other hand, the fact that almost half those on board had lived through what, by all previous airline accident experience, could only be classified as a non survivable accident, offered hope that the very scale of widebodied jet construction provided additional protection against fatal injuries in this type of accident.

The Chairman of the US National Transportation Safety Board, J H

An air safety investigator from the US National Transportation Safety Board surveys the remains of the Tristar's underfloor galley area. The stewardesses who were on duty in the galley during the flight from New York had returned to the passenger cabin before the aircraft crashed, and survived the accident.

Reed, arriving in Miami from Washington DC to face the formidable task of overseeing the investigation of the bewildering disaster, told the press: "It's been felt that the wide-bodied jets had higher survivor features, but unfortunately we had to have an accident to demonstrate it."

The shallow angle of the aircraft's impact, the soft mud of the Everglades swamps, and the large cargo compartments beneath the Tristar's passenger deck had apparently all played their part in contributing to the relatively high survival rate for such a catastrophic aircraft breakup.

By dawn on the Sunday morning, only 30 hours after the crash, a 10 member team of investigators from the National Transportation Safety Board had arrived at the accident site to begin their search for clues. They found the terrain in the impact area to be flat marshland, covered with soft mud under some nine inches (20cms) of water. The elevation of the site was only eight feet above sea level.

The port outer wing structure had struck the ground first, followed by the No 1 engine and the port main undercarriage. The disintegration of the aircraft that followed scattered wreckage over an area 500 metres long and 100 metres wide. No complete cross section of the passenger cabin remained, and both the port wing and tailplane were demolished to fragments. There was no evidence of inflight structural failure, fire, or explosion, and one of the investigators' first successes was the recovery of both the Flight Data Recorder and the Cockpit Voice Recorder from the wreckage.

The extensive breakup of the aircraft structure precluded any physical determination of the integrity of the primary control system before impact. However, the flap lever on the flightdeck was found set at 18 degrees, and the position of the flap jackscrew on the remains of the starboard wing corresponded with this setting. The leading edge slats on the intact portion of the starboard wing were fully extended.

The undercarriage lever on the first officer's side of the flightdeck was in the "down" position. Below it on the instrument panel, the nose undercarriage position indicator lens assembly was found jammed 90 degrees in a clockwise direction from its normal position, and was protruding about six cm. The reason for the failure of the nose undercarriage "down" light to illuminate when the crew lowered the Tristar's undercarriage for landing was now plain to see – the filaments of both its light bulbs had simply burnt out.

The nose and port undercarriage legs had separated from the aircraft as it broke up and both were badly damaged, but the starboard main undercarriage leg, which was still attached to the intact portion of the starboard wing, was in the down and locked position.

The Flight Data Recorder fitted to the Tristar was a new type of Lockheed expandable digital unit, which on this aircraft was programmed to simultaneously record 62 performance parameters. Its successful readout provided a comprehensive and detailed history of the flight and the crew's use of the autopilot and autothrottle systems. The Tristar's Fairchild Cockpit Voice Recorder was also found to be intact and an accurate transcription was made of the voices and sounds on the flightdeck from just before the time of the crew's initial call to Miami Tower.

It was obvious as the investigation progressed that none of the Tristar's flight controls, engines, instruments, or its electrical and hydraulic systems, were factors contributing to the accident, and that the aircraft was flying normally in every way up to the moment the port wingtip gouged into the Everglades mud. Further investigation was therefore focused on the reasons for the aircraft's totally unexpected descent from its holding altitude of 2000 feet. At least three areas immediately suggested themselves for examination:
• Subtle incapacitation of the pilot flying the aircraft at the time.
• A failure in the aircraft's autopilot system.
• Distraction of the crew from adequately monitoring the flight instruments.

Subtle incapacitation had to be included because of the finding, during the postmortem examination of the flight crew's bodies, of a tumour in the captain's cranial cavity which could have affected his peripheral vision. With severely impaired peripheral vision, the captain might not have detected movements in the airspeed and vertical speed indicator needles while he watched the first officer work on the faulty undercarriage indicator lamp assembly.

However, the captain's family, close friends, and company colleagues were all of the opinion that he had shown no sign of visual difficulty in any activity dependent upon peripheral vision. For this reason the investigators concluded that the tumour could not be a factor in the events leading to the accident.

In considering what part, if any, the autopilot could have played in the accident, the investigators noted that the first officer flew the missed

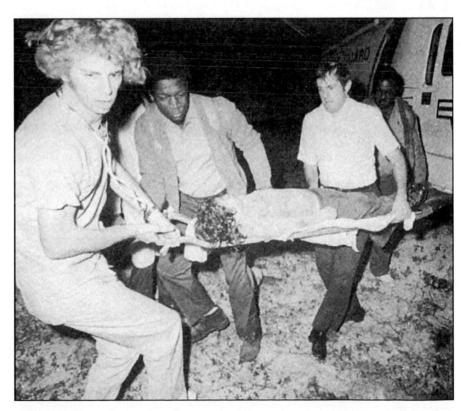

A 10 year old boy, rescued from the wreckage of the Tristar, is carried from a helicopter after being airlifted from the Everglades crash site.

approach at Miami Airport manually, then continued to control the aircraft until just after 11.36pm when the captain ordered him to engage the autopilot. The FDR readout confirmed that he did so at this time, selecting either the "Altitude Hold" or the "Control Wheel Steering" mode. He did not however engage the aircraft's autothrottle system. After the accident, the figure of 2000 feet was found in the "altitude select" window of the autopilot controls.

The advanced autopilot installation in the Tristar – the Lockheed-developed Avionic Flight Control System (AFCS) – comprises two autopilots (one each for captain and first officer), controlled by four major subsystems: autopilot flight director, yaw stability augmentation, speed control, and flight control electronics. The autopilot flight director which provides pitch and steering commands, has two roll and pitch computers, the "A" computer relating to the autopilot on the captain's side and the "B" computer to the first officer's autopilot.

The two autopilots cannot be operated simultaneously except when the AFCS is in the "autoland" mode, when they provide the necessary backup against system failure at critically low altitudes. The modes and functions selected on the AFCS are displayed by warning and annunciator lights located on the glareshield in front of both the captain and first officer, as are the levers and switches for the system.

The basic mode of autopilot operation is Control Wheel Steering (CWS), which provides aircraft attitude stabilisation with attitude changes made possible by the application of light forces to either control wheel by captain or first officer.

The Command mode of autopilot operation provides total control of the aircraft in accordance with selected heading, pitch, or navigational system inputs. Although the system's Altitude Hold mode is a command function, it may also be engaged when the autopilot is selected to CWS. In this mode the autopilot provides pitch inputs to maintain the aircraft altitude at the time of engagement.

While functioning in any mode, the heading or pitch selection may be disengaged by applying a 15 pound (7kg) force to either control wheel. If the force is applied to the aircraft's roll axis when the autopilot is selected to Command, the autopilot engagement lever will revert to the CWS position. If the control wheel force is applied to the pitch axis, only the pitch control system will be

affected, reverting to the basic attitude stabilisation mode.

In this case however, the autopilot engagement lever will remain in the previously selected position – either CWS or Command. In this way it is possible to disengage Altitude Hold without an accompanying "CMD DISC" (Command Disconnected) warning appearing on the pilots' annunciator panels. The disengagement would be indicated only by the extinguishing of the altitude mode light on the glareshield, and the disappearance of "ALT" on both annunciator panels.

During the investigation, it was found that the two pitch control computers fitted to the aircraft were mismatched. The control wheel force required to disengage the Altitude Hold function in computer A on the captain's side was the correct 15 pounds, but for computer B it was no less than 20 pounds. It was thus possible, with the captain's autopilot engaged, to disengage the A computer but not the B computer. In this situation, the altitude mode light would remain on, while the "ALT" annunciator on the captain's panel would go out. Misleadingly however, the ALT annunciator would remain illuminated on the first officer's annunciator panel, giving the first officer the false impression that the autopilot was still in the Altitude Hold mode.

Which of the two autopilots was actually engaged at the time of the accident could not be determined, but the FDR readout showed that at 11.37pm, there was a momentary negative vertical acceleration, resulting in a 200 feet per minute descent for about 30 seconds. Because the timing of this negative vertical acceleration transient coincided with the captain telling the flight engineer to "get down there and see if that damn nosewheel is down", it could quite conceivably have been the result of the captain inadvertently pushing lightly on his control wheel as he turned around to speak to the flight engineer. In doing so, he would have unknowingly disengaged the autopilot's Altitude Hold function, allowing the aircraft to gradually lose height.

The Cockpit Voice Recorder revealed that three minutes after this Altitude Hold disconnection, a half-second C-chord chime, indicating that the aircraft had deviated 250 feet from the selected altitude, sounded on the flightdeck. The chime came from the speaker located on the flight engineer's panel. But at this critical stage Flight Engineer Repo had already gone down

the ladder into the electronics bay to check the position of the nose undercarriage, and both pilots were wearing headsets. The result was that no member of the flightcrew actually heard the warning chime.

But regardless of the way in which the status of the autopilot system was being indicated to the pilots at the time, or the manner in which the Altitude Hold mode was disengaged, the fact that the Tristar was gradually descending should have been evident to the crew from both the captain's and the first officer's altimeters.

Wider inquiries in the airline industry indicated to the investigators that generally, with the new, advanced automatic flight control systems coming into use, flightcrews were relying more and more on sophisticated computerised avionics to fly their aircraft, particularly as the reliability of this new equipment increased. Pilot evidence indicated that dependence on the new autopilots was greater than anticipated when this equipment was being developed, particularly in the cruise phase of flight.

Although formal training on this equipment provided adequate opportunity for crews to become familiar with the new concept of aircraft control, actual in-service operational experience with the new autopilots and their capabilities was often limited by company policy.

For example, Eastern Air Lines' company procedures did not permit the flying of their aircraft in CWS mode, but required all operations to be conducted in the Command mode. The investigators considered it possible that this restrictive policy could have compromised pilots' ability to use and fully understand the unique CWS feature of the Lockheed system. In the case of the crew involved in the accident, it was apparent from the FDR readout that the pilots were not aware of the low control wheel forces required to effect a change in aircraft attitude while in CWS mode.

Further inquiries showed that this lack of knowledge about the capabilities of the new Lockheed autopilot was not limited to the crew of the Tristar involved in the accident.

The investigators also believed that an added crew distraction contributing to the development of the accident, was the flight engineer's unsuccessful attempt to ascertain if the nose undercarriage had extended, after he climbed down into the electronics bay. He was unable to resolve the matter simply because the nosewheel well light had not been turned on and he could not see.

Although the pilots evidently believed the wheel well light was on whenever the undercarriage was down, this was not so. The switch for the wheel well light was in fact on the captain's "eyebrow" panel above the windscreen and had to be turned on manually. It could not be determined if the captain ever turned on the light.

It was obvious to the investigators that the disaster which overtook the Tristar, like so many other major accidents, was not the final result of a single error on the part of the crew, but was the consequence of the sum of several minor distractions from normal operating procedures. Such distractions on their own would not normally affect an aircraft's safety because of their short duration and their integration into the crew's overall task. But in this case their juxtaposition was such as to trigger a disastrous sequence of events:

• The crew's approach procedures were interrupted by an abnormal undercarriage indication.

• Although the aircraft was flown to a safe height and the autopilot engaged, positive responsibility for control of the aircraft was not delegated.

• The first officer became preoccupied with his attempts to deal with the jammed undercarriage position lamp assembly.

• The captain divided his attention between helping the first officer and directions to the flight engineer.

• The crew devoted some four minutes to the distraction, with minimal regard for monitoring the aircraft's flight situation.

There was one other aspect of the accident which merited examination by the National Transportation Safety Board investigators.

Just after 11.40pm, only 42 seconds before the accident, when the Miami approach controller called the Tristar to ask: "How are things coming along out there?", the altitude readout on the controller's radar screen had indicated 900 feet instead of the 2000 feet to which the aircraft had been cleared. Indeed it was this reading which prompted the approach controller to call the aircraft.

Even though the immediate response from the Tristar was obviously untroubled, assuring the controller the aircraft was in no apparent danger, he nevertheless intended to query the Tristar crew on their altitude as soon as he was satisfied it was not a spurious reading. In the event however, he became occupied with other inbound aircraft before he could do so. And when he again turned his attention to the Tristar, its radar image had disappeared from his screen.

The investigators had to consider: Could more timely action by the controller at this point have prevented the accident? Certainly the air traffic control radar system in use was not designed to provide terrain clearance information and there were no procedures requiring controllers to provide such a service. Even so, the National Transportation Safety Board believed there was an inherent responsibility in the overall air traffic control system to alert aircraft crews to any apparently hazardous situation.

The Board concluded its report on the Tristar accident with several recommendations:

• The system for optically viewing the nose leg from the underfloor electronics bay in an emergency should be capable of operation by one crew member only. In other words, the switch for the wheel well light should be located in the electronics bay near the noseleg optical viewing sight, and should be placarded accordingly.

• In addition to the Tristar's aural C-chord warning that the aircraft has deviated plus or minus 250 feet from its selected altitude, the crew should be provided with a flashing amber warning light, to operate continuously until the deviation is corrected.

• Provide for the stowage of portable, high intensity lights at every flight attendant station on the aircraft. This recommendation was prompted by the fact that the total darkness after the accident had seriously hampered survivors' efforts to help themselves or to assist the injured. It had also prevented cabin attendants from taking effective charge of surviving passengers.

On reflection, the fate of Lockheed L-1011 Tristar N310EA seemed all the more tragic because the root cause of the accident could so easily have been avoided. Despite the superb technology incorporated into the magnificent aircraft and its engines, despite its advanced, highly sophisticated, automatic flight control system, it became the victim of a human error as old as the aviation industry itself – inattention to the basic task of safe terrain clearance.

The omission was one that might be expected in an elementary type of aircraft flown by a single, perhaps inexperienced pilot. That it could also occur in a state-of-the-art widebodied jet, carrying nearly 200 people and flown by one of the profession's most experienced crews, was a sobering thought indeed for the airline industry the world over.

A child's mud-encrusted doll, found with other passengers' personal belongings amongst the wreckage of the Tristar. Of the 176 occupants of the aircraft, 77 miraculously survived, despite the total destruction of the fuselage.

CHAPTER 13

"If you pull the N1 tach – will that autothrottle respond ...?"

– DC-10 flight engineer to captain

National Airlines McDonnell Douglas DC-10-10 N6ONA [46700]
Barbara (later *Suzanne*) – November 3, 1973

The profession of airline captaincy is not simply the ability to fly and command a large aeroplane with skill, precision and verve. It also involves self imposed discipline as a way of life, an ongoing resolve – year in, year out – to operate at all times and in all circumstances within defined parameters of safety and aircraft performance.

National Airlines' DC-10 N60NA, the first of 16 of the three engined, wide-bodied type to be delivered to the company, was just two years and two days old on November 3, 1973, the day on which it was scheduled to operate National's Flight 27 from Miami, Florida, to San Francisco, California. The flight was not a direct one, but included en route ports of call at New Orleans, Houston, and Las Vegas.

In command was Captain William Brookes, a highly experienced senior pilot who had been with National Airlines since 1946. His impressive record included ratings on piston-engined Lockheed Lodestars, Curtiss Commandos, Convair 340s and 440s, Douglas DC-6s and DC-7s, turboprop Lockheed Electras, and Boeing 727 jets. He had progressed to DC-10 command 18 months previously and, at the age of 54, had accumulated a total of nearly 22,000 hours' flying.

Captain Brookes' flight crew also had impressive experience. First Officer E H Saunders, 33, had been with the company for eight years, had more than 7000 hours as a pilot, and had completed his DC-10 training more than a year before. Flight

Engineer G W Hanks' experience rivalled that of the captain – 23 years with National Airlines, nearly 18,000 hours total time, and more than 1200 hours on the DC-10.

The routine trip to New Orleans, Louisiana, then on to Houston, Texas, was normal in every way – an everyday, incident free airline flight in fine, moderately cloudy weather under the influence a high pressure system, with a prevailing wind from the northwest – with the DC-10 performing faultlessly.

At 2.40pm local time, the DC-10 took off again from Houston for the next leg of the flight, the long haul to Las Vegas, Nevada, expected to take two hours 50 minutes. For the nine flight attendants on duty in the cabin and the lower deck galley, it promised to be a relatively easy stage – with only 116 of the DC-10's 249 passenger seats filled, the big aircraft was less than half full and, at this time of the day, there were no major meals to be served.

Cleared after departure from Houston to Flight Level 390 (39,000 feet), the crew engaged the autopilot and autothrottle systems for the climb. When the DC-10 had levelled itself out and its cruising speed had stabi-

lised at Mach .82 (257 knots indicated airspeed), the pilots disengaged the autothrottle and the flight engineer reset the power manually to maintain the speed setting. The flight then continued uneventfully at FL 390.

Some two hours later, when the DC-10 was in the vicinity of Socorro, New Mexico, First Officer Saunders left the flightdeck for a routine visit to the passenger cabin. In his absence, the captain and his veteran flight engineer fell to discussing the operation of the DC-10's autothrottle system, speculating on the source from which the system derived the electronic inputs needed to control the engine throttle settings in the various autothrottle modes.

The McDonnell Douglas DC-10 is equipped with two independent autothrottle systems, but only when operating in the autoland mode are both systems engaged simultaneously – to provide the degree of redundancy required for a fully auto-pilot controlled approach to land. In all other phases of flight, the two autothrottle systems – one for each of the two pilot positions – are engaged separately. Each of them has the same function – the capability to

National Airlines DC-10 N6ONA, the actual aircraft on which the No 3 (starboard) engine disintegrated in flight. This company photograph of N6ONA in cruising flight was taken for publicity purposes when the type was introduced to National's routes two years before the accident.

automatically position the aircraft's throttles to maintain either a selected airspeed, or a level of engine thrust based on the engines' low pressure compressor RPM – usually referred to as N1.

Either autothrottle system may be engaged by the pilots and the desired operating mode – airspeed or N1 – selected on the corresponding autothrottle control panel on the pilots' glareshield. When using the airspeed mode, the required airspeed is also selected at the same time, using a control knob on the autothrottle control panel. The speed selected is displayed in a "window" on the autothrottle control panel, and also on an internal "speed bug" on the pilot's airspeed indicator.

After some discussion with Captain Brookes, Flight Engineer Hanks wondered aloud how the autothrottle would respond if the circuit breakers for the N1 tachometers were pulled. Brookes admitted he did not know, but agreed to the flight engineer's suggestion that they try it to see what happened. Mounted on the flightdeck's overhead emergency circuit breaker panel, the N1 tachometer circuit breakers are readily accessible to all three flight crew members.

Brookes therefore re-engaged the autothrottle system in the airspeed mode and selected an autothrottle command speed of 257 knots. After allowing about 10 seconds for the aircraft's speed to stabilise at this figure under autothrottle control, Hanks reached up from his engineer's seat and pulled the N1 tachometer circuit breakers for the No 1, 2, and 3 engines in succession.

The disconnection did not appear to affect the throttle setting at all, convincing Brookes and Hanks that the input for controlling the autothrottle system came from some point other than the N1 tachometers. But to further examine the way the system responded, Brookes then reduced the selected autothrottle speed by about five knots, using the speed bug on his airspeed indicator for reference. He was interested to see that the throttles retarded slightly under this effect. "There it is," he remarked to Hanks with satisfaction.

At this point the captain disengaged the autothrottle system again,

intending to adjust the engine power manually, while Hanks again reached up and reset the N1 circuit breakers. Shortly after he did so there was a loud explosion from the starboard side of the aircraft, and a violent vibration with severe buffetting, accompanied by frightening ratcheting noise, shook the whole aircraft.

"Hell – what was that?" Brookes called to Hanks, his eyes wide with apprehension.

Back in the passenger cabin, all had been serene. The flight from Houston was long and rather boring, but the weather was good and flying

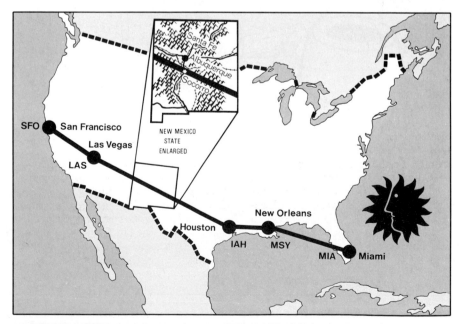

Transcontinental route followed by National Airlines' Flight 27 from Miami, Florida, to San Francisco, California. The inset shows the Socorro-Albuquerque area of south west New Mexico where the accident occurred. (Matthew Tesch)

conditions smooth and comfortable. It was now getting on towards late afternoon, and only another 40 minutes should see them touching down at Las Vegas.

Many of the passengers, utterly relaxed after having been served a pleasant mid afternoon snack by the attentive cabin crew, were now dozing in their chairs; others were reading. Still others, the monotony of their long flight now broken by the light meal, were chatting animatedly again.

In the forward part of the economy section of the cabin on the starboard side, not far behind the first class section bulkhead, Mr G F Gardner was relaxing back in his chair. He was from Beaumont in Texas, and had boarded the flight at Houston. Although he had a window seat for the flight to Las Vegas, there was not a great deal to be seen from his window — sitting in seat 17H, his view downwards was largely restricted by the leading edge of the wing and the huge cowling of the aircraft's starboard underwing engine.

Accepting the sound advice proffered by the captain over the cabin PA system earlier in the flight, he kept his seat belt fastened, but had slackened it several inches to make himself more comfortable.

Around 4.40pm, without any warning, all on board were abruptly jolted out of their reveries by a frightening explosion. It seemed to come from the starboard side and in the same instant a severe buffetting began, shaking the whole aircraft alarmingly. A few seconds later there was a series of rapid, loud bangs against the starboard side of the fuselage.

In the forward section of the economy cabin, the effect was dramatic, something hitting the window alongside the dozing Mr Gardner in seat 17H with a violent impact. The outer window panel splintered and in a moment both outer and inner transparent panels of the window blew out explosively, the noise of the report this time loud in the cabin itself. An enormously powerful rushing of air followed as the entire pressure hull, still buffetting and vibrating, began to depressurise through the windowless aperture.

In another moment, to the traumatised disbelief of all sitting nearby, the hapless Mr Gardner was sucked bodily, head and shoulders first, into the gaping window cutout beside him. He was held there, half in and half outside the aircraft, by his slackened seat belt, as the horrified passenger in the next seat, himself struggling against the powerful blast of the cabin decompression, desperately

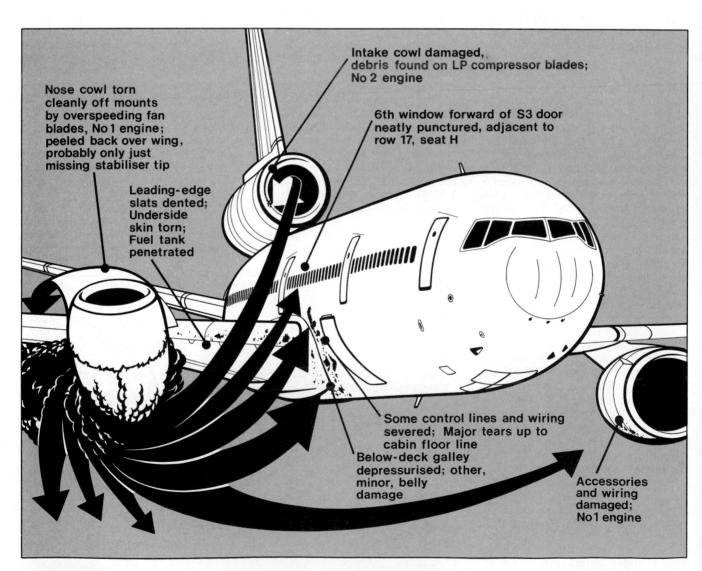

Damage inflicted when the first stage fan of the No 3 engine disintegrated. The unleashed fan blades, flung from the fan disk by enormous centrifugal force, removed the inlet cowl in its entirety, severed electrical wiring, hydraulic lines and control cables, and punctured the upper and lower decks of the pressure cabin. A passenger seated by a cabin window in the plane of the fan's rotation was sucked bodily from the cabin when the window was struck by blade fragments and blew out. Flying debris also struck the No 1 (port side) engine, and was ingested into the air intake of the No 2 (tail mounted) engine. (Matthew Tesch)

Close up of the DC-10's damaged No 3 engine, photographed after the aircraft was hangared for examination at Albuquerque. Only six of the first stage fan's 38 blades remain attached to the fan disk (visible in the 6 and 8 o'clock positions).

Meanwhile on the flightdeck, the flight engineer saw that the fire warning light in the No 3 engine fuel shutoff handle had come on. Attempting to pull the handle, he found it would not move. After several unsuccessful attempts, he pulled the No 3 engine firewall shutoff handle instead and discharged two fire extinguisher bottles into the No 3 engine. Realising also that the cabin was depressurising, he closed the cabin outflow valve and activated the manual release switch for the passengers' oxygen masks.

While Hanks was doing this, First Officer Saunders hurried back to the flightdeck and took his seat, and the pilots began an emergency descent. Radio communications with Air Traffic Control appeared to have failed, but Saunders dialled the emergency code on the aircraft's transponder to alert the Albuquerque Air Route Centre, the ATC unit handling the DC-10 at that stage of the flight.

Warning lights on the engineer's instrument panel now indicated that the No 3 generator (on the starboard engine) had failed, as had both the AC and DC electrical circuits from the No 3 engine. The generator on the No 1 (port side) engine was also showing symptoms of failure, while the oil pressure and hydraulic contents gauges for this port side engine were both giving abnormally low indications.

At 4.45pm, about five minutes after the engine explosion, with electrical power successfully restored to all flightdeck systems, Saunders reestablished contact with Albuquerque Approach Control and the DC-10 was cleared to descend to 8000 feet. Albuquerque, only 60nm north north east of the aircraft's position, offered the nearest major airport suitable for an emergency landing.

In the passenger cabin, the flight attendants, despite the smoke filling the cabin, were now moving among the passengers to assist them with their oxygen masks. Not all the masks had deployed at once and in some sections of the cabin there was a delay ranging from a few seconds to up to three minutes before the masks dropped. In the port side rear cabin, the oxygen masks failed to deploy at all. In this section passengers had either to prise the oxygen compartment doors open themselves, or move to vacant seats in another part of the cabin where oxygen masks were available.

Some passengers obviously did not know how to use the oxygen masks. Some, having removed their mask from its compartment, leant

tried to pull him back. It was like trying to rescue a swimmer from a powerful whirlpool – the forces drawing him were just too great to overcome. Within seconds Gardner's body had slipped completely through the slackened seat belt and in another instant he was gone. There was nothing the awestruck passengers nearby could do.

Further back in the cabin the sudden decompression was filling the aircraft with irritating blue-grey smoke and passenger oxygen masks began deploying from their overhead compartments. In the lower deck galley, the two stewardesses on duty there were sitting in the jump seats when they heard the explosion. Moments later, as the whole aircraft began vibrating severely,

there were loud impacts against the lower starboard side of the fuselage, apparently just beyond the aft wall of the galley. Almost immediately there was a powerful surge of air in the galley, picking up napkins and potholders and drawing them rapidly through the air towards the rear of the compartment. The doors to the storage and serving trolley compartments were pulled open and some of the trolleys drawn into the galley itself.

Realising the pressure hull was depressurising fast, and seeing their overhead oxygen compartments had failed to deploy the masks, the women stood up to go to the portable oxygen equipment stored in the galley. Both lost consciousness before they could reach it.

forward to put it on, rather than pulling the mask towards them. This failed to pull the lanyard activating the oxygen supply, so none was provided. Other passengers stopped trying to use the masks after a short time, either because they could not determine if oxygen was flowing, or because the mask's reservoir bag did not inflate, leading them to believe the equipment was faulty. In three cases, the passengers drew the masks down with such vigour that the oxygen generating cylinders were pulled from their mountings and fell onto the seats, the high temperature chemically generated in the cylinders by the oxygen producing process severely scorching the seat upholstery and creating a danger of fire in the cabin.

The cabin crew also helped to prepare the passengers for an emergency landing, instructing them how to brace themselves when the time came. Down in the lower deck galley, the two stewardesses on duty there regained consciousness of their own accord as the DC-10 descended, and one of them returned to the main cabin via the serving trolley lift.

As the DC-10 continued to descend, Albuquerque Approach Control provided the pilots with vectors for an approach to Runway 26 at Albuquerque International Airport. The airport emergency services were called out to stand by the runway for the DC-10's landing.

Throughout the aircraft's descent and approach on the port and rear engines only, the port engine's oil pressure and hydraulic contents continued to deteriorate, but the operation of the engine and its systems seemed unaffected. The wing leading edge slats and the flaps extended normally when selected, but the undercarriage failed to do so and the flight crew had to lower it using the emergency extension system. Finally at 4.59pm, almost 20 minutes after the onset of the inflight emergency, the DC-10 touched down safely.

Captain Brookes decided to take no more chances, and that the passengers and crew would leave the aircraft immediately via the emergency evacuation equipment. As soon as the DC-10 braked to a stop on the runway therefore, the cabin crew opened the doors and deployed the inflatable escape slides. The slide for the port side forward door was accidentally jettisoned from its door sill, while that for the starboard overwing exit extended uselessly across the top of the wing,

Another view of the damaged No 3 engine. Major punctures caused by flying fan blade fragments can be seen on the side of the fuselage ahead of the leading edge of the wing, and on the still extended wing slat. Despite potentially grave damage to the aircraft's systems, the DC-10 was able to make a safe landing at Albuquerque only 20 minutes after the onset of its problems.

but all the other six slides inflated correctly and the entire evacuation was successfully completed in about 60 seconds.

Only at this point did the cabin and flight crew learn that one passenger had been ejected from the aircraft in flight. They also saw that the massive inlet cowl for the No 3 (starboard) engine was missing, together with the spinner cone, having obviously been torn off in flight.

Twenty passengers and four of the cabin attendants were later examined at the military hospital at the nearby Kirtland Air Force Base. Ten people were treated for hypoxia and decompression sickness, 10 for smoke inhalation, and two for abrasions suffered during the hurried evacuation. The remaining two required no treatment.

Examination of the DC-10 after it had been towed to a maintenance facility at Albuquerque airport, showed that the first stage fan assembly for the No 3 (starboard) engine had disintegrated in flight, carrying away the inlet cowl in its entirety, the spinner cone and all but six of first stage fan blades. A portion of the porous material from the missing inlet cowl's acoustic panels was found jammed against the fan outlet guide vanes. In addition to the inlet cowl, spinner cone and 32 of the 38 first stage fan blades, the fan blade containment ring was missing.

The remaining eight first stage fan blades were all badly damaged. The engine's No 2 and No 3 main bearings had disintegrated, and the N1 shaft which carries the first stage fan assembly had a spiral fracture near its forward end. It was also bent slightly in the area of the crack. Wiring in the No 3 engine nacelle had been torn loose from the AC generator.

In addition to losing the cabin window directly in line with the No 3 engine fan assembly, the aircraft's structure had suffered other serious damage inflicted by the disintegrating fan blades. There were numerous tears and punctures in the lower fuselage, some of them quite major, ranging in size from 540 to 170 square inches (3250 to 1062 square centimetres). Smaller punctures and skin damage were found along the inboard leading edge of the starboard wing and fuselage fillet area. One puncture on the underside of the wing extended into the inboard fuel tank.

The DC-10's No 1 (port) engine had also been struck by fragments from the No 3 engine's fan assembly. Portions of one fan blade had punctured the engine oil tank, and the electrical wiring from the No 1 generator's constant speed drive was severed.

Examination of the No 2 (tail mounted) engine showed that it too had been struck by small fragments from the No 3 engine. A small piece of fan blade was embedded in the forward section of the inlet cowl, and two of the No 2 engine fan blades had sustained damage to their leading edges. Borescope examination of the interior of the engine revealed that three compressor blades had sustained small nicks from ingested fragments.

Internal examination of the affected areas of the aircraft's structure revealed potentially very serious damage. The "up" control cables for the starboard elevator had been severed, as had the "nose left" cables for the rudder trim. In the starboard wing fillet area, the hydraulic lines for the No 3 system were torn and severed, while four of the six No 3 generator feeder cables, together with wiring to the differential current transformer were also cut through.

Damage to wiring and hydraulic lines had also taken place in the No 1 engine nacelle on the port side. The lead connecting the No 1 engine fuel flow transmitter to its associated fuel flow electronics unit was severed, and the hydraulic line from the No 1 hydraulic system for extension of the slats was dented and partly crushed. The Nos 1 and 3 hydraulic reservoirs were both empty, their contents having been discharged through broken hydraulic lines.

The DC-10 was equipped with a multi-parameter Lockheed digital Model 209 Flight Data Recorder similar to that fitted to the Lockheed Tristar N301EA which crashed in the Everglades, near Miami, Florida, almost a year before. The recorder had not been damaged in any way by the engine disintegration, but all attempts to readout what it had recorded during the flight proved fruitless. Unknown to National Airlines or the DC-10 crew, the FDR had been unserviceable for some time before the flight. The complete lack of any data from the FDR added considerably to the complexity of investigating the engine failure and the reasons for it.

Fortunately however, the Sunstrand Cockpit voice Recorder fitted to the DC-10 was fully operational and provided a clear record, not only of the flight deck conversation over the last 30 minutes of flight, but also of the engine sounds prior to the disintegration, the explosion itself, and the vibration and cabin depressurisation noises that followed. This audio record provided valuable data that was to become the basis for a technical assessment of the operating conditions of all three engines before and at the time of the actual failure.

A computer analysis was made of the likely falling trajectories of the missing No 3 engine components, and that of the unfortunate passenger Gardner, ejected from the cabin when the window failed. The results of this were then used by the New Mexico State Police and local organisations in the course of an extensive search of the desert area beneath the flightpath of the DC-10 at the time of the engine disintegration.

Although this analysis proved remarkably successful in helping to locate the separated engine inlet cowl, the fan blade containment ring and even the remains of 18 of the missing fan blades, no trace could be found of the body of the missing passenger and it was never recovered.

The inlet cowl was found relatively intact. It had broken away at its rear attachments and the rearmost section had been crushed when it struck the ground. Numerous fan blade fragments had torn their way through the inner barrel of the cowl and the outer barrel was punctured in eight places. A major portion of the porous sheet from the cowl's first acoustic panel was missing. The acoustic material found wedged against the engine's fan outlet guide vanes at Albuquerque had come from this missing section.

The fan blade containment ring had broken and was torn and distorted. There was evidence that the bolts holding the containment ring to the inlet cowl had sheared off on the direction of engine rotation.

The remains of the 18 first stage fan blades recovered from the desert showed damage consistent with forward movement past the blade restraining devices and out of the blade retaining slots.

★ ★ ★

The investigations to determine the order in which the engine components failed and the precise circumstances that had triggered their failure, were protracted and highly complex.

They involved a study of the entire computer controlled autothrottle system and its limitations, independent analyses of the sounds recorded on the CVR tape by both the Douglas Aircraft Company and the General Electric Company, the manufacturer of the three CF6-6D engines fitted to the aircraft, and a detailed examination of the failed engine. The histories of two previous CF6 fan failures, both of which had taken place while the engines concerned were being run in test cells, were also studied.

Examination of the damaged fan

blades, fan blade disk, and blade retention devices from the DC-10's No 3 engine, revealed that the blades had been forced forward and out of their slots by extremely high dynamic forces. Yet there was no evidence of any mechanical failure which could have resulted in the fan blades leaving the disk slots in the manner they had.

Moreover, a mechanical failure alone could not have caused the type of blade release that occurred. In fact, without high vibratory effects acting to counter the extremely high centrifugal forces on the fan blades and an increase in the forward axial loading on the blades at the same time, it would have been impossible for the fan blades to have moved forward to the point of leaving their slots. The frictional grip of a blade dovetail against the outward surfaces of its slot, resulting from a centrifugal force of some 25 metric tonnes generated by the fan's rotational speed, would normally be greater than any force tending to move the blade forward in its slot. Without the interaction described therefore, a blade operating at high engine power could not move out of its slot.

In this respect the blade loss was similar to the condition experienced in the two test cell failures. In both these failures, the vibratory mechanism which allowed the loss of the blades was the same – resonance between the fan rotor and the fan case resulting from severe rub of the fan blade tips on the fan case.

The severe fan tip rub had in each instance been caused by a rapid fan acceleration and slight extension of the fan blade tips under high centrifugal force. The rocking of the blades in their slots which the combination of these conditions produced, overcame the friction produced by centrifugal force, allowing the blades to move forward until they sheared the blade retainers and left their slots altogether.

From the test cell experience therefore, as well as theoretically, it was clear that a rapid fan acceleration, together with a vibratory condition alternately loading and unloading the blades at high frequency, would have been necessary for the blades to leave their slots. The reason for the onset of the vibratory condition, whatever this proved to be, was thus the initiating factor in the engine disintegration.

National Transportation Safety Board investigators found it difficult to reconcile the actions described by the captain and the flight engineer

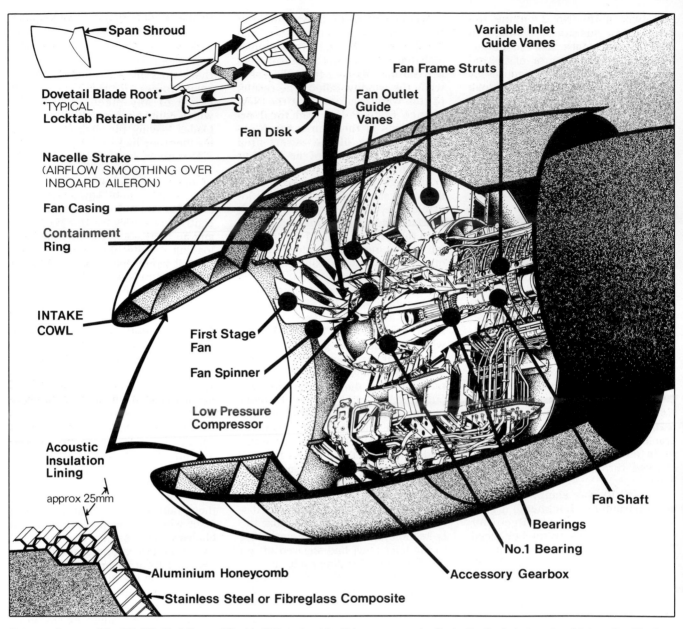

Cutaway diagram of the DC-10's No 3 General Electric CF6 engine, identifying components affected by the first stage fan disintegration. The inset details the attachment of the fan blades to the fan disk. (Matthew Tesch drawing with acknowledgement to Flight International)

with the engine failure sequence. At the time the flight engineer pulled the N1 circuit breakers, the aircraft was in stable flight with its airspeed close to that commanded by the autothrottle system. Although his action would have removed the limiting authority imposed by the autothrottle, the throttles themselves would have advanced only if the aircraft's speed was less than that commanded by the system.

Furthermore, because the captain and the flight engineer were investigating the throttle response with the circuit breakers pulled, they would probably have been on their guard against an undesirable thrust increase. Indeed, the captain's action in retarding the autothrottle command speed by five knots should have produced a retarding of the

throttles. The investigators thus found it difficult to see how the engine could have been operated outside normal cruise power settings.

Even so, it was apparent that such a condition had occurred. Indeed, from the indications of the Engine Pressure Ratio and fuel flow indicators that were effectively "frozen" when the No 3 generator wiring was cut by engine debris, it was evident that all three of the DC-10's engines were operating at abnormally high power at the moment the No 3 engine disintegrated.

It was considered possible that the captain might have inadvertently advanced the levers beyond the required settings while manually adjusting them without the benefit of the N1 tachometers. Or that the autothrottle was still in operation

with the command airspeed setting higher than the existing airspeed, producing a signal for increased thrust. There was no evidence however, to support either of these postulations.

To examine other possible triggering mechanisms for the No 3 engine's disintegration, the analysis of the CVR tape by the General Electric company was studied in detail. This showed that at the time the flight engineer posed the question: "If you pull the N1 tach – will that autothrottle respond to N1?", the No 3 engine's rotational speed was 97% N1 – almost normal for the cruising flight conditions at the time. Twenty-four seconds later the No 3 engine's N1 speed increased to 100% and the power of the other two engines increased in parallel with it. The obvious explanation for this overall increase in power was that it was produced by the autothrottle system.

The CVR analysis also showed that between 31 and 44 seconds after the flight engineer's question, No 3 engine's speed oscillated between 94% and 100% N1. When the explosion occurred forty-eight seconds after the flight engineer's question, the No 3 engine's speed was 99% N1, but in only another 1.42 seconds it had accelerated to 110% N1, after which the sound of No 3 engine was no longer audible. Nos 1 and 2 engines also accelerated to high power (105.5 and 107% respectively) shortly after the explosion and remained at these settings for a further 27 seconds.

Again, the acceleration of the engines to these high power settings would suggest they were being controlled by the autothrottle system, but without the benefit of its thrust limiting feature. Though investigators could not determine what effect this unrestrained N1 acceleration actually had on the disintegration of the No 3 engine, they considered it significant that both previous test cell engine failures had also occurred during rapid engine accelerations.

The investigators thus concluded that the disintegration of the DC-10's No 3 engine had been precipitated by severe rubbing of the fan blade tips on the fan casing, producing a blade exciting sequence that allowed the blades to be forced forward and out of their retaining slots. The blade tip rub was probably caused by an acceleration of the engine to an abnormally high N1 speed, either through an unrestricted power increase by the autothrottle system, or a manual throttle advance by the captain, creating a resonant frequency in the fan section of the engine, and a subsequent destructive vibratory mode.

Regardless of the precise cause of the high fan speed at the time of its failure however, the investigators found that flightcrew of the aircraft were in effect performing an untested failure analysis of the autothrottle system. Such an experiment, without the benefit of training or specific guidelines, should never be conducted during normal airline flying, the investigators commented.

As a result of the accident, the Federal Aviation Administration at once issued an Airworthiness Directive to operators of DC-10 aircraft requiring inspections of engine inlet cowl mountings to correct any possible deficiencies in their structural integrity.

Additionally, the General Electric Company, as a preventative measure against further problems of the same type, immediately stipulated increased fan blade tip clearances inside fan cases. The company also introduced an extensive development and testing programme to increase the effectiveness of blade retention fittings. One of the primary blade retaining devices was quickly redesigned to provide each fan blade with a rearward retaining strength of 60,000 pounds as compared to that of 18,000 pounds in the failed engine. The modified blade retaining devices were promptly incorporated in all General Electric CF-6 engines in service.

In concluding its official report of the investigation of the accident, the National Transportation Safety Board stressed that aircraft operators and pilots-in-command should be fully cognizant of their operational responsibilities for conducting flights in a professional manner. They should never undertake experiments on aircraft systems for which they have not received specific training.

CHAPTER 14

"Keep your eye on it – I'll stay on the gauges ..."

– Boeing 707 captain to third officer in copilot's seat

Pan American Boeing 707-321B N454PA [19376] *Clipper Radiant –* January 30, 1974

A difficult night approach to an island runway, gusting winds with an imminent storm, and a captain who had not made an ILS approach in actual instrument conditions for nearly five months, was an unfavourable enough combination. Add to this a copilot who omitted the required descent calls – and the stage was set for disaster.

Clipper Radiant N454PA was the Boeing 707 scheduled to operate Pan American World Airways' regular trans Pacific service from Auckland, New Zealand, to Los Angeles, California, on the night of January 30, 1974. Designated Clipper Flight 806, it would land at two en route ports of call – Pago Pago in American Samoa, and Honolulu.

Ninety one passengers boarded the flight at Auckland, under the command of 52 year old Captain Leroy Petersen, a senior PanAm pilot of some 23 years' service and more than 17,000 hours' experience. His seasoned flightcrew comprised First Officer Richard Gaines, 37, with more than 5000 hours, Third Officer James Phillips, 43, of similar background, and Flight Engineer Gerry Green, with over 3000 hours. All were well experienced on the Boeing 707. Six female crew members, ranging in age from 24 to 34, looked after the 91 passengers in the cabin.

Although the crew had had almost a full 24 hour day off in Auckland prior to reporting for duty to take Flight 806 as far as Honolulu, the atmosphere on the flightdeck as the aircraft taxied out for departure just after 8pm Central Pacific Time was perhaps not quite as relaxed as usual.

First Officer Gaines, because he was suffering from laryngitis, had been relegated to the jump seat behind the captain, and Third Officer Phillips had taken his place in the copilot's control seat. Not that this should have made any difference – Phillips was a competent flightdeck officer and approved for landings in the course of normal line flying.

But the captain himself was only just getting back into his stride after more than four months off work because of illness. In fact this trans Pacific trip away from the USA to Australia and New Zealand was his first after being returned to flying status by the company's medical department on January 15. Since that time he had undergone refresher training in one of PanAm's flight simulators on January 18, and the following day had completed three actual takeoffs and landings in a Boeing 707 to requalify himself for command flying on the aircraft type. Four days later he left on the first leg of a trip that would take him and his crew to Australia and back over a period of 10 days.

With the captain flying the aircraft from the left hand seat, the Boeing 707 took off from Auckland at 8.14pm Central Pacific Time and was cleared to Pago Pago on its IFR flightplan. The flight continued normally and, three hours 40 minutes later, with the Boeing now cruising at Flight Level 330 (33,000 feet), Third Officer Phillips called Pago Pago Approach Control to report they were 160 nautical miles south.

The approach controller informed the crew that there was overcast cloud at 1000 feet, the visibility was 10 nautical miles (18.5km), the temperature 25 degrees C, light rain was falling, the wind was from the north-northwest at 15 knots, and the altimeter setting was 1016 millibars. Two minutes later at 11.13pm local time, he cleared the aircraft for descent to the Pago Pago VOR and the Boeing reported leaving Flight Level 330 on descent.

At 11.25pm, when the aircraft was descending through 20,000 feet, the controller told the crew: "You're cleared to the ILS DME, Runway 05 – approach via the 20 mile arc, south-southwest. Report the arc, and leaving 5000 [feet]."

Six minutes later, as they de-

Two famous names indelibly linked: As launch customer for the type, PanAm operated no fewer than 137 examples of the Boeing 707, including its eight initial short fuselage 707-120 series, as well as nine of the lesser known Boeing 720Bs. The balance of the fleet comprised B and C variants of the Intercontinental 707-320 series. Typical of the latter is N790PA [18714], the fourth 707-321C delivered to the airline. "Jet Clipper Courser", shown here on a pre-delivery flight, wears PanAm's famous jet era livery of the 1960s, before outline painting of all doors and emergency exists became an ICAO requirement. (Boeing)

scended through 10,000 feet, the crew again requested the wind velocity. The approach controller told them it was now swinging between due north and 020 degrees, fluctuating between 10 and 15 knots.

At 11.35pm the aircraft reported descending through 5500 feet and that it had intercepted the 226 degree radial of the Pago Pago VOR (ie the alignment of the localiser for the Instrument Landing System for Runway 05). The approach controller responded: "Understand inbound on the localiser, report about three [miles] out. No other reported traffic. Wind 010 degrees at 15, gusting to 20."

Four minutes later, the approach controller, looking through the window of his radio room (some 700 metres northeast of the runway) as it began raining heavily, saw that the runway lights were no longer visible and concluded the airport's electrical power supply had failed. Immediately, he transmitted to the aircraft: "Clipper 806, it appears we've had a power failure at the airport."

At this stage the Boeing 707, on final approach, had just descended through 2000 feet, a little over five nm (nine kilometres) from the runway threshold. The crew replied: "We're still getting your VOR and ILS, and the lights are showing."

Approach controller (seeking confirmation): "You can see the runway lights?"

Aircraft: "That's charlie [affirmative]."

Approach controller: "We've got a bad rain shower here – I can't see them from my position here."

Aircraft (just after 11.39): "We're five DME now and they still look bright."

Approach controller: "OK – no other reported traffic. The wind is 030 degrees at 20, gusting to 25. Advise clear of the runway."

The Boeing crew's acknowledgement of this instruction a few seconds before 11.40 proved to be the last transmission from the aircraft. Two minutes later when it had not landed as expected, and the approach controller could make no further radio contact with it, he sounded the airport crash alarm.

Meanwhile, several people waiting at the small airport terminal for the Boeing to arrive were watching an intense rain storm moving across the airport from the northeast. Soon after the rain engulfed the airport buildings, they became conscious of a bright glow beyond the approach end of Runway 05.

In torrential rain shortly before midnight, one small firefighting vehicle, struggling up the narrow jungle

track from the airport towards the ILS middle marker transmitter, finally located the blazing wreckage of the Boeing just under a kilometre short of the runway. Only Third Officer Phillips and nine passengers, all suffering burns, had succeeded in escaping from the fire.

Because of the inaccessibility of the accident site, only one firefighting vehicle at a time was able to approach the wreckage, severely limiting the fire service's effectiveness, and most of the fuselage was gutted before the fire could be extinguished. The 10 survivors were admitted to hospital, but Phillips and four of the passengers died from severe burns over the next three days. Another passenger died nine days afterwards.

Pago Pago International Airport in American Samoa is situated on the southeastern coast of the tiny mountainous tropical island of Tutuila, and its single runway has an elevation of only 30 feet. Aligned northeast-southwest, it is 2750 metres in length and its Runway 05 direction is served by an Instrument Landing System (ILS) and a visual Approach Slope Indicator System (VASIS). A middle marker beacon is located 940 metres from the runway threshold. Although the ILS procedure requires that DME be used to establish the

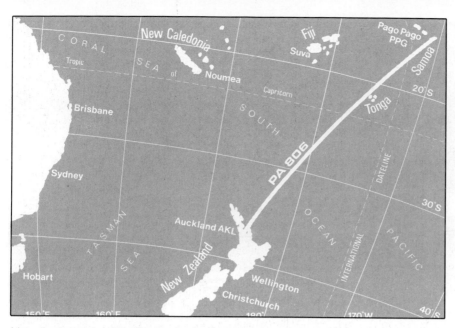

Map showing route of the PanAm Boeing 707 from Auckland, New Zealand, to Pago Pago, American Samoa. (Matthew Tesch)

final approach fix seven nautical miles out, the DME is available only on the VOR frequency and not on the ILS frequency. For this reason aircraft crews are required to monitor the VOR frequency until past the seven DME final approach fix.

The approach to Runway 05 is over the sea until 3.25nm from the threshold, when it crosses the southwestern coast of the island. Some 1.7nm (3000 metres) from the threshold, the approach path crosses Logotala Hill, elevation 400 feet, on which an NDB is located. The sloping terrain between Logotala Hill and the runway is rocky and thickly covered with trees and dense jungle undergrowth.

The airport has no control tower, all communications with aircraft, including approach control, being handled from an airport building 700 metres northeast of the runway.

National Transportation Safety Board investigators who flew to Pago Pago from the US the following day, found that less than a minute after its final, normal and calm radio transmission to the approach controller, the aircraft had, for no obvious reason, descended into trees on this slope. The impact with the trees breached the wing fuel tanks, releasing fuel which immediately caught fire.

Detailed exploration of the environs showed that the Boeing had first contacted 25 foot high trees on the down sloping, jungle covered terrain, 1180 metres short of the runway threshold, where the ground elevation is 88 feet. At a descent angle of about 3.5 degrees, the aircraft then cut a swathe through the trees

and jungle vegetation for a distance of 300 metres. Pieces of nose structure and the radar dome embedded in rocks, marked where the fuselage had first struck the ground itself, 72 metres from the first tree contact.

As it tore its way through the trees and over the rough ground, the aircraft progressively broke up, the outer wings, undercarriage, the inboard wing flaps and all four engines being wrenched off. Towards the end its ground slide, the fuselage hit a low rock wall, severely damaging the underside of the fuselage and dislodging the centre section keel beam. The aircraft finally hit and demolished the middle marker transmitter, coming to rest 940 metres from the runway. Fire was evident over the last 300 metres of the wreckage trail.

All structural failures were clearly the result of impact. The undercarriage was lowered at the time of the accident, with the wing flaps extended to 50 degrees, the normal setting for landing. The spoilers were retracted. The interior of the flightdeck was extensively damaged by fire and many of the instruments had melted. But there was no evidence of pre-impact fire or of failures of the aircraft's engines or systems.

The surviving passengers told investigators that the impact forces they felt in the cabin were small – little more than in a "normal landing", probably because of the cushioning effect of the trees and jungle undergrowth. There was no damage evident in the cabin interior, but they could see a massive fire through the starboard windows.

No one appeared to be injured in

the crash and even before the aircraft actually stopped, numbers of passengers rushed towards the main front and rear doors of the cabin. A passenger sitting on the starboard side opened one of the overwing exits, but promptly closed it again when flames licked inside. Others opened the port side overwing exits, and all the surviving passengers left the aircraft through these. None of them heard any evacuation instructions from the cabin crew, all having been seated near the middle of the cabin. They sustained their burns after they climbed out onto what remained of the port wing.

The surviving passengers told investigators they had listened to the pre-takeoff briefing and read the information card in the aircraft's seat pockets. This had prepared them for what to do when the crash occurred.

Examination of the gutted fuselage showed that none of the main cabin doors had been used for escape. The intense fire on the starboard side could explain why the doors on this side of the fuselage were not opened, but why the main doors on the port side were not used remained a mystery. The forward main door on the port side had been opened about six centimetres, but the aft door on this side remained closed. It was thought that the doors might have been damaged by impact, or that the press of passengers crowding against them prevented the cabin crew from opening them.

The panic movement of passengers to the front and rear doors only, including many who had been seated over the wing, suggested they had not really absorbed the preflight briefing, or that they reacted without thinking. The investigators believed there would have been more survivors if passengers had followed the instructions in the preflight briefing and moved towards their nearest exit.

Third Officer Phillips, the only occupant of the aircraft to have been injured in the actual impact, was assisted by the other flightcrew members to escape from the flightdeck through a hole torn in its starboard side. The others were overcome by smoke and fire before they could follow him. All 91 occupants who failed to escape from the burning aircraft died of smoke inhalation and massive burns.

The Boeing's Flight Data Recorder was recovered undamaged by either impact or heat from its mounting in the tail of the aircraft, behind the rear pressure bulkhead. The Cockpit Voice Recorder, installed further forward in the fuselage, was severely

Another of PanAm's Intercontinental 707-321Cs in the livery of the 1960s, this time N795PA [18765], "Jet Clipper Jupiter Rex". With the arrival of the company's first Boeing 747s in 1970, the fuselage title was abbreviated to "PanAm" and aircraft names lost their "Jet" prefixes.

damaged by fire externally, but its tape was found to be intact and capable of being read out. The two recorders provided the investigators with a detailed "picture" of the aircraft's movements and the crew's actions in the minutes leading up to the accident.

★   ★   ★

It was evident from the CVR transcription that the copilot (in this case Third Officer Phillips), had the runway lights in sight when the aircraft was eight nautical miles out, and that they remained visible throughout the approach.

Although there was nothing to suggest that the airport's radio navigational aids or the aircraft's instruments were faulty, the readouts showed that the captain, who was handling the aircraft, did not intercept the glideslope smoothly.

According to the approach chart, the aircraft could have descended to 2500 feet on being cleared for its approach to the ILS and then intercepted the glideslope at the seven DME (nm) final approach fix. Instead, the Boeing levelled off at 5000 feet for one minute before descending again, this time through the glideslope to some 500 feet below the approach chart intercept altitude of 2500 feet, *before* reaching the final approach fix. On reaching this point, where the stipulated approach chart altitude is 2180 feet, it was 180 feet below the glideslope. Re-intercept-

ing the glideslope at an altitude of 1750 feet as it continued towards the runway, the aircraft then followed a path about 100 feet above it.

From the time the aircraft descended through 2000 feet until it was approaching 1400 feet, the airspeed remained fairly constant at 160 knots.

But from that time on, large variations in airspeed, between 160 and 188 knots, were recorded. These, accompanied by numerous changes in engine power, continued until 30 seconds before the aircraft's first impact with the treetops, by which time the windscreen wipers had been turned on and the flaps extended to 50 degrees, completing the last item in the landing checklist. At this stage the aircraft was descending through 800 feet. There was no change in the approach profile as the flaps went down into the landing setting.

Throughout this time the captain was flying on instruments, and continued to do so until the copilot called, "Now you have the runway"' 23 seconds before impact. At this point the captain evidently "went visual" to complete the landing. Three seconds later the copilot remarked: "You're a little high." Four seconds later again there was the sound of the electric elevator trim, and at the same time there was a major change in the approach profile, the rate of descent suddenly increasing from 690 feet per minute to

nearly 1500fpm. This rate of descent continued for the following 16 seconds until the aircraft struck the trees.

Although the combined readouts of the FDR and the CVR produced a clear reconstruction of the aircraft movements that led to the accident, they gave no hint why such an abrupt descent so late in the approach was allowed to go unchecked. During the final 16 seconds of the approach, there was no comment or remark by any of the four crew members on the flightdeck to point to any developing operational problem.

Indeed, Third Officer Phillips, interviewed in hospital before he succumbed to his injuries, told investigators that "just prior to impact, everything looked normal". He also said the aircraft had encountered some rain, but not heavy rain during the approach. Surviving passengers confirmed that the rain during the approach was light. But they said heavy rain began shortly after the accident.

In view of the fact that this instrument approach was the captain's first in actual instrument conditions for nearly five months, the investigators initially concluded that his instrument flying proficiency was not at its peak.

It was thought probable that from the time the captain "went visual" 23 seconds before impact, he had not again referred to the flight instruments or the ILS indicator, which would have shown the aircraft to be below the glideslope and descending fast.

Another factor probably contributing to the accident in the investigators' view, was that the copilot failed to make all the required altitude and rate of descent calls during the approach.

PanAm's operations manual specified that on an ILS approach in instrument conditions, the aircraft was to be stabilised on the glidepath at the proper rate of descent, with the landing checklist complete, not lower than 1000 feet. The pilot not flying the aircraft was required to make calls at the outer marker, at 500 feet above airfield elevation, and at any time the rate of descent exceeded 800 feet a minute. In addition, the third pilot on the flightdeck and the flight engineer were required to monitor all aspects of the approach procedure. On the approach which culminated in the accident, the landing checklist was not completed until after the aircraft had descended through 1000 feet, and none of the required calls appeared to have been made.

"Proper monitoring of the Vasis lights" would also have provided "a positive visual indication" that the aircraft was descending below the glideslope, the investigators declared.

In concluding their initial report, the investigators commented that many factors could produce visual illusions during an approach to land at night, and these could have caused the Boeing crew to believe they were higher than they were during this approach. The illusion of runway shortening could also have been present. The area of heavy rain, moving slowly down the runway towards the threshold, would have caused an apparent visual decrease in the runway's length, thereby leading the crew to believe they were higher than they should have been. While it was difficult to determine just which factors might have misled the crew, "the possibility of visual illusions could not be dismissed".

The report concluded that "the flightcrew did not adequately monitor the flight instruments after they had transitioned to the visual portion of the ILS approach; they did not detect the increased rate of descent; lack of crew co-ordination resulted in inadequate altitude calls, inadequate instrument cross checks by the pilot not flying the aircraft, and inadequate monitoring by other crew members ... Vasis was available but was apparently not used to monitor the approach."

★   ★   ★

Some time after the National Transportation Safety Board published its official report on the accident, the US Air Line Pilots' Association petitioned the Board to reconsider its finding in the light of other accidents in which transport aircraft had descended into the ground in the vicinity of storms.

As a result, the data derived from the PanAm Boeing 707's FDR and CVR were re-examined in detail, compared with the aircraft's performance capability, and the results analysed to explore the extent to which the weather conditions existing at the time could have affected the captain's efforts to achieve and maintain a stabilised approach.

The performance analysis indicated that about 50 seconds before

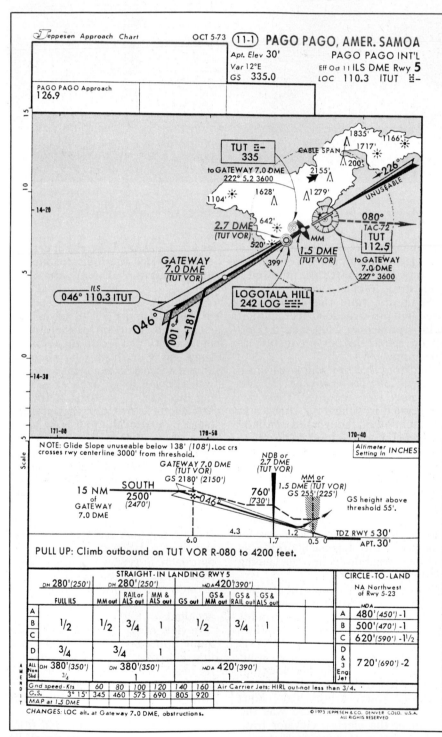

Standard radio navigation aid approach chart, published by Jeppesen & Co, detailing Instrument Landing System approach procedure for Pago Pago International Airport's Runway 05 at the time of the accident. The crew of PanAm's Clipper Flight 806 would have been using an identical chart. Pago Pago Airport is situated on the tiny island of Tutuila, part of American Samoa.

A near perfect flare, with starboard wing slightly down to counter the crosswind on a rain soaked runway, for "Jet Clipper Star of Hope". This aircraft, N428PA [19363], was a near sister to "Clipper Radiant", both of them coming off the Seattle production line in the second half of 1967. The absence of the under tail ventral fin was characteristic of 707s from this production run. Also visible in the picture (below the wings on either side of the runway) are the four box crossbars of the runway's Vasis lights. (via Mike Clayton)

impact, the Boeing 707 encountered gusty wind conditions with a predominantly increasing headwind and an updraught.

The influence of this condition on the aircraft persisted for about 25 seconds, the windshear probably being produced by winds flowing outward from the rainstorm over the airport and being affected by the upsloping ground around Logotala Hill. The windshear was evidenced by a sharp increase in airspeed and a shallowing of the descent path, resulting in the aircraft moving above the glideslope.

At this stage the engine thrust was reduced, evidently to correct the high and fast condition that had developed. But as the aircraft crossed Logotala Hill some 16 seconds before impact, it apparently emerged from the updraught. Not only was the performance advantage suddenly lost – the aircraft then encountered a wind condition having a small negative effect on its performance. With the engine thrust now well below the setting needed for a stabilised approach on the glideslope, the descent rate rapidly increased to about 1500 feet per minute.

At least 12 seconds remained in which to arrest the descent but, at this point in the approach, seven seconds after the copilot called, "Now you have the runway", the captain had just transferred his vision from the instruments to the runway lights ahead, and the aircraft was over a "black hole" – an area

totally devoid of ground lights. In addition, the intense tropical rainstorm moving across the airport towards the approach end of the runway, was probably diminishing the visual cues to the extent that the increased rate of descent would have been almost impossible to recognise while looking through the windscreen.

Although the runway's Vasis was operating at the time, it is likely that, as the rainstorm moved towards the

approach end of the runway, each pair of runway lights would have been progressively obscured until the Vasis itself disappeared from the pilots' sight.

Such a foreshortening of the pilots' "visual segment" – the ground surface distance visible over the nose of the aircraft – could also have been misleading, creating the illusion that the horizon was lowering. This in turn could be interpreted by

This photograph showing investigators examining the wreckage of PanAm's Boeing 707 N454PA where it came to rest a kilometre from the approach end of Pago Pago's Runway 05, belies the true burnt out condition of the fuselage. The fire which erupted on impact, fed by fuel from the aircraft's breached wing tanks, completely gutted the interior of the flightdeck and the passenger cabin, and was responsible for all 97 of the accident's total fatalities. Only four passengers ultimately survived the disaster.

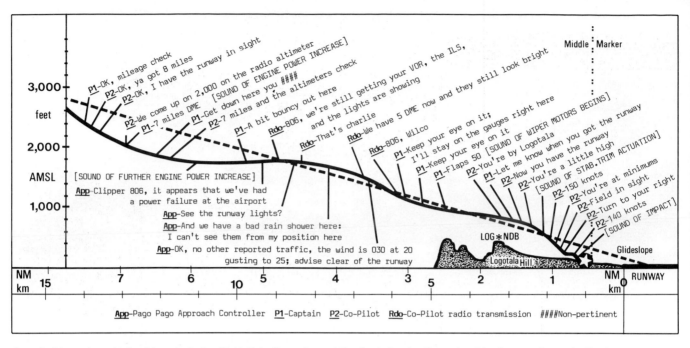

Compiled from data obtained from both the Flight Data Recorder and the Cockpit voice Recorder, this diagram shows the Boeing 707's actual descent profile in relation to the Runway 05's 3.25 degree electronic glideslope. The flightcrew's comments, radio transmissions, and other flightdeck sounds as recorded on the CVR are shown at appropriate points. (Matthew Tesch)

the crew to be the result of the aircraft's nose pitching up. The instinctive reaction would be to lower the nose or to decrease, not increase, engine power.

As a result of its further investigation into the circumstances of the accident, the NTSB conceded that the presence of the severe rainstorm and its influence on surrounding meteorological conditions, together with the timing of its movement across the airport, was certainly a factor in the development of the accident.

Nevertheless the NTSB's investigators were still forced to the conclusion that the accident could have been avoided if the crew had recognised, from all the resources available to them, that the aircraft's rate of descent had dangerously increased. This prompted the NTSB to express its concern generally about flightcrew attitudes to prescribed approach procedures and required altitude and rate of descent callouts.

In this case, the crew were apparently content to intercept the glideslope 500 feet lower than the prescribed altitude; they were also content to cross the final approach fix 180 feet lower than the altitude stipulated on the approach chart. And the copilot who should have made altitude warning calls did not do so. He did call an altimeter check at the final approach fix, but said nothing about altitude.

But even more vital than the need for an awareness of altitude in this "black hole" approach, was the ne-

cessity to be constantly aware of the rate of descent. PanAm operational procedures required that the pilot not flying the aircraft call out the descent rate whenever it exceeded 800fpm, and recommended that it should not be permitted to exceed 1000fpm at any time after the aircraft had descended below 2000 feet.

In the course of the NTSB's performance analysis, it was calculated that if the anticipated headwind component had dissipated sharply during the approach, as apparently occurred after the aircraft passed over Logotala Hill, the rate of descent required to maintain the Runway 05 glideslope at the Boeing's approach speed would have increased to 880fpm. Though this was still less than the recommended maximum of 1000fpm, according to PanAm's procedures it required a callout by the copilot. Such a call could have alerted the captain that the headwind component had changed from that previously passed to them by the approach controller.

Even when the rate of descent increased to 1500fpm, 16 seconds before impact, there was still no callout by the copilot. Had he made the call, the NTSB believed, the accident could have been avoided.

In concluding their revised report on the accident, NTSB investigators commented that flight instruments are more reliable indicators than the senses of pilots, especially during an approach close to the ground, and when visual cues are sparse or di-

minishing. And in severe windshear conditions, the flight director must be used in combination with other flight instruments such as the raw data glideslope needle.

During his interview with investigators in hospital, the copilot recalled that he had not changed his navigational receiver switch from the VOR frequency which also provided the DME reading, to the ILS frequency when they passed the final approach fix. This meant that in monitoring the aircraft's approach relative to the electronic glideslope, he would have had to look across to the captain's side of the instrument panel. It also meant that the copilot's navigational display was not available for cross checking by the captain. To what extent this had contributed to the crew's failure to recognise the final rapid increase in the rate of descent could not be determined' but it was undoubtedly another factor in the development of the accident.

The NTSB concluded that the accident had resulted from the crew's "late recognition of, and failure to correct in a timely manner, an excessive descent rate which developed as a result of the aircraft's penetration of destabilising wind changes ... The captain's recognition was hampered by restricted visibility, the illusory effects of a 'black hole' approach, inadequate monitoring of flight instruments, and the failure of crew to call out descent rate during the last 15 seconds of flight."

CHAPTER 15

"I can't bring it up – she's not responding ..."

*– DC-10 first officer
to captain*

Turk Hava Yollari – THY Turkish Airlines McDonnell-Douglas DC-10-10
TC-JAV [46704] *Ankara* – March 3, 1974

A history of cargo door latching problems on a new widebodied type, and even a near tragedy when a door opened in flight, were insufficient motivation to deal adequately with the problem. It took no less than the worst civil aviation disaster the world had so far seen, to make modifications mandatory.

The assorted crowd of business travellers and casually dressed tourists that thronged the passenger terminal at Paris' Orly Airport was bigger than usual for a Sunday morning, even a fine one in early Spring. Many of them were British tourists, trying to get a seat to London.

It was March 3, 1974, and an unexpected strike had been called by British European Airways ground engineers at London Heathrow Airport. In a month's time their employer was to merge with BOAC to form British Airways, and the industrial action was a gambit to win better pay before they were locked into entirely new working conditions.

The strike stranded many UK bound passengers holding BEA tickets in Europe, and those who could manage to do so had travelled as far as Paris in the hope of being allocated a seat across the Channel to London on other airline flights. The result was an overwhelming demand for seats out of Orly to London.

Among the numerous services operating through Paris to London that morning, one in particular offered hope for some of the frustrated flyers – THY Turkish Airlines Flight 981 from Istanbul to London via Paris.

As international airlines go, THY Turkish Airlines was a small company and its passenger load factors were not normally high. Today Flight TK981 had only 167 passengers aboard the 345 seat DC-10 TC-JAY when it departed Istanbul – and 50 of those were booked only as far as Paris. For the throng of anxious London bound passengers besieging the departure desks in the terminal building at Orly, it looked like the answer to all their hopes for getting home that day.

THY Turkish Airlines was proud of its three McDonnell Douglas DC-10s that had entered service 16 months before, making them the first operator of the widebodied trijet type outside the USA. It was a huge technological step for the small national airline, one which brought with it many new problems. THY flight crews were drawn almost exclusively from the Turkish Air Force, and they had previously operated only DC-9 and F28 twinjets, and smaller turboprop and piston engined aircraft.

The problem was particularly acute in obtaining flight engineers of adequate background for the highly sophisticated DC-10. Most of the

military pilots recruited for the task from fighter and ground attack squadrons of the Turkish Air Force not only lacked a wide aircraft engineering background – they were not really interested in being flight engineers at all, seeing this appointment as but a stepping stone to airline captaincy.

Another major problem the airline had to face was the haste with which the DC-10s were introduced from the time of ordering them in September, 1972. While European airlines like Lufthansa and KLM allowed a full two years for the incorporation of DC-10s into their fleets, with all the crew, engineering, and staff training that this complex process involved, THY's management insisted that at least two of the three aircraft be in service within twelve weeks – an eighth of the time considered adequate by major, experienced airlines in Western countries.

The background to this unseemly haste was the fact that, thanks to Japan's All Nippon Airlines postponing its decision to purchase widebodied aircraft – either the DC-10 or its immediate rival, the Lockheed L-1011 Tristar – the DC-10s McDonnell Douglas had earmarked for Japan

A McDonnell Douglas DC-10-30, similar to the type operated by THY Turkish Airlines.

were available for immediate delivery. In the early 1970s, with so many airlines throughout the world looking to re-equip with the new generation widebodies, the usual delivery time from the placement of an order was at least 18 months.

McDonnell Douglas, with an eye to gaining a crucial DC-10 market foothold in the Middle East was, moreover, offering the aircraft to Turkish Airlines at a highly competitive price, with generous terms, and nearly half a million dollars' worth of crew training thrown in. But to really take full advantage of this windfall, Turkish Airlines needed to have the DC-10s operational in time to catch one of its peak traffic periods just before Christmas, when thousands of Turkish migrant workers in Germany and other European countries would take advantage of the holiday break to travel home to their families. The revenue from this traffic was substantial and not to be missed.

Not without great difficulty on the part of McDonnell Douglas, the seemingly impossible deadline was met and the first aircraft went into service on December 16, 1972. But a McDonnell Douglas support team, including five "flying crew chiefs" (the flight engineer equivalent of an airline training captain) stayed on in Istanbul for six months to provide ongoing training to both ground and flight engineers. For the first weeks of operation of the new DC-10s, one of the crew chiefs travelled on the flightdeck on nearly every trip to assist the Turkish flight engineers.

But all this was in the past when THY Turkish Airlines Flight 981, flown by the DC-10 TC-JAV *Ankara* under the command of Captain Mejat Berkoz, touched down at Orly Airport, Paris, just after 11am local time on the fine, cool, but almost cloudless Sunday morning of March 3, 1974, and taxied to Gate A2 of Orly terminal's west satellite.

The airport is London Gatwick, and the airline Overseas National Airways, but this boarding view in the summer of 1974 captures the feeling of THY Flight TK981's departure from Paris Orly on March 3 of that year. Unusually for contemporary widebody designs, the DC-10's aft underfloor cargo compartment (for loose or last-minute freight), is accessed from the port side, so as not to impede bulk-loading equipment servicing the main rear hold on the starboard side of the fuselage. The aircraft illustrated is ONA's DC-10-30CF, N1032F [46826] 'Holiday Liner Freedom'.

As the passengers disembarked, routine refurbishment of the aircraft was taken over by personnel from the French airline servicing and support contractor SAMOR, the company to whom THY had delegated the responsibility for the unloading, refuelling, cleaning, servicing and loading of its aircraft in Paris. An auxiliary ground power unit was connected to the DC-10, 10,000 litres of jet fuel pumped into its tanks, and its galleys resupplied with food and drinks for the relatively short hop to London.

Meanwhile, the luggage belonging to the 50 passengers who were leaving the aircraft at Paris was unloaded from the underfloor cargo holds, and that of those joining the flight for London progressively put aboard. Here there was some delay because of the sheer number of additional passengers queuing for a seat in the Departures section of the terminal building. This was unusual for the Turkish airline. Normally this Sunday flight would be lucky to have half the DC-10's seats occupied for the last leg to London. But today it looked as though it would depart Paris with a full load.

Most of those who had travelled on the aircraft from Istanbul and were going onto London were Turkish, but the majority of the 216 additional passengers were British: Rugby Union fans returning from watching the annual international

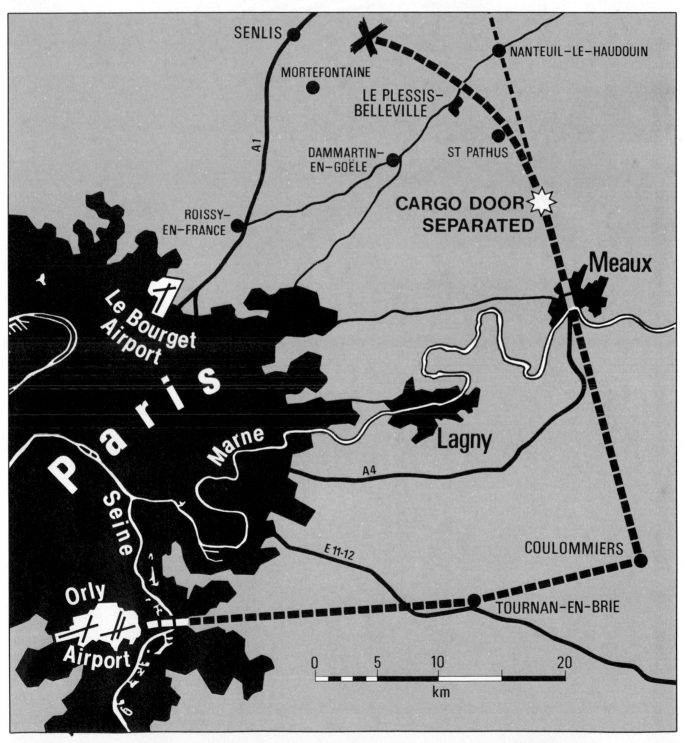

Departure track of DC-10, TC-JAV, from Orly's Runway 08, to the east and north of Paris. Towns and villages referred to in the text are indicated. (Matthew Tesch)

Too low, too late: This striking impression by artist Matthew Tesch depicts TC-JAV hurtling across the treetops of the Grove of Dammartin during its final two seconds of flight. Captain Berkoz's inspired but vain application of power to the wing-mounted engines, together with the DC-10's superb aerodynamic qualities, succeeded in reducing the angle of dive from a steep 20 degrees to only four degrees at the moment of impact.

French-English match in Paris the previous afternoon, including 25 members from one football club at Bury St Edmunds in Suffolk; a party of photographic models returning from an assignment in Spain; various professional people, businessmen and civil servants: tourists returning from a holiday in Europe – some young and single, some families with children, some elderly retired couples.

But not all. The passenger list included a 47 strong party of bank management trainees from Japan, most of them in their early twenties; 16 French men and women: 25 US citizens; two Australian women temporarily resident in England who were returning from a holiday in Spain; a New Zealand man and his two children; an Irish priest; a Swiss racing driver; a Swedish film director; a young German librarian. Other passengers were from Spain, Morocco, South America, India, Pakistan, Ceylon, and Vietnam.

The airline's schedule provided for an hour's stopover at Orly, with a departure time of 12 noon, but the processing of all the additional passengers took longer, and it was 12.20pm by the time all the DC-10's doors were finally closed. Even then some passengers had been turned away because the aircraft was estimated to be full. In the event, the last minute confusion at the departure desks left 10 seats on the aircraft unoccupied – a fateful reprieve for the disappointed few turned back at the departure lounge barrier.

With his flightdeck crew – First Officer Oral Ulusman and Flight Engineer Huseyin Ozer – Captain Berkoz started the engines and at 12.24pm, TC-JAV was cleared to taxi for Runway 08. The surface wind was blowing from the northeast at only 10 knots, and the sky was almost clear with only two oktas of cumulus cloud at 3000, a near perfect early spring day.

As the DC-10 taxied out, in accordance with French airport procedures, it was escorted by a radio car from the Air Transport Gendarmerie (police) to the runway holding point. Meanwhile, Chief Steward Hayri Tezcan and his seven cabin attendants gave the near capacity load of passengers the usual pre-takeoff briefing in Turkish, repeating it in French and English. For the cabin crew the flight promised to be an extremely busy one – with such a load there would barely be time to hand out refreshments to all on board before they would be approaching to land at Heathrow.

Five minutes later, after changing from the surface movement fre-

The great swathe which the DC-10 cut through the trees, deep in the Forest of Ermenonville, as it plunged to destruction at high speed. In this aerial view, two small sections of fuselage are visible – the only remaining parts of the aircraft still recognisable.

quency to the airport control frequency at the runway holding point, the crew were given their airways clearance in the form of Departure Route 18 via Tournan-en-Brie, Coulommiers, thence to Montdidier near Amiens. This standard departure clearance would take the aircraft some 35 nautical miles to the east to avoid overflying the metropolitan area of Paris before setting course to the northwest. The DC-10 was then cleared to line up and subsequently to takeoff, with an initial climb to 4000 feet.

After a faultless lift off, with First Officer Ulusman handling the air-

craft, followed by another frequency change to Orly Departures at 12.33pm, TC-JAV was cleared to continue climbing to 6000 feet. On reporting at 6000 feet one minute later, the DC-10 was transferred to the Northern Area Control frequency, and cleared to climb to its initial cruising level of FL230 (23,000 feet). At 12.36 Northern Area Control instructed it to turn left onto a heading of 345 degrees towards Montdidier. A minute later the aircraft reported climbing through 7000 feet.

But four minutes later (a few seconds after 12.40), disaster struck. An unexpected, confused transmission from TC-JAV containing a heavy background of noise was overlaid by words in Turkish. The transmission continued for almost 30 seconds, the sound of the flightdeck's pressurisation warning becoming audible in the background, followed by the overspeed warning.

Simultaneously, the label with the flight number "981" disappeared from the air traffic controller's secondary surveillance radar screen.

The other label for the aircraft's Flight Level, "130" remained on the screen for a few moments more. On the primary radar screen, the DC-10's echo followed a curved path to the left onto a heading of 280 degrees.

Twenty two seconds after the garbled transmission, there was a another that was brief and unreadable. Two seconds later again a final transmission began which lasted for six seconds. This too was unread-

able. Ten seconds afterwards, the aircraft's echo disappeared entirely from the controller's primary radar screen. Numerous subsequent calls by the controller to the aircraft went unanswered.

At his club in the town of Senlis, 40 kilometres northeast of Paris, Captain Jaques Lannier, officer in charge of the Senlis District of the Gendarmerie Nationale, was enjoying the day off with his family – a fine, crisp, sunny day with the last of the winter snow finally gone.

They had just sat down to lunch in the pleasant dining room when the waiter called the captain to the telephone – a senior police officer in a country community is never really free. It was his duty officer at the Senlis Gendarmerie.

"Captain," he began respectfully, "I have just been told that an aeroplane has crashed between Le Plessis Belleville and Ermenonville." The delightfully unspoilt Forest of Ermenonville, in the hills 50 kilometres northeast of Paris, was a favourite weekend destination for hikers and nature lovers.

(left and below) Police and rescue workers, appalled by the magnitude of the air disaster, comb the still smouldering wreckage of the DC-10 in the eerily silent Forest of Ermenonville, 50km northeast of Paris. The recognisable section of fuselage, one of only two such pieces in the entire wreckage trail, is from the starboard side of the aircraft. The other section (visible in the aerial view on the previous page), lies about 10 metres to the right, out of the picture.

Lannier, from long established habit, looked at his watch. It was just after 12.45pm. "Is it from the flying club?" he asked. There was a small aero club at Le Plessis Belleville and minor accidents requiring police attendance occurred occasionally.

The officer did not know, but would send out a patrol car to investigate. Lannier agreed and went back to join his family at the table.

He had just resumed his meal when the waiter called him back to the telephone. Again it was the duty officer: "Orly Airport has rung to say a Turkish DC-10 with 185 people on board disappeared from radar a short time ago, soon after taking off for London. In addition we've just had a separate report of a violent explosion in the forest near Mortefontaine."

Lannier realised at once this was no ordinary police matter – he had a major international disaster on his hands. What he did not yet know was that Orly Airport's first report underestimated the likely casualties by half.

Instructing his duty officer to immediately alert all available patrol cars, ambulances, civil emergency services and local hospitals, he gave his apologies and left his club at once. Within a few minutes, changed into uniform and at the wheel of a police car, he was threading his way swiftly through the Sunday holiday traffic towards the forest, blue light flashing and two tone siren sounding.

Despite having come down so close to one of the major cities of northern Europe, the site of the disaster at first defied attempts by the police and ambulance ground parties to locate it. The thickly timbered forest covers an area of more than 250 square kilometres and the only vehicle access to it is via a few rough tracks used by the forest rangers' tractors and four wheel drive vehicles. Visibility in the forest is limited to about 50 metres because of the trees.

Finally, early in the afternoon, one of Lannier's staff in a patrol car, accompanied by a four wheel drive vehicle from the Senlis fire station, moving carefully down a narrow forest track into a shallow valley known as the Grove of Dammartin, came upon a scene appalling beyond imagination.

A great swathe up to 100 metres wide had been hacked right across the timbered valley for a distance of more than half a kilometre. At its easternmost end, where the giant aircraft had apparently first brushed the treetops at a shallow angle of descent, only the upper branches had been lopped off. But throughout the remaining length of the swathe, where it had evidently descended into the trees in a westerly direction, the forest devastation rapidly increased, whole trees being flattened, broken up, denuded of foliage, and scorched by fire.

Of the structure of the great aeroplane itself, there was hardly a sign – only a vast, scattered trail of smashed metal, much of it still smouldering, broken looms of electrical wiring, torn cabin furnishings, items of clothing and, to complete the horror, a mind numbing quantity of severely traumatised and fragmented remains of what, until a short time before, had been living human beings.

None of the human remains were badly burnt and only a small proportion bore any sign of being touched by fire. The flash fire that occurred when the DC-10 crashed had obviously been fleeting.

Near where the small party of awed searchers stood, a luggage label, somehow undamaged despite the widespread desolation, lay on the ground. One of them picked it up. On one side were the words: "Turkish Airlines. Paris. Flight TK981. To: LON." The other side showed a small photograph of a DC-10 with the name of the airline in Turkish: "Turk Hava Yollari."

Even the police, accustomed as they were to dealing with the aftermath of violent death, were affected

Clothing of some of the victims of the disaster, left hanging from tree branches as the aircraft descended into the forest and broke up. The foliage of most of the trees near the wreckage trail was consumed by the brief flash fire that occurred on impact.

by the ghastly scale of the disaster and the havoc it had wrought. Captain Lannier, who arrived at the scene soon after the first patrol car, wrote afterwards:

... over a distance of four or five hundred metres, the trees were hacked and mangled, most of them charred but not burnt. Pieces of metal, brightly coloured electric wires, and clothes were literally all over the ground. In front of me in the valley, the trees were even more severely hacked and the wreckage greater. There were fragments of bodies and pieces of flesh everywhere that were hardly recognisable. Not far from where I stood were two hands clasping each other, a man's hand tightly holding a woman's hand, two hands that withstood disintegration ...

★   ★   ★

The aviation world's worst fears had finally been realised: an accident to a fully loaded widebodied jet had killed all on board, in this case some 345 people, though this number still required confirmation because of the confused circumstances of the last minute ticketing arrangements.

But what could have caused it, apparently without any warning, so soon after an obviously perfect take-off on a fine day, while climbing normally to cruising level?

To add to the confusion, a highly agitated farm worker from the village of St Pathus, 15 kilometres south of the crash site, now reported that six bodies had fallen into the turnip field where he was working at about the time of the accident. Police called to investigate found that the six, obviously passengers aboard the stricken airliner, were still strapped to their seats when they struck the ground – two rows of three seats each had somehow been ejected from the aircraft in flight. Small pieces of aircraft structure, later identified as cabin floor panels, had fallen nearby.

The most likely explanation for the accident appeared to be sabotage – had someone placed a bomb aboard the aircraft? It certainly seemed so. Indeed, a media report from Turkey speculated that as many as five of the passengers could have been guerrillas carrying bombs. According to this information, three Japanese and two Arab guerrillas had intended to sabotage a British European Airways flight from Paris to London, but boarded the Turkish aircraft when BEA services were cancelled. These claims were reinforced when French newspapers received telephone calls from two separate terrorist groups claiming responsibility for the disaster.

Critical of an airport security system that could have allowed such an outrage to be perpetrated, editorials in the western world's press thundered against those whose laxity might have been responsible, deaf to French assertions that there could have been no breakdown in security measures at Orly, that all who joined the flight in Paris were thoroughly searched:

The crash of the Turkish airliner killing all 347 [sic] on board has proved that disasters of sufficient magnitude to stun and shock can still occur, declared one newspaper.

What makes it even more horrifying is the suggestion from Turkish airline sources that it may have been caused by the explosion in flight of bombs carried on board by terrorist guerrillas ... the reported finding of bodies and parts of the fuselage some 15 kilometres from the crash scene lend credence to the theory ...

Disclosure of the full facts must of course await the official investigations. But if the guerrilla bomb theory is substantiated, it will reveal an appalling failure of what should have been routine security precautions at Orly Airport ... and the Paris disaster will turn out to be a ghastly scandal as well as a horrible tragedy.

The sabotage theory was one strong possibility to be investigated by the Commission of Inquiry appointed immediately by the French Ministry of Transport. The Commission was to be assisted by representatives from the US National Transportation Safety Board, the US

Because of the high impact speed, the bodies of most of the 346 victims of the accident were severely traumatised, making the task of identification extremely difficult – and in a few cases impossible.

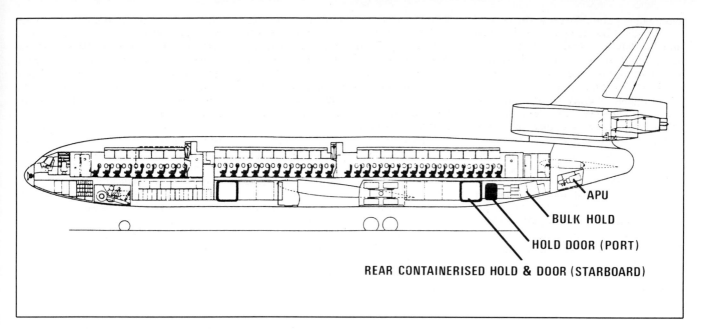

Simplified cross-section of the DC-10's interior, with seat row configuration basically representative of TC-JAV's layout. The location of the rear, "loose" cargo compartment – between aft container hold and the APU bay – is shown, as is the position of the culprit door. (McDonnell Douglas)

Federal Aviation Administration, the Turkish aviation authority, McDonnell Douglas, and General Electric, the manufacturer of the DC-10's engines.

While French air safety investigators began their detailed examination of the accident site and the scattered wreckage, searching particularly in the first instance for the capsules containing the Flight Data Recorder and the Cockpit Voice Recorder, pathologists began wrestling with the daunting, if not overwhelming task of attempting to identify the remains of those killed in the accident – now officially put at 346.

Meanwhile, in Paris' Air Traffic Control centre, other investigators were replaying the video recordings of the Northern Area controller's radar displays at the time of the accident, alert for the slightest additional evidence of what could have overtaken the DC-10 immediately before its crew's garbled emergency transmission, only 10 minutes after takeoff.

Careful examination of the recorded radar displays now revealed that at the time of the emergency transmission, just when the flight number label "981" disappeared from the secondary surveillance radar screen, the aircraft's echo on the primary radar actually split into two. The major echo, that representing the aircraft itself, followed the path seen by the controller on duty at the time, curving left on to a westerly heading before vanishing exactly a minute later. The less prominent echo remained stationary on the radar screen, about 24nm (44km) from

Orly on a bearing of 045 degrees, and persisted for two or three minutes before disappearing.

Was this further evidence of the bomb theory? Had the aircraft begun to break up while still in flight? Were there in fact other bodies and other parts of the aircraft lying somewhere between St Pathus and the crash site? To obtain answers to these possibly vital questions, a police search would now have to be made of the 15 kilometres of country the DC-10 had overflown between these two points.

But at least some progress was being made at the crash site itself – careful combing of the scattered wreckage in the forest had yielded both the Flight Data Recorder and the Cockpit Voice Recorder. And despite the complete disintegration of the aircraft structure, the recording tapes contained in both these instruments were in decipherable condition.

Correlating a readout of the parameters recorded on the FDR with a transcription of the audio recording on the CVR, produced a dramatic reconstruction of the events that took place aboard the DC-10 during its final terrifying minutes of flight.

The FDR indicated that, in accordance with Turkish Airlines' operating procedures, the climb after takeoff was carried out on autopilot. The DC-10 completed its left turn towards Montdidier, becoming stabilised on a heading of 345 degrees, at 12.38pm.

Just a few seconds before 12.40, as the aircraft was climbing through 9000 feet with the airspeed indicating around 300 knots and the flight

proceeding smoothly in every way, there was the noise of a muffled explosion, followed at once by a loud rushing of air – the sound of sudden decompression. At the same moment the throttle lever for the No 2 tail-mounted engine snapped shut, and its rpm indications began to run down. There were involuntary exclamations from the flightcrew and the pressurisation klaxon warning horn began sounding raucously on the flightdeck.

"What's happened?" called Captain Berkoz urgently in Turkish, raising his voice above the noise.

"The fuselage has burst!" cried First Officer Ulusman.

"Are you sure?"

Confused, alarmed voices followed, as the aircraft slowly banked into a descending turn to the left, the nose attitude becoming progressively steeper and the airspeed climbing.

Captain Berkoz pulled the other two throttle levers shut and shouted to Ulusman above the noise: "Bring it up – bring her nose up!"

"I can't bring it up," Ulusman shouted back desperately, "She's not responding!"

By now the DC-10 was diving at an angle of 20 degrees and, as the speed continued to build up frighteningly, one of the crew pressed his microphone button, obviously intending to transmit an emergency call to Air Traffic Control. But in the fear and confusion on the flightdeck, he was apparently unable to frame the words in English.

"Nothing is left!" Ozer yelled from his array of instruments on the flight engineer's panel. Twenty three seconds had now elapsed since the sound of the explosion. "Seven thousand feet!" declared the anguished voice of Captain Berkoz.

Now, 32 seconds after the explosion, a second klaxon began sounding – the horn warning that the aircraft was about to pass its "never exceed" speed.

Both pilots were desperately trying to find some means of regaining control. "Hydraulics?" Berkoz called out, apparently asking the question of Ozer.

"We've lost it …" said another voice, probably Ulusman's. Whether he meant the hydraulics, or the aircraft itself, was uncertain.

"It looks like we're going to hit the ground," said Berkoz more resignedly.

Fifty six seconds into the emergency, Berkoz evidently had an inspiration. "Speed!" he declared, pushing the throttles of the two wing engines open again.

Slowly the DC-10 began to respond, the nose rising and the g forces increasing, pushing the crew and all on board down into their seats, as the aircraft began to ease out of the steep dive.

For 10 seconds that probably seemed an eternity, the crew held their breath as they braced themselves against the mounting g forces – below and ahead of them was a forest – would they level out in time? The noise level was chaotic and the airspeed now greater than ever …

It was too late … the DC-10 was almost level now, but the treetops were rushing at them at incredible speed …

Almost as a reflex action, Captain Berkoz pulled the throttles shut – the last action of his life.

Seventy two seconds after the explosive noise, the DC-10 plunged into the forest at 430 knots – 800 kilometres an hour.

Such clear and dramatic evidence of the DC-10's final moments certainly did nothing to refute the belief that a bomb on board the aircraft was responsible for the disaster. But neither did it positively confirm the theory, though it was difficult to see what else could have suddenly caused a crisis of such magnitude.

The difficulty was that none of the six passengers ejected from the aircraft before the actual crash bore any sign of having been subjected to blast from an inflight explosion. Certainly the bodies had many broken bones, but they were otherwise intact and, unlike the great number of other casualties in the accident, were easily identifiable. Indeed, pathological examination indicated that their injuries were entirely the result of hitting the ground at the end of their fall. Similarly, the six cabin seats ejected from the aircraft with them, and the sections of floor panelling, bore no evidence of explosive blast.

Meanwhile the ground search by parties of police for other components that might have fallen from the aircraft had been continuing beneath the flightpath of the DC-10, particularly in the area where Air Traffic Control's primary radar system had shown the separated section to have disappeared.

Not far from where the sudden arrival of the six bodies and cabin seats from the sky had startled and bewildered the farm worker near the village of St Pathus, searchers found the battered remains of what looked like an aircraft door. It proved in fact to be the door to the rear underfloor cargo hold, located on the port side of the DC-10 beneath the aftermost section of the passenger cabin.

Innocuous though this further piece of wreckage seemed by comparison with the mass devastation in the Forest of Ermenonville 15 kilometres to the north, it would turn out to be the most telling find of the entire investigation.

And for Charles Miller, Director of the Aviation Safety Bureau at the headquarters offices of the US National Transportation Safety Board in Washington DC, news of the discovery would bring a chilling realisation.

Twenty one months previously, on June 12, 1972, American Airlines' Flight 96 from Los Angeles, California to LaGuardia Airport, New York, via Detroit and Buffalo, was being operated by the company's relatively new DC-10-10, N103AA. Captain Bryce McCormick, 52, First Officer Peter Whitney, 34, and Flight Engineer Clayton Burke, 50, typified the experience and background to be expected of a flightcrew belonging to a major, long established US airline flying widebodied aircraft.

An American Airlines' McDonnell Douglas DC-10-10. The company was one of four major US air carriers to introduce the DC-10 to domestic routes in the early 1970s. (McDonnell Douglas)

McCormick had a total of 24,000 hours, Whitney 8000, and the flight engineer almost 14,000 hours flying experience.

The long afternoon trip above cloud across the continent from Los Angeles was normal in every way, the DC-10 touching down after dark at Detroit in overcast but fine weather at 6.35pm.

After the passengers disembarked, the DC-10 was refuelled, cargo unloaded and loaded, and passengers came aboard again. There were only 56 of them for the brief 175nm leg of the flight on to Buffalo, but the aircraft was now carrying a notable addition – a coffin containing a corpse that had been loaded into its rear underfloor cargo hold at Detroit.

The turnaround was a quick one, and at 7.10pm the DC-10 was taxiing out to the holding point for Detroit's Runway 03 Right.

At 7.20, with the first officer at the controls, it was cleared for takeoff.

Five minutes later, when they had almost reached 12,000 feet on autopilot climb to Flight Level 230, (23,000 feet), and were above Windsor, Ontario, on the Canadian side of Lake Erie, the captain sighted the lights of another big aircraft crossing their path well above them. "There goes a big one up there," he remarked conversationally.

The first officer leant forward, close to the windscreen, for a better look.

Suddenly there was loud bang or explosion somewhere behind them in the aircraft. In the same instant a powerful rearwards surge of air threw a cloud of dust up into the crews' faces, pulled off the headphones Captain McCormick was wearing, drew First Officer Whitney sharply back in his seat, and flung open the flightdeck door to the cabin, releasing the dust into it and carrying the flightcrew's caps with it. Almost at the same time the rudder pedals slammed full left, and all three throttle levers snapped closed.

In the passenger cabin, Senior Flight Attendant Cyda Smith, making coffee in the forward galley, was hurled off her feet, papers and all other loose items were snatched up and whisked rearwards, several centre ceiling panels were pulled from their attachments, to be left hanging by their electrical wiring, and a metal floor hatch in the aisle next to seat 4H flew up, striking a woman passenger in the face. All this was accompanied by a loud whistling from the rear of the aircraft.

Momentarily blinded by the shower of dust, the captain's first thought was that the DC-10 had collided with something and that the

Map of the Detroit-Windsor region on the western shores of Lake Erie. The position where the cargo door was found is shown. (Matthew Tesch)

windscreen had shattered. "What the hell was that?" he called out as both the pressurisation warning horn and the fire warning bell began sounding on the flightdeck.

"We've hit something," said Burke from the flight engineer's station.

First Officer Whitney: "We've lost an engine!"

Captain McCormick recovered himself quickly. "Which one is it?"

Whitney: "No 2."

Burke: "No 1 is still good ... but we'll have to check out ..."

Whitney (interrupting): "Yes – we've got engines 1 and 3. Do we have hydraulics?"

McCormick: No – I've got full left rudder here."

Burke: "Hydraulic pressure's OK."

Cabin attendant (entering flight deck): Is everything all right up here?"

McCormick (about to call ATC) yelled at her: "No!" He pressed his microphone button: "Cleveland Centre ... we've got an emergency ..."

Whitney (aside to flight attendant): "You better go back to the cabin."

Back in the chaos of the cabin, now filling with white fog as the result of the sudden decompression, another sort of emergency was being acted out. In the lounge in the aftermost section, fortunately devoid of passengers because the aircraft was so lightly laden, two flight attendants, seated by the two aft cabin doors on opposite sides of the fuselage, were thrown to the floor as it partly collapsed into the cargo hold below. Cabin ceiling panels fell on top of them, temporarily trapping starboard side Flight Attendant Beatrice Copeland by the foot, while a serving bar between the two attendants' seats tore loose and fell into the cavity.

On the port side, as Flight Attendant Sandra McConnell struggled to regain her feet, she found herself staring down amid the collapsed floor panels into the underfloor hold. Where the cargo door on the port side had been was now a howling black void through which the cloud tops were dimly visible far below!

Though Copeland and McConnell both sustained minor injuries, these

"Bouncing over the grass ... the DC-10 finally came to rest, half on and half off the runway." (Matthew Tesch)

did not stop them going on with their work.

Forward in the First Class cabin just behind the flightdeck, the hard pressed cabin crew had to cope with yet another difficulty. The woman struck on the face by the hatch, together with her female companion, had both become hysterical and were screaming, convinced they were about to die.

On the flightdeck, McCormick disconnected the autopilot, and took over control manually. Not that much control was available. Though the rudder pedals were jammed fully to the left, the aircraft was yawing powerfully to the right, requiring about half left aileron to maintain a heading. The elevators were almost jammed and their response extremely sluggish. The throttle lever for the No 2 (tail-mounted) engine could not be moved and the engine itself was dead. But the still idling wing mounted Nos 1 and 3 engines responded as their throttles were opened and McCormick found he was able stabilise the aircraft in level flight at about 250 knots.

Cleared to return for a landing at Detroit (the DC-10 was under the jurisdiction of the Cleveland ATC Centre at the time), McCormick told the controller: "We have no rudder control whatsoever, so our turns have to be very slow and cautious."

Using the wing engines differentially for directional control, all the while holding on left aileron to counteract the right yaw, he gingerly nursed the DC-10 round in a wide shallow turn back towards Detroit.

Then with equal caution, he commenced letting down slowly, fearfully conscious that if the nose lowered too far and the descent rate increased too much, it might be impossible to recover and regain level flight. Handling the aircraft now was akin to walking a tightrope – again he was judiciously juggling engine power, relying primarily on it this time for attitude control.

The DC-10 was now descending at 300 feet a minute at an airspeed of 160 knots. Though they were still above 11,000 feet, McCormick did not dare reduce engine power much further, lest he lose what control he still had. But he needed to increase the rate of descent.

"OK – give me about 15 [degrees] on the flaps now," he instructed Whitney. "Watch it carefully." With this amount of flap and a slight increase in power, McCormick succeeded in stabilising the descent at 800 feet a minute.

"That's a nice rate of descent," Whitney commented encouragingly, "Even if we have to touch down this way, we'll be doing well.

Finding a moment now to make an announcement over the PA system, Captain McCormick, still holding on left aileron, told the passengers there was a "mechanical problem" and that they were returning to Detroit. Apologising for the "inconvenience", he assured them the company would provide a substitute aircraft to fly them on to Buffalo and New York. He also now took time to call Senior Flight Attendant Smith to the flightdeck to brief her on what was happening, and instruct her on preparing the aircraft for an emergency landing.

Returning to the cabin, she made her own announcement to the passengers, gave them a comprehensive briefing on the emergency measures being taken, and the procedures to be followed prior to landing and afterwards.

Her seven flight attendants then dealt with passengers personally, moving some away from the damaged and obstructed areas of the cabin, collecting personal items that could pose a danger at the moment of impact, reassuring those who seemed doubtful about what to do, and having all passengers remove their shoes.

Detroit's Runway 03 Left, 3200 metres in length and 60 metres wide, appeared to be the best option for attempting a landing in the barely controllable aircraft, and at McCormick's request for a long final approach, ATC vectored the DC-10 to intercept the runway localiser 20nm out.

On descending to 6000 feet, the DC-10 was transferred to Detroit Arrivals Control and cleared to continue down to 3000 feet. Deciding not to dump fuel because of unknown damage to the rear fuselage and tail assembly, McCormack carefully manoeuvred the aircraft on to its very long final approach heading.

"Visibility is one and a half miles, breaking, and Detroit is clear of all aircraft," the arrivals controller told them.

"Give me the gear!" McCormick said to Whitney.

As the undercarriage thumped down normally, the descent rate increased and McCormick gently edged the throttle levers forward to stabilise it again.

"OK, we're coming into the ILS,"

Portion of the aft cargo door still attached to NIO3AA's fuselage, after the DC-10 made its emergency landing back at Detroit. The photograph was taken the morning after the near accident.

he said to Whitney, "I'm going to start slowing her down – give me 22 [degrees] on the flaps".

Again there was a judicious juggling of power settings to adjust the aircraft's attitude and rate of descent.

"You're two and a half miles from the outer marker," the controller called. "Contact the Tower now on 112.1." Whitney dialled the Tower frequency. With no further request from the DC-10, the tower controller transmitted: "American 96 – cleared to land!"

"Give me 36 on the flaps," said McCormick tersely.

As Whitney operated the flap lever again, the rate of descent almost doubled to more than 1500 feet a minute. McCormick quickly added more power, bringing it back to 800. But the airspeed had gone up too. They were now approaching at between 160 and 165 knots – 30 knots above the normal approach speed. It would have to do, despite the resulting very flat approach angle – using more flap could be too risky.

"I have no rudder to straighten it out when we hit," McCormick warned his crew ominously as they sank towards the runway lights stretching into the distance ahead of them.

Now came the final test. What would happen if they were not able to check the rate of descent for touchdown? At best it would be an extremely heavy landing. But with both pilots hauling back hard on the near-jammed elevator controls, they succeeded in raising the nose into the landing attitude.

The resulting landing was a good one and McCormick immediately pulled the power levers into reverse thrust. But under the effect of the biased rudder, the DC-10 swung off the runway to the right, bouncing over the grass towards the lights of the airport buildings.

For a moment, desperately trying to counter the swing with full opposite aileron, McCormack thought his battle to save the aircraft was lost after all. But then Whitney grabbed the throttle for the port engine, pull-

ing it hard back beyond the full reverse thrust position, at the same time pushing the starboard throttle out of reverse thrust. His desperate ruse worked, the aircraft swinging back to parallel the runway for 850 metres as it decelerated on the grass airfield surface. As the offset rudder became less effective, the nose-wheel steering, deflected to the left by the jammed rudder pedals, took over and the DC-10 began a gradual turn back towards the runway. It finally came to rest, half on and half off the runway, 2700 metres from the threshold.

Immediately the cabin crew opened all six available doors (avoiding the rear two where the floor had collapsed) and deployed the emergency evacuation slides. In less than a minute all on board had left the aircraft, congratulating themselves on their deliverance – and the crew for their skilled and highly professional handling of the emergency.

Though sabotage was suspected when the inflight emergency devel

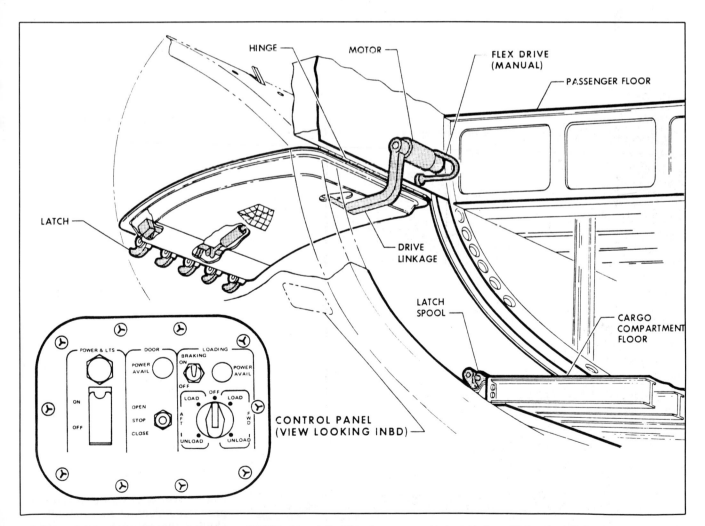

Schematic drawing of the aft cargo door. The angle of view is such that the observers eye is almost in line with the aircraft's keel, slightly below the aft bulkhead of the cargo compartment, looking forward and to port. The inset shows the door's control panel, located beneath a hinged cover on the outside of the fuselage, next to the leading edge of the door. (NTSB)

oped, and FBI agents were already on hand to question passengers when the DC-10 landed, examination of the aircraft quickly revealed the source of the problem was far more mundane – the door to the rear underfloor cargo compartment, located on the port side of the fuselage, had simply opened in flight. Though the door itself had been torn off by aerodynamic forces, much of its battered and folded exterior skin remained attached to the fuselage.

The missing cargo compartment door was later found lying in a field some 30 kilometres from Detroit Airport.

The DC-10's rear cargo compartment door, located on the lower aft section of the fuselage on the port side, is rectangular, hinged at the top, and opens outwards and upwards. It incorporates a vent flap to release any residual pressure in the cargo compartment after the aircraft has landed, thus preventing the possibility of the door flying open uncontrollably when its latches are released.

The door is opened and closed electrically, controlled from an external panel beneath a hinged cover, next to the leading edge of the door. When the switch on the panel is moved to "door close", an electric motor drives the door shut. Continuing to hold the switch in the "close" position for a further seven seconds then operates a screw-type actuator within the door to rotate its four C-latches onto corresponding spools or rollers attached to the door sill, and the driving mechanisms "over-centre", in effect locking the latches in their closed position. At the end of the sequence a green light on the control panel illuminates to indicate the door is closed and locked.

The door's vent flap is then closed manually by pulling down a small hand lever set into the door beside it. Moving the vent flap lever down into its stowed position also slides interconnected locking pins inside the door over the mechanical drive to the four C-latches, further ensuring these door latches are fully home. The lever cannot move to its full travel, closing the vent flap fully, unless the C-latch mechanisms *are* over-centre. Micro switches on the locking pin assembly extinguish a "door open" warning lamp on the flight engineer's instrument panel when the pins slide into position. With the mechanism properly rigged, the manual force on the lever needed to drive the locking pins home is 30 pounds (13.6kg).

Examination of the cargo door recovered from the field, together with its matching structure on the fuselage, showed that the door hinge, door frame and the rollers on the door sill were basically undamaged. But although the C-latches on the door itself had closed over the rollers, the driving mechanisms had not locked over-centre, all four being nearly five millimetres from their fully home positions. The vent flap lever was in its stowed position, but the locking pins had not engaged over the C-latch mechanism, the interconnecting linkage between the hand lever, the vent flap and the locking pins having bent and broken in two places. Bench tests established that the C-latch mechanisms had not gone fully home because of low voltage to the electric actuator.

It was evident to NTSB investigators that, with the C-latches closed on the door sill rollers, but not locked over-centre, the increasing pressurisation load on the cargo door as the aircraft gained height, was progressively transmitted through the latches to the actuator's attachment bolts. When the increasing pressure on the door became too much for the bolts, they sheared, allowing the door to spring open.

The sudden loss of the door violently depressurised the cargo compartment, ejecting its contents, including the coffin being carried as cargo. Because the cargo compart-

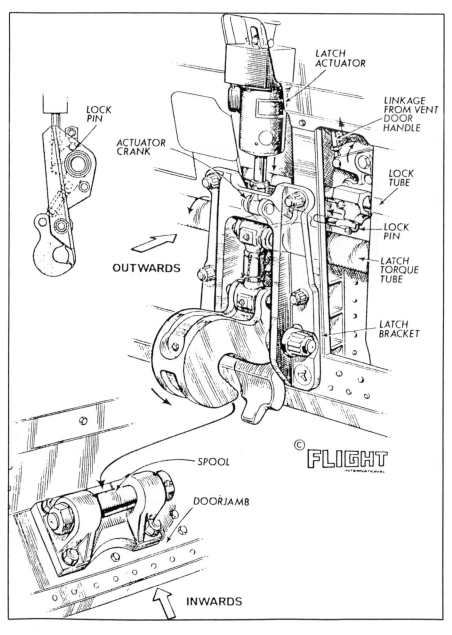

Detailed drawing of one of four C-latches that secure the DC-10's aft cargo door to corresponding rollers or spools on the door sill. The four latches are driven home by a single electric actuator. (With acknowledgement to Flight International)

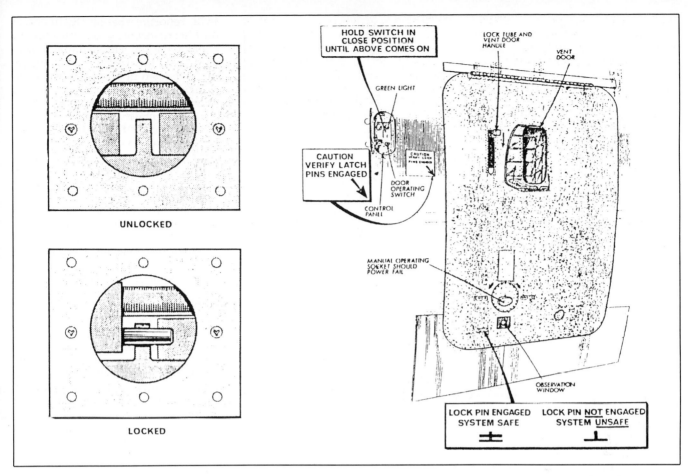

External view of cargo door on the port side of the DC-10's aft fuselage, showing positions of vent flap and lever, door control panel, and viewing window. The window, fitted after the near disaster to American Airlines' N103AA. near Windsor, Canada, on June 12, 1972, enables cargo handlers to ensure that the C-latch locking mechanism is correctly over-centre and locking pins are in place. The two drawings at left show the view through the window, with the locking pins in the unlocked and locked positions. (With acknowledgement to Flight International)

ment was not equipped with pressure relief vents to the cabin above it a powerful pressure differential was immediately created between the compartment and cabin interior. Under the load thus suddenly imposed on the cabin floor, the floor support structure gave way and the floor collapsed downwards into the cargo compartment.

In the DC-10, there is no direct mechanical linkage between the flight controls and the control surfaces themselves. Instead, the control cables from the flightdeck are connected to hydraulic actuators which in turn move the massive control surfaces. The control cables from the flightdeck to the tail surface actuators, as well as to the fin-mounted No 2 engine, are routed through the support beams for the cabin floor, above the underfloor compartments. The collapse of the floor above the rear cargo compartment either snapped or severely jammed these cables. The left rudder cable was broken, while the intact right rudder cable was forced downwards, putting a right signal into the rudder control valve system,

at the same time pulling the flight-deck rudder pedals to full left deflection. Two of the four elevator cables were broken and the other two forced downward, making the pilots' control columns extremely difficult to move. The cables for the No 2 engine power lever and fire shutoff valve were also severed.

Enquiries established that the cargo handler who closed the rear door at Detroit before the DC-10 departed for Buffalo, had experienced difficulty ensuring it was locked. After using the switch to close the door, he had listened for the mechanism to stop running, then attempted to pull down the vent flap lever. It refused to move with the usual hand pressure, so he used his knee to force it. This succeeded in moving the handle into the stowed position, but left the vent flap slightly out of position. He pointed this out to the ground engineer responsible for despatching the aircraft, who gave his approval for its departure in this condition.

Tests on the DC-10 door mechanism at McDonnell Douglas showed that the vent flap lever could in fact

be moved to the stowed position without engaging the locking pins over the C-latch linkages if sufficient force were applied. A force of 120 pounds (55kg) on the hand lever would deform the interconnecting linkage inside the door, giving the impression the C-latches were over-centre and the locking pins in place when they were not. The same mechanical deformation could operate the micro-switches on the locking pins, extinguishing the "door open" warning lamp on the flight engineer's panel, again giving a false impression that the door was safely secured.

The investigators also learnt that the cargo door design had a history of problems, McDonnell Douglas having previously received more than 100 complaints of difficulties with the closing of this door. As a result, on May 30, 1972, only a fortnight before the door failure over Windsor, McDonnell Douglas issued a service bulletin (No 57-27) to all DC-10 operators revising the electrical wiring to the latch actuator to overcome the drop in voltage thought to be the source of the problem.

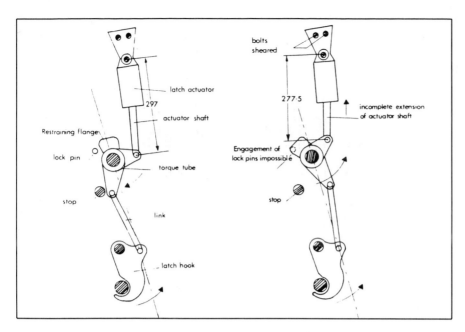

Mechanical schematic drawing of C-latch mechanism, showing how pressure on cargo door can be transferred to actuator securing bolts, if system is not over-centre. The mechanism on the left is in the fully closed and locked position – over-centred, irreversible and safe. That on the right shows the C-latches closed over the rollers on the door sill, but the mechanism not driven fully home over-centre and therefore unsafe. The drawings also show how the locking pins cannot be driven home unless mechanism is over-centre. (With acknowledgement to Flight International)

It was now obvious to the NTSB investigators that the failure of N103AA's door mechanism could easily have had catastrophic consequences. They were also concerned that the loss of pressure in a cargo compartment in flight could so jeopardise the safety of an aircraft.

On completion of the investigation on July 6, 1972, less than three weeks after the DC-10's emergency landing, the National Transportation Safety Board made two urgent recommendations to the Federal Aviation Administration:

• That the DC-10's cargo door locking system be modified to make *it physically impossible* to move the vent flap locking handle to its stowed position unless the C-latch locking pins were *fully* engaged.

• That relief vents be installed between the aft cargo compartment and the cabin above it to minimise the pressure loading of the cabin floor in the event of a sudden depressurisation of the cargo compartment.

FAA officials immediately set about preparing an Airworthiness Directive (AD), binding at law upon all US operators of the DC-10, detailing interim measures to be taken to avoid a repetition of the Windsor experience. But after urgent consultations between the FAA Administrator and the president of the Douglas Division of McDonnell Douglas, also prompted by the dangers manifested

on the night of June 12, it was agreed that the necessary remedies could be promulgated as service bulletins rather than mandatory ADs.

This "gentlemen's agreement" was reached after the FAA Administrator had been assured the door problem could be easily fixed. Though it overruled the decisions of senior FAA technical staff, it was made in deference to the four major airlines now operating the DC-10, whose aircraft utilisation in the middle of the peak summer travel season could be adversely affected by an AD.

Three days later, McDonnell Douglas despatched detailed telegrams to all DC-10 operators recommending the installation of a "lock mechanism viewing window" in the cargo doors. This interim measure would "permit visual inspection to determine the doors are latched and locked prior to flight". As well, it recommended that explanatory placards be placed by the door control panel, the vent flap lever, and the viewing window. The telegram was confirmed a few days later by a further McDonnell Douglas service bulletin, No A52-35, the "A" indicating "Alert" status. The viewing window, a small peephole in the lower part of the door, enabled an observer to actually see if the locking pins for the C-latch mechanism had slid fully into place.

The FAA officially replied to the NTSB's recommendations on July 7,

1972, reporting that all DC-10 operators were carrying out 100 hourly checks on the cargo door system and would incorporate the modifications detailed in the two McDonnell-Douglas service bulletins within 300 flying hours. Additional modifications were under review, and while it might "not be feasible to provide complete venting between cabin and cargo compartment", the NTSB's recommendations would "be considered".

A further service bulletin from McDonnell Douglas at about the same time, No 52-37, provided for the stiffening of the interconnection between the vent flap lever and the locking pin mechanism to withstand deformation of the linkage by excess force on the lever. This bulletin was classified as "recommended" by the FAA, but was not mandatory. Still another service bulletin, No 52-40, issued by McDonnell Douglas on October 27, incorporated a coil spring link in the lever mechanism to act as a safety valve and *prevent* excess force being applied to the linkage. It also altered the wiring of the microswitches to the "door closed" warning lamp on the flight engineer's panel to eliminate the possibility of a false indication.

The final, definitive modification to the troubled cargo door latching mechanism was issued by McDonnell Douglas in the form of service bulletin No 52-49 on October 25, 1973. At last fully meeting the NTSB's recommendation to make it physically impossible to stow the vent flap handle unless the locking pins were fully engaged, it called for major changes to the door locking system that entailed no less than 300 manhours for their installation. Yet again the FAA classified the modification as "recommended" only.

It was against this background that Charles Miller, Director of the Aviation Safety Bureau at the NTSB in Washington, DC, prepared to leave for Paris to join the international team investigating the loss of the Turkish DC-10, TC-JAV.

During a stop in the USA en route to Paris, he noticed another airline's DC-10 on the airport, and took the opportunity to look it over. To his considerable unease, he not only found the viewing window in its rear cargo door so dirty that it was almost impossible to look through: none of the ground staff servicing the DC-10 had any idea what the little window was for!

The next day, March 6, 1974, Miller

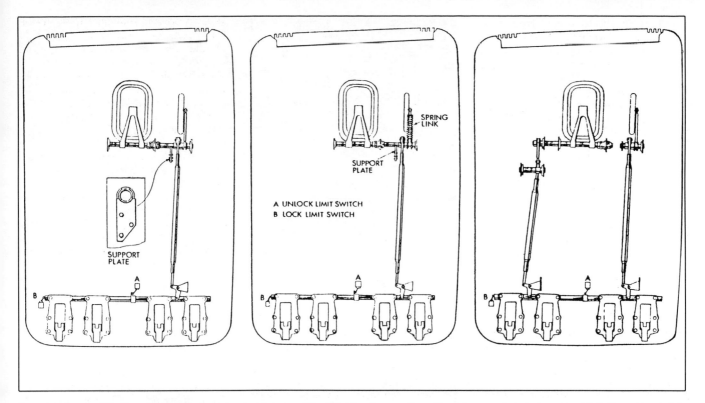

Stages in the modification of the internal mechanical linkage of the DC-10s aft cargo door. The linkage as first designed is at left, the support plate being added after the Windsor incident to stiffen the mechanism against deformation by excessive force on the vent flap lever. A coil spring was later inserted in the linkage to prevent excessive force being applied. The illustration at right shows the final "closed loop" linkage modification required by an FAA Airworthiness Directive after the Paris disaster. This linkage made it physically impossible to close the vent flap and stow its lever unless the locking pins were fully engaged over the C-latch mechanism. (With acknowledgement to Flight International)

arrived in Paris and was able to examine the battered cargo door that had fallen from TC-JAV. The door's latching system itself was little damaged by impact and its general condition almost an exact replication of that of N103AA's separated door when it was examined at Detroit 21 months previously. As with the American Airlines DC-10, there had been no sabotage – at least not by intent and certainly not by any terrorist organisation.

There had been no bomb. Again as in the earlier instance, the actuator had simply failed to drive the C-latch mechanisms over-centre, and the bolts attaching the latch actuator to the door structure had sheared under the increasing cabin pressure as the aircraft climbed.

Because of the complete disintegration of the Turkish aircraft, there was no possibility of determining what had contributed to this failure. Immediately evident to Miller however, was that although the door had the peephole and explanatory placards (in both English and Turkish) recommended by service bulletin A52-35, the stiffening of the internal interconnecting linkage from the vent flap handle had not been incorporated as called for by service bulletin 52-37.

This was surprising in view of the fact that McDonnell Douglas had issued the bulletin three months before TC-JAV was ordered and six months before it was delivered to the Turkish airline. It meant that the locking pin linkage on TC-JAV's aft cargo door was at least as vulnerable to excessive force as N103AA's had been at Detroit, 21 months before.

The cargo handler who closed TC-JAV's aft door at Orly Airport was an Algerian expatriate, who had worked for SAMOR, the French airline servicing company, for six years. He had been given instructions on how to close the DC-10's cargo doors when the aircraft type entered service, being specifically warned against using excessive force on the vent flap handle. He was not instructed on what to look for through the peephole, and this was not part of his duties.

As far as he was concerned, if the vent flap handle clicked down normally into its stowed position and the vent flap closed at the same time, the door was safe. Anything less and he was to call his supervisor.

In any case, THY's Paris based resident ground engineer usually came and made a final inspection before the aircraft departed. Sometimes this was done by the flight en-

gineer too. But no one had ever told the cargo handler what to do if neither engineer was available. And he could read neither the English nor the Turkish placards by the door.

As usual, he followed the procedure for closing the door and it all worked as it had on numerous previous occasions. But this time the resident ground engineer was away on holidays, and the flight engineer chose not to appear for a final pre-flight inspection. In failing to do so, he signed his own death warrant. A look through the peephole would have shown the flight engineer the locking pins had not gone home.

Close examination of the locking pins on the recovered cargo door by Charles Miller and other investigators, showed score marks indicating that the interconnecting linkage had been incorrectly rigged. As a result, only a small additional force on the vent flap lever was necessary to drive it home when the locking pins were not in position – meaning that the Turkish aircraft was exposed to far greater risk of door malfunction than even the American Airlines DC-10 had been.

The events that followed were almost an exact replay of those of 21 months before. The difference was that the rear cabin configuration of the Turkish DC-10 varied from that of American Airlines' N103AA. Instead of a lounge for the passengers above the rear cargo compartment, TC-JAV had seats. Those on the window sides of the two cabin aisles were in sets of three. And they were all occupied, imposing a far heavier load on the cabin floor and its supporting structure.

Undoubtedly, when the cargo door blew off, depressurising the compartment, the resulting collapse of the cabin floor above it was more catastrophic, a fact all too evident from the ejection of two sets of seats, each with three passengers strapped to them, through the cargo door aperture.

Undoubtedly too, this major disruption of the rear fuselage's internal structure would have had a worse effect on the aircraft's control system routed beneath the cabin floor. Just what degree of control was left to the flightcrew can never be known. But from the CVR transcription there was clearly very little, if any.

What can be said with far more certainty is that if the FAA Administrator had heeded the recommendations of the NTSB, and those of his own senior technical staff, after the frightening American Airlines experience over Windsor in 1972, the horrific accident to THY Turkish Airlines Flight TK981 near Paris would probably never have happened.

And what was the immediate FAA reaction to the findings of the Paris investigation?

Like the responsible aviation regulatory body it was, it immediately issued an Airworthiness Directive making mandatory the recommendations of McDonnell Douglas' service bulletin 52-49 of five months previously. Henceforth it would be *impossible* to stow the cargo door's vent flap handle unless the locking pins were engaged.

The FAA was shutting the stable door at last. Unfortunately for Flight TK981 and its 346 hapless occupants, the horse had already bolted.

These two pictures portray "the other side" of the investigation of an accident of the enormity of TC-JAV's – photographs and personal belongings recovered from the vast scatter of charred and muddy debris in the Grove of Dammartin, laid out for identification. The task confronting the various civil authorities responsible for accounting for all on board was made immeasurably more difficult by the violence of the high speed impact, as well as by the last minute confusion that existed at Orly Airport's Departures counter as additional London bound passengers vied for seats aboard Flight TK981.

CHAPTER 16

"By lucky chance this was a ferry flight ..."

– Industry commentator

Northwest Orient Airlines Boeing 727-251 N247US [20296] (F/n 274) –
December 1, 1974

Undue haste in completing the pretakeoff checklist, and a first officer inexperienced on the aircraft type, set the stage for erroneous and misleading airspeed indications. But greater attention to the attitude instruments could have shown the errors for what they were – and averted a tragedy.

On the face of it, it seemed only appropriate that the Northwest Orient Airlines crew rostered for a night charter flight were all enthusiastic young men in their early thirties.

It was December 1, 1974, and the aircraft had been hired by a professional football team to pick up its players and their support team from Buffalo, New York State.

Officially designated Flight NW6231, the aircraft allocated to the task was Northwest Orient's five year old N274US, a Boeing 727-251, under the command of Capt John Lagorio, 35.

With eight years' service with the airline, Captain Lagorio was well experienced on the aircraft type, had a total of about 7500 hours, and had held a command rating for five years. Lagorio's first officer for the flight, Walter Zadra, 32, though only recently upgraded to this position, had been with the company for nearly the same time. A former flight engineer on Boeing 707s, he had become a 727 first officer six weeks previously, and had since flown nearly 50 hours in his new role. Even so, 1500 hours of his total 3700 hours flying time had been logged as a pilot.

Flight Engineer James Cox, 33, had nearly 2000 hours with the airline in this capacity, 1600 of it in Boeing 727s.

To undertake the charter flight, the Boeing 727, based at John F Kennedy International Airport, New York, had first to be ferried to Buffalo, on Lake Erie near the western extremity of New York State, a 40 minute trip over a distance of about 265 nautical miles.

The weather forecast that cold winter evening predicted overcast cloud at 5000 feet, with a wind from the northwest at between 14 and 24 knots. Moderate to heavy rain and scattered thunderstorms, with tops to 28,000 feet, were expected over the eastern portion of the route, while moderate to heavy snowshowers were likely on the western section beyond the Appalachian Mountains. Freezing level was at the surface, with icing likely in cloud.

With only the flight crew on board, the Boeing 727 took off at 7.14pm on a standard instrument departure clearance and, on taking up its northwesterly heading, was cleared to climb to 14,000 feet. At 7.21pm the New York ATC Centre assumed ra-

dar control of the flight, clearing it now to climb to its planned en route Flight Level 310 (31,000 feet).

Only three and a half minutes later, when the Boeing 727's position on the New York ATC Centre's radar was three nm beyond Bear Mountain, 35nm northwest of John F Kennedy Airport, the air traffic controller handling the aircraft was startled to hear it transmit an emergency call.

Aircraft: "Mayday, mayday ...

Controller: "Flight 6231 ... go ahead!"

Aircraft: "Roger ... we're out of control ... descending through 20,000 feet!"

In response to the controller's urgent questions, the flightcrew member operating the radio replied desperately: "We're descending through 12 [thousand feet] – we're in a stall!"

Apart from a brief unmodulated radio transmission 17 seconds afterwards, there were no further calls from the aircraft.

The unburnt wreckage of the Boeing 727 was found in a forest on the side of Bear Mountain later that evening, just over five kilometres west of the town of Thiells and about 35km north of the city of New York. All three flightcrew members, the only occupants of the aircraft, had been killed.

★　★　★

National Transportation Safety Board investigators who reached the crash site later that night found that the Boeing 727 had struck the tree covered 10 degree mountain slope in a slightly nosedown and starboard wingdown attitude at an elevation of 1090 feet.

Detailed examination of the distorted and disintegrated aircraft structure on the frozen ground of the forest early the following morning established that, except for the port side tailplane and the tips of both elevators, all the Boeing's wreckage lay within an area only 55 metres long and 30 metres wide. The missing components were later found scattered between 115 and 1280 metres away from the main wreckage, showing conclusively that they had separated from the aircraft before its impact with the ground.

The Nos 1 and 3 engines had broken away from their tail mounting pylons, but the No 2 engine remained in its mounting in the tail assembly. All the engine damage was clearly the result of impact forces and it was evident that all three were at high power settings when this occurred. The undercarriage and spoilers were retracted at the time, and the flaps lowered two degrees, with Nos 2, 3, 6 and 7 leading edge slats fully extended, positions consistent with the flap setting.

There was nothing to suggest that any of the aircraft's systems had malfunctioned prior to impact with the ground, but two of the aircraft's five pitot heads – the captain's and the port elevator pitot head – were found to contain water or ice. Those for the copilot and the auxiliary system were too severely damaged to be checked for water, while the starboard elevator pitot head, still attached to the fin, was in good condition.

Amongst the remains of the flightdeck, the aircraft's three damaged attitude indicators were all showing 20° nosedown, with the wings almost level. The two pitot head heater switches on the overhead panel above the copilot's seat were in the off position, with the toggles bent backwards, indicating they had been in this position at the moment of impact.

The aircraft's Flight Data and Cockpit Voice Recorders were both damaged, but their tapes were in-

tact. A readout of the FDR traces was found to cover 11 minutes 55 seconds of flight, beginning from shortly before liftoff. The CVR tape began with the crew's conduct of the pretakeoff checklist shortly after 7.00pm, and terminated with the sounds of impact three seconds before 7.26pm.

Air-to-ground communications recorded by the three ATC units that handled the Boeing – Control Tower, Departures Control, and the New York ATC Centre – were correlated with the CVR transcription and FDR readout to give a comprehensive account of what had happened aboard the aircraft in its brief 12 minutes of flight.

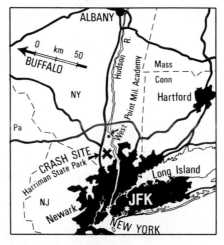

Locality map of New York and adjoining States, showing position of Boeing 727 crash site in Harriman State Park, just beyond the outskirts of greater New York City. The accident occurred less than 12 minutes after departure from John F Kennedy International Airport on a ferry flight to Buffalo. (Matthew Tesch)

The progress of the flight appeared perfectly normal until the aircraft, cleared to Flight Level 310, was climbing through 16,000 feet at an airspeed of 305 knots and at a climb rate of 2500 feet per minute. At this stage, with no change in engine power setting, the airspeed indication began to increase, and with it the rate of climb.

Surprised by this apparent performance, First Officer Zadra, who was flying the aircraft, remarked to the other crew members: "Do you realise we're going 340 knots and climbing 5000 feet a minute?"

The crew talked briefly about the reason for this spirited performance (actually beyond the capability of the aircraft), Flight Engineer Cox concluding: "That's because we're light."

But far from falling off as they gained more altitude, the airspeed and rate of climb continued to increase, despite Zadra exerting back pressure on the control column to prevent the airspeed becoming excessive. By the time the aircraft was climbing through 23,000 feet, the rate of climb was more than 6500fpm and the airspeed indication had risen to 405 knots, triggering the overspeed warning horn. "Would you believe that!" exclaimed Captain Lagorio.

"I believe it," Zadra retorted. "I just can't do anything about it!"

No crewmember suggested that the pitot system could possibly be at fault, causing erroneous readings.

Lagorio: "Pull her back and let her climb."

Again the overspeed warning horn sounded, followed 10 seconds later by the stick-shaker stall warning, accompanied by slight negative g and the altimeter reading levelled at 24,800 feet with the airspeed indicators reading 420 knots.

But the crew, apparently convinced the airspeed was in fact excessive, failed to recognise the continuing stall warning.

Zadra: There's that Mach buffet – I guess we'll have to pull it up [further]."

Lagorio: "Pull it up!"

At this point the undercarriage warning sounded, indicating that one of the pilots had pulled the throttles closed. Two seconds later, there was again a brief period of negative g as the aircraft fell into a spiral dive to the right, the rate of descent rapidly increasing to 15,000fpm as the vertical acceleration increased again to 1.5g, prompting Lagorio to transmit the aircraft's Mayday call.

Just over half a minute later Lagorio reported they were descending through 12,000 feet in a stall and five seconds after this he called to Zadra, "Flaps Two!"

The sound of the flap lever being moved followed, after which there was an immediate further increase in vertical acceleration, with peaks to 3g. But there was no change in the rate of descent, the airspeed indication reduced to zero, and the noise of the stall warning became intermittent.

Five seconds later, Zadra said urgently (obviously to Lagorio): "Pull now! Pull ... that's it!"

The vertical acceleration then increased further to a severe 5g. But the rate of descent lessened only slightly and the dive continued unchecked.

Eighty three seconds after the Boeing fell into the spiral dive at an altitude of 24,800 feet, there was the noise of initial impact as the aircraft struck the mountain treetops at a terrain elevation of 1090 feet. At this point the recording ended abruptly.

At the time of takeoff, the Boeing 727-251 was laden with 22,000kg of fuel and its gross weight was 66,740kg. This weight, as well as the centre of gravity, were within prescribed limits. The aircraft was fully airworthy in all respects.

In the Boeing 727, the pitot-static instruments on the captain's panel, those for the copilot, and the pitot-static instrumentation for the FDR, are connected to separate pitot and static sources in the nose of the aircraft. Each pitot head and static port incorporates a heating element to prevent icing, with the pitot heads also having a small drain hole for exhausting moisture. The three pitot systems are completely independent, as are the three static systems, except for manual selector valves enabling either the captain or the copilot to select the FDR static system as an alternative pressure source if either primary source malfunctions. The copilot's pitot-static system is also connected to the switch activating the overspeed warning horn, and a second warning system switch is incorporated in the FDR pitot-static system.

In addition to these flightdeck pitot-static systems, two further independent systems are connected to the elevator feel mechanism in the aircraft's longitudinal controls, the control column force required to move the elevators varying as a function of the dynamic pressure measured by these two pitot-static systems. The two pitot heads are similar in design to the pitot heads mounted on the nose, and are mounted on either side of the fin. As with the nose mounted pitot-static sources, each of the tail mounted pitot heads and static ports incorporates a heating element to prevent icing.

Northwest Orient Airlines' operational procedures require the flight engineer to read the pretakeoff checklist, to which the captain and the first officer respond as the checklist tasks are accomplished. The portion of the checklist which includes switching on the heaters for the pitot-static system reads as follows:
• Flaps (15 or 25 degrees as required)
• Marked bug (moveable marker on airspeed indicator dial to show rotation speed)
• Ice protection (engine nacelle heat)
• Pitot heat

The CVR transcript showed that after First Officer Zadra responded to Flight Engineer Cox's flap setting call, and Cox called for the "bug" setting, there was no immediate response by either Captain Lagorio or

The flightdeck of a Boeing 727. The switches for the pitot head heaters are on the far right hand side of the overhead panel above the first officer's seat. At the time of the accident, no warning light was provided to indicate the heaters were not activated. The flight engineer's seat is in the right foreground, with his own control panel just out of the picture to the right.

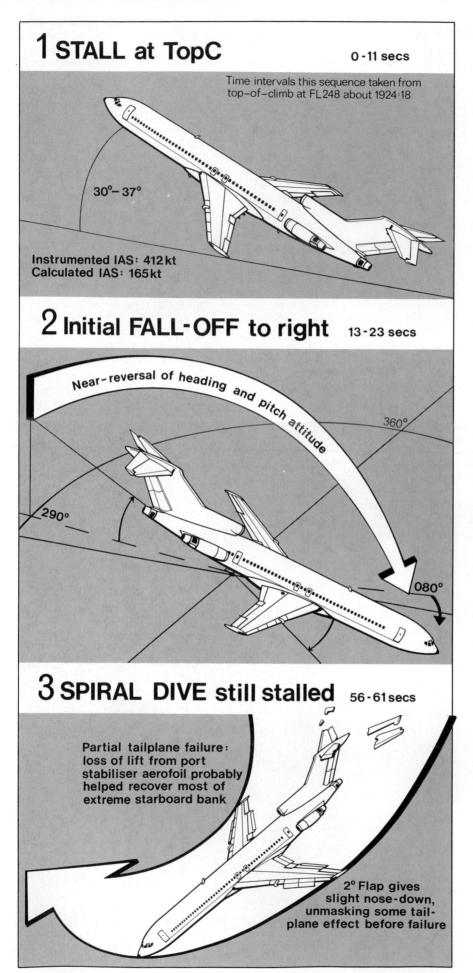

1 STALL at TopC

0-11 secs

Time intervals this sequence taken from top–of–climb at FL248 about 1924:18

30°– 37°

Instrumented IAS: 412 kt
Calculated IAS: 165 kt

2 Initial FALL-OFF to right

13-23 secs

Near–reversal of heading and pitch attitude

360°

290°

080°

3 SPIRAL DIVE still stalled

56-61 secs

Partial tailplane failure:
loss of lift from port
stabiliser aerofoil probably
helped recover most of
extreme starboard bank

2° Flap gives
slight nose-down,
unmasking some tail-
plane effect before failure

Zadra. As a result, the engine ice protection call was missed:

Cox: "Flaps?"

Zadra: "... 15, 15 ... blue"

Cox: "Bug?"

Cox (without waiting for response): "Pitot heat?"

Zadra (apparently responding both to the missed engine anti-ice item and the pitot heat call): "Off and on."

Lagorio: "One forty-two is the bug setting."

Zadra: "Er ... do you want the engine heat on?"

Zadra: "Huh?" (probably responding to Lagorio's nod or hand signal) Sound of five clicks.

A Boeing Company analysis of the data recorded on the FDR and CVR showed that the airspeed and altitude figures were consistent with the aircraft's climb capability until it reached 16,000 feet. But from this point on the simultaneous increases in airspeed and rate of climb began to exceed the theoretical capability of a 727-200, varying directly with the increase in altitude, as would be expected if the pressure in the pitot system remained constant after climbing through 16,000 feet – in other words if the pitot heads had become blocked.

The actual airspeed when the stick shaker stall warning first activated was calculated to be 165 knots, compared to the 412 knots recorded by the FDR, with the aircraft's attitude about 30 degrees noseup.

The normal 1g vertical acceleration acting on the aircraft and its occupants reduced slightly to 0.8g as it levelled out at 24,800 feet, probably because the pilot relaxed the back pressure he was holding on the control wheel, and the stick shaker ceased momentarily. But because of the drag induced by its high nose attitude, the aircraft continued to decelerate, and the stick shaker stall warning was activated again. The second small increment of negative g after the throttles were retarded, coincided with a sudden descent and

Sequence showing inadvertent inflight manoeuvres which led to the loss of the Boeing 727. Exhausting its climb momentum just short of 25,000 feet as a result of the high nose attitude, the aircraft stalled, the nose and starboard wing dropped, and it entered a spiral dive to the right. Within 10 seconds its rate of descent was a staggering 15,000 feet per minute. The attempt to recover from the stall by extending two degrees of flap had little effect. Control column forces applied by the crew finally induced vertical accelerations sufficient to fail the tailplane. (Matthew Tesch)

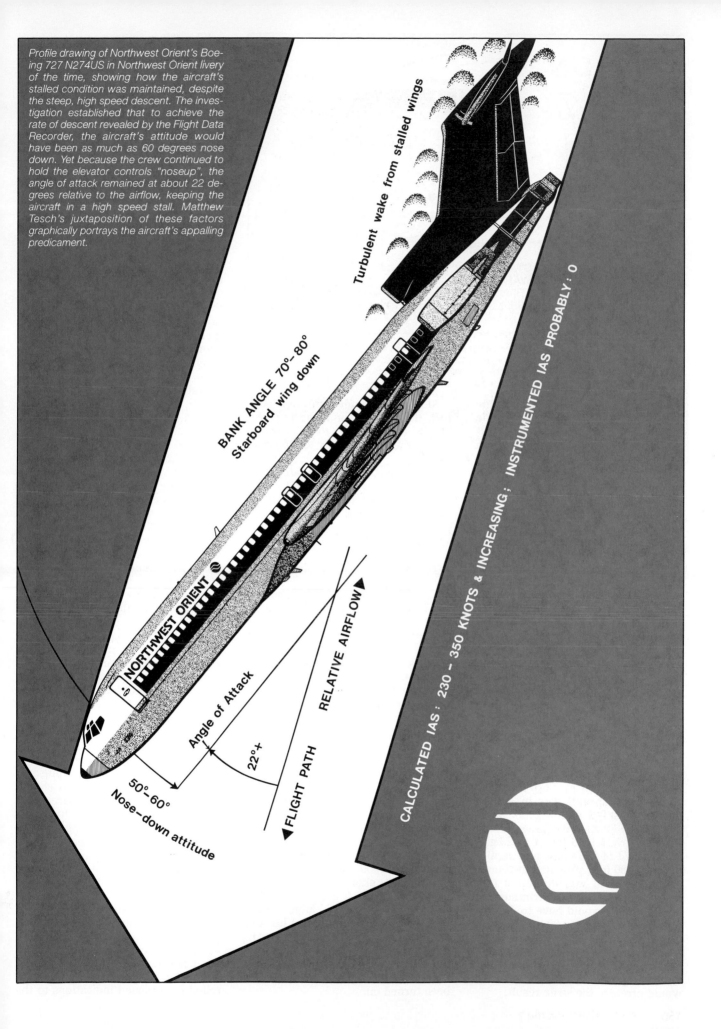

Profile drawing of Northwest Orient's Boeing 727 N274US in Northwest Orient livery of the time, showing how the aircraft's stalled condition was maintained, despite the steep, high speed descent. The investigation established that to achieve the rate of descent revealed by the Flight Data Recorder, the aircraft's attitude would have been as much as 60 degrees nose down. Yet because the crew continued to hold the elevator controls "noseup", the angle of attack remained at about 22 degrees relative to the airflow, keeping the aircraft in a high speed stall. Matthew Tesch's juxtaposition of these factors graphically portrays the aircraft's appalling predicament.

Turbulent wake from stalled wings

BANK ANGLE 70°–80°
Starboard wing down

NORTHWEST ORIENT

RELATIVE AIRFLOW ▲

Angle of Attack

22°+

50°–60°
Nose–down attitude

▲ FLIGHT PATH

CALCULATED IAS : 230 – 350 KNOTS & INCREASING ; INSTRUMENTED IAS PROBABLY : 0

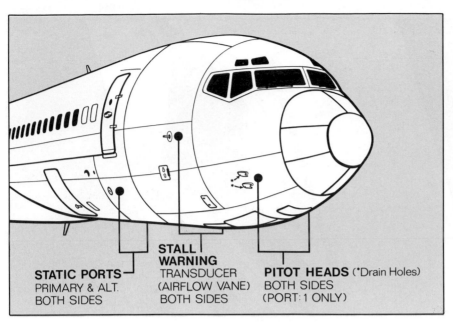

STATIC PORTS
PRIMARY & ALT.
BOTH SIDES

STALL WARNING
TRANSDUCER
(AIRFLOW VANE)
BOTH SIDES

PITOT HEADS (*Drain Holes)
BOTH SIDES
(PORT: 1 ONLY)

Diagram of Boeing 727's nose area, showing position of external sensors for pitot-static and stall warning systems. The stall warning transducer is a pivoting miniature aerofoil which responds to the angle of airflow past either side of the aircraft's nose. (Matthew Tesch)

a rapid change of heading to the right – the result of an aerodynamic stall with a simultaneous loss of lateral control as the aircraft fell into a spiral dive.

The analysis showed that even after the stall, the aircraft reached an angle of attack of 22 degrees or more as it descended. To achieve this angle of attack as well as the measured descent rate of nearly 18,000fpm, the aircraft's attitude would have been more than 60 degrees nosedown at times. The variations in g loadings, averaging about 1.5g at this stage, were probably the result of variations in the aircraft's angle of bank.

As the aircraft descended through 11,000 feet, exceeding 230 knots in a nosedown attitude of at least 50 degrees, the crew extended the flaps to two degrees. The momentary pause in the operation of the stick shaker at this point indicated this had reduced the angle of attack to less than 13 degrees, while the simultaneous increase in vertical acceleration or load factor to more than 2.5g showed the aircraft was in a tight nosedown spiral with a bank angle of between 70 and 80 degrees.

To achieve a load factor of 2.5g at an airspeed of 250 knots and an altitude of 5000 feet, provided the elevator feel system was operating normally and the aircraft trimmed to climb, a pilot would have to exert a pull force of between 20 and 23kg on the control column. However, if the elevator pitot system was blocked, thereby upsetting the elevator feel system, a pull force of less than 14kg would produce the same result.

After it descended through 5000 feet, the load factor being imposed on the aircraft rose to 5g, causing part of the tail assembly to fail structurally.

Boeing engineers calculated that the aircraft's structural limits would have been exceeded at high angles of sideslip and a load factor approaching 5g.

The erroneously high airspeed indications during the aircraft's climb were clearly caused by a complete and nearly simultaneous blockage of all three pitot pressure systems in the nose of the aircraft. The investigators were convinced that the blockages were created by ice forming around the heads, closing the pressure inlet ports and the drain holes.

This conclusion was supported by the moisture found in the pitot heads after the accident, and by the known icing conditions that existed at the time of the flight. The captain of another Northwest Orient aircraft flying the same route behind the Boeing 727 told investigators that he encountered icing conditions and light turbulence during his climb. His aircraft was in solid instrument conditions from 1500 feet to 23,000 feet, except for a short interval between cloud layers.

This ice formation should have been prevented by electrical heating elements in the pitot heads controlled by switches located on the pilots' overhead panel on the flightdeck, but these switches had obviously not been turned on.

Why this was so was not entirely clear. However, in performing the pretakeoff checks required by the Northwest Orient's operational procedures, the crew did not follow the checklist sequence with precision. Because of momentary confusion resulting from an omission in the sequence, it is possible that the switches were positioned incorrectly by a first officer inexperienced as a Boeing 727 copilot.

While reading the checklist, the flight engineer called "Bug?" in the normal way. But before receiving a response from either the captain or the first officer, he omitted the [engine] ice protection call and went on to call, "Pitot heat?"

Apparently responding both to this and the omitted call, the first officer answered, "Off and on". But then, following the captain's late response to the "bug" call, he asked whether engine heat was needed.

To this the captain evidently responded with a nod or a hand movement, because the sound of five switch clicks followed before the first officer returned to setting his airspeed bug. The investigators believed these five clicks might have been the switching of the pitot heaters to their off position, and the engine anti-ice to the on position – an inadvertent reversal of the normal switch positions. Their assumption was supported by the position of the switches in the wreckage, light bulb filament evidence that the engine anti-ice lights were illuminated at impact, and the lack of any reference during the flight to the need for engine ice protection.

No doubt strongly influenced by the fact that both airspeed indicators were showing the same readings, the crew initially attributed the high airspeed and rate of climb to the lightly laden aircraft's low gross weight, in conjunction with encountering a powerful updraught in the prevailing solid instrument conditions, with the presence of thunderstorms forecast.

Even so, the aircraft's attitude as it neared the top of its climb should have told them that the apparent performance was impossible. Its 30 degree noseup attitude was no less than 25 degrees higher than the normal climb attitude, and in this condition the airspeed could never have increased, even if influenced by *extreme* updraughts.

Because the use of attitude references is fundamental to instrument flying, and indeed is stressed in Northwest Orient's own crew training programmes, the investigators concluded that in this case the crew relied on airspeed indications to the

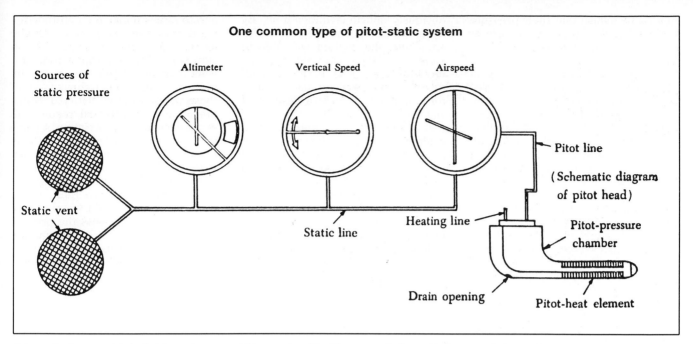

One common type of pitot-static system

Sources of static pressure

Altimeter   Vertical Speed   Airspeed

Static vent

Pitot line

(Schematic diagram of pitot head)

Heating line

Static line

Pitot-pressure chamber

Drain opening

Pitot-heat element

Schematic diagram of typical pitot-static system driving an aircraft's altimeter, vertical speed indicator and airspeed indicator. Blockage of the pitot head by ice would have a negligible effect on altimeter readings as this instrument senses static pressure only.

detriment of what the aircraft's attitude indicators would have been telling them, so missing the vital cues that could have enabled them to recover normal flight.

While the sounding of the overspeed warning horn probably reinforced the crew's belief that they were reacting correctly, the operation of the stick shaker stall warning should have alerted them to the true situation. Yet the first officer misinterpreted this as Mach buffet and the captain agreed.

Certainly the activation of both the overspeed warning horn and the stick shaker stall warning, coming almost simultaneously on top of the erroneous airspeed indications, could have been initially confusing to a crew flying in darkness and cloud. Nevertheless, the differences between the buffet induced by the stick shaker and Mach buffet are substantial and the stall warning should have been easily recognisable. Again, it was apparent to the investigators that the crew were almost totally influenced by the airspeed indicator readings and their related warning systems, and gave no attention to the attitude indicators.

Even when the aircraft stalled – manifested by the negative g, the rapid change of heading, and the sudden descent – the crew still failed to recognise the problem at first, continuing to pull back on the control column. This kept the wings at a high angle of attack, preventing any recovery from the stall, and pulled the aircraft into a tightening

spiral dive, with the actual airspeed building up rapidly.

The combination of the false airspeed indications, the steep nosedown attitude, and the disorienting sensations created by the g forces generated in the spiral dive, would now have been more confusing than ever. In addition, the aircraft's nosedown attitude and angle of bank were now so steep that the horizon references on the attitude instruments would have been almost hidden. But even at this stage, had the pilots been concentrating on the attitude indicators, particularly the position of the "sky pointers", the aircraft could have been recovered to level flight within about 40 seconds.

No doubt because of the now low airspeed indications, the captain finally concluded the aircraft was stalled, and after transmitting a call to this effect, called for two degrees of flap – an appropriate action for stall recovery. But as the actual airspeed was by now in excess of 230 knots and still increasing, the flaps had little effect.

Yet even after the pilots decided the aircraft was stalled, it was evident to the investigators that they continued to react primarily to the high rate of descent indications and their own sensations and continued pulling back on the control column. This was substantiated by the increasing vertical acceleration as the descent continued. But because the wings were not levelled first, this action only tightened the steep spiral descent while leaving the wings aerodynamically stalled.

Because the tail mounted pitot heads for the elevator feel system were also blocked by ice, the control column force required to move the elevators would have increased as the aircraft climbed to high altitude. As it descended however, the force required would have diminished. By the time the aircraft had descended through 5000 feet, the airspeed sensed by the elevator feel system was probably near zero, but the actual airspeed was probably in excess of 350 knots. As a result, a relatively light movement of the control column could apply high vertical acceleration forces to the aircraft.

As the Boeing 727 spiralled steeply down through 3500 feet at high speed, the crew's pull forces on the control column induced accelerations that were sufficient to overload the elevator control assemblies and cause them to fail structurally. This would have immediately produced aerodynamic flutter which in turn quickly failed the elevator spar and led to the port side tailplane breaking away from the fin.

Recovery was now impossible. With the sudden loss of the control surfaces holding it in the spiral dive, the aircraft would probably have rolled level, pitched up steeply, and descended, still in a stalled condition but now at a reduced rate of descent, into the ground.

During the investigation of this accident, other reported instances of probable pitot head icing during flight in freezing conditions were also reviewed. Fortunately in these cases, the crews concerned were able to recognise that their pressure operated flight instruments were at fault in time to take corrective action.

In one case, a DC-9 climbing in cloud was maintaining a four degree noseup attitude at maximum continuous power when the Mach warning sounded and the airspeed indications increased to full scale readings. At the same time, the indicated altitude was decreasing. The crew concentrated on flying the aircraft on attitude indications, then found from ammeter readings that the pitot heaters were not working.

In another instance, a Boeing 707 taking off in a severe snowstorm had climbed to only 400 feet when the pressure instruments began giving obviously spurious indications. By flying the aircraft on the attitude instruments, the captain was able to climb through the cloud until he broke out on top at 10,000 feet. All this time one vertical speed indicator continued to show a descent of 750 feet per minute.

To the NTSB investigators it was evident from these instances that pitot or static icing in flight can and does occur from time to time and that the resulting effect on pitot-static instruments can create at least momentary confusion amongst crews.

There was clearly a need to emphasise the importance of aircraft attitude in determining sources of error if at any time pitot-static instrument indication become suspect, and to stress reliance on attitude flying during instrument flying training as the immediate remedy if pitot-static problems developed in flight.

As a result of the Boeing 727 investigation and the circumstances of these incidents, the National Transportation Safety Board recommended to the Federal Aviation Agency that they issue an Operations Bulletin to the aviation industry. The bulletin, addressed particularly to airline and general aviation operators for incorporation into their operational procedures and training programmes, should stress the primary importance of attitude information whenever pitot-static instrument indications were in any way suspect.

CHAPTER 17

"Let's go around ..."

*– Boeing 727 captain
to first officer*

American Airlines Boeing 727-95 N1963 [19837] (F/n 963) –
April 17, 1976

Because jet services into a small island airport left little margin for error, only experienced captains performed the landings and takeoffs. Yet even this precaution could not prevent a disaster when an error unexpectedly occurred.

For the experienced American Airlines crew of Flight AA625 – the Boeing 727 service from John F Kennedy Airport, New York, to Charlotte Amalie, St Thomas, capital of the US Virgin Islands in the Caribbean – the trip on Tuesday, April 27, 1976 was to be just another routine run.[1] (See footnotes on final page)

There was certainly no reason to suppose otherwise. The weather forecast for the direct 1400 nautical mile flight southeast out over the Atlantic Ocean was benign, with no unpleasant promises, and the terminal forecast for St Thomas' Harry S Truman Airport promised fine warm weather, a southeasterly wind of between 10 and 20 knots, and almost unlimited visibility.

The only slightly disagreeable aspect of the trip for the crew was, as always, the destination itself. The airport had the reputation of being rather "tight" for jet aircraft. The Boeing 727 was in fact the heaviest aircraft type approved to use it.

Built before World War 2 as a Marine Corps base, the airport was set in a pocket of hills on the southwest side of St Thomas, and had a single runway – aligned east-west and only 1420 metres (4660ft) in length, with a 150 metre overrun at the eastern end. Moreover, its location endowed

it with its own peculiar wind conditions, the normally gentle tradewinds increasing in strength and changing as they curled around and over the island's hills.

While airports on neighbouring Caribbean islands might be experiencing east or northeast winds, Harry S Truman Airport on St Thomas could have winds from the southeast. And when winds exceeded 15 knots from the northeast, a 1700 feet ridge three kilometres northeast of the airport could create a mini mountain wave effect on the approach to Runway 09, with turbulence below 1000 feet and a downdraught over the airport.

For all these reasons, American Airlines had some five years previously issued crews engaged in the company's Caribbean services with detailed instructions covering operations at St Thomas. Landings in jet aircraft were permitted only on Runway 09 into the east, and all landing and takeoffs were to be flown exclusively by the captain. VFR approaches were permitted in daylight hours, provided the cloudbase was 3000 feet or more and the visibility was good.

But none of these limitations were cause for great concern on the part of the crew of Flight AA625. All

three flight crewmembers were highly experienced and knew the idiosyncrasies of Harry S Truman Airport well. Captain Arthur Bujnowski, 54, a former US Navy pilot, had been flying Boeing 727s for 11 years, had a total of 22,000 hours, and had made more than 150 landings at St Thomas. First Officer Edward Offchiss, 36, had 8000 hours, 2500 of them in Boeing 727s, and had been into St Thomas 38 times. Flight Engineer Donald Mestler had 9500 hours, nearly all of it on Boeing 727s, and had experienced 125 landings at St Thomas. All three had been into St Thomas a number of times in the preceding month.

Promptly at 12 noon Atlantic Standard Time, N1963 took off from John F Kennedy Airport and was cleared to its flight planned cruising level of FL330 (33,000 feet). On board under the care of the Boeing 727's four flight attendants were 81 passengers – "a cross section of America" as one newspaper later described them. Many of them were on their way to St Thomas to enjoy the island's celebration marking the pause between the harvesting and the planting of successive sugar cane crops.

The en route flight was entirely uneventful and a little less than three

A Boeing 727-100 similar to that involved in the go around accident at St Thomas, retracts its undercarriage as it climbs steeply away after takeoff.

hours later, the aircraft, now in contact with San Juan Air Route Control on the island of Puerto Rico, was cleared to descend into the St Thomas area.

As usual during the descent from cruising level, Flight Engineer Mestler prepared a landing data card for the captain. This showed that the aircraft's estimated landing weight would be 125,000 pounds (56,750kg), and that the flap reference speed (V_{ref}) would be 120 knots for 30 degrees of flap, and 117 knots if 40 degrees were used. Although the use of 40 degrees of flap was the company's standard for St Thomas, 30 degrees was recommended with a headwind component of 20 knots or more on the runway, at the captain's discretion.

When the aircraft was about 20nm north of St Thomas, descending now towards 10,000 feet, the cabin pressure suddenly rose rapidly, causing acute discomfort, ear pain and temporary deafness among passengers and crew alike. Mestler wrestled with the cabin pressurisation controls to correct the problem and allow the pressure to increase at a more comfortable rate, but this proved difficult, apparently because of a lack of co-ordination between engine power and the pressurisation setting.

At 3.04pm, in order to slow the descent for the sake of all on board, the crew cancelled their IFR flightplan with St Juan Control and, from

St Thomas Tower, obtained a clearance for a VFR approach to the airport's Runway 09. They were instructed to call inbound at Savannah, a small island about five nm west of the threshold of Runway 09.

Even though they were cleared for a VFR approach, it was Captain Bujnowski's intention to intercept and use the runway's ILS for vertical guidance to this critical runway.

Progressively bleeding the aircraft's speed off to about 160 knots as the descent continued, Bujnowski called for 15 degrees of flap and intercepted the glideslope smoothly at an altitude of 1500 feet. At the same time Offchiss extended the flaps to 25 degrees and lowered the undercarriage, slowing the aircraft further.

The Tower now reported that the wind was from 120 degrees at 12 knots, and as the Boeing 727 descended through 1000 feet on the glideslope, the captain called for Offchiss to extend the flaps to the landing setting of 30 degrees he had decided to use. The airspeed was now 140 knots, gradually reducing towards the flap V_{ref} speed of 120 knots.

Crossing the threshold at 115 knots, with Offchiss now calling the altitude above the runway in increments of 10 feet, Bujnowski gradually retarded the throttles. Then, when sure of a successful landing, he closed them fully against their stops. But soon after he began to

flare for touchdown, the Boeing flew into a small but sharp patch of turbulence, causing the starboard wing to drop violently and the captain to call out in surprise. For a moment he feared it would strike the runway, but almost full left aileron picked the wing up, and when they emerged into smooth air again the aircraft floated, no longer sinking towards the runway.

"You're still high, Art," called Offchiss a little anxiously eight seconds later and another 500 metres down the runway.

At this point, Bujnowski, concerned that they were rapidly using up the remaining runway length, pushed the Boeing 727 firmly on to the ground. The landing, though hard, was satisfactory, but almost at once the captain had second thoughts about their ability to stop in the distance remaining.

"Let's go round," he declared, at the same time opening the throttles again.

As he did so the takeoff warning horn sounded (indicating that the aircraft was not correctly configured for takeoff), prompting Offchiss to ask: "Flaps 25?"

"Flaps 15!" the captain responded.

Knowing that the correct setting for a missed approach in these circumstances was 25 degrees, and that the captain had called "15" by mistake in the heat of the moment, Offchiss did not argue, but set the flap lever to 25 degrees.

Bujnowski meanwhile had become extremely anxious. There was no sense of the aircraft accelerating, or of the engines developing power, and less than 400 metres of runway remained. Seven seconds after his decision to go around he suddenly pulled off the power again and applied the brakes hard.

It was too late. Two seconds later the aircraft crossed the end of the runway and quickly ate up the 150 metre overrun. Still travelling fast, it demolished the ILS localiser antenna, rode up a shallow embankment to the airport perimeter fence, rupturing the starboard wing and setting it on fire, tore its way through the fence, skated across a road, struck several parked vehicles, and finally impacted violently against a Shell service station, breaking into three sections. A huge fire erupted and the wreckage burnt fiercely to destruction.

Three airport firefighting vehicles were on their way to the accident even before the wreckage slid to a stop. But dense black smoke and fallen live powerlines in the vicinity of the crash delayed them for several minutes before they could fight the fire effectively.

A number of passengers were killed outright in the final impact as the fuselage broke apart at the leading and trailing edges of the wing. Some passenger seats, torn loose from their mountings, were thrown out onto the road through the breaks in the structure. The initial impact with the embankment had broken open the starboard inboard fuel tank, spilling quantities of burning fuel throughout the remainder of the wreckage trail, and as the broken fuselage sections finally came to a stop, black, acrid smoke and intense fire penetrated the forward and centre sections of the cabin.

Passengers and flight attendants lucky enough to survive the impact escaped quickly through the breaks in the fuselage and the port side overwing emergency exits. All but three suffered abrasions, lacerations, fractures, and burns. The three flight crew, who had their seatbelts and shoulder harnesses fastened, escaped through the flightdeck's port side sliding window.

All the survivors, together with a woman who had been sitting in a car at the service station when the aircraft crashed, were rushed to the Knud Hansen hospital on St Thomas. A tally of all those aboard the flight soon established that 35 passengers and two of the four flight attendants were missing. They had all died in the impact and fire.

Thirty two of the survivors, including the three flightcrew, were released after treatment, and two badly burnt passengers were later transferred by air to better hospital facilities at San Juan on Puerto Rico.

★   ★   ★

A team of investigators from the National Transportation Safety Board arrived at St Thomas later that night and were joined the following day by representatives from the FAA, American Airlines, and the Boeing Company. Observers from the pilots', flight engineers' and air traffic controllers' professional associations were also invited to participate in the investigation.

On the face of it, it seemed incredible that such a mature, experienced and competent aircraft commander who had been flying for over 35 years could have made such a basic and fatal error of judgement – the very sort of mistake made sometimes by low time pilots uncertain of themselves and uncertain of their aircraft's capabilities.

Local authorities, the media and even some in the aviation industry were quick to point the finger of blame at the airport itself. It was known to be marginal for operations by jet aircraft and its upgrading had long been a highly political issue in the US Virgin Islands administration.

The busy apron at St Thomas' Harry S Truman Airport handled a wide variety of transport aircraft. The wing in the foreground belongs to a Convair 580, while a Britten Norman Islander and a DC-3 can be seen amongst other types in the background. Just visible at the extreme right is the T-tail of an American Airlines 727, and behind it the fin of a PanAm Airbus. (Osprey Books)

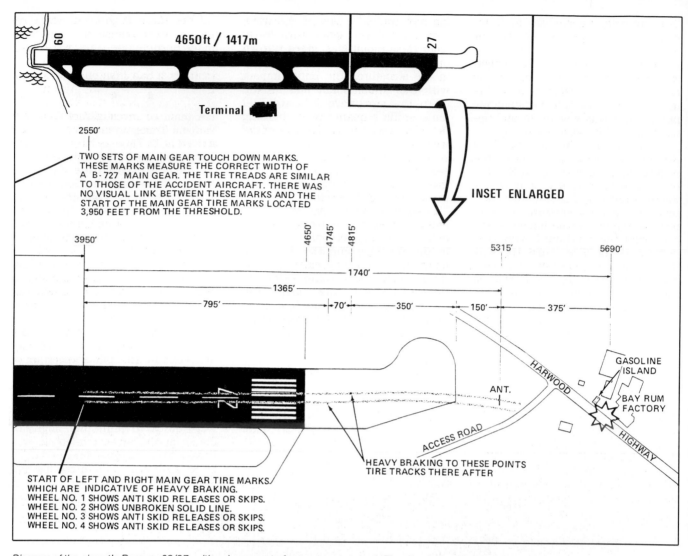

Diagram of the airport's Runway 09/27, with enlargement of area at eastern end. The wheel marks left by the Boeing 727 as it overran the runway, and its point of final impact at the service station on Harwood Highway, are indicated. The approach to Runway 09 is over the sea as shown. (M Tesch)

"In the eyes of numerous air safety experts, Tuesday's plane crash on St Thomas is deemed a textbook example of a crash that was almost bound to happen," declared *The New York Times.* "The reason? Conditions at the Caribbean airport – the short runway and dangerous hills off the east end – provided little safety cushion in case of trouble, even though they met official criteria."

The Washington Post devoted an editorial to the subject, pointing out that the airport had been "the subject of discussions, plans, reports and controversy for 20 years." Many St Croix legislators (a neighbouring island in the group) were "still opposing any funding for St Thomas improvement, contending that all jet traffic should land at St Croix's larger airport, with a shuttle service to St Thomas."

One of the most outspoken critics was Captain J J O'Donnell, president of the Airline Pilots' Union: "There'll be another one there, no question

about it," he told the press. "It's like playing Russian roulette." But improvements would only come slowly because of "local politicians and ecologists."

Another pilots' spokesman pointed out that St Thomas was one of three US airports given a "black star" rating by the International Air Line Pilots' Association as "critically deficient".

But even though St Thomas' airport left a great deal to be desired, Captain Bujnowski was well accustomed to its peculiarities and limitations, flying into it regularly and frequently without any problems in the course of his normal work. So on this occasion what combination of circumstances could have brought about a misjudgement with such terrible consequences?

The three air traffic controllers on duty in the Tower at the time of the accident told the investigators that everything about the Boeing 727's approach looked "normal" until it

reached the runway area where this type of aircraft usually touches down, between 300 and 450 metres from the threshold.

At that stage it began an unusually long float, finally touching down some 900 metres down the runway. Two charter pilots, as well as the airport fireman on duty in the watch tower, described the approach and touchdown in similar terms.

Giving his own account of events leading to the accident, Captain Bujnowski said they were a "shade below" the glideslope as they approached the threshold at about 130 knots (V_{ref} plus 10 knots for a landing with 30 degrees of flap), and they crossed the threshold at a height he estimated at between 30 and 40 feet. The patch of turbulence, which he did not expect "that far down the runway", seemed to buoy the aircraft up. Immediately before touchdown, he decided the aircraft could not be stopped in the distance remaining and, simultaneously with the landing, he called for a go-around and pushed the throttles forward.

He did not see the EPR (engine pressure ratio) needles come up as expected, so he pushed the throttles as far forward as they would go. When there was still no apparent response from the engines and he saw they were "not going anywhere", he immediately closed the throttles and braked hard. He could not recall extending the speed brakes, but thought he "might have actuated the reversers in the final stages."

First Officer Offchiss told investigators the aircraft had "zero sink" for a number of seconds after the turbulence encounter. When the captain "positively put the aircraft on the ground, about 700 metres down the runway", he wasn't worried about the length of the landing. After the captain ordered the go-around, he did not hear a power increase or feel the aircraft accelerate, though

he saw the EPR needles indicating about 1.4. The captain rotated the aircraft to about 11 degrees nose-up during the attempt to go around, and the nose leg was still off the ground when the aircraft overran the runway.

Flight Engineer Mestler also said he saw the same 1.4 reading on the EPR gauges during the go around attempt.

From tyre marks left on the runway and the runway overrun, wheel marks on the embankment, and the wreckage trail itself, it was possible to establish the movements of the aircraft from the moment the captain forced it onto the runway. This information, correlated with data obtained from the aircraft's Flight Data and Cockpit Voice Recorders, both of which were recovered from the wreckage in readable condition, enabled investigators to reconstruct a highly accurate profile of the aircraft's approach, touchdown and attempt to go around.

This showed that the aircraft crossed the threshold at 131 knots at a height of 80 feet, a normal enough approach which should have resulted in a touchdown about 300 metres or a little more beyond the threshold. Instead however, the aircraft floated about 10 feet above the runway for between seven and eight seconds before finally touching down 850 metres beyond the threshold. At this point, 565 metres of runway, plus the 150 metre overrun, remained in which to bring the Boeing to a stop. But by the time the captain said, "Let's go around," the aircraft was 1050 metres beyond the threshold with only 370 metres of runway remaining. Although the captain believed his decision to go around coincided with the touchdown, his words were actually spoken three seconds afterwards.

Five seconds later, and a further 275 metres down runway, the captain abandoned the attempt to go

The fire damaged tail assembly of the Boeing 727, lying where it came to rest on the forecourt of the Shell service station on Harwood Highway – one of the few sections of the aircraft still recognisable when the fire was extinguished.

Taken from the roof of a nearby building, with the Boeing's tail assembly in the foreground, this photograph looks back along the runway towards the west – the direction from which the Boeing 727 was approaching. The camera lens has foreshortened the appearance of the runway's 150 metre overrun.

around and began hard braking because he could neither feel nor see an adequate response from the engines. However, as the time required for a Pratt & Whitney JT8D-1A engine (the type of engines fitted to the Boeing 727) to accelerate from idle power to takeoff thrust is at least 6.3 seconds, the investigators concluded that the crew's observation of a maximum of about 1.4 on the EPR gauges was consistent with the engines' normal acceleration, and that engine performance was not a factor in the accident.

An analysis by the Boeing Company showed that from a go around at idle power, initiated at 110 knots (the speed at which the aircraft was still travelling at touchdown), it would have taken a run of at least 583 metres to lift off again. The required distance would increase if there was any hesitation in moving the throttles to the fully open position.

An inherent danger always present in a go around made in critical circumstances, is that the pilot will rotate the aircraft into the takeoff attitude too early. This would increase the distance required to lift off even further.

The investigators concluded it would have been impossible to carry out a successful go around from the point on the runway where the captain made his decision. However, an analysis of the Boeing 727's braking performance showed that by using maximum braking and spoilers immediately after the late touchdown, the captain should have been able to bring the aircraft to a stop on the runway, and certainly within the confines of the runway overrun.

The guidelines that American Airlines issued to pilots flying the Caribbean routes five years before the accident at St Thomas laid down operational policy on the use of flap, runway aiming point, touchdown point, and going around. They also emphasised the importance of having the aircraft established "in the slot" on final approach, the importance of the 300 metre aiming point, and the possibility of windshear producing a float if the aircraft was landed "long" (ie beyond the 300 metre aiming point). The guidelines further pointed out the necessity for making a prompt decision to go around if the approach was not "in the slot", if the landing was going to be appreciably beyond the 300 metre aiming point, or if the aircraft bounced on touchdown.

The use of 40 degrees of flap was standard practice, but using either 30 or 40 degrees "with strong gusty winds" was optional at the captain's discretion. The use of 30 degrees of flap was recommended when the headwind component on the runway was 20 knots or more.

In an operations bulletin to pilots a year later in 1972, the guidelines on the use of flap were reiterated, but expressed slightly differently. In restating the company's operations policy on the option to use 30 or 40 degrees of flap, the phrase "with strong *or* gusty winds" was used, the word "or" being underlined in the bulletin.

A year before the accident, in 1975, the company issued a further memorandum to Caribbean crews pointing out that the 40 degree flap setting saved 75 metres of runway length and that this was "the reason for requiring 40 degrees of flap when landing at St Thomas in headwinds of 20 degrees or less."

There was no doubt that it was American Airlines' intention to require the use of 40 degrees of flap for all landings at St Thomas in headwinds less than 20 knots. Unfortunately, the ambiguous wording of the 1972 bulletin was misleading and had the effect of extending the option to use 30 degrees if the winds were simply gusty.

Regarding speed control during an approach, American Airlines' operations manual stated that a speed between flap reference speed and that figure plus 10 knots throughout the final approach to touchdown would normally provide "the most stable flight and desired airspeeds." The operations manual did not contain a requirement to bleed off the margin over reference speed before or after crossing the runway threshold, but stipulated that reference speed was to be maintained until the aircraft was flared, when the throttles were to be progressively reduced to idle thrust just before touchdown. The company's 1971 memorandum to pilots added the instruction: "The aircraft must be flown onto the ground – *do not hold it off!*"

The investigators believed that adherence to flap reference speed was most significant for a successful precision touchdown at St Thomas.

In the case of Flight AA625's landing at St Thomas, the Tower controller told the crew on final approach that the wind was from 120 degrees at only 12 to 14 knots, and there was no mention of gusts.

However, Captain Bujnowski told investigators that, from his considerable experience of flying into St Thomas, he knew any southeast wind at the airport would be gusty and that for this reason he decided on the use of 30 degrees of flap. He pointed out that with only this amount instead of 40 degrees, the aircraft was more controllable, easier to manage, and that "you have a greater margin for what is ahead."

But it was evident to the investigators that, having made the decision to use the non standard setting of 30 degrees for this particular landing, the captain and his crew had not checked their American Airlines landing analysis chart for St Thomas to see if such a landing was permissible in the prevailing conditions. Had they done so, they might have been reminded that no less than a 20 knot headwind on the runway was required for a 30 degree flap landing.

The decision to use 30 degrees of flap rather than 40 degrees in fact exposed the Boeing 727 to a landing performance penalty, increasing the theoretical distance required by 75 metres. More significantly as it turned out in this case, the lesser drag of 30 degrees of flap made the aircraft more susceptible to the effects of increased airspeed, with any windshear or gust more likely to produce a float during the flare.

During the approach which culmi-

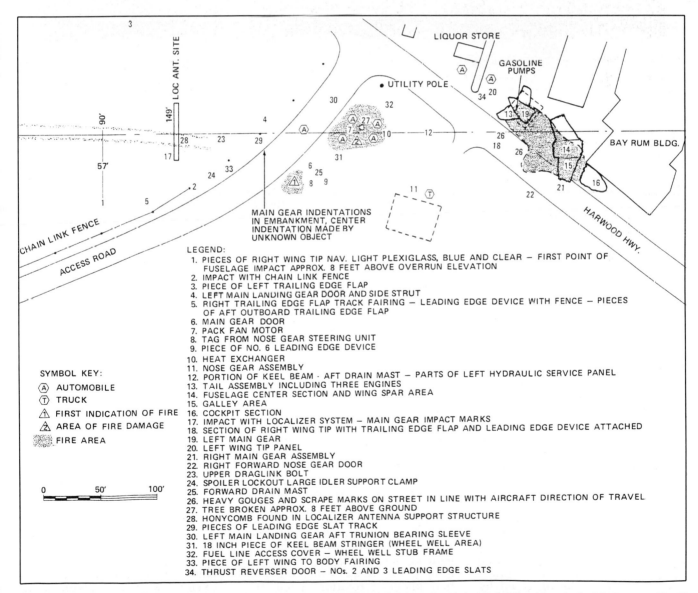

LEGEND:
1. PIECES OF RIGHT WING TIP NAV. LIGHT PLEXIGLASS, BLUE AND CLEAR – FIRST POINT OF FUSELAGE IMPACT APPROX. 8 FEET ABOVE OVERRUN ELEVATION
2. IMPACT WITH CHAIN LINK FENCE
3. PIECE OF LEFT TRAILING EDGE FLAP
4. LEFT MAIN LANDING GEAR DOOR AND SIDE STRUT
5. RIGHT TRAILING EDGE FLAP TRACK FAIRING – LEADING EDGE DEVICE WITH FENCE – PIECES OF AFT OUTBOARD TRAILING EDGE FLAP
6. MAIN GEAR DOOR
7. PACK FAN MOTOR
8. TAG FROM NOSE GEAR STEERING UNIT
9. PIECE OF NO. 6 LEADING EDGE DEVICE
10. HEAT EXCHANGER
11. NOSE GEAR ASSEMBLY
12. PORTION OF KEEL BEAM · AFT DRAIN MAST – PARTS OF LEFT HYDRAULIC SERVICE PANEL
13. TAIL ASSEMBLY INCLUDING THREE ENGINES
14. FUSELAGE CENTER SECTION AND WING SPAR AREA
15. GALLEY AREA
16. COCKPIT SECTION
17. IMPACT WITH LOCALIZER SYSTEM – MAIN GEAR IMPACT MARKS
18. SECTION OF RIGHT WING TIP WITH TRAILING EDGE FLAP AND LEADING EDGE DEVICE ATTACHED
19. LEFT MAIN GEAR
20. LEFT WING TIP PANEL
21. RIGHT MAIN GEAR ASSEMBLY
22. RIGHT FORWARD NOSE GEAR DOOR
23. UPPER DRAGLINK BOLT
24. SPOILER LOCKOUT LARGE IDLER SUPPORT CLAMP
25. FORWARD DRAIN MAST
26. HEAVY GOUGES AND SCRAPE MARKS ON STREET IN LINE WITH AIRCRAFT DIRECTION OF TRAVEL
27. TREE BROKEN APPROX. 8 FEET ABOVE GROUND
28. HONYCOMB FOUND IN LOCALIZER ANTENNA SUPPORT STRUCTURE
29. PIECES OF LEADING EDGE SLAT TRACK
30. LEFT MAIN LANDING GEAR AFT TRUNION BEARING SLEEVE
31. 18 INCH PIECE OF KEEL BEAM STRINGER (WHEEL WELL AREA)
32. FUEL LINE ACCESS COVER – WHEEL WELL STUB FRAME
33. PIECE OF LEFT WING TO BODY FAIRING
34. THRUST REVERSER DOOR – NOs. 2 AND 3 LEADING EDGE SLATS

Diagram showing detail of final impact area, and distribution of wreckage. The end of the runway is just out of the picture to the left. (Matthew Tesch)

Low level aerial photograph of the final impact area as detailed in diagram above. The aircraft's tail assembly can be seen close to the service station's canopy roof.

nated in the accident, the captain deliberately aimed for a 10 knot margin above the flap reference speed, and as the aircraft crossed the threshold the margin was 11 knots. As a result, the investigators believed, when the captain flared the aircraft for touchdown, this excess speed became a factor in overflying the aiming point.

The captain nevertheless flew the approach to the threshold well, with the aircraft stabilised on the glidepath in the landing configuration (ie "in the slot"), and after crossing the threshold began retarding the throttles in the prescribed manner to arrive at the touchdown point with idle power. It was evident that the landing wheels were about 10 feet above the runway at the 300 metre aiming point and, with touchdown apparently imminent, there was no reason to suspect a go around might become necessary.

But just beyond this point the FDR showed two airspeed aberrations as the aircraft apparently encountered an unexpected gust. This was sufficiently powerful to roll the aircraft sharply to the right, prompting the captain to exclaim with surprise, and to increase the airspeed by about five knots. By the time he had

recovered level flight with almost full opposite aileron, the aircraft was well beyond the normal touchdown point, but still at a height of 10 feet above the runway. The investigators believed this gust encounter added to the lift already produced by the rotation of the aircraft into the flared attitude, and caused a prolonged float.

The captain was now suddenly faced with an urgent decision – to land, or to open the throttles and go around. In the event he chose to force the aircraft onto the runway.

But though he knew he was well past the normal touchdown point, the true distance the aircraft had already travelled down the runway only dawned on him after the aircraft was actually on the ground. This prompted him to immediately reverse his decision and call for a go around.

In this he was deceived. From his extensive experience of operating into St Thomas, he saw that the aircraft was still about 150 metres short of the point where it would normally be rotated for liftoff, and its airspeed was still within three or four knots of rotation speed. He therefore assumed a go around was

possible. What he did not take into account was the fact that the aircraft was *decelerating* and the engines, having been at idle thrust for 13 or 14 seconds, were spooled down and would take about seven seconds to redevelop takeoff thrust.

The limited training in touch and go landings given to airline pilots during conversion training on to a new type is usually conducted under ideal operating conditions. Both airspeed and engine rpm are maintained at comfortable levels, and the training takes place at an airfield where the runways are of such length that maximum performance is never needed. Moreover, from the very beginning of their flying careers, pilots are conditioned to the belief that accidents resulting from misjudged approaches can be averted by going around. But as demonstrated all too tragically in this case, they may have little idea of the actual runway distance required to carry out a safe go around under a variety of airfield, aircraft, engine and meteorological conditions.

The final items in the chain of events leading to the accident were played out when the captain realised the rate of engine acceleration could not possibly enable the aircraft to become safely airborne in the short length of runway remaining, and he closed the throttles and applied full braking.

Heavy black tyre marks, indicative of maximum braking, were found over the final 210 metres of runway. Even so, it was evident that the captain did nothing more than brake in his efforts to slow the aircraft, at least until after it left the runway overrun. He did not lower the nosewheel, did not deploy the spoilers, and did not use reverse thrust.

As a result, the Boeing did not decelerate to its full capability. Failing to lower the nosewheel probably had quite a significant effect, as the lift being developed by the wings with the aircraft in a nose high attitude would have reduced the retarding force being transmitted from the wheels to the runway surface. Though reverse thrust was finally applied, this did not occur until just before the final impact. The captain admitted to investigators that he did not know why he hadn't used all the means available to him to slow the aircraft.

The investigators were mindful of research into human behavioural patterns which showed that a person in imminent danger – often regardless of his knowledge, understanding or specialised skills – may undergo behavioural changes resulting in impulsive action intended to extract him quickly from the threat. Tending to cancel the reasoning process, this "emergency mechanism" may be detrimental in situations where deliberate responses are needed.

In this case the captain's "emergency mechanism" was triggered when he realised a go around was impossible and that some sort of accident was inevitable. Probably reacting impulsively and instinctively, he applied full wheel braking, but in the stress of the moment became temporarily oblivious to the need for the more deliberate actions as well – lowering the nose, deploying the spoilers, and applying maximum reverse engine thrust. But had he used all these means of deceleration as soon as he began braking, the aircraft could probably have been brought to a stop within the confines of the airport fence. At the very least, a much less violent impact would have resulted.

In concluding their report, NTSB investigators expressed the view that intensive training was the most effective way to combat such instinctive reactions. In this case, if

---

American Airlines BULLETIN

M. W. EASTBURN
DIR. SAFETY

LA GUARDIA FIELD

TO: Pilots & Flight Engineers   Number 223-76

FROM: Vice President Flight   May 10, 1976

SUBJECT: MANAGING THE APPROACH/LANDING

I'm sure all of you have read and heard a great deal about our tragic accident at St. Thomas.

A great amount of investigative work has been done, but much remains to be done. The ultimate finding as to cause of the accident is of course a decision for the NTSB to render. We therefore do not presume to pre-empt the Board and make a prejudgment in the matter.

However, our daily operations must continue and I would therefore like to take the opportunity to review certain elements of all approaches and landings with you.

We have in our Operating Manuals a graphic depiction (in Section 3A) of what we call the "slot," the beginning of which is the normal decision point with regard to whether to proceed with the landing or to pull up. The target touch-down point, also graphically depicted, is 1000'. Granting that adverse atmospheric conditions may extend this point somewhat, we should virtually always have the airplane on the runway by at least the 1500' point. It's far better to "put it on" the runway, even if it will be a firm landing, than to allow it to float or to hold it off, striving for a smooth landing. Floating "eats up" runway very rapidly. In the case of the 727, deceleration on the runway is about three times greater than in the air.

While the normal decision point, as just stated, is at the beginning of the slot (approximately the middle marker), any necessary go-around should virtually always be initiated no later than the target touch-down area.

In addition to your position down the runway, another important consideration in the go-around decision is the state of the engines at initiation of the go-around. If they are spun down to idle rpm,

remember to count on about eight seconds to obtain go-around power on the 727 and 707 (four to five seconds on the DC-10 and 747). Waiting for this power recovery will rapidly use up runway. Any obstacle beyond the end of the runway will therefore require an earlier decision and initiation of the go-around. Never attempt to salvage a landing from a bad final approach.

Finally, let's all review our standard procedures and practices, and the guidance material in the Operating Technique section of our manuals – all of which represent a lot of thought and inputs from a lot of sources. And let us move forward in the establishment again of a safety record that dispels the notion of the inevitability of an eventual accident in a large operation such as ours. Instead, let's embrace the notion that accidents do not have to happen in our business.

Captain D. E. Ehmann

Distribution
  Lists 12
        13
        14A & B

Bulletin headed "Managing the Approach/Landing", which American Airlines distributed to all its pilots and flight engineers two weeks after the accident at St Thomas.

the captain had been exposed to critical go around situations and made familiar with the maximum performance stopping capabilities of the aircraft by means of lectures and simulator training, he might have reacted appropriately.

The NTSB report summed up:

It was evident that the captain had two opportunities to avoid this accident.

• The first was during the turbulence encounter just after passing the 300 metre touchdown area: he should have followed company procedures and initiated a go around as soon as he regained control.

• The second opportunity came after he landed the aircraft. He should have then applied maximum performance procedures to bring the aircraft to a stop within the remaining runway length. Subsequently, when the accident became inevitable, he could have reduced the severity of the impact by using all available means of deceleration.

So concluded the investigation of the St Thomas accident – to many pilots and others in the aviation industry, a classic example of ascribing the cause to "pilot error" with the enormous advantage of hindsight!

It fell to US aviation psychologist Stanley N Roscoe, dissatisfied with obvious answers to what in reality were quite mystifying departures from sound judgement by exceedingly able flightcrews, to point out in his book, *Aviation Psychology*[2],

that a "pilot error" finding was in no sense an explanation of *why* an accident happened. An explanation, by definition, is the establishment of a cause and effect relationship. "Pilot error" explains nothing – it is simply substituting one mystery for another.

In this case asked Roscoe, what was the *real* reason for Captain Bujnowski's defective control of an aircraft he flew so regularly and so well? Surely something must have *caused* him to react so inappropriately and with such tragic consequences.

Several minutes before the crash, during the aircraft's descent from cruising level, the three flight crew members, together with everyone else on board the Boeing 747, were afflicted by severe pain as a result of an unusually rapid increase in cabin pressure.

A complex combination of equipment design characteristics and adjustments had evidently produced a mismatching of cabin blower output and the manual setting of the pressurisation controls during the rapid descent.

Cancelling the flight's IFR clearance, and obtaining a VFR clearance to descend more gently made the situation more comfortable, but even so, the human effects from the pressurisation problem persisted. So much so that Captain Bujnowski complained about it on the flightdeck.

According to the CVR readout, only four minutes before the crash,

he remarked: "Boy, I'm deaf – I can't hear a goddam thing."

First Officer Offchiss: "Yeah – the bloody thing hurts – my ears hurt."

Flight Engineer Mestler: "Yeah – mine do too."

Apparently concerned for his passengers, Bujnowski said: "I hope nobody ..."

"No, they won't ..." Mestler interrupted, assuring him.

The CVR readout also showed that, immediately following this disjointed exchange, a number of irregularities in crew communication occurred.

On two occasions Mestler called for altimeter cross checks, one of them while flaps were being called for and set, to which there was no discernible response, prompting First Officer Offchiss to comment: "Confusing, isn't it?". Offchiss then made at least three facetious references to Mestler's difficulties in controlling the cabin pressurisation system.

Offchiss also overlooked adjusting his altimeter subscale setting from the standard en route cruise setting of 29.92 inches (1013 millibars) to the St Thomas QNH of 30.00 inches (1015 millibars), while Captain Bujnowski mistakenly set his altimeter to 30.7 inches (1041 millibars) instead of 30 inches.

There was no way a cause and effect relationship could be established between all these difficulties and the events leading to the accident, aviation psychologist Roscoe

After the disastrous Boeing 727 accident, American Airlines refused to operate any more jet services into St Thomas until the airport was upgraded – a major undertaking that was long overdue. Instead, the company's Caribbean subsidiary, American Inter-Island, began regular shuttles to and from St Thomas, connecting with jet flights at neighbouring St Croix Island. The photograph shows one of American Inter-Island's five Convair 440s taxiing out for takeoff at St Croix. (Osprey Books)

pointed out, but there was scientific evidence to suggest an explanation.

The human vestibular (hearing) and oculomotor (seeing) systems respond interactively, and stimuli of the sort experienced in this case by Captain Bujnowski and his crew have been shown to cause over-accommodation in the eyes that can persist for several minutes, inducing errors in size and distance judgements. Such errors could result in a pilot flaring too high above a runway and expecting to touchdown while still above the runway.

With overaccommodation, the curvature of the eye lens increases and the retina stretches, causing the visual image cast on the retina to fall on a slightly smaller area of receptors than normal. The pilot not only perceives the runway to be smaller and more distant – because the entire visual scene appears compressed, the runway appears *higher* than it actually is.

In this case, Roscoe believed, after the rapid increase in the Boeing 727's cabin pressurisation, resulting in blocked ears and head pain, the crew's eyes could have overaccommodated, blurring their vision and causing the runway to initially appear further away than it was – and finally higher relative to the aircraft than it actually was.

Certainly, the possibility that this condition contributed to Captain Bujnowski's tragic error of judgement at St Thomas on April 27, 1976, could not be denied.

Footnotes:

1. *The Boeing 727's route from New York to St Thomas was almost identical to that of the DC-9 described in Chapter 8. See page 69 of Chapter 8 for a map of this route and the St Thomas area of the Caribbean.*

2. *First published by Iowa University Press, 1980.*

CHAPTER 18

"Did he not clear the runway – the Pan American?"

– KLM flight engineer to captain

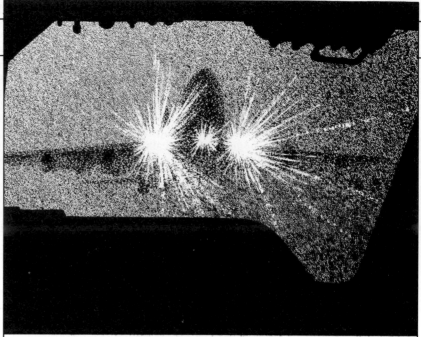

KLM Royal Dutch Airlines Boeing 747-206B PH-BUF [20400] *Rijn (The Rhine)*; and Pan American Airways Boeing 747-121 N736PA [19643] *Clipper Victor* – March 27, 1977

Frustration, fog and fire – how a terrorist bomb blast 100 kilometres away led to the greatest disaster in aviation history, taking the lives of 583 innocent people.

Spain's Canary Islands – Ialas Canarias – an archipelago of seven major volcanic outcrops between 57 and 250 nautical miles out into the Atlantic Ocean from the Moroccan coast of northwest Africa, have long been a tourist destination rivalling the balmy resorts of the Mediterranean. Even ancient Greek and Roman seafarers knew them as "the Fortunate Isles".

Situated around latitude 28 degrees north, their warm and sunny climate is the envy of Northern Europeans, and for many years the group's two principal cities of Las Palmas on Grand Canary and Santa Cruz on Tenerife were regular ports of call for ocean liners en route to South America and South Africa.

As air travel gradually replaced sea transport in the postwar years, major airports were developed to serve Las Palmas and Santa Cruz to cope with the islands' booming tourist trade. New hotels, catering particularly for Scandinavians, Dutch and Germans, proliferated throughout the islands, with Las Palmas, as the Canary Islands' capital, becoming the principal international airport for the group. Strenuous efforts were also made to attract American tourists, the islands' seaports becoming the starting point for luxury cruises of the Mediterranean.

Sunday March 27, 1977 should have been no different to any other spring day at Las Palmas Airport, with the usual frequent international flights coming and going from all over Europe and from the other side of the Atlantic.

But at 1.15pm that afternoon, the bustling life of the airport passenger terminal was thrown into panic and confusion when a small bomb planted by a terrorist exploded in a florist's shop on the terminal concourse. Airport authorities had been warned of the blast 15 minutes before, so although the bomb caused a good deal of damage inside the terminal building, it was being evacuated at the time and there were no fatalities. However, eight people were injured, one seriously.

Telephoning the Spanish airport administration afterwards, a spokesman for a militant Canary Islands independence movement, speaking from Algeria in North Africa, claimed responsibility for the explosion and hinted that a second bomb was planted somewhere in the terminal building.

Unable to tell whether or not this further threat would eventuate, the local police had no alternative but to instruct the civil aviation authorities at Las Palmas to close the airport pending a thorough search for the

second bomb. Their decision inevitably affected far more than airport personnel and waiting passengers: numerous international flights, inbound to Las Palmas from a variety of departure points, were approaching the Canary Islands at the time, some of them within less than an hour's flying time from Las Palmas.

The difficulty was overcome by diverting all inbound Las Palmas traffic to Los Rodeos, the other Canary Islands international airport, serving Santa Cruz on the island of Tenerife, some 50 nautical miles to the northwest (a destination that most, if not all the international flights would be "carrying as an alternate" for Las Palmas in any case).

The only real problem would be one of logistics – the additional traffic would sorely try Los Rodeos airport's capacity for a few hours. The second airport possessed only a single runway, and even its aircraft parking areas had nowhere near the capacity to handle double its normal daily aircraft movements. Even so, it was the only possible option in the circumstances and it was expected that Las Palmas would not be closed for long.

Among the numerous flights from European ports diverted to Los Rodeos was a charter trip flown by KLM's Boeing 747 PH-BUF. Operated by KLM as Flight KL4805 on behalf of the Holland International Travel Group, it had departed Amsterdam's Schiphol Airport that morning at 9.31am local time carrying 234 mostly young passengers escaping the Northern European cold for a holiday in the sunny warmth of the Canaries. They included three babies and 48 children. Most were Dutch, but amongst them were two Australians, four Germans and four Americans.

During the flight, many of the passengers were intrigued to find that their pilot in command was the handsome and esteemed Jacob Veldhuyzen van Zanten, KLM's chief training captain for Boeing 747 aircraft, featured in company advertisements and in the current issue of the company's inflight magazine placed in the back pockets of all the cabin seats.

Captain van Zanten had been flying since 1947 and had been an airline pilot with KLM since 1951 when, as a 24 year old, he commenced duty as a first officer on DC-3s. He now had nearly 12,000 hours' experience, more than 1500 hours of this time as

captain of Boeing 747s. But these days he spent most of his working hours instructing in KLM's simulators.

After its four hour trip from Amsterdam across Belgium, France and Spain, then southwest out over the Atlantic to Tenerife, PH-BUF touched down on Los Rodeos Airport's 3400 metre Runway 30 at 1340 hours GMT (1.10pm local time).

For once the fabled Canary Islands failed to live up to their reputation for fine weather: those on board the KLM Boeing 747 were greeted with the sight of patchy low cloud, light rain, and areas of fog in the distance. The light wind was from the northwest.

The apron area, together with a portion of the main taxiway paralleling the runway, was already fully occupied by diverted aircraft when the KLM 747 arrived at Los Rodeos. The tower controller therefore directed the Dutch crew to vacate the runway via the last intersecting taxiway, continue towards the holding point for the reciprocal Runway 12, and to park the aircraft on the holding area apron next to a Norwegian Boeing 737. A short time afterwards a Dan-

ish Boeing 727 and then a SATA DC-8 also landed at Los Rodeos and were directed to park in the same area.

Meanwhile, Captain van Zanten, not knowing how long the reopening of Las Palmas Airport on Grand Canary was likely to be delayed, but conscious of his need to complete the flight there as soon as possible, had instructed his passengers to remain on board PH-BUF. After about 20 minutes however he relented, and they were transported to the airport terminal by bus.

At 1.45pm local time (a little more than half an hour after PH-BUF's arrival), while the Dutch crew were still on the flightdeck discussing how the delay was likely to affect their stringent company duty time limitations, a Pan American Boeing 747, N736PA, landed and taxied to the same holding area, parking directly behind the KLM Boeing 747. Flying in across the Atlantic from John F Kennedy Airport in New York, it too had been diverted to Tenerife from its original destination of Las Palmas.

The PanAm service, designated

The Pan American Boeing 747, N736PA "Clipper Victor", involved in the accident, is seen here taxiing for takeoff, probably at London Heathrow, sometime before the tragedy at Los Rodeos Airport, Tenerife. The vast bulk of the 747 design, together with the complexity of its 18 wheel undercarriage is evident – factors that probably influenced Captain Grubbs' interpretation of the controller's taxiing instructions on Los Rodeos' relatively narrow pavements a few minutes before the collision. This aircraft was in fact the first Boeing 747 to operate commercially, replacing N735PA "Clipper Young America" at short notice on its inaugural New York/London service in the early hours of January 22, 1970 after teething troubles with the latter's P&W JT9 engines delayed the flight. N736PA's name "Clipper Victor" was hastily overpainted with "Clipper Young America" just for the occasion.

An early model Boeing 747-100 of lead customer, Pan American, during a pre-delivery test flight over the Cascade Mountains. (Boeing)

Flight PA1736, had originated in Los Angeles, where 364 passengers – most of them retirees over 55 years of age – had boarded *Clipper Victor* for the first stage of a charter flight to Grand Canary. Here they were to join the Royal Cruise Line's ship *Golden Odyssey* for a 12 day "Mediterranean Highlights" cruise. Departing Los Angeles late the previous afternoon, they had flown direct to New York, landing at John F Kennedy Airport just under five hours later. The Boeing 747 was refuelled, 14 more passengers came aboard, and there was a change of crew.

After an hour and a half on the ground, the flight took off again for Las Palmas.

Approaching the Canary Islands six hours later, the PanAm flight crew were informed by Air Traffic Control that Las Palmas Airport on Grand Canary was temporarily closed and that their aircraft was to be diverted to Los Rodeos Airport on Tenerife.

For the crew, this was unwelcome news. Already they had been on duty for the best part of eight hours and the diversion would inevitably add several more hours to the trip. And

there were the passengers themselves to consider. It was now nearly 13 hours since most of them had boarded the aircraft at Los Angeles. As well as this, they had experienced an hour and a half's unexpected delay at Los Angeles Airport before their departure late the previous afternoon. They were very tired and the majority of them were no longer young.

The PanAm flight's Captain Victor Grubbs, a 57 year old veteran American pilot of 21,000 hours' experience, sensing from the Spanish air traffic controller's instructions that Las Palmas was expected to reopen before long, therefore asked if, instead of diverting into Los Rodeos, the PanAm flight could continue to Las Palmas and be cleared to join a holding pattern to await the reopening of the airport. N736PA was carrying more than adequate reserve fuel and holding in this way would give them quicker and easier access to a landing at Las Palmas than having to make a further flight from Los Rodeos, with all that entailed in terms of procedures and clearances.

To the disappointment of the seasoned American flight crew – Grubbs, First Officer Robert Bragg, and Flight Engineer George Warns – ATC refused the request, so there was nothing for it but to join the

Subsequent 747s delivered to KLM were mostly Model 206B Combis, named after famous aviators, and wore the company's revised two tone blue cabin top livery. The remaining six aircraft from the first order were later repainted in this modified scheme, but PH-BUF was still carrying its white top livery at the time of the accident. This photograph, taken at Sydney's Kingsford Smith International Airport in 1984, shows the later livery. The smaller twin engined aircraft beside the KLM 747 is a DC-2, the first "modern" type airliner to be operated by the veteran Dutch air carrier. The 50 year old DC-2, flown by a KLM crew, had just completed an epic flight from Amsterdam to commemorate the 50th anniversary of KLM's success in the historic England/Australia MacRoberson Centenary Air Race of 1934. Refurbished by KLM for the 1984 re-enactment at Schiphol Airport, the DC-2 was painted to represent the original KLM DC-2 PH-AJU "Uiver" which came second in the speed section of the race and won the handicap section. In contrast to the enormous capacity of today's 747s, the DC-2 carried a crew of three and had seats for 14 passengers. (Jim Thorn)

numerous other airline aircraft waiting on the ground at Los Rodeos.

Unknowingly echoing Captain van Zanten's initial decision of half an hour earlier, after landing and parking on Los Rodeos' Runway 12 holding apron as directed behind the KLM Boeing 747 PH-BUF, Captain Grubbs announced that the passengers should remain on board in anticipation of an early clearance on to Las Palmas. But the main cabin doors were opened, some passengers taking advantage of this to breathe the fresh Canary Islands air and to take photographs of what they could see from the aircraft.

Meanwhile, on the flightdeck of PH-BUF, Captain van Zanten was becoming increasingly concerned that he and his crew were running out of time as far as their permitted period of duty was concerned. Until a few years previously, a KLM aircraft captain was authorised to exercise his discretion in extending his crew's duty time to meet unforeseen delays and so complete a flight satisfactorily. But because of a number of instances in which serious crew fatigue had jeopardised safety, this provision had been revoked.

Instead, the Dutch civil aviation authority now insisted that flight-crew duty times be rigidly observed, even at the cost of having to delay the completion of a flight. Captains who exceeded the limitations were liable to prosecution.

To add to the difficulty, recent changes to the Dutch aviation legislation had made the calculation of precise duty time limitations a complex matter involving a number of different factors, and KLM had instructed crews that the company should be contacted for a ruling if they were in any doubt.

Aware that if the reopening of Las Palmas Airport was delayed too long, he would be compelled to re-

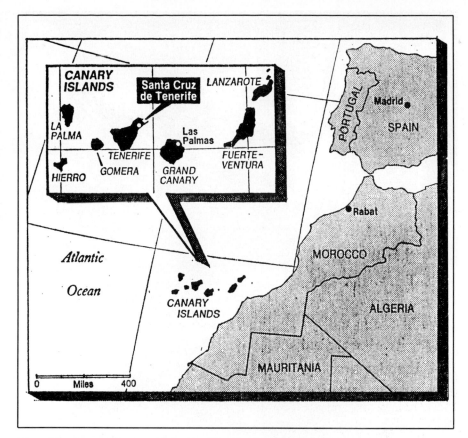

Map of the Canary Islands published by "The New York Times" in its coverage of the Tenerife disaster. Although the islands' subtropical latitude is about the same as Australia's Norfolk and Lord Howe Islands, its weather is constantly affected by the interplay between the warm dry northwest African climate and the cold Canary ocean current flowing from the North Atlantic.

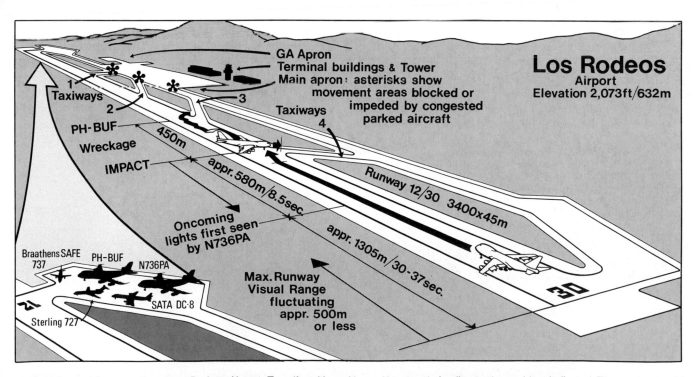

North facing aerial perspective of Los Rodeos Airport, Tenerife, with positions of key events leading to the accident indicated. The reader should not be deceived by the drawing's clarity – horizontal visibility at the time was 500 metres or less in fog. (Matthew Tesch)

Something of the enormous inertia carried by the undercarriage of a Boeing 747 at lift off speed is conveyed by these two pictures. (above) A ground engineer tensions the centre lock system of one of the four landing wheels on each of the 747's four undercarriage bogies – 16 massive wheels and tyres altogether. The size and solidity of the undercarriage leg for each bogie is also evident. (below) A Boeing 747 (this time one of Lufthansa's) lifts into the air after rotation. KLM's PH-BUF would have been at about this height when it collided with PanAm's N736PA at Tenerife, though its nose-up attitude would probably have been more extreme as Captain van Zanten desperately clawed for height. Note how each bogie drops into a "leading wheel up" attitude as the weight of the aircraft is transferred from the wheels to the wings, and the oleo legs and shock absorbing struts fall into their unloaded positions, extending the overall length of the units involved.

The flightdeck of a Boeing 747-200. The flight engineer's control and instrument panel is at right. An instant after impact, PanAm's First Officer Bragg, in the right hand control seat of N736PA, grabbed desperately for the four fire shutoff handles on the overhead panel above him. To his horror they were no longer there – the entire roof had gone. Moments later the flightdeck and what remained of the upper passenger deck collapsed into the first class cabin below. (Boeing)

main overnight at Los Rodeos, with all the burden that would involve in arranging appropriate accommodation at short notice for his passengers and crew, Captain van Zanten decided to contact the KLM operations office in Amsterdam by H/F radio while they were waiting. The captain spoke to the duty operations officer himself, outlined the difficulty in which they were placed, and asked for the precise duty time available to them without any infringement of limitations. KLM Amsterdam's advice when it came back to PH-BUF by radio was something of a relief – the crew had until 1800 hours GMT (6.30pm local time).

Shortly afterwards, Los Rodeos Tower called all waiting aircraft on the ground control frequency to advise that Las Palmas Airport was now open again. Despite a rigorous search, no second bomb could be found, and the police concluded that the warning had been a hoax.

In the Los Rodeos Airport termi-

nal, passengers who had left their various aircraft were called over the PA system to begin boarding again via the airport buses provided. All the passengers from the KLM aircraft did so except a travel guide for the Holland International Travel Group, Miss Robina van Lanschot. Having attended to the needs of her charges on the flight from Amsterdam, she decided to stay overnight at Santa Cruz. Her spur of the moment decision was to save her life.

Meanwhile, out at the holding area apron for Runway 12, Captain van Zanten, his anxiety over flight time limitations now relieved by the advice from his company, decided he would refuel for the return flight to Amsterdam before taking off for Las Palmas. There was time to do so now, whereas at Las Palmas, with the number of aircraft that would be descending on it, there might be delays in obtaining fuel. The Dutch crew accordingly ordered fuel to be brought out to the KLM Boeing 747

in tankers – a decision that was in hindsight to seal the fate of both 747s that day at Tenerife.

A short time later, the three smaller airliners parked by the two Boeing 747s – the Boeing 737, DC-8 and Boeing 727 – started their engines and were cleared to taxi for takeoff, the duty runway still being Runway 30. First manoeuvring carefully around the massive KLM and PanAm aircraft to reach the Runway 12 entrance, they then backtracked on the runway until they had bypassed the centre portion of the parallel taxiway that was still congested by parked aircraft. At this point they rejoined the main taxiway to continue to the holding point for Runway 30.

Although the weather was showing signs of further deterioration and light rain was still falling intermittently, surface visibility remained satisfactory at about 10 kilometres.

Now it was the PanAm Boeing 747's turn to depart. Aboard N736PA,

Captain Grubbs' announcement to his passengers that Las Palmas was finally open for traffic again was greeted with general applause in the cabin – at last they could look forward to joining their cruise ship and getting their heads down for the night, a prospect that seemed almost too good to be true after the best part of 24 wakeful hours since most of them got out of bed at home in California. For the flight on to Las Palmas, N736PA would have two additional passengers – two company staff members had boarded the flight to take advantage of a free ride over to Grand Canary.

But when First Officer Bragg called the tower to request a clearance to start the engines, the ground controller replied that while there was no delay as far as ATC clearances were concerned, the PanAm Boeing 747 could have problems in departing at the moment because the main taxiway was still congested with other parked aircraft. The only way to the holding point for Runway 30 was the route the other aircraft had followed – via the Runway 12 entrance, then backtracking on the runway itself. But KLM's PH-BUF, which was only now beginning to refuel, blocked that way for its PanAm sister ship.

Captain Grubbs somehow contained his frustration. He hadn't wanted to land at Los Rodeos anyway, and if ATC had allowed them to hold in the air as he'd requested, they could be making their approach to Las Palmas by now. To clarify their situation, First Officer Bragg now called the KLM crew on the ground control frequency. "How long will it take you to refuel?" he asked.

"About 35 minutes," he was told with no hint of an apology.

The PanAm crew's only possible alternative was to taxi around the Dutch Boeing 747 as the other three aircraft had done. But this looked doubtful. Los Rodeos Airport had not been designed to handle aircraft as big as the Boeing 747 and the width of the holding area apron did not leave a great deal to spare. Undaunted, First Officer Bragg and Flight Engineer Warns climbed down to the ground to pace out the amount of clearance available. It was insufficient – there was no way N736PA could gain access to the runway until PH-BUF moved out of their way.

Bragg and Warns returned to the flightdeck to convey the unwelcome news to Captain Grubbs – there was nothing they could do but await the pleasure of the Dutch crew.

While the American crew inwardly fumed at this further frustration, the local weather continued to deteriorate. Patches of fog, visible in the distance when they arrived at Los Rodeos, were now blowing in onto the runway. And the low cloud and light rain persisted. Already the surface visibility, which had been some 10 kilometres, was reducing intermittently to between one and a half and three kilometres.

Finally the refuelling of PH-BUF was completed. The tanker vehicles drove away, the doors of the aircraft were closed, and the engines were started. But by the time the Dutch crew called the tower on the ground control frequency of 118.7mhz at 1656 hours GMT (4.26pm local time) for permission to start engines, the patchy fog had moved in across the airport to completely obscure the runway, reducing visibility in some places to as little as 300 metres, though this was fluctuating.

Nevertheless, approval was given and shortly afterwards the KLM aircraft was cleared to taxi to the holding point for Runway 12 and instructed to switch to the aerodrome control frequency of 119.7. Two minutes later at 1658 hours, while standing at the holding point for Runway 12, the KLM aircraft called the Tower on the aerodrome control frequency to request a clearance to enter the runway and backtrack to the beginning of Runway 30 for takeoff.

The communications exchanged in English between the Dutch Boeing 747 and the Spanish tower controller went as follows:

KLM: "We require backtrack on Runway 12 for takeoff on Runway 30."

Tower: "Taxi to the holding position for Runway 30 ... taxi into the runway ... leave the runway third to your left."

KLM: "Roger, Sir. Entering the runway at this time ... and we go off the runway again for the beginning of Runway 30."

Tower: "Correction ... taxi straight ahead ... ah ... for the runway ... make ... ah ... backtrack."

KLM: "Roger, make a backtrack ... KLM4805 is now on the runway."

Tower: "Roger."

KLM (half a minute later): "You want us to turn left at Taxiway 1?"

Tower: "Negative, negative ... taxi straight ahead ... ah ... up to the end of the runway ... make backtrack."

KLM: "OK, Sir."

Meanwhile, the PanAm crew, having also sought a clearance to start engines and to taxi, were about to move their Boeing 747 on to the runway at the holding point for Runway 12. At this stage, the visibility on the

airfield had deteriorated in the fog conditions to the extent that the tower controllers could see neither the runway itself nor the two taxiing Boeing 747s. The PanAm crew therefore sought confirmation that they were to enter the runway while the KLM aircraft was still using it. At 1702 hours GMT, First Officer Bragg, after switching to the aerodrome control frequency of 119.7, called the tower controller:

PanAm: "Ah ... we were instructed to contact you and also to taxi down the runway ... is that correct?"

Tower: "Affirmative ... taxi into the runway and ... ah ... leave the runway third ... third to your left."

PanAm: "Third to the left ... OK."

Tower: "Third one to your left."

Evidently the Spanish controller's English pronunciation was not entirely clear to the American crew, for Captain Grubbs remarked to First Officer Bragg: "I think he said first." Bragg replied: "I'll ask him again."

Both Boeing 747s were now communicating with the Tower on the same frequency and, before Bragg contacted the controller again, the American crew heard him call the KLM aircraft:

Tower: "KLM4805 ... how many taxiway ... ah ... did you pass?"

KLM: "I think we just passed Taxiway 4 now."

Tower: "OK ... at the end of the runway make one eighty and report ... ah ... ready for ATC clearance."

Taxiing in the fog some distance behind the KLM aircraft, the American crew were having some difficulty in clarifying the controller's instruction in their minds. Bragg was studying a small diagram of Los Rodeos Airport which he had opened in the flip chart on his knee.

"This first [intersecting taxiway] is a 90 degree turn." he explained to Captain Grubbs.

Grubbs: "Yeah – OK."

Bragg: "Must be the third [the controller meant] ... I'll ask him again."

Grubbs: "We could probably go in, it's ... ah ..."

Bragg (emphatically): "You've got to make a 90 degree turn!"

Grubbs: (uncertainly) "Yeah ...

Bragg: "Ninety degree turn to get around ... this one further down here is a 45."

Bragg pressed his microphone button and called the Tower: "Would – you confirm that you want us to turn left at the *third* intersection?"

Tower: "The third one, Sir ... one two three ... third one."

Flight Engineer Warns interposed light heartedly to the other crew members: "We'll make it yet."

As the PanAm crew began to go

Artist Matthew Tesch's dramatic impression of the instant of impact between the two Boeing 747 behemoths captures something of the collision's enormity – and the fine knife edge on which the lives of all on board them were momentarily balanced. Investigators calculated that, had PH-BUF succeeded in gaining even an extra 25 feet in height, the outcome would have been totally different. As it was, Captain van Zanten's desperate last moment effort to "leapfrog" his giant aircraft over the PanAm 747 undoubtedly spared its handful of survivors as much as Captain Grubbs' vain attempt, in the scant seconds remaining to him, to move his aircraft off the runway.

550 DIE AS JUMBOS HIT

28/3/77

249 ON DUTCH JET DIE

Air Disaster Is Worst Ever —U.S. Plane Was Taxiing and Other Taking Off

By ROBERT D. McFADDEN

Two Boeing 747 jumbo jets collided and burst into flames on a foggy airport runway in the Canary Islands yesterday, and more than 550 of the 645 people aboard the two aircraft were believed to have been killed. It was the worst disaster in aviation history.

The planes—a Pan American Airways charter flight from Los Angeles and a KLM Royal Dutch Airlines jet carrying tourists from the Netherlands—slammed together on the single destination for the

● *Telegraph artist PAUL LENNON'S impression of the jumbo jet collis*

At least 550 died in the worst crash in a ...mbo jets collided in the Canary Islands toda...

...ARED KILLED ON ...NARY ISLANDS RUNW... ...ON LOS ANGELES JE...

still digging out bodies . . .they ... yet got round to counting them'

...RST EVER

...rican crew members survived ...ved their plane to avoid a

...irline KLM said its aircraft ... as it was taking off.

... poor. Was sea mist the cause

At first it was suspected the smash was a repetition of last September's Yugoslav disaster which was caused by air traffic controllers' errors.

But the governor said the Santa Cruz control tower had given "correct instructions to both planes" and definitely was not at fault.

Jumbo jets in fiery smash

Worst crash of t...

BROADSIDE COLLISION

PAN AMERICAN CREW MEMBERS
DE BEAULIEU, Francoise Colbert, New York, purser
ASAI, Mari, New York, flight attendant
HIRANO, Sachiko, New York, flight attendant
LUKER, Marilyn, Philadelphia, flight attendant
SARP, Aysel, Arlington, Va., flight attendant
EKELUND, Christine, New York, flight attendant

SURVIVING CR...
BRAGG, Robert, Howard Beach...
DONOVAN, Susanne, Harrisburg...
GRUBBS, Victor, Centerport, L...
JACKSON, Joan, Nashville, Te...
JOHNSON, Carla, New York City...
KELLY, Dorothy, New Hampsh...
WARNS, George, B'airstown, N...

...remen drench the smouldering wrecks of the jumbos.

The Pan Am plane was struck broadside by t... KLM jet taking off, Tenerife airport officials sa...

Airport sources said the Pan Am aircraft, which had just landed, missed a turn-off it had been told to take because of bad visibility and had continued along the main runway at Santa Cruz on the island of Tenerife where the KLM jet was taking off.

The KLM jet burst ...to flames on impact. An official of KLM ...id all the people on ...ard its jumbo were ...utch.

He said the Dutch plane was travelling at take - off speed when the accident happened. "The real cause we don't know," he said.

CONTINUED FROM PAGE 1

"But when two ... big planes go a... there is no way t... avoid each other."

Both planes w... charter flight... nearly full loads ... ists.

Airport offi... Tenerife, said th... Am 747 had 381 ...gers and 26 crew ... and the KLM 747 ... 235 passengers ... crew.

Airport officia... the Pan Am jet ... was among the su...

"It was like in ... Bits of the roof w... ing down. The pla... completely in flam...

Canary Island Separatist Says Group Planted Bomb But Did Not Cause Crash

ALGIERS, Monday, March 28 (Agence France-Presse)—Canary Islands separatists here claimed responsibility early today for a bomb explosion at Las Palmas airport, after which two jumbo jets diverted from the airport to Tenerife crashed in the worst accident in aviation history.

Antonio Cubillo, secretary general of the Movement for Self-Determination and Independence of the Canary Islands, disclaimed responsibility for the crash.

"That was the fault of the control tower at Las Palmas," he said. ."We had nothing to do with it."

He added, however, that his movement had warned tourists not to go to the Canaries, "because we are at war with Spain."

The leader of the Algiers-based move-

The unthinkable that became a ghastly reality: the scenario feared since the introduction of "jumbo jets" half a decade earlier had actually happened – not amongst the congested airways of North America or Western Europe as expected – but on the runway of a relatively remote volcanic island in the Atlantic Ocean.

RUNWAY OF DEATH

California Man Says Explosion Threw Him Out

MADRID, March 27 (UPI)—A California man aboard a Pan Am Boeing 747 that collided with another 747 at Santa Cruz de Tenerife today said that he had been blown to the runway by an explosion but had somehow escaped serious injury. James Naik, 37 years old and from Cupertino, Calif., said in a telephone interview from a hospital in the Canary Islands city. "I was

But Di

ALGIERS,
France-Pres
tists here c
day for a b
airport, aft
verted fro
crashed in
history.
Antonio
the Movem
Independer
claimed re
"That

● Remains of the KLM jumbo jet that disintegrated after the collision with the Pan erife.

LITTER OF TRAG

Pieces of rag hanging from a plane's ta flutter in a slight breeze over the twisted debris.

A Red Cross official searches the debris of the world's worst aviation disaster enerife in the Spanish Canary Islands. In the background stands the tail of

Clothes, a high-heeled shoe, two tenn shoes and a can of hair spray stick out of anoth heap of blackened rubble about 300 metr farther down the debris-strewn runway.

The airport officials on the runway of Tenerife Airport on the Canary Islands did not have much to say.

"This was the Pan Am plane," one of them said sadly, pointing to one heap of metal.

★ From Page 3

"And that was the KLM plane," he added, pointing the other way.

The same clouds that shrouded the runway with a ground fog just before Sunday's disaster rose from the coast below and crept along the mountain slopes.

The wings of the Pan Am 747 were all that remained of the plane in which more than 300 Americana died.

The scorched tail of the KLM jumbo still stands 6 m (20 feet) above the main runway, but practically nothing else is left of it after it ploughed through the American plane at 300 kmh (186 miles per hour) and disintegrated farther down the runway.

Twenty - four hours after the crash, some of the rubble was still smoking. No fragment except the KLM plane's tail is more than two metres high.

ened remains of the ies, literally burned yond recognition. looked like a stac burned wood.

Black - hatted guards, the he armed paramilitary lice, guard the airpo

At mid - afte workmen arrived two yellow bulldozer began clearing the way of rubble, exp deep gouges in the ment.

The airport of who predicted Gran Airport would open in two days have been a bit opt tic.

No one is allowe side the airport ter a modern, white storey building 16 (10) miles from centre of Santa Cr Tenerife.

Taxi driver Jo Garcia was waiting fare at the airport the planes collided exploded in a ball of "When I realised had happened, I my cab directly on runway," Garcia sai

Dramatic final radio call by Pan Am jumbo cras

30/3/77

'STOP... I'M ON THE RUNWAY'

610 toll feared

SANTA CRUZ DE TENERIFE (Special). — An error in the Tenerife airport control tower now, increasingly, appears to have caused Sunday's double jumbo jet disaster.

American investigators at the scene have found on tape the Pan Am pilot's last words, which indicate he was given instructions to taxi down the only runway while the Dutch KLM jet was still awaiting take-off.

The American captain's desperate message was: "Stop . . . I'm on the runway . . ."

After that there was thing. The Pan Am pi- Victor Grubbs sur-ed.
t Santa Cruz airport, s normal for the 300-ne jumbos to use the way for taxi-ing since normal taxi-lane was built to take their ight.
he Pan Am jet's cab-voice recorder, which n report claims has n whisked back to erica, out of reach of nish confiscation — arly shows the pilot ew where he was.
But due to enveloping mist and the absence ground radar, it was possible for either he control to "see" the tch jumbo umbering wn the runway on a th to destruction

mostly unrecognisable bodies said as many as 610 people may have died — including a baby who was not on the passenger list of either airline.
A 24-year-old girl travel courier missed

death when she did not rejoin the Dutch jumbo, whose other passengers and crew were all killed. Robina Van Lanschot got off the plane when it landed here and did not board it again.

Spanish, United States, and Dutch investigators yesterday began a technical inquiry.
Some witnesses said the KLM jumbo tried to take off to avoid hitting the Pan Am jet.

TWO-WAY MIX-UP?

The big aviation question remains unanswered — why were two tourist-packed airliners rolling towards each other on the same Santa Cruz runway?

A possibility being considered by the crash investigators is that the two jumbos were each in contact with a

different section of the control tower.

One section instructed the Pan Am flight to taxi down the main runway because of congestion on the usual side lane.

The other section gave the Dutch jumbo the go-ahead for take-off before the American

jet had turned into way.

Surviving Pan Am Victor Grubbs says fo factor. "We did not thing until it happen was quoted as saying

The answers are i the planes' crash-cockpit voice recorde

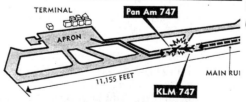

TERMINAL
APRON
11,155 FEET
Pan Am 747
MAIN RU
KLM 747

HOW the two Jumbos may have collided at Santa Cruz.

Contradictions Veiling Cras

But the Prospects for Answers Seem Good

By RICHARD WITKIN

Critical unknowns, confusion and tradictions faced investigators yeste as they set out to reconstruct the ev that led to the collision of two ju jets on a Canary Islands runway. T seemed to be good pros that the cause of the c trophe would emerge electronic recording dev interviews with crew r

News Analysis

through their pretakeoff checks, the tower controller further instructed them to report leaving the runway, and Bragg acknowledged the call. But they were still having difficulty sorting out which taxiway the controller wanted them to use.

"Haven't seen any yet," Grubbs remarked to Bragg as they continued rolling down the runway. "I haven't either," Bragg replied. Then, five seconds later, he exclaimed, "There's one!"

"That's the 90 degree," said Grubbs, as they continued past it. Their pretakeoff checks were almost complete when they heard the KLM Boeing ask the tower controller if the runway centreline lights could be switched on – the KLM crew needed to know if they were available to assess if visibility met their minimum takeoff conditions.

The controller, having checked, replied that the runway centreline lights were out of service. He also passed this information to the PanAm crew. Even so, both crews were evidently satisfied that runway visibility was sufficient for takeoff.

The PanAm crew then sighted the second taxiway through the fog. "That's two!" the captain exclaimed.

Warns: "Yeah ... that's the 45 [degrees] there."

Bragg: "That's this one right here."

Grubbs: "Yeah ... I know "

Warns: "Next one is almost a 45 ..."

Grubbs: "But it does ... it goes ... ahead. I think it's gonna put us on the taxiway."

"Maybe he counts these as three," Bragg said as the PanAm Boeing 747 continued rolling down the runway past the connecting taxiway intersection.

Aboard the KLM Boeing, which had now reached the end of the runway, Captain van Zanten was at this moment manoeuvring his huge aircraft round through 180 degrees to face the direction of takeoff. Just after 1705 hours, as First Officer Klass Meurs finished the pretakeoff check list, van Zanten opened the throttles slightly and the aircraft began to inch forward. Meurs checked him: "Wait a minute – we don't have an ATC clearance."

Van Zanten held the aircraft on the brakes: "No ... I know that. Go ahead and ask."

Meurs called the Tower as the controller instructed: "KLM4805 is now ready for takeoff ... we're waiting for our ATC clearance."

Tower: "KLM4805 ... you are cleared to the Papa beacon ... climb to and maintain Flight Level 90 ... right turn after takeoff ... proceed with heading 040 until intercepting the 325 radial from Las Palmas VOR."

As Meurs began to read back the clearance to the tower controller, van Zanten released the KLM Boeing's brakes and began advancing the throttles to takeoff power. "Let's go," he called to Flight Engineer Willem Schreuder, "Check thrust."

First Officer Meurs, still transmitting to the Tower, continued: "Roger, sir, we are cleared to the Papa beacon, Flight Level 90 until intercepting the 325." By this time the KLM aircraft was six seconds into its takeoff run, so he added: "We are now at takeoff."

Tower: (Interpreting the KLM transmission to mean that the Boeing 747 was *ready* for takeoff): "OK ... standby for takeoff ... I will call you.

Hearing the beginning of this exchange between the KLM aircraft and the Tower, the PanAm crew were understandably alarmed: "We are still taxiing down the runway!" Bragg transmitted urgently.

Tower: "Roger, PanAm 1736, report the runway clear."

PanAm: "OK ... will report when we are clear."

Tower: "Thank you"

Fatefully, PanAm's protesting transmission conflicted with the controller's instruction to KLM. Instead of the words "standby for takeoff ... I will call you," all the KLM crew heard after the controller's first "OK" was a squeal resulting from the two simultaneous transmissions on the same frequency.

The exchange that followed between the Tower and the PanAm 747 was however audible on the KLM flightdeck. But by this time the KLM Boeing was 20 seconds into its takeoff run. With Captain van Zanten and First Officer Meurs both concentrating fully on the takeoff itself, only Flight Engineer Schreuder took in the possible significance of the two transmissions. "Did he not clear the runway then?" he asked the pilots.

The captain, giving all his attention to the takeoff, did not take in the engineer's question either. "What did you say?" he asked over his shoulder.

"Did he not clear the runway – that Pan American?" Schreuder repeated.

"Yes, he did," both pilots answered emphatically.

The KLM takeoff continued.

At this stage, the PanAm Boeing, its crew having missed the intersection for Taxiway 3 which the Tower had directed them to take, and unaware of what the other 747 was doing, was still on the runway, approaching Taxiway 4.

Captain Grubbs, still uneasy about occupying the runway in such poor visibility with the KLM aircraft's takeoff obviously imminent, was keen to be out of its way as soon as possible.

"Let's get the hell right out of here," he remarked to his crew:

"Yeah ... he's anxious, isn't he?" Bragg agreed.

"After he's held us up for all this time," enjoined Warns, "Now he's in a rush."

A few seconds later, the PanAm crew caught sight of lights that were materialising through the fog directly ahead. Hazy at first, they seemed for a long moment to be stationary. But as they continued to brighten, it quickly became obvious they were approaching fast!

Grubbs stared through the windscreen in stunned disbelief. "There he is ... look at him!" he cried out. "Goddamn ... that son-of-a-bitch is coming!" Desperately pushing all four throttles wide open, he attempted to swing the Boeing 747 off the runway to the left.

"Get off! Get off! Get off!" Bragg yelled frantically as he saw the other aircraft's nose begin to rise into the takeoff attitude.

Aboard the hurtling Dutch aircraft, First Officer Meurs' eyes were fixed on his steadily rising airspeed indicator. "V_1!" he finally called.

At the same moment, van Zanten sighted the PanAm 747 slewing, across the runway ahead of them. Instinctively – there was no hope of stopping – he hauled back on the control column to try and lift over the American. But too suddenly – the tail bumper struck the runway, emitting a shower of metallic sparks.

But lift the KLM aircraft did – just before reaching the other – only it was too late. Its nose leg cleared the PanAm fuselage, but at 140 knots the main undercarriage slammed into it, slicing off the fuselage top as the No 4 engine demolished the hump just behind the flightdeck, and both aircraft exploded into flames.

For a few seconds more the burning Dutch aircraft remained in the air, then fell back on to the runway, slewing through 90 degrees before coming to rest with its engines torn off, 150 metres further along the runway. None of the fuselage doors were opened before its fuel tanks exploded, enveloping the entire aircraft in a raging fire.

Aboard the PanAm aircraft, the nightmare of impacts, flash fires, smoke and explosions created utter

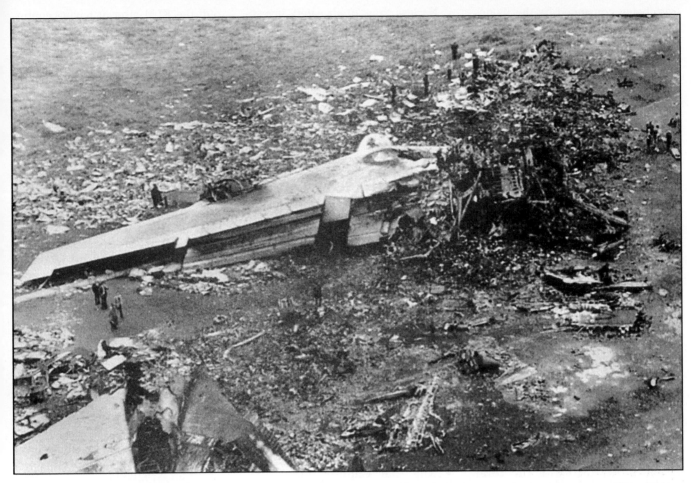

Thanks to the efforts of the Los Rodeos Airport fire service, the large amount of fuel contained in the port wing of the PanAm Boeing 747 was prevented from adding to the inferno. Between 15 and 20 tonnes of jet fuel was later recovered from the wing tanks – the only portion of the structure of the two Boeing 747s' to survive the accident.

terror and confusion. Momentarily, First Officer Bragg grabbed for the engine fire shutoff handles above his head. They were not there – the entire top of the fuselage had been carried away!

Moments later the flightdeck floor, together with that of the wrecked upper deck, collapsed, spilling the uninjured flightcrew and the traumatised bodies of passengers who had been seated in the upper deck lounge into the main deck First Class cabin below. Together with passengers from this section of the aircraft, the crew escaped down on to the ground through a hole torn in the port side of the fuselage.

For once, those in the nose of the aircraft proved to be the lucky ones. Many of those seated on the starboard side of the main cabin in the areas of the initial impact were killed outright. On the port side, and further back in the main cabin, many other passengers who were initially spared injury were trapped and prevented from escaping by collapsed sections of the starboard fuselage side. They were soon overcome by the rapidly spreading fire.

Despite a fire under the port wing, where the engines were still running down, many managed to escape through the port side overwing exits on to the wing. But they then had to jump to the ground, some sustaining broken legs or other injuries. Still others jumped 20 feet to the ground from a rear door. Within one minute, the evacuation of survivors was effectively over. Fire had now overwhelmed the fuselage and starboard wing of the PanAm Boeing, and those who had not already made their escape would never do so.

Because of the fog, the tower controllers did not see the collision of the two huge aircraft. They heard only the series of explosions, unable to localise them or know their cause. Moments later, the crew of one of the aircraft on the parking apron reported seeing a fire through the fog, but again was unable to specify its exact location or cause.

Immediately the tower controllers sounded the fire alarm, instructing the fire service to be ready for an urgent departure as soon as the position of the fire was known. Shortly afterwards an airport workman

came running to the fire station to say there was a fire "to the left of the aircraft parking area."

Vague though this was, it was the first indication of the fire's location. Fire fighting vehicles left at once, but had to pick their way carefully through the congested apron to avoid colliding with parked aircraft. Finally they were able to make out a bright light through the fog, and as they approached, were able to feel the heat. Then they saw the fire itself – it was a big aircraft totally enveloped in fierce flames, the only part visible being the fin and rudder.

As the fire service began fighting the fire, the fog cleared slightly and they sighted another bright light further away. Taking it to be a separated section of the burning aircraft, some fire vehicles went on to this fire, only to discover it was a second large aircraft burning fiercely. All the fire vehicles then moved to concentrate on this second aircraft because the first was obviously now utterly beyond saving.

As a result of this decision, the fire service were there in time to prevent the port wing of the PanAm Boeing from being consumed by the flames (between 15 and 20 tonnes of fuel were subsequently recovered from it). It was not until the early hours of the following morning that the KLM aircraft fire was totally extinguished.

Because of the dense fog, the tower controllers remained unaware of the exact location of the fire for some minutes, and whether one or two aircraft were involved. But there were five ambulances at the airport at the time and these, following the firefighting vehicles, were soon on the scene. A standing airport emergency plan designed to cope with a major disaster was quickly implemented, with further medical and ambulance assistance coming from the city of Santa Cruz, and all the injured survivors were soon on their way to hospitals in the city.

When a tally could finally be taken of the cost of the horrific disaster in terms of casualties, it was found that all 234 passengers and 14 crew members aboard KLM's PH-BUF had perished in the intense fire. Another 326 aboard PanAm's N736PA died in the actual crash, including nine members of the cabin crew. Amazingly, there were 70 survivors from the PanAm aircraft, but nine of these later succumbed to their injuries and severe burns, bringing the total number of deaths to 583. The PanAm flight crew all survived, together with the two company staff who had boarded the aircraft at Tenerife and were occupying jump seats on the flightdeck, this nose section of the aircraft having just missed being struck by the KLM Boeing's No 4 engine.

Because of the magnitude of the disaster, it was agreed by the Spanish Justice Department that pathologists from Holland and the US should work as a team with Spanish medical authorities in the enormous task of body identifications and, where possible, autopsies. The state of the bodies made it impossible to perform autopsies on the remains of the KLM flight crew.

Not far from the site of the collision, in one of Los Rodeos Airport's cavernous hangars, mute evidence of the worst disaster in aviation history gradually accumulated. As emergency and medical workers completed their tasks, row after row of dark wooden coffins progressively filled the entire floor of the makeshift morgue in the 2500 square metre building – by far the greatest number of fatalities that had ever resulted from one aviation accident.

★　　★　　★

No less than 70 air safety investigators – from Spain, The Netherlands, the USA, and from the two airline companies involved – descended upon Los Rodeos Airport to probe the cause of this most disastrous of all air accidents.

They found the airport to be located on a plateau, 2000 feet above sea level, with hills lying on either side, a factor that gives rise to somewhat unpredictable weather and frequent low cloud in the vicinity of the airport.

Los Redoes' single runway, aligned southeast-northwest (Runways 12 and 30), was 3400 metres long and 45 metres wide, with 60 metre overruns at both ends. The terminal area lies on the northeastern side of the runway, with a main taxiway parallel to the runway connecting the main apron to holding points at both ends of the runway (see diagram). Adjacent to both runway holding points were smaller apron areas capable of accommodating several airline aircraft at once. In between the runway holding areas, four separate short taxiways linked the main taxiway with the runway.

Three questions were uppermost in the investigators' minds as they began their formidable task:
• Why had Captain Jacob van Zanten, a senior, highly experienced training captain, who had been with the respected KLM, an airline renowned for its safety record, for 25 years, commenced takeoff on Runway 30 without the control tower's clearance to do so?
• Why had Captain Victor Grubbs been instructed by the tower controller to vacate the runway at Taxiway 3, one that led back towards the main apron at an angle of 135 degrees from the runway, rather than the far more conveniently placed 45 degree angled Taxiway 4, leading towards the holding point for Runway 30? And unexpected as this instruction was, why had Captain Grubbs disregarded it? If he had made the earlier turn, the PanAm aircraft would probably have been clear of the runway by the time the KLM Boeing reached that point on its takeoff run.
• Why did the KLM crew not grasp the significance of the PanAm aircraft's report that it had not yet cleared the runway, and would report again to the Tower when it did?

Beginning their inquiry at the crash site itself, the investigators found that the distance of the KLM wreckage from the commencement of Runway 30 was around 1835 metres. The PanAm wreckage lay 450 metres closer to the runway thresh-

old, the KLM aircraft having continued in flight for about 150 metres after striking the upper fuselage of N736PA, before falling back on to the runway and sliding a further 300 metres. Both aircraft were completely destroyed, only the outer two thirds of the port wing of N736PA surviving the fire.

At the moment of impact, the PanAm aircraft was slewed across the runway at an angle of about 45 degrees, as its crew desperately tried to manoeuvre out of the path of the oncoming KLM Boeing. The latter was fully airborne, its tail bumper having scraped the runway as a result of over-rotation for a distance of 20 metres before it finally lifted off only 80 metres short of N736PA.

But it was too late. Although PH-BUF's nose undercarriage cleared N736PA's fuselage, its main undercarriage did not, impacting initially against the PanAm aircraft's No 3 engine and fuselage. One of the KLM's undercarriage bogies was wrenched off, but the rest of the main undercarriage and the underside of PH-BUF's rear fuselage rode across the cabin top of N736PA, shearing it off. As both aircraft exploded into flames, the port wing of PH-BUF sliced off N763PA's tail fin.

As there was no evidence of any failure in either aircraft prior to the impact, and there was every reason to suspect that the accident had resulted from misunderstandings or a lack of adequate communication, the key to the cause of the disaster would most probably be found in the transcriptions of the two Boeing 747's Cockpit Voice Recorders and the continuous tape recording of the Los Rodeos air traffic controllers' communications.

Fortunately the CVRs of both aircraft were recovered from the wreckage and both proved capable of being read out satisfactorily. These readouts were correlated with that of the control tower recording to produce a complete, accurately timed record of all that took place on the flightdecks of both Boeing 747s and in the Los Rodeos Control Tower, from before the time the two aircraft started their engines, up to the instant of impact.

It was evident from a careful analysis of all the recorded exchanges that Captain van Zanten, as soon as he heard the ATC clearance being passed to his crew, believed that PH-BUF had been cleared for takeoff and immediately opened the throttles to do so.

But the clearance given them was

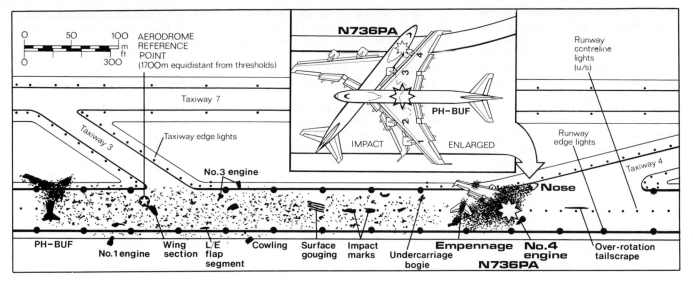

Diagram compiled by accident investigators showing the relative positions of the burnt out wreckage of the two Boeing 747s on Los Rodeos Airport's Runway 30. (Matthew Tesch)

an *airways* clearance, applicable only *after* the aircraft was airborne from Los Rodeos Airport, and *not* clearance to takeoff.

Thus the fundamental factors in the development of the accident were that PH-BUF:
• Took off without being cleared to do so.
• Did not heed the tower controller's instruction to "standby for takeoff"
• Did not abandon the takeoff when it became apparent that N736PA might still be on the runway.

But how could a senior airline pilot with the technical capacity and experience of Captain van Zanten, whose demeanour during his time on the ground at Los Rodeos seemed perfectly normal, commit such a basic error only a few minutes afterwards – despite several warnings addressed to him?

There were a number of factors that could have contributed to his situation:
• An increasing feeling of tension as the imperative to depart increased. Though reassured by the information radioed from KLM Amsterdam about the duty time still available to him and his crew, they were nevertheless committed to leaving Los Rodeos within a relatively short time, if the flight was not to remain there overnight – with all the resulting inconvenience to the passengers and expense to the company.

The weather conditions at the airport had suddenly deteriorated and the runway visibility was already uncomfortably close to the minimum specified by KLM for takeoff. For Captain van Zanten it would have seemed important to get airborne quickly, especially as the runway centreline lighting was out of service.

Otherwise they might have to wait for an improvement in the weather, with the risk of exceeding the crew's duty time limit. This anxiety to depart was apparent even to the PanAm crew, as was evident from the latter's flightdeck conversation while they themselves were taxiing for takeoff.
• Although Captain van Zanten had flown for many years on KLM's European and intercontinental routes, he had been an instructor for 10 years, spending much of his duty time during those years in the company's simulators at Schiphol Airport in Amsterdam. This tended to reduce his day to day familiarity with route flying and its procedures.

At the same time his experience and high standing in the company probably made his crew reluctant to question his decisions. In addition, his first officer was a former DC-8 captain who had only recently qualified to crew Boeing 747 aircraft and whose experience on the type was limited to only 95 hours. Having now found himself flying with the training captain who had given him his Boeing 747 rating, he would have been even more circumspect in his attitude to Captain van Zanten.
• While the KLM crew were taxiing for takeoff, the tower controller offered them their ATC [airways] clearance. They declined to accept it at the time, presumably because they were engrossed in performing their pretakeoff checks and it would have distracted them from this vital task.

But this meant that when they had finally lined up on the runway and were in all other respects ready for takeoff, they still had to obtain both their airways and takeoff clearances. This fact was perhaps ob-

scured by First Officer Meurs when, after Captain van Zanten began to let the aircraft roll forward on completion of the pretakeoff checks, he told the captain: "Wait ... we don't have an ATC [airways] clearance".

First Officer Meurs' subsequent transmission to the Tower, "KLM4805 is now ready for takeoff and we are waiting for our ATC clearance," though ambiguous, was in effect a simultaneous request for both clearances. That is evidently how Captain van Zanten interpreted it, for when the Tower transmitted the airways clearance only, he immediately accepted it as the takeoff clearance, released the brakes and opened the throttles. Meurs, if he in fact realised the captain's error at this stage, did nothing more to bring it to his attention.

For Captain van Zanten, the misunderstanding resulted in his believing they were cleared both for takeoff and for the airway route. For the controller on the other hand, it resulted in the conviction that PH-BUF was still awaiting its takeoff clearance at the runway threshold.

The further transmission by First Officer Meurs on completing the mandatory readback of the airways clearance when the aircraft was already six seconds into its takeoff run, "We are now at takeoff", was then interpreted by the controller as confirming that the aircraft was at the "takeoff position" on the runway, awaiting its clearance to begin rolling.

Because it was probably the last possible opportunity to avert the unfolding disaster, it was nothing less than tragic that the PanAm crew's understandably alarmed response to these transmissions, "We are still taxiing down the runway!", coincided with the controller's further transmission: "OK ... standby for takeoff ... I will call you." The result was that the KLM crew heard only the controller's "OK", followed by a squeal resulting from the simultaneous transmissions.

The brief exchange that followed between the Tower and the PanAm crew, concerning reporting when the runway was clear, apparently fell on deaf ears as far as the two KLM pilots were concerned, concentrating as they were on their takeoff. But Flight Engineer Schreuder was sufficiently concerned to query the captain about it. What prompted both pilots to give him such an emphatic assurance that the runway was already clear, can never be known. However, the KLM crew's overall failure to monitor the radio communications between the Tower and the PanAm Boeing while both aircraft were taxiing resulted in their having no mental "picture" of its whereabouts on the airfield – a "picture" that could have prevented the accident.

It could also be said that a contributing factor to the accident was the fact that the PanAm crew, while taxiing on the runway in the severely limited visibility, bypassed Taxiway 3 where they had been instructed to turn off and were only 150 metres from Taxiway 4. As a result of a careful analysis of the PanAm aircraft's movements, the investigators found that if it had in fact turned off at Taxiway 3, in all probability no collision would have occurred.

The PanAm crew obviously had difficulty interpreting the tower controller's instruction. In the first place, because of language difficulties, they were unsure whether the controller had nominated Taxiway 1 or Taxiway 3 and, after a further exchange clarified this, they experienced problems in identifying the actual taxiways in the reduced visibil-

ity. Their efforts were probably not helped by the pretakeoff checks they were conducting at the same time, and First Officer Bragg had only a small diagram of the airport.

But none of the taxiway intersections on the airport were indicated by markers, and the fact that the third taxiway they saw appeared to lead back towards the congested airport apron at an angle of 135 degrees from the direction in which they were heading, convinced them it was inactive and could not be the taxiway the controller meant.

Apart from the congestion on the apron which they were backtracking on the runway to avoid, it seemed to the PanAm crew that the controller would not ask an aircraft as big as a Boeing 747 to make such a tight turn on to a comparatively narrow taxiway, requiring a similarly tight 135 degree turn in the opposite direction to regain the main taxiway leading to the runway.

Their belief was further reinforced when they saw from the airport diagram that the next taxiway led off the runway at a comfortable 45 degree angle to connect with the main taxiway leading to the holding point for Runway 30. Though they had been careful to query the Tower's initial instruction to backtrack on the runway in the poor visibility before presuming to enter the runway, they did not do so on this occasion, but continued towards Taxiway 4, believing it to be the one nominated.

A final consideration in the fateful sequence of events leading to the disaster were the actions and decisions of the tower controllers themselves. In the first place, the airfield controller's command of English left something to be desired, resulting in misunderstandings on the part of both the American and the Dutch crews. Secondly, the controller, as with the KLM first officer, did not

adhere to standard terminology in his communications, giving further opportunity for misunderstanding and misinterpretation.

The tower controller's decision to allow two aircraft to use the runway at the same time was undoubtedly a dangerous one in weather conditions which prevented the controller and the two aircraft concerned from seeing one another.

In the circumstances that had overtaken Los Rodeos Airport, there was little choice but to do so, but the lack of visibility could have been offset by having the aircraft readback all the Tower's instructions and subsequently confirm their various movements and positions.

As it was, with none of the parties in visual contact, the tower controller and the two aircraft were depending entirely on radio communication for a knowledge of position. Only by careful readbacks, and confirmation of instructions therefore, could safety have been assured.

Against all this, it has to be said that the controller had been on duty all day, during which he had been under pressure handling an unusually high workload because of the number of aircraft diverted to Los Rodeos. He also had relatively little experience in handling Boeing 747 aircraft. His instruction to the PanAm crew to vacate the runway at Taxiway 3 was thus a consequence of his limited appreciation of the manoeuvrability of the aircraft type. He had not asked the impossible however, as taxiing tests with a Boeing 747 during the investigation subsequently established.

Overall, the investigation determined that, even apart from the shortcomings that existed in the radio communications and the misunderstandings that arose from them, the accident was the final outcome of an unfavourable coincidence of a

The charred skeleton of KLM's PH-BUF blocks Los Rodeos' single runway the day after the accident. In the background on the still congested apron, a British Airways L-1011 Tristar, a Sabena Boeing 747, two DC-8s and a Boeing 707 await the clearing of the disaster's massive debris before they can depart.

(Clockwise from top left): Probably the best known of all the harrowing images of the Tenerife disaster is this photograph of the scorched fin and the twisted, burnt out empennage of KLM's PH-BUF.

A woman's wig, bedraggled by the efforts of firefighters, lies atop a passenger's suitcase which has somehow escaped the devouring flames. In the background is a section of N736PA's massive triple slotted port wing flaps, lowered ready for takeoff just prior to the collision.

PH-BUF's starboard outboard main undercarriage bogie, sheared off when it struck the fuselage top of N736PA, bears mute testimony to the devastation wrought by the collision!

whole chain of circumstances that individually were relatively insignificant. If any one of these circumstances had not been in place, the accident would not have happened.

It was the seemingly predestined way in which these largely everyday circumstances happened to coincide at Los Rodeos on Sunday, March 27, 1977, that developed the accident to its terrible inevitability.

Above all however, the accident was an appallingly tragic lesson on the danger of depending on radio communication alone for the safe operation and regulation of air traffic. The facts of the accident show that information transmitted by radio communication can be understood in a different way to that intended, as a result of ambiguous terminology and/or the obliteration of key words or phrases. They demonstrate beyond doubt that the oral transmission of essential information, via single and vulnerable radio contacts, carries with it great potential dangers.

The primary safety message drawn from the accident was the urgent need to improve communication between aircraft and Tower. Such communications lagged far behind the fail-safe principle applied to other aspects of aviation. Radio communication, as it existed at Los Rodeos Airport on the day of the accident, was not fail-safe.

Operational measures recommended for immediate adoption as a short term improvement included:

• The use of concise and unambiguous terminology.
• Avoiding the expression "takeoff" in airways clearances.
• Allowing a distinct time interval between the transmission of an airways clearance and a takeoff clearance.

These recommendations were referred to the Air Navigation Commission of the International Civil Aviation Organisation (ICAO) for study.

Longer term improvements for the introduction of fail-safe principles in communication between aircraft and Tower were also considered. In its most simple form, this could be no more than a red-green light at the threshold of the runway to confirm the controller's oral takeoff clearance. The FAA in the USA had been testing this system at Atlantic City Airport with encouraging results.

For all who lost loved ones, or were injured, or who were involved in other ways in the horror at Los Rodeos Airport that fateful Sunday afternoon on the island of Tenerife, there would have been a seemingly endless sense of recrimination as they thought over what had happened. There were so many "ifs" – so many small coincidences that need not have compounded to make the tragedy inevitable.

If the bomb had not gone off at Las Palmas, if the PanAm Boeing had been permitted to hold instead of landing at Los Rodeos, if the KLM crew had not decided to refuel, if the PanAm aircraft could have squeezed past its KLM sistership without having to wait for it to move, if the weather had not deteriorated, if the PanAm crew had not bypassed the No 3 taxiway, if they had not transmitted at the moment they did when they feared the KLM aircraft was about to takeoff, if the KLM captain had taken more notice of his flight engineer's doubt ... any of these factors could have altered the whole course of events as they unfolded.

But no amount of speculation could now change even one of them, much less bring back those who were lost.

The best that could be hoped for was that 583 people had not died in vain – that the sheer magnitude of the disaster would forcibly sheet home to all involved in aviation that, by its very nature, flying abounds with countless opportunities for "little" things to go wrong.

That, to be routinely safe, aviation requires constant and unswerving vigilance on the part of all its professionals – and that those who carry such responsibilities can never afford to take *anything* for granted.

GLOSSARY OF AERONAUTICAL TERMS AND ABBREVIATIONS

ADF: Automatic Direction Finder. Previously known as radio compass.

Aileron: Control surfaces on outer sections of wing trailing edges, controlling bank and roll of aircraft.

Airspeed Indicator (ASI): Instrument measuring speed of aircraft through air, expressed in knots.

Air Traffic Control: System of directing all aircraft operating within designated airspace by radio. Divided into sectors such as Tower (aerodrome control for takeoffs and landings), Departures, Control (en route aircraft), and Approach.

Angle of attack: Angle at whichh wings meet airflow.

Artificial horizon (AH): Instrument displaying aircraft attitude in relation to real horizon.

Asymmetric flight: Multi engined aircraft flying with one engine inoperative.

ATIS: Automated terminal information service. Continuous, recorded radio transmission of meteorological conditions at airport.

Attitude: Lateral and longitudinal relationship of aircraft to horizon.

Attitude indicator: See artificial horizon and flight director.

Bunt: Sudden nose down manoeuvre of aircraft, usually producing uncomfortable negative G.

Clearance: Approval by Air Traffic Control for aircraft to taxi, takeoff, enter controlled airspace, or to land.

Control Area: Designated area of airspace in which all aircraft movements are under radio direction of Air Traffic Control.

Directional gyro (DG): Instrument accurately registering direction aircraft is heading. When aligned with compass, provides immediate indication of changes In magnetic heading.

DME: Distance Measuring Equipment. Radio navigation aid providing pilot with constant readout of distance from selected radio beacon.

Elevation: Height of terrain above mean sea level. Abbreviated AMSL.

Elevators: Control surfaces at rear of horizontal tail (tailplane), controlling nose attitude of aircraft.

Endurance: Time (expressed in minutes) aircraft can theoretically remain in air before fuel is exhausted.

ETA: Estimated time of arrival.

ETD: Estimated time of departure.

Flaps: Adjustable surfaces on aircraft's wing trailing edge. When lowered, flaps increase lift of wing, thereby reducing stalling speed, and increase drag, steepening aircraft's glide angle.

Flight Director: Complex, computer controlled flying instrument combining inputs of other flying and radio navigation instruments in single large dial located directly in front of each pilot.

Flightplan: Document prepared by pilot on official form providing full details of proposed flight.

"G" (gravities): Expression of force acting on aircraft and its occupants in flight, measured in multiples of earth's gravitational force.

GMT (Greenwich Mean Time): Standard time used for navigation regardless of location of ship or aircraft.

Ground speed: Actual speed of aircraft over ground. May be greater or less than airspeed, according to wind.

Instrument Flight Rules (IFR): Stipulated procedure for navigating aircraft by reference to cockpit instruments and radio navigation aids alone. Enables flight regardless of visibility.

Knot: One nautical mile per hour. Equivalent to 1.853kmh

Lowest Safe Altitude (LSA): Designated minimum altitude for particular air route, providing minimum of 1,000 feet clearance above underlying terrain.

Mach number: Figure expressing relationship between true airspeed of aircraft and speed of sound.

Mach buffet: Turbulence like condition, felt initially in flying controls at high Mach numbers (ie as aircraft approaches speed of sound). As Mach number increases, manifestations can include large changes of trim and heavy buffeting of the aircraft itself.

Mayday (repeated three times): Radio telephony version of former morse code "SOS" distress call. Derived from the French "m'aidez" – "help me".

Nautical mile (nm): Measure of distance used for navigation in the air and at sea. Equal to one minute of an arc of latitude on the earth's surface. Is 800 feet longer than statute mile and equivalent to 1.853km.

Navaid: Radio navigation aid.

NBD: Non directional beacon. Ground based medium frequency radio transmitter sending continuous signals for use by aircraft fitted with ADF (radio compass).

Pitot-static system: System of instruments, connecting tubes and air sensors for measuring altitude, airspeed, and rate of climb or descent.

Precipitation: (Meteorological) Rain, hail, sleet or snow in or falling from cloud.

Preflight (inspection): "Walk around" inspection of aircraft by pilot, usually immediately prior to flight.

QFE: Code expression designating altimeter setting in millibars for particular airport. When set on subscale of altimeter, instrument reads aircraft's height above that airport.

QNH: Code expression designating altimeter setting in millibars – when set on subscale of aircraft's altimeter, instrument reads aircraft's height above mean sea level.

Radial: Bearing to or from VOR radio range.

Radio Compass: See ADF above.

Radio Range: Type of radio beacon providing defined aircraft tracks to or from that navigation aid.

Rate One turn: Shallow standard rate turn used in instrument flight conditions.

RPM (rpm): Measure of engine speed expressed in revolutions per minute.

Rudder: Control surface at rear of vertical tail (fin) – controls yawing movement of aircraft.

Sigmet: Warning signal issued by Aviation Meteorological Service when weather conditions suddenly deteriorate.

Slats: Aerodynamic device fitted to leading edge of wings to delay onset of stall.

Trim: Adjusting control of aircraft in climb, level flight and descent, so pilot is not required to maintain continuous pressure on elevators, ailerons or rudder.

Turn and bank indicator: Instrument displaying rate of turn and if turn is "balanced" with correct amount of bank – ie neither skidding outwards nor slipping inwards.

SAR: Search and Rescue.

Spot height: Height noted on chart showing elevation of prominent mountain peak.

Stalling speed: Low airspeed at which aircraft wings suddenly lose lift. No connection with engine "stall". Is absolute minimum airspeed at which aircraft can maintain flight.

V (code): Schedule of indicated airspeeds stipulated for different phases of flight (see following).

V_1: Decision speed during takeoff. Aircraft is committed to fly when this speed is passed.

V_r: Rotation speed. Speed at which aircraft is "rotated" into liftoff attitude by raising the nosewheel off the runway.

V_2: Takeoff safety speed. Minimum control speed plus safety margin to allow for engine failure and other contingencies.

V_{ne}: Never exceed speed.

V_{ref}: Flap reference speed. Landing speed for stipulated number of degrees of flap extension.

Vasis: Visual approach slope indicator. System of lights located on ground on either side of runway to indicate correct angle of descent to approaching aircraft.

Vertical Speed Indicator (VSI): Instrument displaying rate of climb or descent in feet per minute.

VHF: Very High (radio) Frequency. In general use for inflight radio communications.

Visual Flight Rules (VFR): Stipulated flight procedure for navigating aircraft visually, clear of cloud, in Visual Meteorological Conditions (VMC).

VOR: Very High Frequency Omni directional Radio Range.

NOTE ON UNITS OF MEASUREMENT USED IN THIS BOOK

Units of measurement used in Australian civil aviation have undergone a number of changes since World War 2. Originally the same as for land transport, distance was in statute miles, speed in miles per hour, and altitude in feet.

The first change came in the early postwar years when expression of distance and speed was changed to nautical miles and knots – a logical move, since air navigation has much in common with navigation at sea, and one nautical mile is one minute of an arc of latitude on the earth's surface.

Major changes (creating great confusion for non-aviation writers and readers!), came when Australia "went metric" in 1970. The committee charged with determining standards for aviation then decreed that horizontal distances less than three nautical miles (runway lengths, visibility in fog, etc), would be expressed in metres and kilometres. But nautical miles and knots would continue to be used for navigation, while altitude would continue to be measured in feet!

The units of measurement quoted in this book conform with current Australian and ICAO aviation practice. Conversions are included when it is necessary to quote other units from overseas accident reports.

PORT AND STARBOARD – OR LEFT AND RIGHT?

A word on the usage and historical perspective of these terms may help avoid confusion.

As aviation developed in the English speaking world, the new transport medium adopted nautical terminology to express relative position and direction – ahead, abeam, astern, port and starboard. Hence port engine, starboard wing and so on. But with the advent of two crew cockpits with pilots side-by-side, the terms did not translate so well *inside* the aeroplane. The command seat became the "left-hand seat" not the "port seat", with the copilot or first officer in the "right hand seat". References to the *flying* controls soon followed this practice, eg in a twin engined aircraft with mechanical trouble, a pilot might hold on "right rudder" to counter-act a loss of power on the "port" engine which he shut down by retarding the "port" throttle.

Further erosion from the nautical ideal came with the introduction of airfield circuit procedures. A standard circuit became a "left hand circuit", not a "port circuit". Air traffic control by radiotelephony took the rot further: it was less likely to be misunderstood if the controller told an aircraft to "turn right", rather than "turn to starboard". Even so, tradition died hard and a wind encountered in flight might still cause "starboard" drift; likewise an en route check point might still be sighted "to port".

With their penchant for pragmatism, the Americans finally and thankfully put an end to this ambiguity by abandoning all nautical influence, "left" and "right" becoming standard in all their aviation references. In recent years, this practice has become increasingly accepted in British and Australian aviation and today, however traditionalists may regret their passing, the terms "port" and "starboard" are used less and less.

The usage of such terminology in this book follows the style in use in Australia at the time of the events described.